DANIEL HERAUD

The 2003 Canadian Used Car Guide

trader

classified media

Daniel Heraud

CREDITS

The photographs appearing on the cover and inside pages were provided by the manufacturers' press services and Daniel Heraud.

Project Manager: Michel DOYON
Chief Editor: Daniel HERAUD
Assistant: Julien CHAMPAGNE
Coordinator: Lyse HERAUD
Proofreaders: Claude BOUCHER

"Le Guide Des Autos Usagées" and "The Canadian Used Car Guide" are registered trademarks and published by Trader Publications a Division of Classified Media (Canada) Holdings Inc.

Legal deposit: First quarter of 2003
Bibliothèque nationale du Québec
National Library of Canada
ISBN: 1-895729-44-0
Printed and bound in Canada

HOW TO USE THIS GUIDE

Please consider the following instructions to use this guide efficiently:

1. All models are sorted in alphabetical order as to the companies that manufacture them rather than those that sell them.
2. Always refer to the index to rapidly locate the model you are interested in.
3. In the case of American manufacturers, models are grouped according to their platform which is identified by a letter.
4. Crosses indicating the type of problem experienced during the year in question point to reliability issues.
5. Recall campaigns are those signaled by Transport Canada.
6. Models illustrated on certain photos may appear differently depending on the origin of the said photos.
7. Before adding or subtracting the value of an equipment indicated at the top of page 9, make sure that the equipment was not standard on certain special editions (e.g., air conditioning or power steering).

ABBREVIATIONS

ENGINE TYPES

H	Horizontal engine
L	In-line cylinders
V	V-shaped cylinders
R	Rotary piston
Cyl	Cylinder
L.	Capacity in liters
hp	Horsepower

CARBURATION

SOHC	Single overhead cam
DOHC	Double overhead cam
OHV	Overhead valve
T.	Turbocharger
C.	Supercharged

TRANSMISSIONS

M4	Manual 4-speed
M5	Manual 5-speed
M6	Manual 6-speed
A3	Automatic 3-speed
A4	Automatic 4-speed
A5	Automatic 5-speed

MODELS

con	Convertible
cpe	Coupe
sdn	Sedan
a.p.v	All-purpose vehicle

wgn	Station wagon
m.v.	Mini-van
p.u.	pickup truck
2dr	2-door
3dr	3-door
4dr	4-door
5dr	5-door
2x4 or 2WD	2-wheel drive
4x4 or 4WD	4-wheel drive
AWD	permanent 4-wheel drive

MEASURES

mm	Milimetre
kg	Kilogram
km/h	Kilometers per hour
l./100 km	Liters per 100 km

OTHERS

NA	Not available
Cd	Coefficient drag
dc	Disc
dr	Drum
r&p.	Rack & Pinion
bal.	Recirculating balls
w&r	Worm & Roller
fr.	Front
rr.	Rear
pwr.	Power assistance
ABS	Anti-lock brake system

INDEX

Credits	2
How to use this guide	
Abbreviations	3
Index	4-5
Few tips	6
Price adjustment charts	7

ACURA

CL	8
EL	10
Integra	12
MDX	14
RL	16
RSX	18
TL	20

AUDI

A4	22
A6/S4/S6	24
A8	26
Allroad	28
TT	30

BMW

3-Series	32
5-Series	36
7-Series	38
8-Series	40
X5	42
Z3	44

BUICK

Century	142
Le Sabre	116
Park Avenue	106
Regal	142
Rendezvous	136
Riviera	108
Skylark	128

CADILLAC

Escalade	148
Catera	140
DeVille	120
Eldorado/Seville	120

CHEVROLET

Astro	126
Blazer S-10	112
Camaro	110
Cavalier	118
Corvette	146
Impala	142
Lumina	142
Malibu	122
Metro	124
Monte Carlo	142
Suburban	148
Tahoe	148
Trailblazer	132
Tracker	304
Venture	134

CHRYSLER

300M	54
Cirrus	50
Concorde	52
Concorde LTD	54
Intrepid	52
Neon	62
LHS	54
PT Cruiser	56
Sebring	48
Town & Country	60

DAEWOO

Lanos	66
Leganza	68

Nubira	70

DODGE

Avenger	48
Caravan	58
Durango	46
Grand Caravan	60
Neon	62
Stratus	50

EAGLE

Talon	64
Vision	52

FORD

Aerostar	72
Contour	74
Crown Victoria	76
Escape	78
Escort	80
Excursion	82
Expedition	84
Explorer	86
Focus	88
Mustang	90
Probe	92
Taurus	94
Thunderbird 1997	96
Thunderbird 2002	98
Windstar	104

GEO

Metro	124
Tracker	304

GMC

Envoy	132
Jimmy S-15	112
Safari	126
Suburban	148
Yukon	148
Yukon XL	148

HONDA

Accord	150
Civic	152
CR-V	154
del Sol	156
Insight	158
Odyssey	160
Prelude	162
S2000	164

HYUNDAI

Accent	166
Elantra	168
Santa Fe	170
Sonata	172
Tiburon	174
XG300-350	176

INFINITI

G20	178
I30-I35	180
J30	182
Q45	184
QX4	186

ISUZU

Rodeo	188
Trooper	190

JAGUAR

S-Type	192
X-Type	194
XJ	196
XK8	198

JEEP

Cherokee	200
Grand Cherokee	202

INDEX

Liberty	204
TJ	206

KIA

Magentis	208
Rio	210
Sedona	212
Sephia-**Spectra**	214
Sportage	216

LADA

Niva	218
Samara	220

LEXUS

ES	222
GS	224
LS	226
LX	228
RX	230
SC	232

LINCOLN

Continental	234
LS	236
Mark VIII	238
Navigator	240
Town Car	242

MAZDA

Miata	244
Millenia	246
MPV propulsion	248
MPV traction	250
Protegé	252
626/MX-6	254
Tribute	256

MERCEDES-BENZ

C-Class	258
CLK-Class	260
E-Class	262
M-Class	264
S-Class	266
SL-CL-Class	268
SLK-Class	270

MERCURY

Cougar XR7	96
Cougar	100
Grand Marquis	76
Mystique	74
Sable	94
Villager	102

NISSAN

Altima	272
Maxima	274
Pathfinder	276
Quest	278
Sentra	280
Xterra	282
200SX	280
240SX	284

OLDSMOBILE

Achieva	128
Alero	128
Aurora	114
Bravada	132
Cutlass	142
Intrigue	142
Silhouette	134
88	116

PLYMOUTH

Breeze	50
Grand Voyager	60
Neon	62
Voyager	58

PONTIAC

Aztek	138
Bonneville	116
Firebird	110
Firefly	124
Grand Am	128
Grand Prix	142
Montana	134
Sunfire	118
Sunrunner	304
Trans Sport	134

SAAB

900-9^3	286
9000-9^5	288

SATURN

L	290
S	292
Vue	294

SUBARU

Forester	296
Impreza	298
Legacy	300

SUZUKI

Esteem	302
Sidekick	304
Swift	306
Vitara-Grand Vitara	308
X-90	310
XL7	308

TOYOTA

Avalon	312
Camry	314
Celica	316
Corolla	318
Echo	320
Highlander	322
Paseo	336
Previa	324
Prius	326
RAV4	328
Sequoia	330
Sienna	332
Solara	314
Supra	334
Tercel	336
4Runner	338

VOLKSWAGEN

Eurovan	340
Golf	342
Jetta	344
New Beetle	346
New Golf	348
New Jetta	350
New Passat	352
Passat	354

VOLVO

40-Series	356
60-Series	358
70-Series	360
80-Series	362
850-Series	364
900/90-Series	366

A FEW TIPS ON BUYING A USED CAR

WHERE CAN YOU FIND THE BEST BARGAINS?

- At dealerships which offer the best choice of recent model vehicles, with low kilometrage, but available at higher prices.
- At independent resellers, but beware of those who have no repair facilities on the premises or who offer recent model vehicles with high kilometrage.
- Through individuals, where prices are more affordable, but where no other warranties are available except the remainder of the vehicle's original warranty.
- In all cases, make sure that the vehicle's origin is correctly stipulated on the documents supplied to you, that the maintenance record is up-to-date and that copies of all major repair bills have been supplied.

VEHICLE INSPECTION

- Check the body in full daylight, look for repainting, any indication of previous accidents and make a detailed evaluation of the degree of rust present, especially on doors and the trunk lid.
- Wear patterns on tires are an indication whether balancing is good, tar residues on the end of the exhaust pipe indicates that the engine is burning oil because valves or other parts need replacement. Test shock absorbers by leaning hard on the vehicle, which should not bounce more than twice, and examine the exhaust system.

TEST DRIVING THE VEHICLE

- After examining the vehicle while it is standing still, you should insist on test driving it yourself. Take someone with you and have them sit in the back of the vehicle to detect any suspicious noises. As a first step, press down on pedals before starting the engine. The gas pedal and the clutch pedal should be firm and should return quickly to their normal position when released. Verify controls and dials on the instrument panel, check inside lights, headlights, and taillights: everything should be in good working order.
- The engine should start smoothly, with no unusual noises, knocking, whistling or rattling. Engage the handbrake and try to accelerate. The vehicle should go forward slightly, if not, the clutch or the transmission needs adjusting. When in motion, gear shifting should be smooth on automatic transmissions. It should be easy and precise on manual transmissions and the clutch pedal should not need excessive pressure.
- Use a clear area to apply brakes at 50 km/h; they should respond energetically and the vehicle should not deviate from its trajectory. On an incline, it should not move any further when the handbrake is engaged.
- When you return from the test drive, let the engine idle for a few minutes, move the vehicle forward, and check the ground for evidence of leaks.

THINGS TO REMEMBER

- Verify the origin of the vehicle with the manufacturer and with your insurance agent.
- When purchasing a privately owned vehicle, draw up a sales contract and include all pertinent details: the names and addresses of both parties, the vehicle's description, its serial number, the price you have actually paid.
- After the purchase, in writing, notify the manufacturer that you are the new owner of the vehicle and include its serial number; this will ensure that you can take advantage of the remainder of the original warranty and that you will receive notice of any future recalls.

IMPORTANT

Minimum and maximum price quotations provided in this Guide reflect the condition of cars built between 1997 and 2002, at the time of the purchase transaction.

The lowest value quoted applies to a vehicle in poor condition and the highest value quoted applies to a vehicle in the best possible condition.

The average of these two values can be considered to apply to a vehicle in normal condition given its age.

1) Average annual kilometrage is less than 20,000 km.
2) The body and mechanical system should not require any major repairs, nor should painting be necessary.
3) All accessories included as equipment should be in good working order.
4) Tires, shock absorbers and brake linings should have a potential that is equal to or greater than 50%.
5) If in doubt, have a professional proceed with a detailed evaluation to determine the true value of the vehicle you are considering.

Depending on the case, adjust the value using the following charts:

ADJUST THE PRICES ACCORDING TO THE KILOMETRAGE						
Km	2002	2001	2000	1999	1998	1997
			ADD IN $			
10 000	225	370	475	625	770	850
20 000	0	275	375	550	650	750
30 000	375	175	250	375	475	550
40 000	500	0	175	275	400	500
50 000	650	300	125	225	325	425
60 000	850	450	0	150	225	350
70 000	1100	650	275	125	175	275
80 000	1275	825	450	0	125	225
90 000	1400	1100	600	250	100	175
100 000	1575	1250	950	400	0	125
110 000	1750	1300	1025	600	225	100
120 000	2000	1525	1125	750	475	0
130 000	2100	1725	1300	925	600	175
140 000	2300	2000	1400	1100	650	300
150 000	2525	2100	1650	1250	875	500
			DEDUCT IN $			

EQUIPMENT
ADD IN $ IF NOT DELIVERED STANDARD

Equipment	1997	1998	1999	2000	2001	2002
Automatic transmission	225	325	475	625	800	900
Cruise control	75	100	125	150	175	200
Air conditioning	425	525	650	750	850	950
Electric windows	75	100	125	150	175	200
Electric door locks	100	125	150	175	200	225
Electric seats	100	125	150	175	200	225
Leather seats	175	225	275	325	400	500
Radio-cassette	175	200	225	250	275	325
CD player	225	250	275	325	350	425
Sunroof or T-top	325	425	525	675	750	800
Light alloy wheels	200	225	250	275	300	325

ACURA   CL

2001 ACURA 3.2 CL Type-S

The Acura CL is a two-door 2+2 based on the Honda Accord's platform. It was inaugurated in 1997, renewed in 2001 and slightly improved in 2002.

PROS

• **Streamlined style** with a futuristic look, especially the taillamps. The overall effect is quite elegant, more so than are most of its rivals.

• **Comfortable drive**. The cabin seats four passengers with room to spare, but head room is a bit tight. The suspension handles big road faults like a charm, even though there's only average wheel travel.

• **A lot of commodities**, on a car of this like. The trunk is a nice size, and there's plenty of storage space everywhere.

• **Driving** is pleasant even with the 4-cylinder the car makes quick moves and the suspension really controls car path. Steering is great, it's clean, though slightly firm and benefits from a good reduction ratio.

• **The cabin interior** is quite classy with the wood appliques, leather trim seats, meticulous finish details and nice plastic trim that for once looks really neat.

• **The V6 engine** is smooth and quiet, puts out very good accelerations and pick-up, but only the Type-S move like a Sportscar.

• **Brakes** are good and firm, ABS helps achieve emergency stops of around 40 meters and are easy to apply.

CONS

• **The 4-cylinder engine** is a wimp, it's so smooth that it purrs like a big tabby, it never achieves the speed you'd expect on a sports coupe in this price category.

• **Maneuverability** isn't great with a 11.9 m steer angle diameter and you have to take several cracks at most moves.

• **Rigidity isn't enough**, with the groans and rattles we heard on our two test cars when we hit the rippled road section on our test course.

• **The trunk** isn't convertible, it only connects to the cabin via a ski-sized pass-through and the trunk door is pretty narrow.

• **ABS** is somewhat unpredictable, sometimes it's slow on the trigger, and wheel lock occurs over several meters.

• **Unbelievable**: front seat belts that aren't height-adjustable and the poor quality of the standard sound system installed on the first generation models.

VERDICT

All in all, this sports coupe is built more for civilized comfort than for wild sporty behavior.

RECALLS

2002 Defective water pump.

RELIABILITY PROBLEMS

	1997	1998	1999	2000	2001	2002
Engine:	-	-	-		-	-
Transmission:	X	-	-		-	-
Suspension:	-	-	-		-	-
Steering:	-	-	-		-	-
Brakes:	-	-	-		-	-
Electricity:	X	X	X		X	-
Body:	X	X	X		-	-
Accessories:	X	-	X		X	X
Fit/finish:	X	-	-		-	-

POWERTRAIN

Year	Type/ L/Camshaft/bhp	Drivetrain & gearbox	Acceler. 0/100 sec.	Top. speed km/h	Ave. Fuel consp. l./100 km
1997	L4/2.2/SOHC/145	front-M5	9.0	190	9.5
		front-A4	10.0	180	10.5
98-99	L4/2.3/SOHC/150	front-M5	9.0	190	9.6
		front-A4	10.0	180	10.4
97-99	V6/3.0/SOHC/200	front-A4	8.5	200	12.0
01-02	V6/3.2/SOHC/225	front-A5	8.2	200	12.0
	V6/3.2/DOHC/260	front-A5	7.5	220	12.2

PERFORMANCE

SPECIFICATIONS

Model	Wlb. mm	Lght. mm	Cb.wt kg	Brakes fr/rr	Steering type	Standard tires
cpe. 2dr. 2.2	2715	4826	1365	dc/ABS	pwr.r&p.	205/55R16
cpe. 2dr. 2.3	2715	4830	1362	dc/ABS	pwr.r&p.	205/55R16
cpe. 2dr. 3.0	2715	4830	1466	dc/ABS	pwr.r&p.	205/55R16
cpe. 2 dr. 3.2	2715	4877	1574	dc/ABS	pwr.r&p.	205/60R16
cpe. 2 dr. 3.2 S	2715	4877	1592	dc/ABS	pwr.r&p.	215/50R17

PRICES

Model / version		1997	1998	1999	2000	2001	2002
cpe. 2dr. 2.2	mini	10500					
	maxi	14100					
cpe. 2dr. 2.2 Prem	mini	12600					
	maxi	15100					
cpe. 2dr. 2.3	mini		15700	17850			
	maxi		18400	20600			
cpe. 2dr. 3.0	mini	14200	17850	19950			
	maxi	16700	19950	22700			
cpe. 2dr. 3.2	mini					26100	29600
	maxi					28750	32500
cpe. 2dr. Type S	mini					27100	31300
	maxi					29800	34650

See page 7 to adapt these figures.

ACURA EL 2001

The Acura EL is a dressed up Honda Civic loaded with equipment.

PROS

• **Roadhandling** benefits from the excellent original tires and 15-inch wheels. Equipped with two standard stabilizer bars, the EL models take curves very nicely and they're quite agile on slalom runs.

• **Comfort** is good because the suspension handles bumps beautifully and there's less engine roar and vibration. Seats offer good support, but the upholstery is firm.

• **The VTEC engine** is fuel-efficient for normal driving, for the performance it delivers.

• **Commodities**, the trunk is roomy enough when at full passenger capacity and it can also be extended. There are a goodly number of storage compartments in the cabin, but they aren't terribly generous.

• **Build quality** and finish details are scrupulously executed and the cabin interior is spiffy, especially the seat coverings and plastic trim on the dashboard that's the same as on the Civic.

• **This car has inherited** some nice features from the Civic: an ergonomic dashboard, clear outward view and simple gauges and controls.

• **These cars** are really plush-looking, even with the nothing-new body design. Dressed up in certain colors, the EL looks like a little gem.

CONS

• **Performance** are so-and-so because of vehicle weight, due to the rich equipment and safety-oriented vehicle rigidity.

• **Brakes** on the base model are poor, because they aren't linked to ABS, front wheels lock on emergency stops.

• **The EL body** design isn't unattractive, but it's just as nondescript as that of the Civic.

• **The engine** isn't at all well-mannered, it screeches and snorts whenever your toe touches the gas pedal.

• **The automatic shifter** is jumpy and cuts out a few precious horsepower, especially when the air conditioner is functioning.

VERDICT

The Acura EL isn't a bad idea in this day and age when everyone wants to drive a ritzy car, but can't always afford one.

RECALLS

97-98   Right frontal air bag needs to be repaired.
2001   Corroded fuel pump and loose hose clamp will be checked by dealers.

RELIABILITY PROBLEMS

	1997	1998	1999	2000	2001	2002
Engine:	X	X	X	X	-	-
Transmission:	-	-	-	-	-	-
Suspension:	X	-	-	-	X	-
Steering:	-	-	-	-	-	-
Brakes:	X	X	-	-	-	-
Electricity:	X	X	-	X	-	-
Body:	X	X	X	-	-	-
Accessories:	X	X	X	X	X	X
Fit/finish:	X	X	-	-	-	-

POWERTRAIN

Year	Type/ L/Camshaft/bhp	Drivetrain & gearbox	Acceler. 0/100 sec.	Top. speed km/h	Ave. Fuel consp. l./100 km
97-00	L4/1.6/SOHC/127	front-M5	8.8	190	8.3
		front-A4	10.0	180	9.1
01-02	L4/1.7/SOHC/127	front-M5	9.5	190	7.7
		front-A4	10.5	185	8.0

SPECIFICATIONS

Model	Wlb. mm	Lght. mm	Cb.wt kg	Brakes fr/rr	Steering type	Standard tires
97-00						
sdn. 4dr.base/SE	2620	4478	1124	dc/dr	pwr.r&p.	195/55R15
sdn. 4dr. Sport	2620	4478	1144	dc/dr/ABS	pwr.r&p.	195/55R15
sdn. 4dr. Prem.	2620	4478	1162	dc/dr/ABS	pwr.r&p.	195/55R15
01-02						
ber. 4 p. Tour.	2620	4488	1155	dc/dr/ABS	pwr.r&p.	185/65R15
ber. 4 p. Prem.	2620	4488	1172	dc/dr/ABS	pwr.r&p.	185/65R15

PRICES

Model / version		1997	1998	1999	2000	2001	2002
sdn. 4dr.	mini	9450	10700				
	maxi	11450	12600				
sdn. 4dr. SE	mini			12100	14400		
	maxi			13950	16100		
sdn. 4dr. Sport	mini	10500	11750	13100	15450		
	maxi	12600	13650	15100	17200		
sdn. 4dr. Premium	mini	10500	12500	14200	16700	17200	18600
	maxi	13550	14700	16100	18200	19300	21500
sdn. 4dr. Touring	mini					16700	20150
	maxi					18900	22900
sdn. 4dr. LTD	mini						21950
	maxi						25400

See page 7 to adapt these figures.

ACURA   Integra

2000 ACURA Integra GSR

The Acura Integra was first sold in Canada in 1987 and its body design got the latest face-lift in '94. The 4-door model was abandoned in 1997.

PROS

• **Topnotch** reliability, akin to that of Honda products.
• **The 1.8L engine** is more muscular than the former generation 1.6L, especially the latest Type-R's which its 195-hp offers some rather exotic accelerations.
• **Sportscar-like handling** is great with the well-adjusted suspension.
• **The comfy cluster** of seat, steering wheel and instrument panel makes for pleasant driving.
• **The 4-disc brakes** are very effective.
• **Rack and pinion** steering is precise, well-calibrated and has a good reduction ratio.
• **Equipment** is more complete on the LS and GS models.
• **The modular rear seatbench** allows for trunk extension and for greater luggage capacity.

CONS

• **Rear seats** on the coupes are snug and hard to get to.
• **The sedan** body design is too blah and run-of-the-mill for a car of this class.
• **Some trim** materials look chintzy.
• **The automatic gear box** siphens off a lot of power and makes the engine roar and sputter.
• **The sporty suspension** isn't terribly smooth.
• **Soundproofing** on lower-end models isn't what it should be.
• **The poorly upholstered seats** are a pain on long trips.
• **The high trunk** opening doesn't make for easy luggage handling.

VERDICT

The Integra, a reliable, economical car with a Sportscar character, doesn't depreciate or lose its stylish charm as much as its main rivals.

RECALLS

None over this period.

Integra   ACURA

RELIABILITY PROBLEMS

	1997	1998	1999	2000	2001	2002
Engine:	X	X	-	-	-	
Transmission:	-	-	-	-	-	
Suspension:	-	-	-	-	-	
Steering:	-	-	-	-	-	
Brakes:	X	X	X	X	-	
Electricity:	-	-	-	X	-	
Body:	X	-	-	-	-	
Accessories:	X	X	X	X	X	
Fit/finish:	-	-	-	-	-	

POWERTRAIN

Year	Type/ L/Camshaft/bhp	Drivetrain & gearbox
97-01	L4/1.8/DOHC/130-139	front-M5
		front-A4
	L4/1.8/DOHC/170	front-M5
		front-A4
98-01	L4/1.8/DOHC/195 (R)	front-M5

PERFORMANCE

Acceler. 0/100 sec.	Top. speed km/h	Ave. Fuel consp. l./100 km
8.8	200	9.3
9.6	190	9.8
7.5	210	9.3
8.6	200	9.5
7.0	220	9.5

SPECIFICATIONS

Model	Wlb. mm	Lght. mm	Cb.wt kg	Brakes fr/rr	Steering type	Standard tires
97-01						
cpe. 2dr.RS/SE	2570	4380	1147	dc/dc	pwr.r&p.	195/60R14
cpe. 2dr. LS	2570	4380	1170	dc/dc	pwr.r&p.	195/60R14
cpe. 2dr. GS	2570	4380	1197	dc/ABS	pwr.r&p.	195/55R15
cpe. 2dr. GS-R	2570	4380	1214	dc/ABS	pwr.r&p.	195/55R15
cpe. 2dr.Type R	2570	4380	1161	dc/ABS	pwr.r&p.	195/55R15

PRICES

Model / version		1997	1998	1999	2000	2001	2002
cpe. 2 dr. RS	mini	10000	11350				
	maxi	11950	13250				
cpe. 2 dr. LS	mini	12100					
	maxi	14100					
cpe. 2 dr. GS	mini	13100	13950	15750	17100	19400	
	maxi	15100	15750	17650	18700	21500	
cpe. 2 dr. SE	mini			13100	14500	16000	
	maxi			15000	16000	18400	
cpe. 2 dr. GS-R	mini	14200	15000	17450	19200	21000	
	maxi	16300	16800	19200	21000	23100	
cpe. 2dr. Anniv.Ed.	mini	10500					
	maxi	12600					
cpe. 2 dr. Type R	mini	16300	18150	20600	21800	23600	
	maxi	18900	20600	22350	23600	25700	

See page 7 to adapt these figures.

2001 ACURA MDX

Acura took its sweet time to develop its high-end sport-utility vehicle. The result is than much more competitive.

PROS

- **The sober and classic lines** are nevertheless modern and will pass the test of time better than some of its competitors that are already outdated.
- **The MDX has enough interior room** to accommodate seven people in three rows of seats; this makes it about as roomy as a compact minivan.
- **The very sophisticated engine** cranks out brilliant performance, and Honda is the only one to know its secrets since it also equips the Odyssey.
- **The brakes** are powerful, efficient and perfectly balanced. As a result, the hefty MDX comes safely to a stop over short distances. However, fade resistance could be improved.
- **The MDX** is closer to an automobile than a utility vehicle when it comes to ride comfort, because it benefits from a supple suspension as well as efficient shock absorbers and soundproofing.
- **The bin** housed in the floor under the luggage compartment is useful to keep valuables away from prying eyes.

CONS

- **The rear seats** are not comfortable because the benches' cushions are very short, the seatbacks too flat and rear legroom is at a premium.
- **The windshield wipers** are terribly slow and are unable to provide adequate visibility in pouring rain.
- **The plastic materials** look rather cheap; they have a utilitarian look to them that sticks out like a sore thumb in a vehicle of this status and price.
- **Front-seat access** is hindered by the lack of grab handles. Acura could have installed some on the A pillars as most of the competition does.
- **The ridiculous compact spare tire** has no place on a vehicle of such luxury. Here again, Acura shows a lack of judgement in a market segment where competition is fierce.

VERDICT

Technically speaking, the MDX is a remarkable SUV, but its equipment is unfortunately tarnished by certain annoying details.

RECALLS

2002   Defective water pump.

RELIABILITY PROBLEMS

	1997	1998	1999	2000	2001	2002
Engine:						
Transmission:						
Suspension:						
Steering:						
Brakes:		**Insufficient data**				
Electricity:						
Body:						
Accessories:						
Fit/finish:						

POWERTRAIN / PERFORMANCE

Year	Type/ L/Camshaft/bhp	Drivetrain & gearbox	Acceler. 0/100 sec.	Top. speed km/h	Ave. Fuel consp. l./100 km
01-02					
base	V6/3.5/SACT/240	all-A5	8.5	185	14.0

SPECIFICATIONS

Model	Wlb. mm	Lght. mm	Cb.wt kg	Brakes fr/rr	Steering type	Standard tires
01-02						
wgn. 4 dr.	2700	4789	1965	dc/ABS	pwr.r&p.	235/65R17

PRICES

Model / version		1997	1998	1999	2000	2001	2002
wgn. 4 dr.	mini					41600	45700
	maxi					44400	48800

See page 7 to adapt these figures.

2001ACURA MDX

2002 ACURA 3.5RL

Put on the market in 1987, the Legend was the very first Japanese luxury car. It underwent some design modifications in 1991 and in 1996, when it was named the RL.

PROS

• **It is one of the most reliable** car on the market.
• **Its body design** is elegant, but it doesn't have an ounce of character.
• **Driving** is much more enjoyable at the wheel of a coupe powered by a manual transmission.
• **The driver is really spoiled** with such a good driver's position, convenient instrument panel and clear all-round visibility.
• **Build quality** is topnotch.
• **Handling** is generally clean and crisp.
• **Driving** is cushy in such a quiet, spacious interior; there's no vibration whatsoever and seats are well-designed.
• **Fuel consumption** is very reasonable for a car of such displacement and size.

CONS

• **Even the new 210-bhp** V6 engine only yields fair to middling power and torque, it's really quite gutless.
• **Braking power** is generally rather poor because of vehicle weight but stops are mostly straight or predictable, thanks to the ABS.
• **The automatic** siphens off engine output and shifting speeds can be pretty rough and uneven; the 6-speed manual is imprecise and nothing special, given the speed limits that have to be respected by law-abiding citizens.
• **Steering** is over-assisted and crippled by a too high reduction ratio.
• **The terribly** "synthetic"-looking instrument panel on the RL.
• **Trunk capacity** isn't proportional to interior cabin space.
• **The seats** aren't terribly comfortable, for they're poorly contoured and upholstered, and the seat on the seatbench is too short.

VERDICT

The Legend-RL models really lack charisma and character and they trail far behind their Lexus and Infiniti rivals, as far as luxury, comfort or power go.

RECALLS

97-98 Front suspension lower ball joints may prematurely wear out.
00-02 Dealers must clean brake pedal assembly and replaced the brake lights switch full of antirust oil on some vehicles.

RELIABILITY PROBLEMS

	1997	1998	1999	2000	2001	2002
Engine:	X	X	-	-	-	-
Transmission:	-	-	-	-	-	-
Suspension:	X	X	-	-	-	-
Steering:	-	-	-	-	-	-
Brakes:	-	-	X	-	-	-
Electricity:	X	X	X	X	-	-
Body:	X	X	-	-	-	-
Accessories:	-	X	X	X	X	-
Fit/finish:	-	-	-	-	-	-

POWERTRAIN

Year	Type/ L/Camshaft/bhp	Drivetrain & gearbox
97-02	V6/3.5/SOHC/210-225	front-A4

PERFORMANCE

Acceler. 0/100 sec.	Top. speed km/h	Ave. Fuel consp. l./100 km
8.5	200	12.6

SPECIFICATIONS

Model 97-02	Wlb. mm	Lght. mm	Cb.wt kg	Brakes fr/rr	Steering type	Standard tires
sdn. 4dr. RL	2910	4995	1768	dc/ABS	pwr.r&p.	225/55R16

PRICES

Model / version		1997	1998	1999	2000	2001	2002
sdn. 4dr. RL	mini	18400	22400	25800	30150	35100	40400
	maxi	22000	25800	29200	33600	38800	44600

See page 7 to adapt these figures.

2000 ACURA 3.5RL

ACURA   RSX

2002 ACURA RSX

The RSX coupe replaced the Integra in 2002. It is fitted with a 2.0-liter engine and available in base or sport trim.

PROS

• **The dynamic body styling** looks very sporty and is very popular with young drivers.

• The Type S whose engine generates more muscular performance than the base model is fun to drive.

• **The competent handling** is ensured by a very rigid body and sophisticated suspension components. The setup is conducive to fun and safe driving.

• **The attention to assembly** and finish is obvious, with tight tolerances and an impeccable presentation.

• The popularity of Honda products stems mainly from their notorious reliability and durability.

• **The driving position** is comfortable and the cockpit achieves ergonomic perfection.

CONS

• **The base engine's** performance is rather disappointing and does not reflect the vehicle's racy styling.

• **The VTEC engines** deliver their power at high engine speeds that are not always easy to reach in North American driving conditions.

• **The mediocre brakes** produce long stopping distances and models without ABS cannot brake in a straight line.

• The thin cloth upholstery and plastic materials look rather cheap.

• **The rear seats** are suited only for children given leg and headroom are at a high premium.

• **The trunk's** sill is too high and hinders baggage handling.

VERDICT

As was the case with the Integra, the RSX is aimed at young drivers. However, its price and insurance costs are not within everyone's budget.

RECALLS

None over this period.

RELIABILITY PROBLEMS

	1997	1998	1999	2000	2001	2002
Engine:						-
Transmission:						-
Suspension:						-
Steering:						-
Brakes:			Insufficient data			-
Electricity:						-
Body:						-
Accessories:						-
Fit/finish:						-

POWERTRAIN

Year	Type/ L/Camshaft/bhp	Drivetrain & gearbox	Acceler. 0/100 sec.	Top. speed km/h	Ave. Fuel consp. l./100 km
2002					
base	L4/2.0/160	M5-front	9.6	200	8.8
Type S	L4/2.0/200	M5-front	8.2	210	9.7

SPECIFICATIONS

Model 2002	Wlb. mm	Lght. mm	Cb.wt kg	Brakes fr/rr	Steering type	Standard tires
base	2570	4375	1197	d/d	pwr.r&p.	195/65R15
Premium	2570	4375	1260	d/d	pwr.r&p.	205/55R16
Type S	2570	4375	1257	d/d	pwr.r&p.	205/55R16

PRICES

Model / version		1997	1998	1999	2000	2001	2002
cpe. 2 dr. Premium	mini						23600
	maxi						26700
cpe. 2 dr. Type S	mini						26800
	maxi						29900

See page 7 to adapt these figures.

2002 ACURA RSX

2000 ACURA 3.2TL

The TL is built on the Honda Accord platform. It replaced the Vigor in 1996 and was equipped with the V6 Legend engine in 1999. The Type S version was introduced in 2001.

PROS

• **Its clean, classic body** design isn't sensational, but it never goes out of style.
• **The 3.2L V6 engine** has sure added character to the TL, due to a better power to weight ratio, mostly on the Type S.
• **Handling is fine**, but the supple suspension doesn't make for crisp Sportscar moves or maneuvers.
• **Build quality**, fit and finish and materials are absolutely topnotch.
• **Well-designed** suspension and soundproofing make long drives enjoyable and fatigue-free.
• **A rigid frame** resists impact and enhances safety features.
• **The sequential automatic gearbox** that equipped the 99 TL, logically delays upshifting when climbing an incline and applies braking effect by automatically downshifting when going downhill.

CONS

• **The 5-cylinder** engine is a real wimp compared to the V6.
• **Cabin space** is snug, especially in the rear seats where there isn't much head room or leg room.
• **Steering** the Vigor-TL makes you feel like you're driving one of those big American cars of the '70's, for it's over-assisted and has too high a reduction ratio.
• **Vehicle weight** really affects engine performance, especially with four passengers aboard and a trunk chock-full of luggage.
• **Brakes lack** gripping power, the pedal is soft and takes a while to get used to.
• **Aerodynamic efficiency** is disappointing (0.37), given that the car was designed in the nineties.

VERDICT

Unlike the Vigor, the TL has encountered a smashing success, for its performance and driving pleasure, and can be compared to upper crust models in its category.

RECALLS

1998 Front suspension lower ball joints may prematurely wear out.
2002 Defective safety belt buckles on 1081 vehicles (Type S). Power windows mechanism can be corroded by humidity and must be inspected and replaced by dealers if necessary. Inspection and replacement, if necessary, of the water pump and timing belt.

RELIABILITY PROBLEMS

	1997	1998	1999	2000	2001	2002
Engine:	X	X	-	-	-	-
Transmission:	-	-	-	-	-	-
Suspension:	-	X	-	-	-	-
Steering:	-	-	-	-	-	-
Brakes:	-	-	-	-	-	-
Electricity:	X	X	X	X	-	-
Body:	X	X	-	-	-	-
Accessories:	-	X	X	X	X	-

POWERTRAIN

Year	Type/ L/Camshaft/bhp	Drivetrain & gearbox	Acceler. 0/100 sec.	Top. speed km/h	Ave. Fuel consp. l./100 km
97-98	L5/2.5/SOHC/176	front-A4	9.3	200	11.9
97-00	V6/3.2/SOHC/200-225	front-A4	8.6	220	12.3
2001	V6/3.2/DOHC/260 (S)	front-A5	7.2	220	13.4

PERFORMANCE

SPECIFICATIONS

Model	Wlb. mm	Lght. mm	Cb.wt kg	Brakes fr/rr	Steering type	Standard tires
97-98						
sdn. 4dr. 2.5TL	2840	4865	1480	dc/ABS		205/60R15
98-02						
sdn. 4dr. 3.2TL	2745	4900	1565	dc/ABS	pwr.r&p.	205/60R16
01-02						
sdn. 4dr. 3.2TLS	2745	4900	1614	dc/ABS	pwr.r&p.	215/50R17

PRICES

Model / version		1997	1998	1999	2000	2001	2002
sdn. 4dr. 2.5	mini	13100	16000				
	maxi	16100	19550				
sdn. 4dr. 3.2	mini	15200	18150	22000	24500	27700	31300
	maxi	18300	21650	25000	27300	30500	35000
sdn. 4 dr. 3.2 S	mini						33400
	maxi						37200

See page 7 to adapt these figures.

2000 ACURA 3.2 TL

AUDI   A4

2000 AUDI S4

The A4 has replaced the 90 in 1996 with 1.8T L4 and 2.8L V6 engines and has been renewed in 2002 with 1.8T L4 an 3.0L V6 engines and an optional continuously variable automatic transmission.

PROS
- **A nicely shaped**, striking body design.
- **With the right tires**, the Quattro all-wheel drive makes for safer handling in winter conditions, and the A4 really holds the road in most cases.
- **Engine performance** are impressive, thanks to a good power to weight ratio and to a well-suited 5-speed automatic gear box.
- **The build is very rigid**, fit and finish are meticulous and materials are top-notch, and reliability is no longer a problem.
- **Monocoque body** is made entirely of galvanized steel, so it provides one of the best warranty in the world to win the war against rust.
- **Overall comfort** is great due to a supple suspension, contoured and well-cushioned seats and effective soundproofing that blocks out engine and road noise.
- **A comfortable driver's position**, good visibility and a straightforward and practical instrument panel make for pleasant driving.
- **There are plenty** of good-sized storage compartments and the trunk is expandable and of easy access with its large opening.

CONS
- **Price tag** isn't too popular and the V6 sure guzzles the gas and of course, upkeep and repairs can cost an arm and a leg.
- **Cabin space** is quite snug in the rear seat, there's more head room and hip room, but leg room is quite tight.
- **Steering** is a bit over-assisted and becomes light and sensitive at high speeds. Luckily the body isn't sensitive to wind.
- **The typically European** controls take getting used to.
- **The Audi service** network is quite limited, which makes upkeep a bit touchy.

VERDICT
People who are out to impress others will opt for this high-tech sophisticated model, but their choice won't be cheap...

RECALLS
1997 Airbags are defective.
1998 Air flow meter's screen is defective.
97-99 Possible loss of power brake assist at low temperatures.

RELIABILITY PROBLEMS

	1997	1998	1999	2000	2001	2002
Engine:	X	X	X	-	-	-
Transmission:	X	X	-	-	-	-
Suspension:	-	-	-	-	-	-
Steering:	-	-	-	-	-	-
Brakes:	X	X	X	X	X	-
Electricity:	X	X	X	X	X	-
Body:	-	-	-	-	-	-
Accessories:	X	X	X	X	X	X
Fit/finish:	-	-	X	-	-	-

POWERTRAIN

Year 97-01	Type/ L/Camshaft/bhp	Drivetrain & gearbox	Acceler. 0/100 sec.	Top. speed km/h	Ave. Fuel consp. l./100 km
1.8T	L4T/1.8/DOHC/150	ft./all-M5	9.0	200	13.2
		ft./all-A5	10.0	200	12.1
2.8	V6/2.8/DOHC/172-190	ft./all-M5	10.0	200	12.2
		ft./all-A5	10.5	190	13.5
2002					
1.8T	L4/1.8/DOHC/170	ft./all-M5	8.2	210	11.0
		ft./all-TVC	8.5	200	11.5
3.0	V6/3.0/DOHC/220	ft./all-M6	7.4	220	13.5
		ft./all-TVC	7.6	210	12.5

SPECIFICATIONS

Model 97-01	Wlb. mm	Lght. mm	Cb.wt kg	Brakes fr/rr	Steering type	Standard tires
sdn. 4dr. 1.8	2617	4522	1305	dc/ABS	pwr.r&p.	205/60R15
sdn. 4dr. 1.8 q.	2607	4522	1420	dc/ABS	pwr.r&p.	205/60R15
sdn. 4dr. 2.8	2617	4522	1400	dc/ABS	pwr.r&p.	205/55R16
sdn. 4dr. 2.8 q.	2607	4522	1505	dc/ABS	pwr.r&p.	205/55R16
2002						
sdn. 4dr. 1.8T	2650	4547	1475	dc/ABS	pwr.r&p.	205/65R15
sdn. 4dr. 1.8Tq.	2650	4547	1610	dc/ABS	pwr.r&p.	205/65R15
sdn. 4dr. 3.0	2650	4557	1570	dc/ABS	pwr.r&p.	215/55R16
sdn. 4dr. 3.0 q.	2650	4557	1625	dc/ABS	pwr.r&p.	215/55R16

PRICES

Model / version		1997	1998	1999	2000	2001	2002
sdn. 4dr. 1.8T	mini	15850	16150	19300	24250	28250	
	maxi	19200	19400	22450	27100	30900	
sdn. 4dr. 1.8T q.	mini	13450	17100	20250	26900	30700	33600
	maxi	16700	20350	23500	29900	33600	36750
sdn. 4dr. 1.8T FT	mini						31500
	maxi						35100
sdn. 4dr. 2.8	mini	14900	18900	21750	26350	30350	
	maxi	18300	22250	25000	29200	33100	
sdn. 4dr. 2.8 q.	mini	15800	19850	22700	29500	33450	
	maxi	19300	23100	26150	32500	36350	
sdn. 4dr. 3.0 q.	mini						37800
	maxi						41350
wgn. 4dr. 1.8T q.	mini						35700
	maxi						39300
wgn. 4dr. 3.0 L q.	mini						39900
	maxi						43450

See page 7 to adapt these figures.

AUDI   A6/S4-S6

2000 AUDI A6

The A6, redesigned in '95, is available with front-wheel drive or quattro all-wheel drive and are driven by the 2.8L V6, while the sporty S4 is powered by a 2.2L 5-cylinder. The A6 was renewed in 1998 and a 2.7 V6 Turbo and a V8 engines where added in 2000 and the 3.0L V6 in 2002.

PROS

• **The Quattro system** provides excellent traction in all kinds of weather, which makes for remarkable handling, especially in snow.
• **The sporty S4/S6/2.7/4.2** models are thrilling to drive and they are real spoilers too, because they are so plush.
• **In some respects**, build quality and fit and finish are superior to that of BMW and Mercedes cars.
• **The body shape** of the 1998 A6 is classic yet has a lot more character than its predecessors.
• **The cabin comfortably** seats five adults and the trunk is spacious and of easy access, even if it isn't expandable.
• **Equipment** is very lush and a real treat.
• **The 6-cylinder** engine is smooth, powerful and economical.
• **As far as rust goes**, you don't have a care in the world with a completely galvanized steel body. A world first.

CONS

• **With such a heavy vehicle**, the V6 seems to strain and sputter and performance is at the base limit of what you'd expect for a model of this price...
• **Steering** is terribly over-assisted, so you have to really keep an eye on it.
• **The suspension** is too flexible and causes a lot of sway.
• **Some of the controls** are quite unconventional and require getting used to.
• **Maintenance** isn't cheap when the warranty runs out and resale value plummets, so you don't see too many of these cars on the road.

VERDICT

In spite of its high-tech features, build quality and reliability, this model isn't too popular as a new or used car because of consumer mistrust of Audi products.

RECALLS

1997 Airbags are defective.
1998 Air flow meter's screen is defective.
98-00 Defective fuel tank sensors give false indications about the real amount of fuel.

RELIABILITY PROBLEMS

	1997	1998	1999	2000	2001	2002
Engine:	X	X	X	-	-	-
Transmission:	-	-	X	X	X	-
Suspension:	-	X	X	-	-	-
Steering:	-	X	X	-	-	-
Brakes:	X	X	X	X	-	-
Electricity:	X	X	X	X	X	X
Body:	-	-	-	-	-	-
Accessories:	X	X	X	X	X	-
Fit/finish:	-	-	-	-	X	-

POWERTRAIN

Year	Type/ L/Camshaft/bhp	Drivetrain & gearbox	Acceler. 0/100 sec.	Top. speed km/h	Ave. Fuel consp. l./100 km
1997					
base	V6/2.8/SOHC/172	front-A4	10.0	210	13.3
quat.	V6/2.8/SOHC/172	all-A4	11.2	210	12.6
S4-S6	L5T/2.3/SOHC/227	all-M5	7.0	210	12.7
98-01					
base	V6/2.8/DOHC/193-200	front-A5	9.6	230	13.4
quat.	V6/2.8/DOHC/193-200	all-A5	11.0	225	13.8
2.7T	V6T/DOHC/250	all-A5	7.2	210	13.5
4.2	V8/4.2/DOHC/300-340	all-A5	6.7	210	14.0
2002					
3.0	V6/DOHC/220	ft./all- A5	9.0	200	12.5

SPECIFICATIONS

Model 1997	Wlb. mm	Lght. mm	Cb.wt kg	Brakes fr/rr	Steering type	Standard tires
sdn. 4dr.	2692	4892	1535	dc/ABS	pwr.r&p.	195/65R15
sdn. 4dr. q.	2692	4892	1665	dc/ABS	pwr.r&p.	195/65R15
wgn. 4dr.	2692	4892	1685	dc/ABS	pwr.r&p.	195/65R15
sdn. 4dr. S4	2692	4892	1715	dc/ABS	pwr.r&p.	225/50R16
sdn. 4dr. S6	2692	4892	1715	dc/ABS	pwr.r&p.	225/50R16
98-02						
sdn. 4dr. 2.7 q	2760	4878	1705	dc/ABS	pwr.r&p.	215/55R16
sdn. 4dr. 3.0 q	2760	4878	1650	dc/ABS	pwr.r&p.	215/55R16
sdn. 4dr. 4.2 q	2759	4878	1825	dc/ABS	pwr.r&p.	255/40R17

PRICES

Model / version		1997	1998	1999	2000	2001	2002
A6							
sdn. 4dr.	mini		23750	29300	29700	37600	
	maxi		27700	33700	33700	40400	
sdn. 4dr. quat.	Mini	19950	24800	32850	32850	40700	
	maxi	23850	28700	36950	36950	43600	
sdn. 4dr. 2.7 q.	mini				36750	44500	50400
	maxi				40500	47250	53950
sdn. 4dr. 3.0 L frtrk	mini						43600
	maxi						47000
sdn. 4dr. 3.0 L q	mini						46700
	maxi						50300
sdn. 4dr. 4.2 q.	mini				47800	54800	61950
	maxi				51850	57750	65500
wgn. 4dr. q.	mini	22000					
	maxi	25700					
wgn. 4dr. q. IV	mini				30650	34950	44400
	maxi				34650	38950	47250
wgn. 4dr. Av. quat	mini						48800
	maxi						52400
S4							
sdn. 4dr. 2.7 q.	mini				39700	45450	48800
	maxi				43800	48000	52300
S6							
sdn. 4dr.	mini	25400					
	maxi	28550					
wgn. 4dr. 4.2 L quat	mini						76850
	maxi						80750

See page 7 to adapt these figures.

2001 AUDI S8

The first V8-powered Audi came on the market towards the end of 1992, whereas the A8 has been sold since 1997 and makes more than one dream about. The stretch L version was introduced in 2000 and the sporty S8 in 2001.

PROS

- **Roadability** with the exclusive Torsen quattro system is super, especially in winter conditions.
- **The remarkable V8** engine pumps out real sporty zoom, yet these roomy sedans are luxurious and practical.
- **The 4.2L** engine is smooth and zippy and fuel consumption is reasonable with the front-wheel drive mode.
- **Four-disc brakes** provide honorable braking, but linings wear out quickly and have to be replaced often.
- **The cabin comfortably** seats five passengers and the trunk holds quite a bit of luggage.
- **Steering** is smooth and precise.
- **The galvanized** steel body on the first models or aluminum body on the more recent models holds up well against rust.
- **The array** of equipment is lush and refined.

CONS

- **Maintenance and repairs** are pricy, so the privilege of driving such a high-tech vehicle doesn't come cheap.
- **Driving pleasure** is a mixed bag with the A8, due to the prim and proper behavior of such a perfect specimen that seems to lack soul.
- **Body and cabin design** are rather blah, which doesn't quite match the modern engineering that comes with the package.
- **The quattro versions** are gas guzzlers due to the hefty weight and its all-wheel drive mechanism.
- **These heavy, bulky cars** can't boast of athletic agility on slalom runs.

VERDICT

The innovative features of the V8-powered Audi cost a bundle when it comes to upkeep and repairs. Best to think twice before making such an investment.

RECALLS

1997 Airbags can be defective on some models.

RELIABILITY PROBLEMS

	1997	1998	1999	2000	2001	2002
Engine:						
Transmission:						
Suspension:						
Steering:						
Brakes:						
Electricity:		**Insufficient data**				
Body:						
Accessories:						
Fit/finish:						

POWERTRAIN / PERFORMANCE

Type/ L/Camshaft/bhp	Drivetrain & gearbox	Acceler. 0/100 sec.	Top. speed km/h	Ave. Fuel consp. l./100 km
97-02 V8/4.2/DOHC/300-310	all-A5	7.5	210	14.0
01-02 V8/4.2/DOHC/360 (S8)	all-A5	6.5	240	16.0

SPECIFICATIONS

Model	Wlb.	Lght.	Cb.wt	Brakes	Steering	Standard
97-02						
sdn. 4dr. A8	2882	5034	1770	dc/ABS	pwr.r&p.	225/60R16
00-02						
sdn. 4dr. A8L	3010	5164	1885	dc/ABS	pwr.r&p.	225/60R16
01-02						
sdn. 4dr. S8	2880	5034	1845	dc/ABS	pwr.r&p.	245/45R18

PRICES

Model / version		1997	1998	1999	2000	2001	2002
A8							
sdn. 4dr. q. A8	mini	30550	35800	43000	49750	55950	61950
	maxi	34850	40850	47900	55100	60600	66000
sdn. 4dr. quat . L	mini					60900	66150
	maxi					64800	70350
S8							
sdn. 4dr. q.	mini					75600	85800
	maxi					78700	89200

See page 7 to adapt these figures.

2001 AUDI S8

AUDI   Allroad

2001 AUDI Allroad

The Allroad is based on the A6 Avant and equipped with a height-adjustable suspension that enables it to travel "somewhat" off the beaten path, somewhat being the key word because it's not a true all-terrain vehicle.

PROS
• The model is a shining example of **active and passive safety**, a rarity among multi-purpose vehicles.
• **It's remarkably versatile**, combining luxury and utility features.
• **Assembly and finish quality** are remarkable, and the Audi even outclasses its reputed German rivals in this respect.
• **The twin-turbo V6** cranks out high performance and makes this luxurious utilitarian feel like an exotic.
• **The generous cabin and cargo bay** make it possible for five people to travel aboard in full comfort and bring their luggage along with them.
• **The extended warranty** will keep bad surprises due to defects at bay for original owners.
• **Audi models' resale value** is progressing quite well, but many potential buyers fear the high repair costs associated with these technological marvels.

CONS
• This luxury car comes with a **high price tag** and commands expensive maintenance costs, placing it out of the financial reach of most buyers.
• **The Allroad's off-road capabilities** are limited, and it's far from being a real all-terrain vehicle.
• **The turbocharger** is plagued by an annoyingly long turbo lag; making the most of the engine's power therefore takes some getting used to.
• **The Tiptronic shifter** is not as practical to use as other similar systems on the market.
• **The harsh suspension** and extremely firm seats are not very comfortable but typical of German automobiles.
• **The steering** is too light and fuzzy because it's overassisted. Drivers must exercise caution when travelling in strong crosswinds or on slippery surfaces.
• **The windshield wipers** are terribly slow and do not provide adequate visibility in heavy rain.
• **The digital information display** housed in the middle of the instrument panel is completely impossible to decipher during the day.

VERDICT
The Allroad remains a marginal model that will interest only the make's fanatics, because other auto makers offer models that are just as good but far less expensive.

RECALLS
None over this period.

RELIABILITY PROBLEMS

	1997	1998	1999	2000	2001	2002
Engine:						
Transmission:						
Suspension:						
Steering:						
Brakes:		Insufficient data				
Electricity:						
Body:						
Accessories:						
Fit/finish:						

POWERTRAIN

Year	Type/ L/Camshaft/bhp	Drivetrain & gearbox
01-02		
base	V6T/2.7/DOHC/250	all-M6

PERFORMANCE

Acceler. 0/100 sec.	Top. speed km/h	Ave. Fuel consp. l./100 km
7.5	210	15.0

SPECIFICATIONS

Model	Wlb. mm	Lght. mm	Cb.wt kg	Brakes fr/rr	Steering type	Standard tires
wgn. 4dr.	2757	4810	1890	dc/ABS	pwr.r&p.	225/55R17

PRICES

Model / version		1997	1998	1999	2000	2001	2002
wag. 4dr. Quat.	mini					37700	43000
	maxi					40750	46000

See page 7 to adapt these figures.

2001 AUDI Allroad

AUDI   TT

2000 AUDI TT coupe

Derived from the A4 in 1999, the TT coupe and convertible are available with FWD or AWD and a 1.8L L4T engine giving 180 or 225 hp.

PROS
- **The bulky style** of this speedster that looks solid as a rock.
- **Safety** is insured by the extremely stiff body and front and side-impact airbags.
- **Performance** of the base engine are fun but its 225 hp version seems sometimes too powerful...
- **Handling** of the quattro version is impressive, because the car seems to be literally glued to the road.
- **Brakes** are easy to adjust, grip smoothly and progressively. Stopping distances are short and fade resistance very good.
- **The suspension** isn't really too supple, but it benefits from enough travel to take a bruising from the bumps, without jostling occupants.
- **Cabin design** is gorgeous since it imitates race car stylistics with all this polished metal inserts.
- **High quality** of engineering, assembly and finish which is simply flawless.
- **Convenient** storage bins and the regular shapes of the trunk.

CONS
- **Steering** system springs and lacks of accuracy on FWD.
- **Visibility** isn't ideal because the seating position is low , the body belt high and roof pillars are very thick.
- **Access** to the rear seats is no picnic and their use is very limited.
- **Center console** gobbles up a lot of space, especially the aluminum bar that forms a handle that you're always hitting your knee against.
- **Remote-control** switches to open the rear hatch door, gas tank filler hole cap and to deactivate the alarm system are hard to reach, hidden in a compartment at the extremity of the center console.

VERDICT
Against its competitors the TT coupe offers the advantage of year-round driveability thanks to a very reliable quattro AWD system.

RECALLS
1999 The highly sensible steering system hampered stability in curves on the FWD version.

RELIABILITY PROBLEMS

	1997	1998	1999	2000	2001	2002
Engine:					-	-
Transmission:					-	-
Suspension:					-	-
Steering:					-	-
Brakes:					X	
Electricity:					X	X
Body:					X	-
Accessories:					X	-
Fit/finish:					-	-

POWERTRAIN

Year	Type/ L/Camshaft/bhp	Drivetrain & gearbox
00-02	L4/1.8/DOHC/180	front-M5
	L4/1.8/DOHC/180	all-M5
	L4T/1.8/DOC/225	all-M5

PERFORMANCE

Acceler. 0/100 sec.	Top. speed km/h	Ave. Fuel consp. l./100 km
8.4	200	11.0
9.0	190	11.5
7.8	210	12.0

SPECIFICATIONS

Model 00-02	Wlb. mm	Lght. mm	Cb.wt kg	Brakes fr/rr	Steering type	Standard tires
cpe. 2 dr. FWD	2429	4041	1325	dc/ABS	pwr.r&p	205/55R16
cpe. 2 dr. AWD	2429	4041	1485	dc/ABS	pwr.r&p.	225/45R17
conv. 2 dr.FWD	2429	4041	1420	dc/ABS	pwr.r&p	205/55R16
conv. 2 dr.AWD	2429	4041	1575	dc/ABS	pwr.r&p.	225/45R17

PRICES

Model / version		1997	1998	1999	2000	2001	2002
cpe. 2 dr. 180	mini				32350	39150	44000
	maxi				36100	42500	47150
cpe. 2 dr. q. 180	mini					41250	46150
	maxi					44300	49250
cpe. 2 dr. q 225	mini					41150	47450
	maxi					44100	50600
conv. 2 dr. q. 225	mini					42850	54000
	maxi					46000	57200
conv. 2 dr. 180	mini						53350
	maxi						56400

See page 7 to adapt these figures.

2000 AUDI TT convertible

BMW   3 Series

2001 BMW 330i

The last revamped of the 3 Series occured in 1999 with 2.5 and 3.0L engines and, since then, the model range has widened considerably. AWD versions arrived in 2001.

PROS

• **Handling** on s and M3 models is much more stable than on the basic i model whose rear end tends to swing.

• **The engines** are really gutsy and silky smooth except for the 1.8L.

• **The M3 sports** model is incredible and worth every cent.

• **Brakes** are absolutely sensational, for they're powerful and stop on a dime.

• **You can't beat** the fun of driving with such a good seating position and a well-organized instrument panel at your fingertips.

• **The well-adjusted** suspension and plush seats make for a great blend of Sportscar capabilities and luxury sedan comfort.

CONS

• **The really snug** rear seat on the 94 models and predecessors.

• **Overall build** quality isn't as good as for other cars available in this model range.

• **The trunk** isn't too roomy and is hard to get to because of the high opening.

• **Whistling** wind noise around the windshield and sunroof.

• **Plastic trim** on the instrument panel looks pretty chintzy.

VERDICT

The 3 Series is the most affordable BMW vehicle for Sportscar enthusiasts who never give up on their dream of owning such a car...

RECALLS

1997 Cruise control is defective.

1999 Airbag control module must be reprogrammed to avoid inadvertent side airbags and head protection system.
The retaining clip that secures the brake booster pushrod to the brake pedal arm may be incompletely seated.

2001 Some defective rims will be checked by dealers.

RELIABILITY PROBLEMS

	1997	1998	1999	2000	2001	2002
Engine:	X	X	X	X	X	-
Transmission:	-	-	-	-	-	-
Suspension:	-	-	-	-	-	-
Steering:	-	-	-	-	-	-
Brakes:	-	-	X	-	-	-
Electricity:	X	X	X	X	X	-
Body:	X	X	X	X	X	-
Accessories:	X	X	X	X	X	X
Fit/finish:	X	X	-	-	-	-

POWERTRAIN

Year	Type/ L/Camshaft/bhp	Drivetrain & gearbox	Acceler. 0/100 sec.	Top. speed km/h	Ave. Fuel consp. l./100 km
97-99	L4/1.9/DOHC/138 (318)	rear-M5	9.8	187	10.2
98-02	L6/2.5/DOHC/184 (323)	rear-M5	NA	NA	11.6
97-00	L6/2.8/DOHC/190 (328)	rear-M5	8.0	206	11.9
1997	L6/3.2/DOHC/321 (M3)	rear-M5	6.0	230	13.0
98-99	L6/3.2/DOHC/240 (M3)	rear-M5	7.0	220	11.8
01-02	L6/2.2/DOHC/168 (320)	rear-M5	NA	NA	11.5
	L6/3.0/DOHC/225 (ix)	rr./all-M5	8.5	205	12.0

PERFORMANCE

(merged into POWERTRAIN table above)

SPECIFICATIONS

Model 97-98	Wlb. mm	Lght. mm	Cb.wt kg	Brakes fr/rr	Steering type	Standard tires
cpe. 2dr. 318i	2700	4210	1260	dc/dr/ABS	pwr.r&p.	185/65R15
sdn. 4dr. 318is	2700	4433	1300	dc/ABS	pwr.r&p.	205/60R15
sdn. 4dr. 320i	2700	4433	1370	dc/ABS	pwr.r&p.	205/60R15
sdn. 4dr. 323i	2725	4471	1430	dc/ABS	pwr.r&p.	195/65R15
cpe. 2dr. 325is	2700	4433	1370	dc/ABS	pwr.r&p.	205/60R15
sdn. 4dr. 325i	2700	4433	1405	dc/ABS	pwr.r&p.	205/60R15
sdn. 4dr. 328i	2725	4471	1450	dc/ABS	pwr.r&p.	205/55R16
cpe. 2dr. M3	2710	4433	1440	dc/ABS	pwr.r&p.	225/45R17
sdn. 4dr. M3	2700	4433	1440	dc/ABS	pwr.r&p.	225/45R17
99-02						
sdn. 4dr. 320i	2725	4471	1440	dc/ABS	pwr.r&p.	195/65R15
sdn. 4dr. 325i	2725	4471	1470	dc/ABS	pwr.r&p.	205/55R16
cpe. 2dr. 325iCi	2725	4471	1490	dc/ABS	pwr.r&p.	205/55R16
sdn. 4dr. 330i	2725	4471	1505	dc/ABS	pwr.r&p.	205/50R17
conv. 2dr.330Ci	2725	4488	1645	dc/ABS	pwr.r&p.	205/50R17

2000 BMW 323Ci convertible

2001 BMW 330Ci coupe

PRICES

Model / version		1997	1998	1999	2000	2001	2002
cpe. 2dr. 318i	mini	10100	13450	16000			
	maxi	12800	16600	18400			
cpe. 2dr. 318S	mini	13850	18900	20500			
	maxi	17450	22350	23000			
cpe. 2dr. 318ti Active	mini	11000	15450	17000			
	maxi	13850	18500	19400			
cpe. 2dr. 318ti Sport	mini	12100	16800	19200			
	maxi	14900	19950	21500			
con. 2dr. 318C	mini	20000	24450	27600			
	maxi	24800	29200	31500			
cpe. 2dr. 323i	mini		19550				
	maxi		24150				
cpe.2dr. 323Ci	mini				29400		
	maxi				33400		
cpe. 2dr. 323iS	mini			27600			
	maxi			31500			
con. 2dr.323CI	mini		26900	31800	38300		
	maxi		31500	35700	42300		
cpe. 2dr. M	mini			39150	46000		
	maxi			43000	50700		
cpe. 2dr. M3	mini	30000	37800	42300		61950	64600
	maxi	34700	40900	46200		65400	68250
con. 2dr. M3	mini					70350	74000
	maxi					73800	77700
cpe. 2dr. 325Ci	mini					34100	36200
	maxi					37500	39900
con. 2dr. 325Ci	mini					45350	48300
	maxi					47800	52500
cpe. 2dr. 328iS	mini	19750	25100	28650			
	maxi	24550	28650	32550			
cpe. 2dr. 328Ci	mini				38000		
	maxi				42000		

3 Series   (cont.)   BMW

PRICES

Model / version		1997	1998	1999	2000	2001	2002
con. 2dr. 328Ci	mini	26000	31500	38100			
	maxi	30750	36550	42000			
cpe. 2dr. 330Ci	mini					40250	43600
	maxi					43600	47250
con. 2dr. 330Ci	mini					54400	59200
	maxi					57750	63000
sdn. 4dr. 318i	mini	12900	18000				
	maxi	16400	22000				
sdn. 4dr. 320i	mini					26000	27800
	maxi					29400	32000
sdn. 4dr. 323i	mini			26550	27800		
	maxi			30450	31800		
sdn. 4dr. 325i	mini					32850	33600
	maxi					35700	37800
sdn. 4dr. 325i touring	mini						35700
	maxi						40400
sdn.4dr. 325xi	mini						37800
	maxi						42000
sdn. 4dr. 325xi touring	mini						36750
	maxi						43000
sdn. 4dr. 328i	mini		19750	18600	30350	35700	
	maxi		24600	22150	34100	39700	
sdn. 4dr. 330i	mini	40200	42000				
	maxi	43600	46200				
sdn. 4dr. 330 xi	mini						44100
	maxi						49350
sdn. 4dr. M3	mini	30000	37600				
	maxi	34750	41600				

See page 7 to adapt these figures.

2000 BMW 323Ci

2000 BMW 530i

The 5 Series ranks between the lower-end 3 Series and the upper-end 7 Series. The last generation was born in 1996 when the V8 engine was available along with the traditional 6-cylinder engine. Since 1999, two new and improved wagons were introduced, powered by either a 6 or a 8 cylinders. The M5 version appeared in 2000 and the 2.5L and 3.0L in 2001.

PROS
• **The clean**, classic look is elegant and even the station wagon has a charming design.
• **The engines** have gutsy get up and go, especially the V8 or the M5 model, which even at normal speeds, make for a really thrilling ride.
• **This car** is state-of-the-art high-tech, body is robust and rustproof.
• **The car handles** smoothly and evenly and traction is sensational for these rear-wheel drive vehicles, even on slippery roads.
• **Comfort** is getting cushier and cushier, with smoother suspensions and plusher seats and the interior cabin design has improved.
• **Steering** and brakes are simply perfect and completely reliable.
• **The interior cabin** is less plain than on the former 500 Series, build quality and fit and finish are clean as a whistle.
• **The trunk** is roomy and nicely shaped and the cabin has lots of well-designed storage compartments.

CONS
• **Vehicle weight**, price tag and high cost of upkeep.
• **The manual transmissions** are poorly calibrated for they're geared to driving at top speeds on the "autobahn", which really affects torque at low rpm.
• **The cabin** is still snug even with the bigger body.
• **Fuel consumption** varies according to the engine performance: so the 525i/ 528i are the most economical models to run.

VERDICT
Even used, 5 Series cars are pretty pricy and you should think twice about investing in one.

RECALLS
1998 Transmission gear position switch is defective (528i). Some defective differential assemblies must be replaced.

RELIABILITY PROBLEMS

	1997	1998	1999	2000	2001	2002
Engine:	X	X	X	X	X	-
Transmission:	-	X	-	-	-	-
Suspension:	-	-	-	-	-	-
Steering:	-	-	-	-	-	-
Brakes:	-	-	X	-	-	-
Electricity:	X	X	X	X	X	X
Body:	X	X	X	X	X	-
Accessories:	X	X	X	X	-	-
Fit/finish:	X	X	-	-	-	-

POWERTRAIN

Year	Type/ L/Camshaft/bhp	Drivetrain & gearbox	Acceler. 0/100 sec.	Top. speed km/h	Ave. Fuel consp. l./100 km
01-02	L6/2.5/DOHC/184(525i)	rear-M5	8.6	206	11.5
97-00	L6/2.8/DOHC/190 (528i)	rear-M5	8.0	206	11.9
01-02	L6/3.0/DOHC/225(530i)	rear-M5	8.0	206	12.0
99-02	V8/4.4/DOHC/282 (540i)	rear-M6	6.7	250	15.5
00-02	V8/5.0/DOHC/400 (M5)	rear-M6	5.5	250	15.0

PERFORMANCE

SPECIFICATIONS

Model	Wlb.	Lght.	Cb.wt	Brakes	Steering	Standard
97-02						
sdn. 4dr. 525i	2830	4775	1575	dc/ABS	pwr.bal.	225/55R15
sdn. 4dr. 528i	2830	4775	1585	dc/ABS	pwr.bal.	225/60R15
sdn. 4dr. 530i	2830	4775	1600	dc/ABS	pwr.bal.	225/66R16
sdn. 4dr. 540i	2830	4775	1700	dc/ABS	pwr.bal.	235/45R15
wgn. 4dr. 525il	2830	4805	1690	dc/ABS	pwr.bal.	225/60R15
wgn. 4dr. 528iT	2830	4805	1690	dc/ABS	pwr.bal.	225/60R16
wgn. 4dr. 540iT	2830	4805	1840	dc/ABS	pwr.bal.	225/55R16
00-02						
sdn. 4dr. M5	2830	4785	1720	dc/ABS	pwr.bal.	245/40R18 275/35R18

PRICES

Model / version		1997	1998	1999	2000	2001	2002
sdn. 4dr. 525i	mini					44700	47900
	maxi					48300	51450
wag. 4dr. 525T	mini					44950	48400
	maxi					48500	52000
sdn. 4dr. 528iA	mini	23100	29000	36950	41250		
	maxi	29100	34100	41600	45800		
wgn. 4dr. 528iT	mini			38000	41600		
	maxi			42650	46400		
sdn. 4dr. 530i	mini					53250	55350
	maxi					56400	59900
sdn. 4dr. 540iA	mini	29600	35700	42000	47450	61500	65100
	maxi	34650	41150	47250	53250	65300	69300
sdn. 4dr. M5	mini			74550	81900	86100	
	maxi				81250	88500	93450
wgn. 4dr. 540iT	mini			42200	48600	62800	67200
	maxi			47550	54300	66700	70900

See page 7 to adapt these figures.

1999 BMW 750iL

Launched in 1986, the 7 Series vehicles come in short or long body styles, driven by a 6-cylinder in-line engine, a V8 or a V12. They were redesigned in 1995.

PROS

• **State-of-the-art technology** is the name of the game, like the anti-skid system, the electronically controlled suspension and other expensive high-tech items that are simply amazing.

• **Engine performance** are awesome, especially with the V12 that takes you away into another dimension.

• **Handling** is just sensational and works like a charm, no matter what the driving style.

• **Driving** is safe and sure, thanks to near-perfect steering and clean, crisp brakes.

• **The electronically controlled** suspension, plush seats and quiet as a mouse soundproofing make for a regal ride.

• **Equipment** is very extensive and includes various sophisticated devices.

CONS

• **The high price** tag and expensive upkeep after the warranty runs out.

• **Vehicle weight** and size are awkward at times and affect maneuverability.

• **Pick-up** is pretty soft and lazy with the automatic, and gears take quite a while to wake up and kick in.

• **Some of the controls** are unusual and/or complicated and take time getting used to.

VERDICT

The BMW 7 Series is the top-end and top-price model range produced by the carmaker. Yet, you have to be wary of buying one of the older models that cost a small fortune to keep in good running order.

RECALLS

1997 Defective front suspension springs.

1998 Some defective differential assemblies must be replaced.

RELIABILITY PROBLEMS

	1997	1998	1999	2000	2001	2002
Engine:	X	X	X	X	X	-
Transmission:	X	-	-	-	-	-
Suspension:	X	X	X	-	-	-
Steering:	-	-	-	-	-	-
Brakes:	X	X	X	X	-	-
Electricity:	-	X	X	X	X	X
Body:	X	X	-	-	-	-
Accessories:	X	X	X	X	X	X
Fit/finish:	X	X	-	-	-	-

POWERTRAIN

Year	Type/ L/Camshaft/bhp	Drivetrain & gearbox	Acceler. 0/100 sec.	Top. speed km/h	Ave. Fuel consp. l./100 km
97-02					
740i	V8/4.4/DOHC/282	rear-A5	8.5	206	13.9
750i	V12/5.4/SOHC/322	rear-A5	7.8	206	16.2

SPECIFICATIONS

Model 97-02	Wlb. mm	Lght. mm	Cb.wt kg	Brakes fr/rr	Steering type	Standard tires
sdn. 4dr.740i	2930	4984	1930	dc/ABS	pwr.bal.	235/60HR16
sdn. 4dr.740iL	3070	5124	1945	dc/ABS	pwr.bal.	235/60HR16
sdn. 4dr.750iL	3070	5124	2068	dc/ABS	pwr.bal.	235/60HR16

PRICES

Model / version		1997	1998	1999	2000	2001	2002
sdn. 4dr. 740i	mini	29400	35900	45250	52700	58800	
	maxi	33900	40400	50700	58150	65950	
sdn. 4dr. 740iL	mini	32000	38100	47450	55100	64700	71400
	maxi	36550	42600	52700	60700	69300	77700
sdn. 4dr. 745 L	mini						89250
	maxi						94500
sdn. 4dr. 745 ll	mini						96600
	maxi						101850
sdn. 4dr. 750iL	mini	47800	56900	66350	74750	87800	
	maxi	56200	64900	74350	82950	92200	

See page 7 to adapt these figures.

2000 BMW 750iL

1997 BMW 850i

Built on the 7 Series platform and sharing the same mechanical features, the 8 Series is an exotic GT cocktail.

PROS

• **An upper-crust** model belonging to a very select club of cars driven by a V12 (850).
• **The body design** isn't too bold and brassy and hasn't really gone out of style.
• **Engine performance** are pretty impressive, considering vehicle weight and size.
• **High-tech features** provide top-notch control and handling.
• **Road stability** is just outstanding in most situations, but these coupe are more suited to highway driving.
• **It's really a thrill to drive** a vehicle dressed up with such extensive and high-tech equipment.
• **Driving** is quite comfortable, even with the snug interior, stiff suspension and a higher noise level than on a 750 sedan.
• **With such a top-notch design**, build and finish quality and such lavish materials, the vehicle is, of course, quite pricy.

CONS

• **Sky-high costs** go with the territory, for depreciation is high and it costs an arm and a leg to run, maintain and repair such a vehicle, so much so that even the most enthusiastic potential buyers might walk away from it.
• **Maneuverability** isn't really great, given vehicle weight and size.
• **Sportscar performance** aren't up to par on curved roads and the 850 just doesn't go through the paces it should, which takes all the fun out of being at the wheel.
• **Rear seats** are cramped and hard to get to, head room and leg room are tight.
• **There aren't enough** storage compartments in the cabin interior and the trunk is low and quite small.

VERDICT

The 840 / 850 coupe have never been too popular and aren't the best used car buy either, for the most affordable among them aren't really a steal, because they'll rob your pocketbook.

RECALLS

1997 Defective cruise control.

RELIABILITY PROBLEMS

	1997	1998	1999	2000	2001	2002
Engine:	X					
Transmission:	X					
Suspension:	-					
Steering:	-					
Brakes:	X					
Electricity:	X					
Body:	X					
Accessories:	X					
Fit/finish:	-					

POWERTRAIN

Year	Type/ L/Camshaft/bhp	Drivetrain & gearbox		
1997				
840i	V8/4.4/DOHC/285	rear-A5		
850i	V12/5.4/SOHC/322	rear-A5		

PERFORMANCE

	Acceler. 0/100 sec.	Top. speed km/h	Ave. Fuel consp. l./100 km
840i	7.8	250	14.4
850i	6.5	250	17.1

SPECIFICATIONS

Model 1997	Wlb. mm	Lght. mm	Cb.wt kg	Brakes fr/rr	Steering type	Standard tires
cpe. 2dr. (840i)	2684	4780	1870	dc/ABS	pwr.bal.	235/50R16
cpe. 2dr. (850i)	2684	4780	1950	dc/ABS	pwr.bal.	235/50R16

PRICES

Model / version		1997	1998	1999	2000	2001	2002
cpe. 2dr. 840i	mini	26150					
	maxi	34650					
cpe. 2dr. 850i	mini	41600					
	maxi	49900					

See page 7 to adapt these figures.

1997 BMW 850i

BMW   X5

1999 BMW X5 4.0i

Keeping in step with Mercedes-Benz, BMW has come up with its own all-terrain SUV in the form of the X5, a car specifically designed for the North American market which is also built in North America.

PROS

• **Aesthetically**, the X5 is a sure-fire hit and its flamboyant presentation contrasts a great deal with that of the more reserved Mercedes ML.

• **The V8 engine** churns out sports-car performance; full-stop and passing accelerations are quite impressive, mostly with the 4.6is.

• **The brakes** are very efficient and bite into the pavement when pushed hard. In emergency situations, they quickly bring the X5 to a perfectly controlled stop.

•**The X5 handles** extremely well for a vehicle of this sort, despite its high center of gravity and bulky weight.

• **The HDC** (Hill Descent Control) system replaces the low first gear when descending a steep grade without applying the brakes.

• **Getting into** the X5 is easy despite its generous road clearance.

• **Its interior** is just as luxurious as that of any BMW automobile.

• **The extensive equipment** list compares well with that of the automobiles produced by the Munich-based manufacturer.

• **Practical storage** space abounds in front.

• **The exhaust note** resembles that of a sports coupe.

CONS

• **The high sticker price**, of this vehicle which is a gas guzzler and costs a fortune in maintenance.

• **The ideal driving position** is low and hard to find.

• **The dashboard** is not very ergonomic on center.

• **The two-part liftgate** is not very practical to use.

• **The roof pillars** are devoid of access handles.

VERDICT

The X5 is more synonymous with luxury than utilitarianism and—just as is the case with BMW automobiles—it targets an elite clientele who has the financial means of keeping it on the road. . .

RECALLS

2000 The steering rack input shaft collar will be inspected and repositioned if necessary.

2001 Steering spindle will be inspected and fastening bolt replaced. Some safety belt lower anchorage may not have been secured. The nut that secures the axial joint of the left steering rod may not have been tightened properly.

RELIABILITY PROBLEMS

	1997	1998	1999	2000	2001	2002
Engine:				X	X	-
Transmission:				X	-	-
Suspension:				X	X	-
Steering:				-	-	-
Brakes:				-	-	-
Electricity:				X	X	X
Body:				X	-	-
Accessories:				X	X	X
Fit/finish:				X	-	-

POWERTRAIN

Year	Type/ L/Camshaft/bhp	Drivetrain & gearbox	Acceler. 0/100 sec.	Top. speed km/h	Ave. Fuel consp. l./100 km
01-02	L6/3.0/DOHC/225 (3.0i)	all-A5	9.0	190	14.0
		all-M5	8.6	200	13.8
00-02	V8/4.4/DOHC/290 (4.4i)	all-A5	7.3	210	16.5
2002	V8 /4.6/DOHC/340 (4.6is)	all-A5	6.5	230	18.0

PERFORMANCE

SPECIFICATIONS

Model 00-02	Wlb. mm	Lght. mm	Cb.wt kg	Brakes fr/rr	Steering type	Standard tires
wgn. 4dr. 3.0i	2820	4667	2050	dc/ABS	pwr.r&p.	235/65R17
wgn. 4dr. 4.4i	2820	4467	2175	dc/ABS	pwr.r&p.	255/55R18
wgn. 4dr. 4.6is	2820	4467	2188	dc/ABS	pwr.r&p.	275/40R20

PRICES

Model / version		1997	1998	1999	2000	2001	2002
wgn. 4dr. 3.0i	mini					52900	55650
	maxi					57750	61950
wgn. 4dr. 4.4i	mini				56400	61300	63000
	maxi				61850	66000	69300
wgn. 4dr. 4.6is	mini						73500
	maxi						84000

See page 7 to adapt these figures.

2000 BMW X5 4.0i

2000 BMW Z3

In 1996, BMW came up with a roadster derived from the 3 Series platform. The first models were equipped with a 1.9L L4 engine, 2.8L and M 3.2L L6 engine. In 99, a 2.5L replaced the 1.9L and a 3.0L replaced the 2.8L in 2001. The M Roadster was discontinued in 2001.

PROS

• **Its bold and lively** body design is a looker, yet it's nice and traditional with those little retro grilles along the fenders.
• **It is fun driving** this car, for engine response is clean and crisp and you feel like you're king of the road with the wind and exhaust roaring.
• **The 6-cylinder** engines, especially the M version's, makes for a much more exciting driving experience than the 4-cylinder offers.
• **Power steering** is smooth and right on with such a good reduction ratio and small steer angle diameter.
• **Handling** is terrific and taking those curves is a real thrill with so much grip and power at your fingertips.
• **Brakes are impressive**, making for smooth, straight, short stops, and they don't heat up with intensive use.
• **Driving comfort** is quite good for a vehicle of this type, the suspension is smooth and noise level is at a minimum.
• **Wind isn't a problem** with the top down, thanks to a net placed vertically behind the passengers' heads.
• **The convertible top** is a breeze to open and close and bolts clamp down easily.
• **The trunk** is practical, even if it's smallish.

CONS

• **The price tag**, given the poor quality of the original equipment.
• **Engine performance** of the 1.9L are very run-of-the-mill and similar to those of the Miata.
• **The convertible top** isn't lined, it isn't too rain-proof (above the side windows) and the rear panel is made of plastic.
• **Some of the controls** aren't within easy reach, like the power window locks located on the center console and especially the steering column that stays just where it is, because you can't adjust it even an inch!
• **Seats are flat** and don't provide much lateral support.
• **Overall quality** could be ritzier, considering the price.

VERDICT

BMW really didn't make a good move by first putting on the market a lower-end roadster which is really nothing special.

RECALLS

1997 Defective cruise control.

RELIABILITY PROBLEMS

	1997	1998	1999	2000	2001	2002
Engine:	X	X	X	X	X	X
Transmission:	-	-	-	-	-	-
Suspension:		X				
Steering:	-	X	-	-	-	-
Brakes:	X	X	X	X	-	-
Electricity:	X	X	X	X	X	-
Body:	-	X	-	X	-	-
Accessories:	X	X	X	X	X	X
Fit/finish:	-	-	-	X	-	-

POWERTRAIN

Year	Type/ L/Camshaft/bhp	Drivetrain & gearbox
97-98	L4/1.9/DOHC/138	rear-M5
99-02	L6/2.5/DOHC/168-184	rear-M5
97-00	L6/2.8/DOHC/193	rear-M5
01-02	L6/3.0/DOHC/225	rear-M5
98-01	L6/3.2/DOHC/240	rear-M5

PERFORMANCE

Acceler. 0/100 sec.	Top. speed km/h	Ave. Fuel consp. l./100 km
9.0	190	10.2
8.0	200	11.6
6.7	210	12.3
7.5	206	11.5
5.4	220	11.8

SPECIFICATIONS

Model 97-01	Wlb. mm	Lght. mm	Cb.wt kg	Brakes fr/rr	Steering type	Standard tires
con. 2dr. 1.9	2445	4025	1210	dc/ABS	pwr.r&p.	225/50R16
con. 2dr.2.3-2.5	2445	4025	1220	dc/ABS	pwr.r&p.	225/50R16
con. 2dr.2.8-3.0	2445	4025	1300	dc/ABS	pwr.r&p.	225/45R17
con. 2dr. 3.2	2445	4025	1350	dc/ABS	pwr.r&p.	245/40R17

PRICES

Model / version		1997	1998	1999	2000	2001	2002
2dr. 1.9i	mini	19500	23800				
	maxi	24450	27750				
2dr. 2.3i	mini			27500	31500		
	maxi			31500	35500		
2dr. 2.5i	mini					35200	38850
	maxi					38650	42000
2dr. 2.8i	mini	22700	30000	33400	37300		
	maxi	27600	34000	37400	41250		
2dr. 3.0i	mini					44600	48800
	maxi					48300	52000
2dr. 3.2i	mini		34850	39150	44600		
	maxi		38850	43150	48600		
2dr. M Roadster	mini						58300
	maxi						69800

See page 7 to adapt these figures.

1999 BMW Z3

CHRYSLER D Series   DODGE Durango

2000 DODGE Durango

The Durango is a 4-door rear or all-wheel drive multipurpose vehicle, derived from the Dakota pick-up, equipped with a 3.9L V6 or a 4.7L, 5.2L and 5.9L V8.

PROS

• **A great-looking design** with a zoomy, virile character is a definite ace in the hand.

• **Cabin space** is remarkable since the Durango is the only vehicle in its category to be able to accommodate eight passengers.

• **Its mid-size format** between that of the Blazer-Explorer and Tahoe-Expedition seems ideal for available engine power.

• **Load and trailering** capabilities are almost equivalent to those of an Expedition, yet it's less cumbersome.

• **Build is solid** all-round and the stiff chassis makes for super-smooth handling prowess.

• **The suspension** is cushy in spite of its rustic leaf springs and it provides ride comfort comparable to that inside a minivan.

• **The dashboard** is neat and logical, but it's rather basic and homespun.

• **Nice feature**: modular seats and trunk located under the cargo hold floor.

CONS

• **Fuel consumption** is never cheap even with the base model V6, since this vehicle weighs well over 2 tons when at full load capacity.

• **Brakes** aren't at all up to snuff, either when slowing down in normal conditions or in emergency situations, causing vehicle lurch and sway.

• **Front seats** are barely contoured and rear seats are awfully flat and thinly upholstered.

• **Recirculating** ball steering on the 4X4 model is vague and lacks spontaneity due to the big, springy tires.

• **Technical features** seem a bit too bare-boned basic for such a recent vehicle

VERDICT

The Durango is more of a workhorse than a luxury all-terrain vehicle. Regular use should depend on its load and trailering capabilities, for fuel consumption is far from frugal.

RECALLS

1998   The fasteners which secure the alternator and the battery cables may have insufficient clamp load.

2001   Defective electric shift transfer case on 4-wheel drive models.

RELIABILITY PROBLEMS

	1997	1998	1999	2000	2001	2002
Engine:		X	X	-	-	-
Transmission:		X	X	X	-	-
Suspension:		X	X	-	-	-
Steering:		-	-	-	-	-
Brakes:		X	X	X	X	-
Electricity:		X	X	-	X	X
Body:		-	X	X	X	-
Accessories:		X	X	X	X	X
Fit/finish:		X	X	X	-	-

POWERTRAIN

Year	Type/ L/Camshaft/bhp	Drivetrain & gearbox	Acceler. 0/100 sec.	Top. speed km/h	Ave. Fuel consp. l./100 km
98-00	V6/3.9/OHV/175	rear/all	12.0	150	15.4
	V8/5.2/OHV/230	rear/all	9.5	185	17.8
00-02	V8/4.7/SOHC/235	rear/all	10.5	175	18.5
98-02	V8/5.9/OHV/245	rear/all	9.3	180	20.5
2002	V8/5.9/OHV/250	rear/all	9.0	180	20.5

SPECIFICATIONS

Model 98-02	Wlb. mm	Lght. mm	Cb.wt kg	Brakes fr/rr	Steering type	Standard tires
wgn. 4dr. 4x2	2951	4915	1932	dc/dr/ABS	pwr.r&p.	235/75R15
wgn. 4dr. 4x4	2951	4915	2112	dc/dr/ABS	pwr.bal.	235/75R15

PRICES

Model / version		1997	1998	1999	2000	2001	2002
wgn. 4dr. SXT	mini						31800
	maxi						35500
wgn. 4dr. SLT	mini		19850	23500	26150	32550	35600
	maxi		22250	26450	28900	36550	39500
wgn. 4dr. SLT+	mini		21000	25400		26250	38200
	maxi		23400	28000		29600	42300
wgn. 4dr. Sport	mini				24800	26250	
	maxi				27500	29600	
wgn. 4dr. R/T	mini				28450	33000	39900
	maxi				33300	36950	44100

See page 7 to adapt these figures.

2001 DODGE Durango

CHRYSLER FG Series

1998 Dodge Avenger

These coupes replaced the former Le Baron and Daytona in 1995. They're built in the United States by Mitsubishi and equipped with 2.0L or 2.4L L4 engine and 2.5L or 2.7L V6. The Sebring convertible launched in 1996 is also derived from the Cirrus-Stratus. They were renewed in 2000 and the Sebring sedan replaced the Cirrus.

PROS

• **Their attractive look** with their hulky, bold shape up front reminiscent of the Viper.
• **The cabin comfortably** seats 4 adults with plenty of head room and leg room. Rear seats are quite high, but lean too far back.
• **Driving** is fine rather than fun, for you don't get that zesty, spirited Sportscar feeling with such smooth power steering and brakes.
• **The ergonomic instrument** panel is straightforward. It's actually the Eagle Talon design that the Sebring-Avengers share along with many other features.
• **The top** on the convertible is well-designed for it handles well and its glass rear window comes with an electric defroster.

CONS

• **The V6** just doesn't cough up the goods compared to the 4-cylinder Neon, even if the power to weight ratio in both cases is affected by heavy vehicle weight.
• **The interior cabin** design is terribly blah and not even the imitation wood trim on the Sebring can liven things up.
• **Outward view** is only fair because of the low front seat, high trunk, minuscule rearview mirror up front and C-pillar which affects rearward view at quarterback.
• **If you want to store things**, there's the reasonably sized glove box, but the door side-pockets are hard to reach and the compartment on the center console is tiny.
• **To be improved upon**: climate control venting system strains in extreme temperatures, rear windows don't open and there's quite a bit of body rattle and chatter.

VERDICT

These models have an attractive body design, but the cabin design is quite colorless. There's nothing sporty about them, except for the name, for none of the engines really have the muscle that Sportscar dreams are made of...

RECALLS

1997   Defective control arm ball joint due to loss of lubrication.
Headrest support bracket weld might fail on some vehicles.
1998   Failing aspirator system increases nitrous oxide emissions.
Dash panel may sag and interfere with the accelerator pedal.
Safety belts anchors may have not been properly installed.
Shift lever lock mecanism may get stuck.

2001 On some vehicles the passenger side airbag module may not retain the airbag door during deployment.
The automatic transmission cooler hoses may not meet winner wall thickness requirements.
Crankshaft position sensor wiring harness must be rerouted.
Dealers must inspect fuel return hose date code and replace it if required.

RELIABILITY PROBLEMS

	1997	1998	1999	2000	2001	2002
Engine:	X	-	-	X	-	-
Transmission:	X	-	-	-	-	-
Suspension:	-	-	-	-	-	-
Steering:	-	X	-	-	-	-
Brakes:	X	X	X	X	X	-
Electricity:	X	X	X	X	X	X
Body:	-	-	-	-	-	-
Accessories:	X	X	X	X	X	X
Fit/finish:	-	X	-	X	X	-

POWERTRAIN

Year	Type/ L/Camshaft/bhp	Drivetrain & gearbox	Acceler. 0/100 sec.	Top. speed km/h	Ave. Fuel consp. l./100 km
97-99	L4/2.0/DOHC/140	front-A4	11.8	160	11.1
97-02	L4/2.4/DOHC/150	front-A4	10.7	170	11.3
97-00	V6/2.5/SOHC/163-168	front-A4	10.2	175	12.2
00-02	V6/2.7/SOHC/198-200	front-A4	9.0	180	12.5

PERFORMANCE

SPECIFICATIONS

Model Sebring	Wlb. mm	Lght. mm	Cb.wt kg	Brakes fr/rr	Steering type	Standard tires
cpe. 2dr. LX	2635	4850	1346	dc/dr	pwr.r&p.	195/70R14
cpe. 2dr. LXi	2635	4850	1453	dc/dr	pwr.r&p.	215/50R17
con. 2dr. JX	2692	4893	1511	dc/dr	pwr.r&p.	205/65R15
con. 2dr. JXi	2692	4893	1534	dc/dr/ABS	pwr.r&p.	215/55R16
con. 2dr. JXiLTD	2692	4893	1545	dc/ABS	pwr.r&p.	215/55R16
sdn. 4dr. LX	2743	4844	1479	dc	pwr.r&p.	205/65R15
sdn. 4dr. LXI	2743	4844	1504	dc	pwr.r&p.	205/60R16
Avenger						
cpe. 2dr.base	2635	4830	1314	dc/dr	pwr.r&p.	195/70R14
cpe. 2dr. ES	2635	4830	1359	dc/dc	pwr.r&p.	205/55R16

PRICES

Model / version		1997	1998	1999	2000	2001	2002
Sebring							
cpe. 2dr. LX	mini	7350	9150	11000	13350	15100	
	maxi	10300	12100	13850	16150	18150	
cpe. 2dr. LXi	mini	8925	10700	12600	14900	16700	
	maxi	11850	13650	15450	17850	19750	
con. 2dr. JX	mini	11000	13350	15200	17850		
	maxi	13950	16300	18000	20350		
con. 2dr. JXi	mini	13100	15450	17300	19750		
	maxi	16000	18700	20150	22450		
con. 2dr. LX	mini					20300	22350
	maxi					23600	26250
con. 2dr. LXi	mini					22450	54550
	maxi					25600	28350
con. 2dr. Ltd	mini					26000	28150
	maxi					29200	32000
sdn. 4dr. LX	mini					14000	17200
	maxi					17100	21000
sdn. 4dr. LXi	mini					15650	18700
	maxi					18100	22600
Avenger							
cpe. 2dr. base	mini	5800	7550	9450			
	maxi	8950	10500	12300			
cpe. 2dr. ES	mini	7350	9150	11000			
	maxi	10500	12100	13850			

See page 7 to adapt these figures.

CHRYSLER JA Series

1998 CHRYSLER Cirrus

The Cirrus-Stratus models replaced the Le Baron-Acclaim's in 1995. They're driven by a 2.0L or 2.4L 4-cylinder engine, or by a 2.5L V6.

PROS
• **Advanced technical** features such as rigid build, MacPherson suspensions that muffle wheel vibration and superb rear end follow-through, as well as state-of-the-art engines.
• **Original design** and resemblance to other members of the Chrysler car family.
• **Good handling**, in spite of the sensitive suspension, for there isn't much sway or body roll.
• **The cushy suspension** and comfy, well-shaped seats that provide good support.
• **The interior cabin** is really much nicer than that of their direct rivals, the Contour-Mystique's, for even tall rear seat passengers have enough head room and leg room.

CONS
• **The V6 engine** isn't as muscular as that of the competition.
• **The 4-speed automatic** is a hassle because the shifter design doesn't provide any real braking effect.
• **Stops** are very long, but they're smooth and straight with ABS.
• **Some trim materials** and poor fit of some components aren't up to par for such a car.
• **Rearward visibility** is poor because of the high, narrow rear window.
• **Soundproofing** could be beefed up, for there's a lot of road and wind noise.
• **The instrument panel** deck reflects too much into the windshield and blinds the driver in bright sun.

VERDICT
These are good cars that made more of a splash before they hit the market than since, because of certain inconsistencies. Basic models are the best buy.

RECALLS
1997   Defective control arm ball joint due to loss of lubrication.
Oil leakage on cylinder head.
Premature rusting on the ABS unit.
Risk of possible brake fluid leakage on master cylinder.
Defective primary & secondary hood latch spring.

97-98 Safety pin in the automatic transmission shift lever may break.
1998 Premature failure of the catalytic converter assembly.
2000 A brake line bracket will be added to the right front brake tube, because of a defective weld.
Incorrect child lock instruction label.

RELIABILITY PROBLEMS

	1997	1998	1999	2000	2001	2002
Engine:	-	-	-	-		
Transmission:	X	-	X	X		
Suspension:	-	X	-	-		
Steering:	-	-	-	-		
Brakes:	X	-	X	-		
Electricity:	X	X	X	X		
Body:	X	-	-	-		
Accessories:	X	X	X	X		
Fit/finish:	X	X	-	-		

POWERTRAIN / PERFORMANCE

Year	Type/ L/Camshaft/bhp	Drivetrain & gearbox	Acceler. 0/100 sec.	Top. speed km/h	Ave. Fuel consp. l./100 km
97-00	L4/2.0/SOHC/132	front-M5	11.3	165	8.7
		front-A4	12.0	160	10.4
	L4/2.4/DOHC/150	front-A4	10.4	175	11.3
	V6/2.5/SOHC/168	front-A4	9.7	180	12.2

SPECIFICATIONS

Model	Wlb. mm	Lght. mm	Cb.wt kg	Brakes fr/rr	Steering type	Standard tires
Cirrus						
sdn. 4dr.LX	2743	4750	1395	dc/dr/ABS	pwr.r&p.	195/65R15
sdn. 4dr.LXi	2743	4750	1428	dc/ABS	pwr.r&p.	195/65R15
Stratus						
sdn. 4dr.base	2743	4725	1325	dc/dr	pwr.r&p.	195/70R14
sdn. 4dr.ES	2743	4725	1391	dc/dr/ABS	pwr.r&p.	195/65R15
Breeze						
sdn. 4dr.	2743	4742	1327	dc/dr	pwr.r&p.	195/70R14

PRICES

Model / version		1997	1998	1999	2000	2001	2002
Cirrus							
sdn. 4dr. LX	mini	5250		7350	9150		
	maxi	8400		10800	11950		
sdn. 4dr. LXi	mini	6300	7050	8950	11250		
	maxi	9450	10000	11750	13550		
Stratus							
sdn. 4dr. base	mini	4200	6000	7900			
	maxi	7250	8950	10700			
sdn. 4dr. ES	mini	5800	7550	9450			
	maxi	8700	10500	12300			
Breeze							
sdn. 4dr.	mini	4200	6000	7900			
	maxi	7350	8950	10800			

See page 7 to adapt these figures.

CHRYSLER LH Series

CHRYSLER Concorde
CHRYSLER Intrepid
EAGLE Vision

1999 CHRYSLER Intrepid

The Chrysler Concorde, Intrepid and Eagle Vision were first sold in 1993 and share the same platform and mechanical features. In 1998, a facelift was given to the Chrysler and Dodge but the Eagle didn't make it and has been terminated in 1997. In 2002 the 3.2L V6 was replaced by a 3.5L and the R/T version was introduced.

PROS
• **The unique style** of the latest Concorde, sporting a more retro look, and the Intrepid's daring panache.
• **The cab forward design** that was first used on these models has since been copied by many competitors.
• **The cabin** is akin to that of a luxury car, which is a nice surprise for a mid-size car.
• **The rigid frame**, dual airbags and on the upper-end model, 4-disc brakes with ABS, are excellent safety features.
• **The adaptive suspension**, well-cushioned seats and superb sound-proofing make for a smooth ride.
• **Handling** is stable and neutral in most situations, as long as the car is equipped with good-quality tires.
• **Engine performance** are quite good especially given the fact that fuel consumption is reasonable for the vehicle size.
• **Build quality** and tight fit and finish are on a par with Japanese products sold at similar or higher prices.
• **Convenient**: huge trunk and scads of storage compartments.

CONS
• **The automatic shifter** that doesn't come through with vital braking effect and whose unreliability made for lots of repairs under warranty.
• **The plastic materials** used for the dash board seem a little cheap for models in this price range.
• **Rear drum brakes** on the base model Intrepid make for longer stops and don't hold up as well.
• **To be improved upon**: no headrests in the rear, seatbench that can't be folded down, handbrake located under the instrument panel and poor headlights on the Intrepid.

VERDICT
The LH Series models have a lot of good features: an attractive body, tight fit and finish, a roomy cabin, all at an affordable price. They're popular cars and don't depreciate too much.

RECALLS
1997 Rubber compound rings on the fuel injector feed may leak.
1998 Airbag module's initiator is incomplete and may not work.
99-00 A defective adjustable turning loop on the shoulder belt will be replaced.
2000 Defective master cylinder will be replaced on some vehicles. Left front retractor assemblies must be replaced on some vehicles.

RELIABILITY PROBLEMS

	1997	1998	1999	2000	2001	2002
Engine:	X	X	X	-	-	-
Transmission:	X	X	X	X	-	-
Suspension:	X	X	X	X	-	-
Steering:	X	-	-	-	-	-
Brakes:	X	X	X	X	X	-
Electricity:	-	X	X	X	X	-
Body:	X	X	X	-	-	-
Accessories:	X	X	X	X	X	X
Fit/finish:	-	X	-	X	-	-

POWERTRAIN

Year	Type/ L/Camshaft/bhp	Drivetrain & gearbox	Acceler. 0/100 sec.	Top. speed km/h	Ave. Fuel consp. l./100 km
1997	V6/3.3/OHV/161	front-A4	10.8	175	12.4
	V6/3.5/SOHC/214	front-A4	9.0	210	13.7
98-02	V6/2.7/DOHC/200	front-A4	10.5	180	11.3
	V6/3.2/SOHC/225	front-A4	9.3	200	12.6
2002	V6/3.5/SOHC/234	front-A4	9.0	200	12.6
	V6/3.5/SOHC/242 (R/T)	front-A4	8.8	220	13.0

SPECIFICATIONS

Model 1997	Wlb. mm	Lght. mm	Cb.wt kg	Brakes fr/rr	Steering type	Standard tires
Concorde						
sdn. 4dr. LX	2870	5119	1584	dc/ABS	pwr.r&p.	225/60R16
sdn. 4dr. LXi	2870	5119	1611	dc/ABS	pwr.r&p.	225/60R16
Intrepid						
sdn. 4dr. base	2870	5126	1549	dc/dr	pwr.r&p.	205/70R15
sdn. 4dr. ES	2870	5126	1599	dc/ABS	pwr.r&p.	225/60R16
Vision						
sdn. 4dr. ESi	2870	5121	1563	dc/dc	pwr.r&p.	205/70R15
sdn. 4dr. TSi	2870	5121	1600	dc/ABS	pwr.r&p.	225/60R16
98-02						
Concorde						
sdn. 4dr. LX	2870	5311	1563	dc	pwr.r&p.	205/70R15
sdn. 4dr. LXi	2870	5311	1613	dc/ABS	pwr.r&p.	225/60R16
Intrepid						
sdn. 4dr. base	2870	5175	1552	dc	pwr.r&p.	205/70R15
sdn. 4dr. ES	2870	5175	1596	dc/ABS	pwr.r&p.	225/60R16
sdn. 4dr. R/T	2870	5175	1621	dc/ABS	pwr.r&p.	225/55R17

PRICES

Model / version		1997	1998	1999	2000	2001	2002
Concorde							
sdn. 4dr. LX	mini	6300	8200	10900	13100	16150	18700
	maxi	9450	10600	13350	15750	18800	21500
sdn. 4dr. LXi	mini	8400	9750	12900	15250	18250	20800
	maxi	10500	12600	15450	17850	20900	23600
Intrepid							
sdn. 4dr. base	mini	5800	7350	9850	12100		
	maxi	8400	10000	12300	14700		
sdn. 4dr. ES	mini	7350	8900	11550	13650	16700	19950
	maxi	10000	11850	13550	16300	19950	23100
sdn. 4dr. R\T	mini				14700	17200	20250
	maxi				17300	20450	23600
sdn. 4dr. SE	mini					15100	18400
	maxi					18400	21500
Vision							
sdn. 4dr. ESi	mini	6300					
	maxi	8400					
sdn. 4dr. TSi	mini	7350					
	maxi	9450					

See page 7 to adapt these figures.

CHRYSLER   LHS-300M-Concorde Limited

1999 CHRYSLER 300M

Designed in 1994, these deluxe Chrysler sedans were built on the LH series platform. The New Yorker and LHS are quite similar but they have a different body design and array of equipment. The 300M joined the last LHS in 1999 replaced by the Concorde Limited in 2002.

PROS

• **The sensational body design**, especially the rear window design, reminiscent of upper-crust models; more particularly the 300M look.
• **Price, upkeep and fuel** consumption are very reasonable.
• **The spacious cabin** seats five passengers and the huge trunk can hold all their luggage.
• **Handling** is cool and smooth with such a well-balanced vehicle that moves all of a piece and engine performance are really quite impressive. The 300M is a lot of fun to drive with its roaring 253-bhp.
• **Well-contoured** and cushioned seats, a smooth as silk suspension and superb soundproofing put you on cloud nine.
• **Build quality**, fit and materials are top-notch.
• **Equipment is extensive**, both safety-wise and convenience-wise for there are a reasonable number of storage compartments.

CONS

• **The shifter** on the automatic doesn't provide for anywhere near enough braking effect and has caused a lot of hassles.
• **The body is starting** to show its age for there's quite a bit of wind noise blowing about (except for the 300M).
• **The cruise control** button isn't conveniently located and the shape of the steering wheel doesn't allow for resting one's hands on the spokes.
• **Some finish** details could be improved upon.
• **Storage compartments** are small, the glove compartment is tiny and there's no compartment in the rear elbowrest.
• **There aren't any headrests** in the rear.

VERDICT

These cars are a good buy, for they're lavish, comfortable and quite economical.

RECALLS

1999   Wrong Vehicle Emission Control Information (VECI) label.
2000   Left front retractor assemblies must be replaced on some vehicles.

RELIABILITY PROBLEMS

	1997	1998	1999	2000	2001	2002
Engine:	X		X	-	-	-
Transmission:	X		X	-	-	-
Suspension:	-		-	-	-	-
Steering:	-		X	-	-	-
Brakes:	X		X	-	-	-
Electricity:	X		X	X	X	X
Body:	X		X	-	-	-
Accessories:	X		X	X	X	-
Fit/finish:	-		X	X	-	-

POWERTRAIN

Year	Type/ L/Camshaft/bhp	Drivetrain & gearbox
1997	V6/3.5/SOHC/214	front-A4
99-02	V6/3.5/SOHC/250-255	front-A4

PERFORMANCE

Acceler. 0/100 sec.	Top. speed km/h	Ave. Fuel consp. l./100 km
9.2	200	13.7
8.5	220	13.3

SPECIFICATIONS

Model 99-02	Wlb. mm	Lght. mm	Cb.wt kg	Brakes fr/rr	Steering type	Standard tires
LHS						
sdn. 4dr.	2870	5276	1623	dc/ABS	pwr.r&p.	225/55R17
300M						
sdn. 4dr.	2870	5023	1618	dc/ABS	pwr.r&p.	225/55R17
Concorde Ltd						
sdn. 4dr.	2870	5076	1618	dc/ABS	pwr.r&p.	225/55R17

PRICES

Model / version		1997	1998	1999	2000	2001	2002
LHS	mini	7900		16300	19650	23950	
sdn. 4dr.	maxi	11550		18900	22450	26200	
300M	mini			18400	22800	25400	
sdn. 4 dr.	maxi			21200	23400	29400	
sdn. 4 dr. Special	mini						31500
	maxi						35000
Concorde limited							
sdn. 4dr.	mini						18700
	maxi						21500

See page 7 to adapt these figures.

1999 CHRYSLER LHS

CHRYSLER

PT Cruiser

2001 CHRYSLER PT Cruiser

The PT Cruiser is difficult to fit into an one category: it's a versatile 4-door wagon based on the Neon's platform and equipped with the base Sebring's mechanical components.

PROS
• **This vehicle's irresistible styling** explains half of its success. Combining modern and retro styling cues, it's unique on the North American market.
• The other half of the PT Cruiser's success can be attributed to its **versatility**. The front portion of the cabin is highly modular and easy to adapt according to the circumstances.
• **The PT Cruiser drives** with surprising aplomb, despite its higher-than-average center of gravity. It could even be considered sporty if its engine were more powerful.
• **The base model packs plenty of equipment** for the price and is an affordable small utility vehicle.
• **The cabin** will seat 4 adults comfortably, and room is ample in all directions. Furthermore, cabin access is made easy by the large doors that open wide.
• **With loads of storage space** and a shelf that can be installed in various ways and even be used as a picnic table, this car has an undeniably practical side.

CONS
• **With the timid performance** of the automatic version, due to a poor weight-to-power ratio, it's a shame that a small V6 engine (2.5 L) is not available.
• **Rearward visibility** is hindered by the headrests and narrow rear window.
• **Some of the ergonomics** need improving.
• **The automatic version** is not as maneuverable as the manual, whose turning radius is narrower.
• **The mechanical components** are almost inaccessible, which makes basic maintenance and simple repairs difficult. Indeed, there's hardly a square inch of unused space under the hood.

VERDICT
The PT Cruiser is a marketing phenomenon that also has the advantage of being practical and sure-footed.

RECALLS
2002 Possible fuel pump leak in the event of a collision.
Faulty instrumentation software.
Possible fuel tank leak.

RELIABILITY PROBLEMS

	1997	1998	1999	2000	2001	2002
Engine:					-	-
Transmission:					-	-
Suspension:					-	-
Steering:					-	-
Brakes:					-	-
Electricity:					-	-
Body:					-	-
Accessories:					-	-
Fit/finish:					-	-

POWERTRAIN

Year	Type/ L/Camshaft/bhp	Drivetrain & gearbox	Acceler. 0/100 sec.	Top. speed km/h	Ave. Fuel consp. l./100 km
01-02	L4/2.4/SOHC/150	front-M5	10.5	175	12.5
		front-A4	11.7	170	12.0

PERFORMANCE

(See table above)

SPECIFICATIONS

Model 01-02	Wlb. mm	Lght. mm	Cb.wt kg	Brakes fr/rr	Steering type	Standard tires
wgn. 4dr.base	2616	4288	1421	dc/dr	pwr.r&p.	195/65R15
wgn. 4dr.Touring	2616	4288	1421	dc/dr	pwr.r&p.	205/55R16
wgn. 4dr.Limited	2616	4288	1448	dc/dr	pwr.r&p.	205/55R16

PRICES

Model / version		1997	1998	1999	2000	2001	2002
sdn. 5dr.	mini					19650	20800
	maxi					22100	24700
sdn. 5dr. Ltd	mini					21000	22600
	maxi					23400	26250
sdn. 5dr. Touring	mini						21500
	maxi						25200

See page 7 to adapt these figures.

2001 CHRYSLER PT Cruiser

CHRYSLER S Series

**DODGE Caravan
PLYMOUTH Voyager**

1998 PLYMOUTH Voyager

Chrysler minivans opened up a new and highly successful market segment in the '80's and '90's. Driven by 4 and 6-cylinder engines, they hail back to 1984, were upgraded in 1991 and 1994, and completely redesigned in 1996 and 2001.

PROS
• **Wide choice** range of models and mechanical features at a competitive price.
• **Their varied uses** have made all sorts of people very happy.
• **The driver's position** is reassuring for it provides an excellent outward view and makes for virtually fatigue-free driving on long hauls.
• **With its front-wheel** and all-wheel drive, it handles safely and surely, especially in winter conditions.
• **It's a comfortable** vehicle with such a roomy interior, smooth suspension, well-upholstered seats and good soundproofing.

CONS
• **Its leaf springs** and rigid axle rear suspension are jumpy and bumpy on rough pavement and can be quite unpleasant.
• **Limited maneuverability** on extended models due to a large turning radius.
• **The frame** rattles and chatters, especially when it comes to the touchy sliding doors.
• **Headlights** don't have good luminosity or reach.
• **Limited load** and pulling capabilities in spite of the V6.
• **The weak 4-cylinder** engines and their automatic gear boxes.
• **To be improved upon**: emergency brake and next to no storage compartments.

VERDICT
The basic models are the best buy and the 3.0L V6 coupled with a 3-speed automatic is the most reliable combination.

RECALLS
97-00 An external seal will prevent fuel leakage that could occur as the «O-Ring» degradation.
1997 Tires on vehicles with steel road wheels may have been damaged during mounting.
Master cylinder of the brakes is defective.
1998 Seat belt not properly installed on child's seats and locking mechanism may malfunction.
2000 Left front retractor assemblies will be replaced on some vehicles.
2001 Dealers will replace the lower control arm bolts and nuts.
On some vehicles the daylight running lamps do not function when the switch is in the park lamp position.

RELIABILITY PROBLEMS

	1997	1998	1999	2000	2001	2002
Engine:	X	X	X	X	-	-
Transmission:	X	X	X	X	X	-
Suspension:	X	X	X	X	-	-
Steering:	-	-	X	-	-	-
Brakes:	X	X	X	X	X	X
Electricity:	X	X	X	X	X	X
Body:	X	X	X	X	X	X
Accessories:	X	X	X	X	X	-
Fit/finish:	-	-	X	-	-	-

POWERTRAIN

Type/ L/Camshaft/bhp	Drivetrain & gearbox	Acceler. 0/100 sec.	Top. speed km/h	Ave. Fuel consp. l./100 km
97-02 L4/2.4/DOHC/150	front-A3/A4	NA	NA	11.8
V6/3.0/OHC136-150	front-A3/A4	12.0	165	12.7
V6/3.3/OHV/150-180	front-A4	11.7	170	13.3
V6/3.8/OHV/162-215	front-A4	11.0	175	13.8

PERFORMANCE Year

SPECIFICATIONS

Model	Wlb. mm	Lght. mm	Cb.wt kg	Brakes fr/rr	Steering type	Standard tires
Caravan/Voyager 97-00						
m.v. 4dr.	2878	4733	1682	dc/dr/ABS	pwr.r&p.	215/65R15
Caravan 01-02						
m.v. 4dr.	2878	4803	1755	dc/dr/ABS	pwr.r&p.	215/70R15

PRICES

Model / version		1997	1998	1999	2000	2001	2002
Caravan/Voyager							
m.v. 4dr. 5 st.	mini	6700	8100	10100	12900		
	maxi	9450	10300	11850	14700		
m.v. 4dr. 5 st. SE	mini	7900	10200	12100	15450		
	maxi	10000	12100	13850	17200		
m.v. 4dr. 5 st. LE	mini	10500	13650	15750			
	maxi	12600	16300	17650			
m.v. 4dr. 5 st. LX/ES	mini	11550					
	maxi	13650					
m.v. 5dr. 5 st. SE	mini	8400	10700	12700	16100	18900	21750
	maxi	10500	12300	14600	17950	21850	24750
m.v. 5dr. 5 st. Sport	mini					19950	23100
	maxi					22600	25900
m.v. 4dr. 7 st. SE	mini	8250	11150	12500	15950		
	maxi	10300	13000	14400	17750		
m.v. 4dr. 7 st. LE	mini	10850	14000	16200			
	maxi	13000	16700	18000			
m.v. 4dr. 7 st. ES	mini	11850					
	maxi	13950					
m.v. 5dr. 7 st. SE	mini	8800	11350	13150	16600	19400	22350
	maxi	11000	13450	15100	18500	22350	25200
m.v. 5dr. 7 st. LE	mini	11400	14600	16700			
	maxi	13550	17100	18800			
m.v. 5dr. 7 st. Sport	mini					20500	23750
	maxi					23100	26550
AWD							
m.v. 4dr. 7 st. SE	mini	9250	12200	13350	17000		
	maxi	11350	14100	15450	18800		
m.v. 4dr. 7 st. LE	mini	11800	14700	17200			
	maxi	14100	17750	19100			
m.v. 4dr. 7 st. ES	mini	12900					
	maxi	15100					
m.v. 5dr. 7 st. SE	mini	12900	13650	14200	17650	20350	24150
	maxi	14600	15550	16150	19850	24000	27100
m.v. 5dr. 7 st. LE	mini	12400	15650	17750			
	maxi	14600	18150	19850			
m.v. 5dr. 7 st. Sport	mini					21950	25400
	maxi					24550	28350

See page 7 to adapt these figures.

CHRYSLER S Series

1998 DODGE Grand Caravan

Chrysler minivans hail back to 1984, were upgraded in 1991 and 1994, and completely redesigned in 1996 and 2001.

PROS

• **Wide choice** range of models and mechanical features at a competitive price.
• **Their varied uses** have made all sorts of people very happy.
• **The driver's position** is reassuring for it provides an excellent outward view and makes for virtually fatigue-free driving on long hauls.
• **With its front-wheel** and all-wheel drive, it handles safely and surely, especially in winter conditions.
• **It's a comfortable** vehicle with such a roomy interior, smooth suspension, well-upholstered seats and good soundproofing.

CONS

• **Its leaf springs** and rigid axle rear suspension are jumpy and bumpy on rough pavement and can be quite unpleasant.
• **Limited maneuverability** on extended models due to a large turning radius.
• **The frame** rattles and chatters, especially when it comes to the touchy sliding doors.
• **Headlights** don't have good luminosity or reach.
• **Limited load** and pulling capabilities in spite of the V6.
• **To be improved upon**: emergency brake and next to no storage compartments.

VERDICT

The basic models are the best buy and the 3.0L V6 coupled with a 3-speed automatic is the most reliable combination.

RECALLS

1997   Tires on vehicles with steel road wheels may have been damaged during mounting.
Cylinder of the brakes master is defective.

1998   Seat belt not properly installed on child's seats and locking mechanism may malfunction.

97-00   An external seal will prevent fuel leakage that could occur as the «O-Ring» degradation.

2000   Left front retractor assemblies will be replaced on some vehicles.

2001   Dealers will replace the lower control arm bolts and nuts.
On some vehicles the daylight running lamps do not function when the switch is in the park lamp position.

RELIABILITY PROBLEMS

	1997	1998	1999	2000	2001	2002
Engine:	-	-	-	-	X	-
Transmission:	X	X	X	X	-	-
Suspension:	-	-	-	-	-	-
Steering:	X	X	X	-	-	-
Brakes:	X	X	X	X	X	X
Electricity:	-	-	-	-	X	X
Body:	X	X	X	X	X	X
Accessories:	-	-	-	-	-	-
Fit/finish:	X	-	-	-	-	-

POWERTRAIN

Year	Type/ L/Camshaft/bhp	Drivetrain & gearbox	Acceler. 0/100 sec.	Top speed km/h	Ave. Fuel consp. l./100 km
97-02	V6/3.0/OHC/136-150	front-A3/A4	12.0	165	12.7
	V6/3.3/OHV/150-158	front-A4	11.7	170	13.3
	V6/3.8/OHV/162-180	front-A4	11.0	175	13.8

SPECIFICATIONS

Model 97-99	Wlb. mm	Lght. mm	Cb.wt kg	Brakes fr/rr	Steering type	Standard tires
Town & Country						
m.v. 4dr. base	2878	4735	1795	dc/dr/ABS	pwr.r&p.	215/65R16
m.v. 4dr. AWD	3030	5073	1971	dc/ABS	pwr.r&p.	215/65R16
Gd Caravan-Gd Voyager						
m.v. 4dr. base	2853	4468	1499	dc/dr/ABS	pwr.r&p.	195/75R14
m.v. 4dr. SE/LE	2853	4468	1515	dc/dr/ABS	pwr.r&p.	195/75R14
Gd Caravan/Gd Voyager						
m.v. 4dr. SE/LE	3030	5070	1671	dc/dr/ABS	pwr.r&p.	215/70R15
m.v. 4dr. ES	3030	5070	1837	dc/dr/ABS	pwr.r&p.	215/60R17
Gd Caravan 01-02						
m.v. 4dr. base	3030	5070	1671	dc/dr/ABS	pwr.r&p.	215/70R15

PRICES

Model / version		1997	1998	1999	2000	2001	2002
Gd Caravan/Gd Voyager							
m.v. 4dr. 7 st.	mini.	7350	10000	11550	15000		
	maxi	9450	12400	13550	17300		
m.v. 4dr. 7 st. SE	mini.	9000	12400	13650	16800		
	maxi	12150	14400	15750	18700		
m.v. 4dr.7 st. LE	mini.	12150	15100	17300	18700		
	maxi	14200	17100	19200	20600		
m.v. 4dr. 7 st. ES	mini.	13450	16600	17850	21200		
	maxi	15100	18700	19950	23400		
m.v. 4dr. 7 st. SE AWD	mini.	10100	13400	14700	18000		
	maxi	13200	15450	16600	19950		
m.v. 4dr. 7 st. LE AWD	mini.	13100	16150	18350	19850		
	maxi	15250	18150	20650	22050		
m.v. 4dr. 7 st. ES AWD	mini.	14500	17350	18050	22450		
	maxi	16800	19750	21000	24700		
m.v. 5dr. 7 st.	mini.	7700	10240	12210	15650		
	maxi	9800	12800	14210	17850		
m.v. 5dr. 7 st. SE	mini.	9350	12800	14300	17450		
	maxi	12450	14800	16400	19300		
m.v. 5dr. 7 st. LE	mini.	12450	15550	17850	19300		
	maxi	14750	17550	19850	21850		
m.v. 5dr. 7 st. ES	mini.	13750	17000	18500	21850	30750	33600
	maxi	16000	19100	20600	24000	33300	36750
m.v. 5dr. 7 st. Sport	mini.					22800	26250
	maxi					25600	28750
m.v. 5dr. 7 st. SE AWD	mini.	10500	13850	15300	19300		
	maxi	13500	15800	17300	21250		
m.v. 5dr. 7 st. LE AWD	mini.	13650	16600	18900	21250		
	maxi	15750	18600	20900	23100		
m.v. 5dr. 7 st. ES AWD	mini.	15400	18000	19550	23750	32000	35200
	maxi	17300	20150	21650	25900	34500	38300
m.v. 5dr. 7 st. Sport AWD	mini.					24000	27800
	maxi					26900	30350
Town & Country							
m.v. 5dr. 7 st. LXi	mini.	13650	15600	19300	22800	25400	30250
	maxi	16300	18150	21950	25950	28850	33600
m.v. 5dr. 7 st. LXi AWD	mini.	14700	16700	20350	23950	26950	31800
	maxi	17300	19200			30350	35200
m.v. 5dr. 7 st. LTD	mini			21300	24450	29600	34450
	maxi			24150	27800	32950	37800

See page 7 to adapt these figures.

CHRYSLER TL Series

1999 PLYMOUTH Neon

After retiring the Colt, the Neon is now the smallest model in the Chrysler line. It is available either as a 4-door sedan with a 2.0L 130-hp or a 2-door coupe with 150-hp.

PROS

• **The amusing looks** which have contributed significantly to its success.
• **Efficient handling** due to moderate lean and good quality shocks.
• **The power steering**, precise and direct, which makes driving much nicer than with the manual found in the older base model.
• **The decent performance**, in spite of a larger engine and greater fuel consumption than the average.
• **The interior space** which is decent, although it does lack leg room in the rear.
• **The price** of the base model, the only one which is really attractive.

CONS

• **The 2.0L engine** which is rough, noisy and lacks refinement. In addition, we are not sure it produces the advertised power.
• **The price** of the Highline version which isn't a miracle car and is as expensive as some competitive models.
• **The firm rear suspension** with limited wheel movement.
• **The average brakes** which lack stability without the ABS and the spongy pedal which makes precise braking difficult.
• **The overall quality** which still isn't as good as Japanese products.
• **The front seats** which are uncomfortable for big people and in the rear, the bench is short and lacks padding.
• **A note**: the steering wheel is not very practical and visibility to the front is affected by dashboard reflection in the front windshield.

VERDICT

The Neon isn't the miraculous vehicle that Chrysler had originally announced. Simply put, it is an honest and reliable mode of transportation.

RECALLS

1997 Defective circuit design may cause inadvertent airbag deployment.
1998 Engine's fan is malfunctioning.
Rear suspension crossmember may be missing spot welds.
2001 Brake booster hose may swell and loosen from the intake manifold.
Some vehicles may have wrong tire label.

RELIABILITY PROBLEMS

	1997	1998	1999	2000	2001	2002
Engine:	X		X	X	X	X
Transmission:	X	-	-	-	-	-
Suspension:	X	X	-	-	-	-
Steering:	-	-	-	-	-	-
Brakes:	X	X	X	X	-	-
Electricity:	X	X	X	X	X	X
Body:	X	-	X	X	X	
Accessories:	X	X	X	X	X	X
Fit/finish:	X	X	X	X	-	-

POWERTRAIN

Year	Type/ L/Camshaft/bhp	Drivetrain & gearbox	Acceler. 0/100 sec.	Top. speed km/h	Ave. Fuel consp. l./100 km
97-02	L4/2.0/SOHC/132	front-M5	9.5	185	8.2
		front-A3	10.6	180	10.1
	L4/2.0/DOHC/150	front-M5	8.5	195	9.1
		front-A3	9.4	190	9.8

PERFORMANCE

SPECIFICATIONS

Model	Wlb. mm	Lght. mm	Cb.wt kg	Brakes fr/rr	Steering type	Standard tires
97-99						
cpe. 2dr. base	2642	4364	1082	dc/dr	pwr.r&p.	185/65R14
cpe. 2dr. Sport	2642	4364	1120	dc/dr	pwr.r&p.	185/65R14
cpe. 2dr. R/T	2642	4364	1120	dc/dc	pwr.r&p.	185/65R14
sdn. 4dr. base	2642	4364	1063	dc/dr	pwr.r&p.	185/65R14
sdn. 4dr. High	2642	4364	1096	dc/dr	pwr.r&p.	185/65R14
sdn. 4dr. Sport	2642	4364	1137	dc/dr	pwr.r&p.	185/65R14
00-02						
sdn. 4dr. LE	2667	4430	1164	dc/dr	pwr.r&p.	185/65R14
sdn. 4dr. LX	2667	4430	1193	dc/dr	pwr.r&p.	185/60R15
sdn. 4dr. R/T	2267	4430	1229	dc/ABS	pwr.r&p.	195/50R16

PRICES

Model / version		1997	1998	1999	2000	2001	2002
cpe. 2dr.	mini	3200	4200				
	maxi	5800	6800				
cpe. 2dr. Highline	mini	3700		5250			
	maxi	6300		7650			
cpe. 2dr. EX	mini		4750	5800			
	maxi		7350	8100			
cpe. 2dr. Sport	mini	4200	5400	6850			
	maxi	6800	7900	9350			
cpe. 2dr. Compet.	mini		5800	6650			
	maxi		8400	9150			
cpe. 2dr. R/T Expr.	mini		6100	7150			
	maxi		8600	9650			
sdn. 4dr.	mini	3350	4200				
	maxi	6000	6800				
sdn. 4dr. Highline	mini	3900		5450			
	maxi	6500		7900			
sdn. 4dr. EX	mini		4500	6000			
	maxi		7350	8300			
sdn. 4dr. Sport	mini	4200	5100	7050			
	maxi	6800	7650	9650			
sdn. 4dr. Compet.	mini		6100	6850			
	maxi		8600	9450			
sdn. 4dr. R/T Expr.	mini					12600	15000
	maxi					15200	17850
sdn. 4dr. LE	mini				8400	10500	13100
	maxi				10500	13100	16300
sdn. 4dr. LX	mini				9450	11550	13950
	maxi				11550	14200	16800

See page 7 to adapt these figures.

1997 EAGLE Talon ESi

The Talon sports model coupes, the first vehicles to be equipped with all-wheel drive, were built on the Mitsubishi Galant platform. They were designed by Chrysler and have been built by Diamond Star in Illinois since 1990.

PROS

• **Such a bold**, gutsy look has a lot to do with vehicle sales.

• **What you get** for your money goes a long way: the TSi Turbo 4WD model is less expensive than rival imports.

• **Handling** on the all-wheel drive model is clean as a whistle with the high-tech rear suspension and large tires.

• **The 2.0L Turbo** is a mean engine, and with the well-adjusted suspension as a sidekick, the sky's the limit.

• **The ride** is quite smooth, for the suspension never bounces and the front contour seats are comfortable.

CONS

• **There's a heck of a torque** wallop on the Turbo-driven 4X4's when you gun it.

• **Rear passengers** suffer from cramped head and leg room.

• **The noise level** is more noticeable on more recent models.

• **Only tall passengers** will be really comfortable in the front because seats are low and the body frame is high.

• **The trunk** on the AWD model is small and hard to get to.

• **The second generation** car interiors are plain and colorless.

VERDICT

These sports model coupes have been a smashing success because of all-wheel drive and because they're relatively cheap to buy and keep in good running order.

RECALLS

97-98 On AWD models, the oil level of the transfer case may be too low resulting in seizure and wheel lock-up.

Damaged rubber boot on the lower lateral ball joint may cause an extraordinary wear on the ball joint and a possible separation.

1998 Dash panel may sag interfering with the accelerator pedal. (on the Talon).

Talon   EAGLE

RELIABILITY PROBLEMS

	1997	1998	1999	2000	2001	2002
Engine:	X	X				
Transmission:	X	-				
Suspension	-	-				
Steering:	-	-				
Brakes:	X	X				
Electricity:	X	-				
Body:	-	-				
Accessories:	X	X				
Fit/finish:	-	X				

POWERTRAIN

Year	Type/ L/Camshaft/bhp	Drivetrain & gearbox	Acceler. 0/100	Top. speed	Ave. Fuel consp.
97-98		front/all-A4	7.2	215	12.0
ESi	L4/2.0/DOHC/141	front-M5	9.5	175	9.0
		front-A4	10.8	170	10.0
TSi	L4T/2.0/DOHC/210	front/all-M5	7.0	225	11.0
		front/all-A4	7.2	215	12.0

PERFORMANCE

(see table above)

SPECIFICATIONS

Model	Wlb.	Lght.	Cb.wt	Brakes	Steering	Standard
97-98						
cpe. 3dr. ESi	2510	4340	1286	dc/dc	pwr.r&p.	195/70R14
cpe. 3dr. TSi	2510	4340	1315	dc/dc	pwr.r&p.	205/55R15
cpe. 3dr. TSi/AWD	2510	4340	1470	dc/dc	pwr.r&p.	215/55R17

PRICES

Model / version		1997	1998	1999	2000	2001	2002
cpe. 3dr. base	mini	6850	8900				
	maxi	8400	11550				
cpe. 3dr. TSi AWD	mini	10500	13350				
	maxi	13650	16300				
cpe. 3dr. ESi	mini	8400	10500				
	maxi	10500	13150				

See page 7 to adapt these figures.

1997 EAGLE Talon ESi

DAEWOO   Lanos

2001 DAEWOO Lanos

The Lanos is the smallest Daewoo commercialized in North America. Since 1999 it is available as a 2-door coupe and 4-door sedan.

PROS

• **Its attractive asking price** encourages consumers to disregard its limited equipment level. This in turn gives the Lanos an edge over its Korean and Japanese competitors.
• **Its body** features flowing lines and has an original shape.
• **The engine** is surprisingly modern, the controls enjoyably accurate and the handling pleasantly composed for a car in this price range.
• **With good quality tires**, the Lanos provides good handling despite its smooth suspension.
• **The well-gauged suspension** and properly padded seats combine to produce quite a comfortable ride.
• Even without ABS, the **brakes** bring the Lanos to a stable and straight stop; also, the pads are quite durable and resist well to fading.
• **The rigorous quality**, attention to detail, and materials used are attractive to the eye and the touch.
• **The well-proportioned trunk** can fit a good amount of luggage.

CONS

• **Stopping distances** are above-average, because of the threshold braking system designed to prevent the wheels from locking.
• **Acceleration** and pick-up are laborious when the vehicle is loaded.
• **The engine** and tires are loud, and wind leaks can be heard around the windshield.
• **The suspension** is too soft on smooth roads and has a tendency to go wild on rough surfaces, which in turn creates some jumping.
• **The rear seats** are minuscule and hard to access, and the storage space is limited to a cup holder. . .
• **Performance** is compromised by the gap between the second and third gears on the automatic transmission.
• **A few drawbacks** worth pointing out are the fact that the instrument panel is not equipped with an indicator to show which gear the automatic transmission is in, the huge blind spot created by the windshield wipers and the lack of storage space.

VERDICT

After Daewoo's bankruptcy, this model has no commercial value, despite its virtues.

RECALLS

99-00 Wheel bolt torque will be increased to 88 lb/pi.
2001 Extra protection will be applied to the ECM wiring harness which will be rerouted too.

Lanos   DAEWOO

RELIABILITY PROBLEMS

	1997	1998	1999	2000	2001	2002
Engine:			-	-	-	-
Transmission:			-	-	-	-
Suspension:			-	-	-	-
Steering:			-	-	-	-
Brakes:			-	-	-	-
Electricity:			X	-	-	-
Body:			X	X	X	-
Accessories:			X	-	-	X
Fit/finish:			-	X	-	-

POWERTRAIN

Type/ L/Camshaft/bhp	Drivetrain & gearbox
99-02 L4/1.6/DOHC/105	front-M5
	front-A4

PERFORMANCE Year

	Acceler. 0/100 sec.	Top. speed km/h	Ave. Fuel consp. l./100 km
	11.2	165	9.2
	12.3	160	10.4

SPECIFICATIONS

Model 99-02	Wlb. mm	Lght. mm	Cb.wt kg	Brakes fr/rr	Steering type	Standard tires
cpe. 2 dr.	2520	4076	1110	dc/dr	pwr.r&p.	185/60R14
sdn. 4 dr.	2520	4237	1144	dc/dr	pwr.r&p.	185/60R14

PRICES

Model / version		1997	1998	1999	2000	2001	2002
cpe. 2dr. S	mini			5250	6100	8400	9450
	maxi			7350	8400	10500	12600
cpe. 2dr. SX	mini				5550	6600	10000
	maxi				7900	8800	12400
sdn. 4dr. S	mini			5450	6300	8900	10000
	maxi			7550	8600	11350	13100
sdn. 4dr. SX	mini				5800	6800	10300
	maxi				8100	9100	12600

See page 7 to adapt these figures.

2001 DAEWOO Lanos

DAEWOO   Leganza

2001 DAEWOO Leganza

The Leganza which was Daewoo's luxury model in North America was introduced in 1999. It exists as a 4-door sedan available in two versions.

PROS

• **The lines** are elegant and reserved.
• **The CDX version** features all of the equipment typical of a luxury car.
• **The Leganza is fun to drive** because of its precise steering system, good braking power that's easy to gauge and impeccable ergonomics.
• **Performance** levels are comparable to the Infiniti G20's, and acceleration and pick-up are strong enough.
• **The car is stable** on the road in spite of its mediocre tires.
• **The volume** of the cabin and trunk can easily accommodate four adults and their luggage.
• **The rear seats** are easy to get into thanks to long doors that open wide, and the windows roll all the way down.
• **The comfort level** is decent for a car of this calibre, and the noise level remains reasonable even on the highway.
• **The lightweight panels** are carefully assembled and the finish is impeccable, with several unusual features for a car sold at this price.
• **The full-size spare wheel** and the quality of the Sony radio-cassette player with multiple speakers.

CONS

• **The seats** are insufficiently padded, and the front seat adjustments are very strange. Furthermore, the ideal driving position is hard to find.
• **The Korean tires** that equip the Leganza have a long way to go before equalling the quality of their American or European counterparts.
• **Storage spaces** are few and far between in the rear, where even cup holders are lacking.
• **Oversights**: the windshield wipers have a hard time handling heavy rain and the headlights are not bright enough.

VERDICT

Despite its virtues, this model has no commercial value, after Daewoo's bankruptcy.

RECALLS

2001   Dealers will install padding to A-pillar to reduce the risk of injury in case of a crash.

RELIABILITY PROBLEMS

	1997	1998	1999	2000	2001	2002
Engine:			X	-	-	-
Transmission:				-	-	-
Suspension:				-	-	-
Steering:				-	-	-
Brakes:			X	X	-	-
Electricity:			X	X	X	-
Body:			X	-	-	-
Accessories:			-	X	X	X
Fit/finish:				-	-	-

POWERTRAIN

Year	Type/ L/Camshaft/bhp	Drivetrain & gearbox
99-02	L4/2.2/DOHC/131	front-A4

PERFORMANCE

Acceler. 0/100 sec.	Top. speed km/h	Ave. Fuel consp. l./100 km
11.5	175	12.0

SPECIFICATIONS

Model 99-02	Wlb. mm	Lght. mm	Cb.wt kg	Brakes fr/rr	Steering type	Standard tires
sdn. 4dr. SX	2670	4671	1415	dc/dc	pwr.r&p.	205/60R15
sdn. 4dr. CDX	2670	4671	1420	dc/ABS	pwr.r&p.	205/60R15

PRICES

Model / version		1997	1998	1999	2000	2001	2002
sdn 4dr. SX	mini			8000	9650	13650	15750
	maxi			10300	11950	17300	19400
sdn 4dr. CDX	mini			10000	11850	15550	18400
	maxi			12300	13850	18300	22000

See page 7 to adapt these figures.

2001 DAEWOO Leganza

DAEWOO   Nubira

2001 DAEWOO Nubira

The Nubira is the mid-range model in Daewoo's line-up. It is sold as a 4-door sedan and a wagon, both models sharing the same mechanical components.

PROS

• **The engine** is a real workhorse and both acceleration and pick-up are more than satisfactory. However, certain passing maneuvres will need to be planned well in advance.

• **Braking** is among the most efficient in this class: stopping distances are short and power is well-balanced and easy to gauge.

• **The passenger compartment** is roomy enough to accommodate four adults comfortably, and access to the front and rear seats is easy.

• **The dash** is conservatively presented, controls are ergonomic and materials generally look good.

• **The equipment** is very adequate on the SX models, which feature power controls and a good quality radio.

• **Nubira is fun to drive** because it reacts quickly and consistently. Braking is reassuring and the precise steering system produces a car that is easy to handle.

• **Good road stability** despite being equipped with average quality tires, the Nubira offers and corners with only moderate roll.

• **The wagon's trunk** features many compartments around the emergency wheel. It also includes a baggage cover.

CONS

• **The suspension** is harsh even though its travel and smoothness are average and shock absorption is effective.

• **Engine and road noise** is omnipresent, pointing to a serious lack of soundproofing especially in the case of the wagon.

• **Storage space** is kept to a minimum, both in front and back.

• **The wagon's bench seat** is positively rustic; its cushion is short, padding is minimal and the back is almost perfectly vertical.

• **The radio** is maddeningly busy and controls are microscopic and hard to master.

• **The reliability** of these new models remains to be proven.

• **The shattered network** complicate the scheduled maintenance of these vehicles.

VERDICT

Despite its virtues, this model has no commercial value, after Daewoo's bankruptcy.

RECALLS

00-02 Dealers must inspect and replaced flexible front brake lines on some vehicles if necessary.

RELIABILITY PROBLEMS

	1997	1998	1999	2000	2001	2002
Engine:			X	-	-	-
Transmission:			-	-	-	-
Suspension:			X	-	-	-
Steering:			-	-	-	-
Brakes:			X	X	-	-
Electricity:			X	X	-	-
Body:			-	X	X	X
Accessories:			-	-	-	-
Fit/finish:						

POWERTRAIN

Year	Type/ L/Camshaft/bhp	Drivetrain & gearbox	Acceler. 0/100 sec.	Top. speed km/h	Ave. Fuel consp. l./100 km
99-02	L4/2.0/DOHC/129	front-M5	9.5	170	11.0
		front-A4	10.7	165	11.0

(PERFORMANCE)

SPECIFICATIONS

Model 99-02	Wlb. mm	Lght. mm	Cb.wt kg	Brakes fr/rr	Steering type	Standard tires
sdn. 4 dr.	2750	4470	1165	dc/dr/ABS	pwr.r&p.	185/65R14
wgn. 4 dr.	2750	4514	1222	dc/dr/ABS	pwr.r&p.	185/65R14

PRICES

Model / version		1997	1998	1999	2000	2001	2002
sdn. 4dr. SX	mini			5800	6500	7350	12100
	maxi			7900	9450	8900	15200
sdn. 4dr. CDX	mini			6300	7550	10000	13100
	maxi			9100	12300	11550	16300
wgn. 4dr. SX	mini			6300	7000	8400	13200
	maxi			8400	10000	10000	16500
wgn. 4dr. CDX	mini			6800	8100	11000	14200
	maxi			9650	11000	12600	17300

See page 7 to adapt these figures.

2001 DAEWOO Nubira

FORD   Aerostar

1997 FORD Aerostar

This minivan was first available in 1985. It comes in base, extended and 4WD models, powered by 3.0L and 4.0L V6 engines.

PROS

• **Its body** mounted on an H-frame provides a good cargo capacity or pulling power for heavy loads.

• **The ride** is smooth, more so on the highway than on bumpy roads, because of the rigid rear axle.

• **The instrument panel** is practical, the driver's position is comfortable and the digital gauges are convenient.

• **Steering** is clean and crisp.

• **Noteworthy**: a really huge baggage compartment on the extended model, adjustable bucket seats and optional «captain's chairs», convenient hand-brake and sliding side windows.

CONS

• **Hit and miss** reliability on the first models.

• **High fuel bills** because of excessive vehicle weight.

• **Handling** is pretty sloppy with all that swing and sway, and the ride is bumpy with the rigid rear axle and poor-quality shock absorbers.

• **The thick A-pillar** obstructs peripheral vision, rearview mirrors are tiny and those small triangular windows up front are a pain.

• **Cabin space** is cluttered with the large seats and low ceiling clearance.

• **Body height** makes parking a problem, if you try to park in a private garage or in some indoor public parking lots.

• **Brakes** are sluggish and unreliable because of chronic front-wheel lock.

• **Things to be considered**: some inconveniently located controls, the cumbersome shifter on the floor, hard-to-get-to mechanical components and very heavy rear hatch.

VERDICT

The Aerostar is a sturdy all-purpose vehicle, whose 4WD extended model is a good buy if you need to tow heavy loads.

RECALLS

1997 Possibility of transmission case assembly failure on all-wheel drive vehicles.

A short circuit could occur at the accessory terminal in the ignition switch when it is in the "on" position causing overheating and the potential for a vehicle fire.

RELIABILITY PROBLEMS

	1997	1998	1999	2000	2001	2002
Engine:	X					
Transmission:	-					
Suspension:	-					
Steering:	-					
Brakes:	-					
Electricity:	X					
Body:	X					
Accessories:	-					
Fit/finish:	-					

POWERTRAIN   PERFORMANCE

Year	Type/ L/Camshaft/bhp	Drivetrain & gearbox	Acceler. 0/100 sec.	Top. speed km/h	Ave. Fuel consp. l./100 km
1997	V6/3.0/OHV/140	rear-A4	12.7	160	13.7
	V6/4.0/OHV/152	rear-A4	10.0	175	14.4
		all-A4	11.2	165	15.6

SPECIFICATIONS

Model	Wlb. mm	Lght. mm	Cb.wt kg	Brakes fr/rr	Steering type	Standard tires
m.v. 4dr.short	3020	4442	1545	dc/dr	pwr.r&p.	215/70R14
m.v. 4dr.AWD short	3020	4442	1570	dc/dr/ABS	pwr.r&p.	215/70R14
m.v. 4dr.long	3020	4834	1655	dc/dr	pwr.r&p.	215/75R14
m.v. 4dr.AWD long	3020	4834	1695	dc/dr/ABS	pwr.r&p.	215/75R14

PRICES

Model / version		1997	1998	1999	2000	2001	2002
4x2							
m.v. 4dr. XLT 7st.	mini	5250					
	maxi	7550					
m.v. 4dr.XLTlwb 7st.	mini	6600					
	maxi	8950					
4x4							
m.v. 4dr.XLT 7st.	mini	6300					
	maxi	8600					
m.v. 4dr.XLTlwb 7st.	mini	7650					
	maxi	10000					

See page 7 to adapt these figures.

1997 FORD Aerostar

FORD-MERCURY Contour-Mystique

1998 FORD Contour

The Contour-Mystique replaced the Tempo-Topaz models in 1995. They're more high-tech 4-door sedans that come in GL, LX and SE trim levels at Ford and in GS and LS trim levels at Mercury.

PROS

• **A rugged build** provides good passenger protection and excellent road stability.

• **Construction quality** is solid, fit and finish are meticulous and materials and parts are top-notch.

• **The 4-cylinder** engine and the SVT model are really quite powerful.

• **The "oh so" charming SVT** with its daring look and buffed up engine letting out a very noticeable purr.

• **The SE** has the best braking system of the lot, thanks to 4-disc brakes, but stops are more predictable with ABS.

• **You can be sure** of a regal ride with such a smooth suspension, well-contoured seats and low noise level.

• **The car handles** beautifully, it stays good and neutral before going into understeer, which is easy to readjust.

• **The instrument panel** is ergonomic and has a good lay-out, with a style midway between Ford European and American cars.

• **Good fuel economy** with the reasonably powerful 4-cylinder engine, especially when it's coupled to a manual transmission.

• **Bonus points** for some practical items like the inside door handles that light up and are easy to find at night, and the rear seatback control located in the trunk.

CONS

• **Snug room** in the rear seats, both head and leg room are cramped, which is surprising for this type of car, especially when compared to its Cirrus-Stratus rivals.

• **The V6 engine** performance are pretty disappointing, for both accelerations and pick-up are no more muscular than those of the 4-cylinder engine which doesn't burn as much gas.

• **The awkward maneuverability** of the SE model due to its large steer angle.

• **These cars aren't stunning** enough to attract much notice in this day and age, when body design is such a decisive purchase factor.

VERDICT

The Contour-Mystique are solid and safe. But it's too bad the rear seats are so cramped...

RECALLS

97-98 Automatic floor shift control may not correctly indicate the actual gear position.
Defective headlight switch and wiring harness connectors.

1997 Throttle cables to be replaced. (models with traction control).

1998 A burr on the accelerator cable may cause the accelerator not to return to idle when the pedal is released.

1999 Rear fuel lines may allow dangerous evaporative emissions.
Ignition key can be removed from the steering column without the shift lever and transmission being in "PARK".

RELIABILITY PROBLEMS

	1997	1998	1999	2000	2001	2002
Engine:	X	X	X			
Transmission:	X	-	-			
Suspension:	-	-	-			
Steering:	X	-	-			
Brakes:	-	-	X			
Electricity:	X	X	-			
Body:	-	-	X			
Accessories:	X	X	X			
Fit/finish:	X	-	-			

POWERTRAIN   PERFORMANCE

Year	Type/ L/Camshaft/bhp	Drivetrain & gearbox	Acceler. 0/100 sec.	Top. speed km/h	Ave. Fuel consp. l./100 km
97-99	L4/2.0/DOHC/125	front-M5	10.0	175	9.6
		front-A4	11.1	170	9.9
	V6/2.5/DOHC/170	front-M5	8.8	180	11.5
		front-A4	9.4	175	10.9
98-99	V6/2.5/DOHC/200 (SVT)	front-M5	7.7	220	11.9

SPECIFICATIONS

Model Contour	Wlb. mm	Lght. mm	Cb.wt kg	Brakes fr/rr	Steering type	Standard tires
sdn. 4dr. GL	2705	4671	1256	dc/dr	pwr.r&p.	185/70R14
sdn. 4dr. LX	2705	4689	1256	dc/dr	pwr.r&p.	185/70R14
sdn. 4dr. SE	2705	4689	1285	dc/dc	pwr.r&p.	185/70R14
sdn. 4dr. SVT	2705	4671	1392	dc/dc/ABS	pwr.r&p.	215/50ZR16
Mystique						
sdn. 4dr. GS	2705	4694	1272	dc/dr	pwr.r&p.	185/70R14
sdn. 4dr. LS	2705	4694	1272	dc/dc	pwr.r&p.	205/60R15

PRICES

Model / version Contour		1997	1998	1999	2000	2001	2002
sdn. 4dr.	mini	3250	5050	7350			
	maxi	6300	8000	10300			
sdn. 4dr. GL	mini	3700	5550				
	maxi	6850	8400				
sdn. 4dr. LX	mini	4200	6000				
	maxi	7350	9000				
sdn. 4dr. SE	mini	4750		8000			
	maxi	7900		10700			
sdn. 4dr. LX V6	mini		6600				
	maxi		8900				
sdn. 4dr. SE V6	mini		6200				
	maxi		9000				
sdn. 4dr. SVT V6	mini		7350	9000			
	maxi		10100	11750			
Mystique							
sdn. 4dr.	mini	3350	5050				
	maxi	6300	8000				
sdn. 4dr. GS	mini	3700	5550	7350			
	maxi	6850	8400	10200			
sdn. 4dr. LS	mini	4200	6100	7900			
	maxi	7350	9000	10700			

See page 7 to adapt these figures.

FORD-MERCURY

Crown Victoria
Grand Marquis

1998 FORD Crown Victoria

Launched in 1978, these models were redesigned in 1991 and got a face-lift in 1992 and 1997. In 1999, the antilock braking device becomes standard feature on these rear wheel-drive vehicles.

PROS

• **The cabin** is really roomy and can accommodate up to six adults and the huge trunk can gobble up all their luggage.
• **Their rather fluid** and flowing body design is sure more striking than those on the defunct GM rivals...
• **Standard dual airbags** and rigidified body structure are good preventive safety features.
• **The smooth suspension** gently rocks passengers in the quiet, calm cabin interior where next to no noise can creep in.
• **Engine performance** are quite impressive and out of the ordinary for such heavy cars.
• **The newly designed Intech engine** is more economical on gas than were its gas-guzzling predecessors.
• **The plush ride** you've come to expect in such luxury cars.

CONS

• **The jumpy rear axle** is an indicator that mechanical components are a bit outdated and on bad roads, wheels bounce a lot.
• **Steering** is quite vague and is problematic in crosswinds and on slippery roads.
• **Brakes** just don't grip as they should, even with 4-disc brakes, and long stops are proof positive of same.
• **The suspension** with such flexible wheel travel causes quite a sway, but it's really more annoying than dangerous.
• **The seats** are nicely shaped, but they don't provide much lateral or lumbar support.

VERDICT

These cars are the last living specimens of a dying breed, but they still provide a very cushy form of travel.

RECALLS

97-99 Eventual cracking of the lower control arm ball joints.
98-00 Replacement of the label regarding the jacking operation of the car, by a more detailed one.
2000 Inspection and if necessary replacement of the wiper control module on some vehicles.
2001 Dealers will inspect RCM, side and front crash sensor and replace them if necessary.
Restraint Control Module will be replace.

RELIABILITY PROBLEMS

	1997	1998	1999	2000	2001	2002
Engine:	X	X	X	X	X	-
Transmission:	-	X	X	-	-	-
Suspension:	-	-	X	X	-	-
Steering:	X	X	X	-	-	-
Brakes:	X	X	X	-	-	-
Electricity:	X	X	X	X	X	-
Body:	X	-	X	X	X	X
Accessories:	X	X	-	X	X	X
Fit/finish:	X	X	X	X	-	-

POWERTRAIN

Year	Type/ L/Camshaft/bhp	Drivetrain & gearbox	PERFORMANCE Acceler. 0/100 sec.	Top. speed km/h	Ave. Fuel consp. l./100 km
97-02	V8/4.6/OHC/175-235	rear-A4	8.8	175	13.5

SPECIFICATIONS

Model 1997	Wlb. mm	Lght. mm	Cb.wt kg	Brakes fr/rr	Steering type	Standard tires
sdn. 4dr. base	2906	5395	1713	dc/dc	pwr.bal.	215/70R15
sdn. 4dr. LX/LS	2906	5395	1750	dc/dc	pwr.bal.	215/70R15
98-02						
sdn. 4dr. base	2913	5385	1776	dc/ABS	pwr.bal.	225/60SR16
sdn. 4dr. LX/LS	2913	5385	1781	dc/ABS	pwr.bal.	225/60SR16

PRICES

Model / version		1997	1998	1999	2000	2001	2002
Crown Victoria							
sdn. 4dr. base	mini	7350	10700	14200	17550	21000	25700
	maxi	10000	13850	17000	20950	24000	29400
sdn. 4dr. LX	mini	8900	12300	16300	19400	23950	27800
	maxi	11950	15250	19000	22600	26000	31500
Grand Marquis							
sdn. 4dr. GS	mini	8400	11750	15450	18600	21850	28150
	maxi	11550	14700	18000	21500	25200	31000
sdn. 4dr. LS	mini	10000	13350	17550	20250	24450	32250
	maxi	13150	16300	20700	23800	27300	33100

See page 7 to adapt these figures.

1998 MERCURY Grand Marquis

FORD   Escape

2001 FORD Escape

The identical twin of the Mazda Tribute, the Escape arrived just at the right time to complete Ford's line-up and allay suspicion from the Explorer's setbacks. At once compact and modern, the Escape is a good choice in mechanical terms.

PROS
• **The compact size** is current and practical, and the youthful styling is highly successful within the otherwise very conservative line-up.
• **The Escape handles** as safely as a car, to the great delight of female drivers.
• **The overall comfort** level is quite adequate for a utility vehicle, thanks to efficient seats and soundproofing.
• **The brakes** are powerful and easy to modulate. Stops are short and straight, even without ABS.
• **The V6** cranks out honorable performance levels, and output is quite reasonable under load.
• The simple and efficient **all-wheel traction system** requires no driver intervention.
• **The Escape's off-road capabilities** are adequate to allow it to travel over quite hilly terrain, but it's not a real 4x4.
• **The powerful headlights** provide good visibility even in poor weather.

CONS
• **The 4-cylinder's** limited performance is adequate only with front-wheel drive and the manual transmission.
• **Rear-seat** roominess is limited. Indeed, rear accessibility and legroom are at a premium.
• **The standard tires** are of poor quality because their provide mediocre grip even on dry roads.
• **The suspension** reacts harshly on poor roads where the occupants get jostled around without mercy.
• **Ford's plastics** look very cheap and give the dashboard a very utilitarian look to it.
• **The windshield wipers** operate too slowly to ensure adequate visibility in rainy conditions.

VERDICT
The Escape is a very successful compact vehicle that will represent for many a more realistic alternative to the purchase of an Explorer . . .

RECALLS
None over this period.

RELIABILITY PROBLEMS

	1997	1998	1999	2000	2001	2002
Engine:					-	-
Transmission:					-	-
Suspension:					-	-
Steering:					-	-
Brakes:					-	-
Electricity:					X	X
Body:					X	-
Accessories:					X	-
Fit/finish:					-	-

POWERTRAIN

Year	Type/ L/Camshaft/bhp	Drivetrain & gearbox	Acceler. 0/100 sec.	Top. speed km/h	Ave. Fuel consp. l./100 km
01-02	L4/2.0/SOHC/125	av./all-M5	12.0	160	10.0
	V6/3.0/OHV/200	av./all-A4	10.0	175	13.0

SPECIFICATIONS

Model 01-02	Wlb. mm	Lght. mm	Cb.wt kg	Brakes fr/rr	Steering type	Standard tires
wgn. 4dr. 4x2	2618	4395	1390	dc/dr	pwr.r.&p.	225/70R15
wgn. 4dr. 4x4	2618	4395	1568	dc/dr	pwr.r.&p.	235/70R15

PRICES

Model / version		1997	1998	1999	2000	2001	2002
wgn. 4dr. XLS	mini					20800	23600
	maxi					24900	27950
wgn. 4dr. XLT	mini					25200	28100
	maxi					28350	30250

See page 7 to adapt these figures.

2001 FORD Escape

2000 FORD Escort SE

The last Escorts have been singularly improved. Unlike their predecessor, they owe less to the Mazda 323-Protegé and have unveiled a new 2.0L engine before their retirement. The ZX2 coupe derived from the Escort has been produced between 1998 and 2000.

PROS

• **Handling** is more sure and stable than on former models because of smoother suspension, greater wheel travel and upgraded shock absorbers.

• **These models** are more reliable, which may not mean much, given the plethora of problems that afflicted their predecessors.

• **Cabin space** and trunk capacity are roomier, which puts these models in the upper-crust compact car range.

• **The 1.8L engine** is gustier with its improved torque and power.

• **Brakes are easier** to control and are sturdier than before.

• **Comfort** on the road is more noticeable on the latest models whose suspension absorbs shocks better and the front seats are more stuffed and comfy.

CONS

• **Assembly quality** is still the pits, for body fit is far from tight or straight and materials aren't ritzy-looking at all, quite the contrary.

• **Speeding along** in a GT model isn't always care-free on poor roads, for road stability is a bit iffy.

• **The 1.9L and 1.8L engines** coupled to the automatic aren't lively at all and performance can be quite inconsistent, so driving becomes a real drag.

• **Brakes** are quite poor, achieving only long stopping distances.

VERDICT

Escort sales are really quite good, because the Escort is what you could call the typical economical family car.

RECALLS

1999   Belt buckle assemblies will be inspected and replaced if necessary.

RELIABILITY PROBLEMS

	1997	1998	1999	2000	2001	2002
Engine:	X	X	X	-		
Transmission:	-	-	-	-		
Suspension:	-	-	X	-		
Steering:	X	-	-	-		
Brakes:	-	X	-	X		
Electricity:	X	X	X	X		
Body:	-	X	X	-		
Accessories:	-	X	X	-		
Fit/finish:	-	-	-	-		

POWERTRAIN

Year	Type/ L/Camshaft/bhp	Drivetrain & gearbox	Acceler. 0/100 sec.	Top. speed km/h	Ave. Fuel consp. l./100 km
97-00	L4/2.0/SOHC/110-130	front-M5	9.5	180	9.1
		front-A4	10.0	175	9.3

PERFORMANCE

SPECIFICATIONS

Model	Wlb. mm	Lght. mm	Cb.wt kg	Brakes fr/rr	Steering type	Standard tires
97-99						
sdn. 4dr. base	2499	4428	1119	dc/dr	pwr.r&p.	185/65R14
sdn. 4dr. LX/LS	2499	4428	1121	dc/dr	pwr.r&p.	185/65R14
wgn. 5dr. LX/LS	2499	4386	1148	dc/dr	pwr.r&p.	185/65R14
98-00						
cpe. 2dr. ZX2	2499	4450	1124	dc/dr	pwr.r&p.	185/65R14

PRICES

Model / version		1997	1998	1999	2000	2001	2002
cpe. 2dr. ZX2 cool	mini		5450	7350			
	maxi		8400	10200			
cpe. 2dr. ZX2 hot	mini		6000	7900	9150		
	maxi		8900	10700	11750		
sdn. 4dr. LX	mini	3700	4400	6300			
	maxi	6800	7350	9150			
sdn. 4dr.GL	mini	3200					
	maxi	6300					
sdn. 4dr. SE	mini		4950	7350			
	maxi		8400	10200			
wgn. 4dr. LX	mini	4200					
	maxi	7350					
wgn. 5dr. SE	mini		5450	7900			
	maxi		8400	10700			

See page 7 to adapt these figures.

FORD   Excursion

2002 FORD Excursion

A champion of the sport-utility market, Ford wanted to crown its success by creating the ultimate SUV ever marketed. Derived from the Super-Duty pickup, the Excursion comes in XLT and Limited trim levels and is available with a RWD or AWD transmission.

PROS

• **The ultimate expression** of the largest civilian vehicle on the market after the Hummer.

• **A large choice** of mechanical components makes it possible to tailor the vehicle's performance to specific uses.

• **The cavernous cabin**—with its three rows of seats—and baggage compartment can fit up to eight people and their luggage.

• **The load and traction capacities** allow it to carry or pull heavy loads.

• **The rear hatch** features an original design that makes it practical and easy to handle.

• **The thickly upholstered seats**—is comfortable, and the soundproofing is effective even with the diesel engine aboard.

• **The dashboard** is nevertheless ergonomic and provides ample storage space.

CONS

• **This vehicle's overall dimensions** and hefty weight limit its use in both on- and off-road conditions.

• **Maneuverability** is hindered by the wide steer angle diameter.

• **The different engines** are veritable gas guzzlers, because of the indecent weight and size of the Excursion.

• **The hefty weight** translates into wimpy performance levels. Accelerations and pick-up are more of a chore, and the driver must plan passing maneuvres well in advance.

• **Braking is mediocre**, with emergency stop distances that are longer than average. This in turn requires the driver to adopt a defensive driving style.

• **Reselling** the Excursion will be problematic in regions where gasoline does not come cheap.

VERDICT

The out-of-the-ordinary Excursion is the fare of the professional crowd given the amount of cash it takes to buy and operate this vehicle.

RECALLS

None over this period.

RELIABILITY PROBLEMS

	1997	1998	1999	2000	2001	2002
Engine:						
Transmission:						
Suspension:						
Steering:						
Brakes:		Insufficient data				
Electricity:						
Body:						
Accessories:						
Fit/finish:						

POWERTRAIN   PERFORMANCE

Year	Type/ L/Camshaft/bhp	Drivetrain & gearbox	Acceler. 0/100 sec.	Top. speed km/h	Ave. Fuel consp. l./100 km
00-02	V8/5.4/SOHC/255	rr./all-A4	14.5	165	17.0
	V10/6.8/OHC/310	rr./all-A4	12.5	175	20.0
	V8TDI/7.3/OHC/250	rr./all-A4	16.0	165	18.0

SPECIFICATIONS

Model 00-02	Wlb. mm	Lght. mm	Cb.wt kg	Brakes fr/rr	Steering type	Standard tires
wgn. 4dr. 4x2	3480	5758	3016	dc/ABS	pwr.ball	LT265/75R16
wgn. 4dr. 4x4	3480	5758	3487	dc/ABS	pwr.ball	LT265/75R16

PRICES

Model / version		1997	1998	1999	2000	2001	2002
wgn. 4dr. XLT	mini				30450	34000	39300
	maxi				33500	36750	42000
wgn. 4dr. LTD	mini				34550	37250	42200
	maxi				36500	39900	45150

See page 7 to adapt these figures.

2002 FORD Excursion

FORD   Expedition

1999 FORD Expedition

The Expedition is a RWD or AWD sport utility vehicle that comes as a large 4-door station wagon XLT or Eddie Bauer.

PROS

• **The spacious cabin** can welcome six, even seven passengers aboard and if the middle individual seats are replaced by a seatbench, an eighth passenger can be accommodated.
• **You'll be amazed** at the cool comfort you get in this sport ute. The suspension is silky smooth even on the 4X4 models. The thickly upholstered seats are comfortable, though cushions are a bit short and soundproofing provides a nice, quiet travel environment.
• **Maneuverability** is amazing for such a humungous vehicle and with such a short turning diameter.
• **Handling** is a breeze with the new sophisticated front suspension and steering is slick, clean and benefits from a good reduction ratio.
• **The rear hatch** is fitted with a window that opens for handier cargo area access, so you don't have to open the hatch door to load or unload various and sundry objects inside the cabin.
• **The drive is super-comfy**, controls and responses are incredibly smooth, the quiet ride is soothing and handling is a piece of cake.
• **Kudos for**: the simple Control-Trac control that's equipped with a 4X4 automatic function and for the safer, lit-up running boards and the sound system and climate control dials in the rear seat area.
• **Workmanship** is very good for a domestic product. The build is robust, clean finish details and trim materials are as classy.

CONS

• **Fuel consumption** is far from frugal, as is to be expected on such a heavyweight that can tow a trailer weighing up to 8,000 lb. But the gas tank capacity does allow for good road autonomy.
• **Brakes** aren't the best with those long emergency stops.
• **Parking** such a big brute in the city isn't a treat, when parking spots are in shrink mode.
• **Pick-up** isn't as peppy as accelerations and so you have to be pretty careful when passing because this maneuver takes more room.
• **The poorly** designed third seatbench isn't too comfy and it's tough as heck getting to it.

VERDICT

This vehicle is as civilized as a limo practical and really versatile.

RECALLS

1997   Transmission shifter cable must be inspected and reinstalled.
97-99 The lug nuts of the wheels must be inspected and replaced.
1999   Missing or partially installed retainer clip that holds the master cylinder pushrod to the brake pedal arm.
Defective fuel line assemblies that could develop a leak.
17-inch chrome steel wheels can separate from the vehicle due to insufficient wheel contact area with the hub and lack of lug nuts torque.
2001   Driver airbag module can be defective and will be replaced.
The wiper motor gear case will be inspected and replaced on suspect time frame vehicles.

RELIABILITY PROBLEMS

	1997	1998	1999	2000	2001	2002
Engine:	X	X	X	X	X	-
Transmission:	X	-	X	-	-	-
Suspension:	X	X	X	-	-	-
Steering:	X	-	-	-	-	-
Brakes:	X	X	X	X	-	-
Electricity:	X	X	X	X	X	X
Body:	-	X	X	X	X	-
Accessories:	X	X	X	X	X	-
Fit/finish:	X	X	X	X	-	-

POWERTRAIN

Year	Type/ L/Camshaft/bhp	Drivetrain & gearbox	Acceler. 0/100 sec.	Top. speed km/h	Ave. Fuel consp. l./100 km
97-01	V8/4.6/SOHC/214-240	rear/all-A4	11.5	170	16.9
	V8/5.4/SOHC/235-260	rear/all-A4	11.0	175	18.2

SPECIFICATIONS

Model 4x2	Wlb. mm	Lght. mm	Cb.wt kg	Brakes fr/rr	Steering type	Standard tires
wgn. 4dr. XLT	3025	5197	2199	dc/ABS	pwr.bal.	255/70R16
wgn. 4dr. E.B	3025	5197	2220	dc/ABS	pwr.bal.	255/70R16
4x4						
wgn. 4dr. XLT	3025	5197	2300	dc/ABS	pwr.bal.	255/70R16
wgn. 4dr. E.B	3025	5197	2350	dc/ABS	pwr.bal.	265/70R17

PRICES

Model / version		1997	1998	1999	2000	2001	2002
4x2							
wgn. 4dr. XLT	mini	17750	21000	24900	26250	29900	
	maxi	20500	23750	27300	29400	33600	
wgn. 4dr. E.B.	mini	20800	24150	28150	31500	34650	
	maxi	22800	26800	30850	34650	38850	
4x4							
wgn. 4dr. XLT	mini	19200	22500	26450	27800	31500	35700
	maxi	21950	25200	28900	31000	35200	37800
wgn. 4dr. E.B.	mini	21650	25600	29700	33100	36200	40400
	maxi	24150	28250	32450	36200	40400	43600

See page 7 to adapt these figures.

1999 FORD Expedition

1998 FORD Explorer

The Explorer replaced the Bronco II in 1991 and was renewEd in 1997 and 2002. The Sport Trac version was introduced in 2001.

PROS
• **Its more modern look** has a lot to do with its popularity.
• **The interior cabin** is very much like that of a car.
• **Road stability** on straight runs and overall handling are better on the 4-door model with its longer body frame.
• **The V8** engine is super with its surging torque and power.
• **This vehicle** is more comfortable because of its longer wheelbase and better designed soundproofing.
• **Reliability** is better than most of its competitors.

CONS
• **The hefty price** of the Eddie Bauer and Limited models that cost as much as upper-end luxury cars.
• **Touch and go handling** on the 2-door model in crosswinds.
• **The ride** in the base models is as smooth or as rough as the road you're travelling on.
• **Brakes** could be improved, stops are long and unpredictable and brake pads don't have too much lasting power.
• **The manual shifter** is imprecise and quite unpleasant to use.
• **The driver's position** is far from perfect with the long steering column, high instrument panel and low-slung seat. Besides, the windshield pillars obstruct visibility on both sides.
• **Rear seats** are tough to get to without a step to climb up on, because of high ground clearance.

VERDICT
The Explorer is more refined than the Bronco II, for handling and comfort are of higher caliber, but by opting for luxury, it's become an expensive vehicle to run.

RECALLS
1997	Ice may form around the throttle plate while driving at temperatures under 29°C and at highway speeds. Antipollution device does not correspond to established standards.
97-98	Fuel line may be damaged if used as ground while jump starting the vehicle.
1998	Warning chime for opened doors may not work on some vehicles.
98-99	Speed control cable may interfere with the servo pulley and not allow the throttle to return to idle when disengaging the unit. Secondary hood latch may corrode and cause a hood fly-up.
1999	Right front brake line attachment may separate from the ABS hydraulic control unit resulting in a loss of brake pressure.
2000	Belt buckle assemblies will be inspected and replaced if necessary. Dealers will install a relay and wring on affected vehicles. Side crash sensor will be replaced with a revised design. Dealers will insta a resistor on GEM (Generic Electronic Module) to prevent electronic noise.
2001	Dealers will install a revised seat back hinge.
2002	Dealers will inspect tires and replace them if they are slashed.

Explorer FORD

RELIABILITY PROBLEMS

	1997	1998	1999	2000	2001	2002
Engine:		X		X	X	-
Transmission:	X	X				-
Suspension:	X	X	X	X		-
Steering:	-	-	-	-		-
Brakes:		X				-
Electricity:	X	X	X	X	X	-
Body:						-
Accessories:	X	X	X	X	X	-
Fit/finish:	-	X		X		-

POWERTRAIN

Year	Type/ L/Camshaft/bhp	Drivetrain & gearbox	PERFORMANCE Acceler. 0/100 sec.	Top. speed km/h	Ave. Fuel consp. l./100 km
1997	V8/5.0/OHV/210-215	rear/all-A4	10.0	175	17.7
97-02	V6/4.0/OHV/145-210	rear/all-M5	9.0	170	15.1
		rear/all-A4/5	8.5	175	15.5
2002	V8/4.6/SOHC/240	rear/all-A5	9.0	175	17.0

SPECIFICATIONS

Model	Wlb. mm	Lght. mm	Cb.wt kg	Brakes fr/rr	Steering type	Standard tires
97-01						
wgn. 2dr.	2583	4893	1765	dc/ABS	pwr.r&p.	225/70R15
wgn. 4dr.	2835	4844	1880	dc/ABS	pwr.r&p.	255/70R16
2002						
wgn. 2dr.	2583	4893	1765	dc/ABS	pwr.r&p.	225/70R15
wgn. 4dr.	2889	4813	1970	dc/ABS	pwr.r&p.	255/70R16
wgn. 4dr.SporTrac	3198	5230	1929	dc/ABS	pwr.r&p.	255/70R16

PRICES

Model / version		1997	1998	1999	2000	2001	2002
4x2							
wgn. 2dr. XL	mini	7350					
	maxi	10000					
wgn. 2dr. XL Sport	mini	8000	11250	14200	17300	19200	23100
	maxi	10500	13450	16300	19200	21950	26150
wgn. 4dr. XL	mini	8400	11250	3650			
	maxi	11000	13350	15750			
wgn. 4dr. XLT	mini	10200	13650	16800	20150	22000	26150
	maxi	13600	15950	18900	22250	24700	29300
wgn. 4dr. E.B	mini	12800	14900	18400	21700	23600	27700
	maxi	15200	17300	20700	23750	26250	30900
wgn. 4dr. XLT	mini	14100	16500	19400	22900	24700	28750
	maxi	16800	18900	21650	25000	27300	32000
wgn. 4dr. XLS	mini				18100	19950	24000
	maxi				20250	22700	27200
4x4							
wgn. 2dr. XL	mini	8400					
	maxi	11000					
wgn. 2dr. XL Sport	mini	8000	11750	15750	18900	20800	24700
	maxi	11550	14000	17800	20800	23500	27800
wgn. 4dr. XL	mini	9450	12700	15200			
	maxi	12100	14700	17300			
wgn. 4dr. XLT	mini	11250	15100	18400	21750	23600	27700
	maxi	13650	17450	20500	23850	26250	30900
wgn. 4dr.E.B.	mini	13850	16400	19950	23300	25200	29300
	maxi	16300	18800	22000	25500	28300	32450
wgn. 4dr. LTD	mini	15100	17850	21000	24450	26250	30350
	maxi	17850	20400	23000	28900	28900	33600
wgn. 4dr. XLS	mini				19400	21500	25600
	maxi				21850	24150	28750
wgn. 4dr. XLT V8	mini	11750	15750	19100	22700	24700	
	maxi	14200	18150	21200	24800	27300	
wgn. 4dr. E.B. V8	mini	14400	17100	20700	24250	26250	
	maxi	16800	19500	22800	26450	28900	
wgn. 4dr. LTD V8	mini	15700	18600	21700	25400	27750	
	maxi	18400	21000	23850	27500	29900	
Sport Trac							
wgn. 4dr. 2WD	mini					23100	25200
	maxi					26600	29400
wgn. 4dr. 4WD	mini					26250	28350
	maxi					29900	32550

See page 7 to adapt these figures.

FORD   Focus

2001 FORD Focus wagon

The Focus replaced the Escort in 2000 and is available as a 3-door coupe, a 4-door sedan and a wagon. It shares its mechanical components with its predecessor.

PROS

• **The Focus is competitively priced**, but to the detriment of its equipment and the fact that a number of practical features haven't been included.

• **Rounded lines** and other styling touches make the Focus look bigger than most of its rivals.

• **Stopping distances** are short, power is progressive and easy to gauge. The brake pads resist well to heat.

• **The Zetec engine** offers better performance.

• **The Focus handles** with assurance and efficiency, and is well-balanced in curves when equipped with good quality tires.

• **The trunk** can take on a fair amount of baggage, but its narrow opening makes it hard to load large items.

• **The quality** of the radio on our test drive models was remarkable, especially when compared with other equipment that was mediocre at best.

CONS

• **The dashboard's tortured lines** make it a nightmare to look at, and it is already seriously outdated.

• **The disappointing quality** of the finish and the quality of materials, fabrics and plastics create an overall look that is decidedly inexpensive.

• **The rear seats** are hard to get into because of limited space and the narrow opening of the doors.

• **The base engine** provides mediocre performance, especially when coupled with the automatic transmission. Also, it produces as much noise as it does vibration.

• **The suspension** is too soft, and the poor shock absorbers cause the front wheels to hop on bad road surfaces.

• **Visibility** is not ideal because of the thick A-and C-pillars; the small triangular windows are a further drawback.

• **Major road, wind and engine noise** points to very poor soundproofing.

• **A number of practical features have been left out**: the driver has no dummy pedal, there is no gear indicator for the automatic transmission, and rear-seat passengers have no headrests or storage spaces.

VERDICT

Like the Escort, the Focus is relatively inexpensive, but it is not worth much more.

RECALLS

2000   Speed control cable will be inspected and replaced if necessary.
Vehicles will be inspected and rear wheel hub assembly replaced if necessary.
Dealers will replace the IPS (Injector Pressure Sensor) on some vehicles.

2001   Seat back recliner handle spring will be replaced on both front seats.

2002   Dealers must check the cruise control cable location.

RELIABILITY PROBLEMS

	1997	1998	1999	2000	2001	2002
Engine:				X	X	-
Transmission:				-	-	-
Suspension:				-	-	-
Steering:				-	-	-
Brakes:				X	X	-
Electricity:				X	X	X
Body:				X	X	-
Accessories:				X	X	X
Fit/finish:				X	-	-

POWERTRAIN   PERFORMANCE

Year Type/ L/Camshaft/bhp	Drivetrain & gearbox	Acceler. 0/100 sec.	Top. speed km/h	Ave. Fuel consp. l./100 km
00-02				
LX/SE L4/2.0/SOHC/110	front-M5	11.2	170	8.5
	front-A4	12.0	165	9.2
ZX5/ L4/2.0/DOHC/130	front-M5	9.5	180	9.2
ZTS/ZTW	front-A4	10.5	175	9.6

SPECIFICATIONS

Model 00-02	Wlb. mm	Lght. mm	Cb.wt kg	Brakes fr/rr	Steering type	Standard tires
cpe. 2 dr.	2616	4270	1157	dc/dr	pwr.r&p.	175/70R14
sdn. 4 dr.	2616	4526	1163	dc/dr	pwr.r&p.	195/60R15
wgn. 4 dr.	2616	4526	1232	dc/dr	pwr.r&p.	195/60R15

PRICES

Model / version		1997	1998	1999	2000	2001	2002
cpe. 3dr. ZX3	mini				7550	10500	12600
	maxi				10500	13650	16300
cpe. 3dr. ZX5	mini						13100
	maxi						16800
sdn. 4dr. LX	mini				6600	9450	11550
	maxi				9450	12600	15200
sdn. 4dr. SE	mini				7550	11000	13100
	maxi				10500	14200	16800
sdn. 4dr. SE Sport	mini						13650
	maxi						17300
sdn. 4dr. ZTS	mini				8600	11550	14200
	maxi				11550	14700	17850
wgn. 4dr. Se	mini				9150	12100	13650
	maxi				12100	15200	17300
wgn. 4dr. Se Sport	mini						13850
	maxi						17550
wgn. 4dr. ZW5	mini						15200
	maxi						18900

See page 7 to adapt these figures.

2000 FORD Focus

FORD   Mustang

FORD Mustang convertible 1998

Renewed in 1994, the latest Mustang is offered with a V6 or V8 engine, as a coupe or a convertible, as a base or a GT version. To celebrate its 35th anniversary in 2000, a new body design has been introduced.

PROS
• **The sassy body** design is a winner for the young and young at heart.
• **The V6 and V8 engines** are quite different one from the other, but they put a lot of fun and frolic into driving.
• **The latest generation** vehicle is more stable because of its beefed up body.
• **Brakes are gutsy** and stop-on-a-dime dependable, but they're over-assisted so they can be a bit tricky.
• **Driving** is a treat with such spirited, straight-on steering and clean gears.
• **More recent models** are more comfy for there's more room in the rear seat, the suspension is never brutal and there are just enough decibels to add zest to the drive.

CONS
• **Road stability** can be touch and go on slippery roads, for wheels skid and the rigid rear end gives you a Jolly Jumper workout.
• **Steering** is fine at low speeds, but it becomes vague and out of touch at high speeds, so the driver has to watch what he's doing.
• **Fuel consumption** is high with all engine models.
• **The 3.8L engine** doesn't have much get up and go, so driving becomes rather dull and run-of-the-mill.
• **The really stiff suspension** and seats, along with high noise level, make for pretty tiring trips in the older GT.
• **Rear seat** access is awkward and the trunk is hard to get to as well.
• **The trunk** on the convertible model is pretty small.

VERDICT
The Mustang is a versatile and affordable Sportscar that's way ahead in the race against its rivals, yes, even when it comes to the Probe...

RECALLS
1998   The 4.6L engine's fuel rail could separate.
98-99 Speed control cable may interfere with the servo pulley and not allow the throttle to return to idle.
2001   Dealers will modify the parking brake to control the self adjustment mechanism.

Mustang   FORD

RELIABILITY PROBLEMS

	1997	1998	1999	2000	2001	2002
Engine:	X	X	X	X	X	X
Transmission:	X	-	X	-	-	-
Suspension:	X	X	X	X	X	-
Steering:	-	-	-	-	-	-
Brakes:	X	X	X	X	X	-
Electricity:	X	X	-	-	-	-
Body:	X	X	X	X	X	X
Accessories:	X	X	X	X	X	-
Fit/finish:	X	-	X	X	-	-

POWERTRAIN

Year	Type/ L/Camshaft/bhp	Drivetrain & gearbox	Acceler. 0/100 sec.	Top. speed km/h	Ave. Fuel consp. l./100 km
97-02	V6/3.8/OHV/145-190	rear-M5	8.2	170	11.6
		rear-A4	9.0	165	12.3
	V8/4.6/SOHC/215-260	rear-M5	6.7	190	13.7
		rear-A4	7.5	180	13.7
97-99	V8/4.6/DOHC/305	rear-M5	6.0	225	13.4

SPECIFICATIONS

Model 97-02	Wlb. mm	Lght. mm	Cb.wt kg	Brakes fr/rr	Steering type	Standard tires
con. 2dr.	2573	4653	1392	dc/dc	pwr.r&p.	205/65R15
cpe. 2dr.	2573	4653	1456	dc/dc	pwr.r&p.	205/65R15
97-99						
cpe. 2dr. Cobra	2573	4610	1540	dc/ABS	pwr.r&p.	245/45ZR17
con. 2dr. Cobra	2573	4610	1600	dc/ABS	pwr.r&p.	245/45ZR17

PRICES

Model / version		1997	1998	1999	2000	2001	2002
cpe. 2dr.	mini	7350	9750	12100	14400	16150	17850
	maxi	10500	12600	14900	17300	19400	21500
cpe. 2dr. GT	mini	10500	12300	15700	18150	23100	24700
	maxi	13600	15200	18400	21500	26250	28350
cpe. 2dr. Cobra	mini	15750	18150	20500		27300	
	maxi	18900	21000	23400		30450	
con. 2dr.	mini	8900	11250	13650	15950	20500	22600
	maxi	12100	14200	16500	18900	25200	26250
con. 2dr. GT	mini	13100	16000	18600	21000	25700	27300
	maxi	16300	18400	21200	24150	28900	31000
con. 2dr. Cobra	mini	17300	19650	22000		30950	
	maxi	20400	22600	24000		34100	

See page 7 to adapt these figures.

FORD   Probe

1997 FORD Probe GT

Of Ford and Mazda design, the Probe coupe shares its platform and mechanical components with the MX-6. It was touched up in '93 along the same lines. The former conventional and Turbo 2.2L and the 3.0L V6 engines were later replaced by the 2.0L 4-cylinder and 2.5L V6.

PROS

- **Its unique design** once created quite a sensation.
- **The nicely designed** cockpit is the icing on the cake when you're at the wheel of such a fun vehicle.
- **The V6 engines** are thrilling with the manual transmission.
- **Road stability** is better on the GT models, because shock absorbers are better adjusted than on the base models, and these models stay neutral longer.
- **Fuel consumption** is economical if you're not too rough and ready a driver.
- **This is a pretty comfortable** sportswear, even with the stiff suspension and it can accommodate four adults, even with the low ceiling clearance in the rear seat.

CONS

- **Excessive vehicle weight** explains why the base engine model isn't too spirited.
- **Rear seats** are quite cramped on the latest model.
- **The muscular V6 accelerations** can cause walloping torque, which can be hazardous on slippery roads.
- **Brakes** on the base model are definitely less effective than those on the GT that comes equipped with rear disc-brakes.
- **The narrow windows** obstruct vision and the driver is seated low, so it's hard to get a good outward view.
- **The high trunk** opening doesn't make luggage handling easy.

VERDICT

The Probe coupe doesn't have what it takes any more, for former owners are now buying multipurpose sports vehicles that better meet their varied needs.

RECALLS

1997 Fuel cap must be replaced to prevent fuel vapor leak.
2.0L engine timing belt auto tensioner may break resulting in possible engine stalling.

RELIABILITY PROBLEMS

	1997	1998	1999	2000	2001	2002
Engine:	X					
Transmission:	-					
Suspension:	X					
Steering:	-					
Brakes:	-					
Electricity:	X					
Body:	X					
Accessories:	X					
Fit/finish:	-					

POWERTRAIN   PERFORMANCE

Year	Type/ L/Camshaft/bhp	Drivetrain & gearbox	Acceler. 0/100 sec.	Top. speed km/h	Ave. Fuel consp. l./100 km
1997	L4/2.0/DOHC/118	front-M5	9.9	180	9.2
		front-A4	11.0	175	10.5
	V6/2.5/DOHC/164	front-M5	7.9	210	11.4
		front-A4	8.8	200	11.8

SPECIFICATIONS

Model 1997	Wlb. mm	Lght. mm	Cb.wt kg	Brakes fr/rr	Steering type	Standard tires
cpe. 3dr.base	2611	4539	1220	dc/dr	pwr.r&p.	195/65R14
cpe. 3dr.GT	2611	4559	1325	dc/dc	pwr.r&p.	225/50R16

PRICES

Model / version		1997	1998	1999	2000	2001	2002
cpe. 3dr. base	mini	5250					
	maxi	8400					
cpe. 3dr. GT	mini	6850					
	maxi	9850					

See page 7 to adapt these figures.

1997 FORD Probe

FORD-MERCURY   Taurus-Sable

1998 MERCURY Sable

The Taurus and Sable are the most popular cars in North America. Launched on the market in 1986, they were redesigned ten years later and got a serious remodelling in 1998 and 2000.

PROS

• **Sumptuous,** clean lines that are just a bit sassy.

• **With such firm shock** absorbers and such a smooth independent suspension, road stability is just great.

• **The ride is silky** smooth, thanks to well-adjusted suspension, cushy seats and dead on soundproofing.

• **The SHO engine** is thrilling and has great thrust, power steering is smooth and clean as a whistle and the tires are perfect for Sportscar maneuvers.

• **Finish is spiffy** and construction build is tight, yet some of the plastic moldings are really quite awful-looking.

CONS

• **The first generation models** weren't always reliable and build quality was never quite topnotch.

• **The 3.0L engine** puts out only fair to middling performance.

• **The models equipped** with rear drum brakes are iffy when it comes to clean stops or right-on road stability because ABS is only standard on SHO models.

• **Items to consider**: the impractical parking brake, poor maneuverability, rearward vision on the station wagons, not enough and weirdly designed storage compartments and the smaller trunk on the latest models.

VERDICT

The Taurus-Sable have a fresh body design, are good cars and are still quite affordable.

RECALLS

97-98   Transaxle's cover can separate while car is being driven.

1998   Attaching stud on front seat belt buckle defective.

2001   Brake lamp will be replaced and excess grease wiped off the adjustable pedal assembly.
Dealers will install a jumper/resistor assembly at the spoiler.
Dealers will replace driver and front passenger seat belt buckles.

Taurus-Sable — MERCURY-FORD

RELIABILITY PROBLEMS

	1997	1998	1999	2000	2001	2002
Engine:	X	X	X	X	X	-
Transmission:	X	X	-	-	-	-
Suspension:	-	-	-	X	-	-
Steering:	-	-	X	X	-	-
Brakes:	-	-	-	-	-	-
Electricity:	X	X	X	X	X	X
Body:	X	X	X	X	X	X
Accessories:	X	-	-	X	-	-
Fit/finish:	X	X	X	-	-	-

POWERTRAIN / PERFORMANCE

Year	Type/ L/Camshaft/bhp	Drivetrain & gearbox	Acceler. 0/100 sec.	Top. speed km/h	Ave. Fuel consp. l./100 km
97-99	V6/3.0/OHV/145	front-A4	10.6	165	12.4
	V6/3.0/DOHC/200	front-A4	9.4	175	12.7
	V8/3.4/DOHC/235	front-A4	8.0	200	14.2
00-02	V6/3.0/OHV/145-155	front-A4	10.2	165	12.5
	V6/3.0/DOHC/200	front-A4	9.0	175	12.8

SPECIFICATIONS

Model	Wlb. mm	Lght. mm	Cb.wt kg	Brakes fr/rr	Steering type	Standard tires
97-99						
sdn. 4dr. GL/GS	2756	5017	1510	dc/dr	pwr.r&p.	205/65R15
sdn. 4dr. SHO	2756	5039	1504	dc/ABS	pwr.r&p.	225/55ZR16
wgn. 4dr. LX/LS	2756	5070	1579	dc/dr	pwr.r&p.	205/65R15
00-02						
sdn. 4dr.	2756	5019	1550	dc/dr	pwr.r&p.	205/65R15
wgn. 4dr.	2756	5022	1585	dc/dr	pwr.r&p.	205/65R15

PRICES

Model / version		1997	1998	1999	2000	2001	2002
Taurus							
sdn. 4dr. GL	mini	4750					
	maxi	7350					
sdn. 4dr. LX	mini	5250	6300	7350	9450	12100	14200
	maxi	7900	8900	10500	12100	15200	17300
sdn. 4dr. SHO	mini	7900	12100	14700			
	maxi	11000	15250	17850			
sdn. 4dr. SE	mini		7350	8400	11550	14200	16300
	maxi		10500	11550	14200	17300	19400
sdn. 4dr. SEL	mini				13100	15750	17850
	maxi				15750	18900	21000
wgn. 4dr. GL	mini	5250					
	maxi	7900					
wgn. 4dr. LX	mini	5800					
	maxi	8400					
wgn. 4dr. SE	mini		7900	9450	12600	15200	17300
	maxi		11000	12600	15200	18400	20500
wgn. 4dr. SEL	mini				13650	16300	18900
	maxi				15750	19400	22000
Sable							
sdn. 4dr. GS	mini	4950	6800	8400			
	maxi	7900	6450	11000			
sdn. 4dr. LS	mini	5800	7900	9450			
	maxi	8900	10500	12600			
wgn. 4dr. GS	mini	5450					
	maxi	8400					
wgn. 4dr. LS	mini	6300	8900	10500			
	maxi	9450	11550	13650			

See page 7 to adapt these figures.

FORD-MERCURY

1997 FORD Thunderbird

These mid-size coupes that hail way back to 1954 have had quite an erratic and bumpy career. They were last revamped in '89 in a still very large format before disappearing in '98 due to poor sales. In 99, the Cougar is reintroduced on the market but this time, in a much smaller format and in a very different style; all of this based on the Contour-Mystique platform.

PROS

• **Lots of folks are still wild** about their clean and classic body design.
• **A comfortable ride** with spacious cabin, sensitive suspension, well-upholstered seats and low noise level.
• **Muscular accelerations** and pick-up on the SuperCoupe and XR7 with supercharged engine.
• **Handling** is good with the independent rear suspension and good-sized original tires.
• **Steering is quick**, crisp and smooth.
• **There are lots of storage** compartments and the trunk holds an amazing amount of luggage.

CONS

• **High fuel consumption**, especially with the Thunderbird's V8.
• **Maneuverability** and ability to make quick moves aren't perfect because of vehicle size and very large steer angle.
• **The cabin interior** is rather dull and some items just aren't the right design for a so-called Sportscar.
• **Brakes are smooth**, but they don't have much lasting power and emergency stops are too long.
• **No shifter position** indicator among the instruments and poorly located air-conditioner controls.

VERDICT

Even though they're quite winsome, these models have fewer and fewer takers, because engine performances aren't really of Sportscar caliber. If only their famous name can evoke more than good old memories...

RELIABILITY PROBLEMS

	1997	1998	1999	2000	2001	2002
Engine:	X					
Transmission:	-					
Suspension:	X					
Steering:	X					
Brakes:	-					
Electricity:	X					
Body:	-					
Accessories:	-					
Fit/finish:	X					

POWERTRAIN / PERFORMANCE

Year	Type/ L/Camshaft/bhp	Drivetrain & gearbox	Acceler. 0/100 sec.	Top. speed km/h	Ave. Fuel consp. l./100 km
1997	V6/3.8/OHV/140	rear-A4	11.5	165	11.0
	V8/4.6/SOHC/205	rear-A4	9.0	195	13.0

SPECIFICATIONS

Model 1997	Wlb. mm	Lght. mm	Cb.wt kg	Brakes fr/rr	Steering type	Standard tires
cpe. 2dr. LX	2870	5047	1641	dc/dr	pwr.r&p.	205/70R15
cpe. 2dr. SC	2870	5047	1728	dc/ABS	pwr.r&p.	225/60R16
Cougar / XR7						
cpe. 2dr. XR7	2870	5047	1739	dc/ABS	pwr.r&p.	225/60R16

PRIX

Model / version		1997	1998	1999	2000	2001	2002
Thunderbird							
cpe. 2dr. LX	mini	8400					
	maxi	11000					
Cougar / XR7							
cpe. 2dr. XR7	mini	7350					
	maxi	10500					

See page 7 to adapt these figures.

1997 MERCURY Cougar

FORD   Thunderbird

2002 FORD Thunderbird

It is back to the basics for this model which had disappeared from the catalog several years beforehand. It is now more reminiscent of the original fifties model and borrows its mechanical components from the Lincoln LS.

PROS

• **The original styling**, featuring a host of evocative details, is very reminiscent of the first T-Bird.

• **The driving pleasure** is ensured by a rigid chassis, well-adapted controls and the powerful engine.

• **The V8 engine** cranks out excellent performance and produces enthusiastic acceleration as well as an evocative exhaust note.

• **The road handling** is competent due to the rigid structure and sophisticated suspension components.

• **The excellent brakes** produce short and straight stopping distances whereas the pads are quite fade resistant in intensive use.

• **The overall comfort** is surprising for a sport-tuned model. The supple suspension does a good job of absorbing road defects.

• **The well-designed** soft top is electrically assisted and is easy to stow away.

CONS

• **The body styling** is controversial because the stylists seem to have contented themselves with simply imitating the original's without innovating.

• **The brakes** are difficult to gauge and the pedal is easily provoked and sensitive.

• **The small trunk** and storage spaces hindered the vehicle's practicality.

• **The doors** shake on poor road surfaces, which points to a faulty platform design and inadequate rigidity at this level.

• **The tonneau cover** is poorly designed and difficult to install.

• **The limited access** to the engine bay complicates maintenance tasks because the main components are hidden from view.

• **The cheap finish** is clearly unacceptable for a specialty model that commands a high price tag.

VERDICT

The latest Thunderbird will satisfy neither the make's purists nor auto collectors or driving enthusiasts.

RECALLS

None over this period.

RELIABILITY PROBLEMS

	1997	1998	1999	2000	2001	2002
Engine:						-
Transmission:						-
Suspension:						-
Steering:						-
Brakes:		Insufficient data				-
Electricity:						-
Body:						-
Accessories:						-
Fit/finish:						-

POWERTRAIN

Year	Type/ L/Camshaft/bhp	Drivetrain & gearbox
2002		
base	V8/3.9/DOHC/280	A5-rear

PERFORMANCE

Acceler. 0/100 sec.	Top. speed km/h	Ave. Fuel consp. l./100 km
7.2	210	14.4

SPECIFICATIONS

Model 2002	Wlb. mm	Lght. mm	Cb.wt kg	Brakes fr/rr	Steering type	Standard tires
con. 2 dr.	2723	4732	1712	d/ABS	pwr.r&p	235/50R17

PRICES

Model / version		1996	1997	1998	1999	2000	2001
con. 2dr.	Mini						55100
	maxi						68700

See page 7 to adapt these figures.

2002 FORD Thunderbird

FORD-MERCURY   Cougar

2000 MERCURY Cougar

The compact Cougar was introduced to the market in 1999. It's a completely different model from the one that bore the same name for a long time in Mercury's line-up. Its platform and mechanical components are derived from the defunct Contour/Mystique.

PROS
• **The modern styling** of the first model was slightly exaggerated, but it has since been slightly redesigned and has become more sober.
• **The compromise** between comfort and handling is unusual for a car whose intentions are sporty, because the suspension, seats and sound level are surprisingly civilized.
• **The large modular trunk** is a very appreciated practical touch in an era where versatility is a must for any vehicle.
• **The well-contoured front seats** provide great lateral and lumbar support, and they are consistently padded.
• **The V6** engine's sporty exhaust note makes driving this car addictive.
• **The equipment** list is extensive, despite a few oddities.

CONS
• **The V6's performance** is disappointing; the Cougar accelerates no quicker that the former Contour/Mystique. Ford could have given it more character by entrusting it to its SVT guys.
• **The manual gearbox** is fuzzy and does not encourage sporty driving. This is in direct contradiction with the vehicle's mission.
• **Torque steer** becomes a problem when accelerating and can prove to be downright dangerous on slippery roads.
• The irrational equipment list contains many oddities, but there is no tilt steering column or ABS.
• **The rear seats** are rather useless, as is often the case in such coupes. Only small children or pets will have enough room in back.
• **Rearward visibility** is greatly hindered because of the small exterior mirrors, sharp slope of the rear window and thickness of the B and C pillars.
• **The high trunk** sill seriously complicates the loading and unloading of luggage.

VERDICT
Ford failed to seize a great opportunity to launch an interesting vehicle. It missed its target market and chose components that produce a vapid cocktail.

RECALLS
None over this period.

RELIABILITY PROBLEMS

	1997	1998	1999	2000	2001	2002
Engine:			X	X	-	-
Transmission:			-	-	-	-
Suspension:			X	-	-	-
Steering:			-	X	-	-
Brakes:			X	X	X	-
Electricity:			X	X	X	-
Body:			X	X	X	X
Accessories:			X	X	-	-
Fit/finish:			X	-	-	-

POWERTRAIN

Year	Type/ L/Camshaft/bhp	Drivetrain & gearbox	Acceler. 0/100 sec.	Top. speed km/h	Ave. Fuel consp. l./100 km
99-00	L4/2.0/DOHC/125	front-M5	11.0	175	9.7
99-01	V6/2.5/DOHC/170	front-M5	9.0	185	12.0
		front-A4	10.4	180	11.4

PERFORMANCE

SPECIFICATIONS

Model 99-01	Wlb. mm	Lght. mm	Cb.wt kg	Brakes fr/rr	Steering type	Standard tires
cpe. 2dr. 2+2 L4	2703	4699	1312	dc/dr	pwr.r.&p.	205/70R15
cpe. 2dr. 2+2 V6	2703	4699	1363	dc/dr	pwr.r.&p.	205/60R15

PRICES

Model / version		1997	1998	1999	2000	2001	2002
cpe. 2dr. I4	mini			10100	12600		
	maxi			13100	15200		
cpe. 2dr. V6	mini			11550	14200	15750	
	maxi			14700	16800	18600	
cpe. 2dr. V6-S	mini					18400	
	maxi					21500	
cpe. 2dr. Sport	mini						21000
	maxi						24700

See page 7 to adapt these figures.

2000 MERCURY Cougar

FORD-MERCURY   Villager

1998 MERCURY Villager

Designed by Nissan and built by Ford, this front-wheel drive minivans derived from a former Maxima. They were first sold in 1993, redesigned in '99 with the addition of a second sliding door. Last production year a 3.3L V6 engine replaced the former 3.0L V6.

PROS

• **They look great** both inside and out and the body design is clean and elegant.

• **Modular rear seats** are unique and cleverly designed and besides, they're easy to adjust.

• **Driving comfort** is enhanced by a well-adjusted combination of springs and shock absorbers and by good rear end follow-through.

• **Handling** is stable even though there's some sway due to the soft suspension and rustic rear axle design.

• **Safety features** are great with such a rigid cabin frame, standard airbags and headrests as well as standard ABS on Ford products and on the Nissan GXE.

• **Build and finish** quality and spiffy materials are more like those of a luxury car rather than a sports utility vehicle.

• **These two models** come loaded with a lot of standard equipment, which explains why they're pricier than the equivalent competitor models.

CONS

• **Excessive vehicle weight** affects engine performance and fuel consumption.

• **Brakes** don't have much grip or lasting power, because it is not equipped with 4-disc brakes, like its Japanese counterpart the Quest.

• **Engine performance** is weak when vehicle is loaded or when pulling a trailer.

• **Trunk and rear seat** are cramped with seven persons aboard.

• **Maneuverability** isn't great with such a large steer angle.

• **Better soundproofing** would make for a more comfortable ride.

• **Some of the controls** and storage areas are inconvenient.

VERDICT

These vehicles are perfect for people looking for the kind of space and comfort that you used to get in the large station wagons no longer on the market.

RECALLS

1997   Defective battery.

RELIABILITY PROBLEMS

	1997	1998	1999	2000	2001	2002
Engine:	X	X				
ansmission:	X	-				
Suspension:	-	-				
Steering:	X	X				
Brakes:	-	-				
Electricity:	X	X				
Body:	X	X				
Accessories:	X	X				
Fit/finish:	X	X				

POWERTRAIN

Year	Type/ L/Camshaft/bhp	Drivetrain & gearbox
1997	V6/3.0/SOHC/151	front-A4
1998	V6/3.3/SOHC/170	front-A4

PERFORMANCE

	Acceler. 0/100 sec.	Top. speed km/h	Ave. Fuel consp. l./100 km
	12.0	180	13.0
	11.0	180	13.8

SPECIFICATIONS

Model 97-98	Wlb. mm	Lght. mm	Cb.wt kg	Brakes fr/rr	Steering type	Standard tires
m.v. 4dr. GS	2850	4831	1810	dc/dr/ABS	pwr.r&p.	205/75R15
m.v. 4dr. LS	2850	4831	1848	dc/dr/ABS	pwr.r&p.	205/75R15
m.v. 4dr. Nautica	2850	4831	1848	dc/dr/ABS	pwr.r&p.	205/75R15

PRICES

Model / version		1997	1998	1999	2000	2001	2002
m.v. 4dr. GS	mini	7550	10500				
	maxi	10000	12600				
m.v. 4dr. LS	mini	9250	12600				
	maxi	11550	15100				
m.v. 4dr. Nautica	mini	11750	13650				
	maxi	14200	16300				

See page 7 to adapt these figures.

1998 MERCURY Villager

FORD   Windstar

1999 FORD Windstar

It took Ford ten years to come up with a front-wheel drive minivan with a long wheelbase and driven by a V6 engine. Remolded in '99, it offers a left side sliding door to follow the competition.

PROS
• **It's well-designed** to accommodate seven passengers and the huge baggage compartment holds all their luggage.
• **Brakes are effective**, emergency stops are normal, ABS comes as standard equipment and the brake pedal is responsive and smooth.
• **The 3.8L V6** engine puts out 200-hp and far outstrips performance of its main rivals.
• **The ride** is cushy with such a smooth suspension, thickly upholstered seats and low noise level.
• **The elegant**, even though a bit blah, look and spiffy design down to the smallest details.
• **Fuel consumption** is quite economical even with the muscular 3.8L engine that isn't too gas-thirsty.
• **Driving is pleasant** with such crisp steering, smooth engine and good road stability, even though there is a bit of sway.
• **Build is solid**, fit and finish are clean and tight, materials are nice and the overall design is simple and straightforward.
• **Convenient**: the well-designed hand brake and rear hatch handle.

CONS
• **Its bland body** design and conventional technical features put the Windstar far behind in the race against its Chrysler and GM rivals (no second sliding door before 1999, no short body style model, etc.)
• **The far-fetched** instrument panel is neither convenient nor ergonomic.
• **Seats** are heavy and hard to handle, the seat is short but there are standard headrests.
• **There aren't enough** storage compartments in the front seat area.
• **To be improved upon**: the off-center rear windshield wiper and it isn't intermittent either.

VERDICT
The Windstar is a solid and powerful (3.8L engine) minivan, but its design and equipment aren't at all interesting or innovative.

RECALLS
97-98	May have faulty front brake rotors and pads.
97-99	The brake fluid warning statement embossed on the reservoir. is not clearly visible by direct view. New label required.
97-98	Transaxle's cover can separate while car is being driven.
1998	Headrest's lock defective on second row bench seat. Rack and pinion steering gears may be damaged.

2001 Dealers will inspect the Restraint Control Module or crash sensors and if necessary replace them.

Dealers will replace both front driver and passenger floormat of some vehicles equipped with adjustable pedal option.

RELIABILITY PROBLEMS

	1997	1998	1999	2000	2001	2002
Engine:	X	X	X	X	-	-
Transmission:	X	X	X	X	X	X
Suspension:	X	X	X	X	-	-
Steering:	-	-	-	-	-	-
Brakes:	X	X	X	X	X	-
Electricity:	X	X	X	X	X	X
Body:	X	-	X	X	X	-
Accessories:	X	X	X	X	X	-
Fit/finish:	X	X	X	X	-	-

POWERTRAIN

Year	Type/ L/Camshaft/bhp	Drivetrain & gearbox
97-99	V6/3.0/OHV/150	front-A4
97-02	V6/3.8/OHV/155-200	front-A4

PERFORMANCE

	Acceler. 0/100 sec.	Top. speed km/h	Ave. Fuel consp. l./100 km
	NA	NA	NA
	9.8	175	13.6

SPECIFICATIONS

Model 97-02	Wlb. mm	Lght. mm	Cb.wt kg	Brakes fr/rr	Steering type	Standard tires
m.v. 4dr. 3.0	3066	5103	NA	dc/dr/ABS	pwr.r&p.	205/70R15
m.v. 4dr. LX	3066	5103	1671	dc/dr/ABS	pwr.r&p.	215/70R15
m.v. 4dr. GL	3066	5110	1681	dc/dr/ABS	pwr.r&p.	215/70R15
m.v. 4dr. LTD	3066	5110	NA	dc/dr/ABS	pwr.r&p.	225/60R16
m.v. 4dr. SE	3066	5103	NA	dc/dr/ABS	pwr.r&p.	215/70R15
m.v. 4dr. SEL	3066	5103	NA	dc/dr/ABS	pwr.r&p.	225/60R16

PRICES

Model / version		1997	1998	1999	2000	2001	2002
m.v. 4dr. 7 st. 3.0	mini		8400	10500			
	maxi		11000	13650			
m.v. 4dr. 7 st. GL	mini	7350	9750				
	maxi	9450	12400				
m.v. 4dr. 7 st. LX	mini	10500	12600	12200	14700	19400	
	maxi	13200	15200	15200	17300	22600	
m.v. 4dr. 7 st. LTD	mini		15000		21750	28000	
	maxi		17850		24150	31000	
m.v. 4dr. 7 st. SE	mini			14700			
	maxi			17300			
m.v. 4dr. 7 st. SEL	mini			17850	18900	24800	
	maxi			20500	21500	27800	
m.v. 4dr. 7 st. Sport	mini					21750	
	maxi					24700	
m.v. 5dr. 7 st. LX	mini				15200	21000	23000
	maxi				17800	23100	26250
m.v. 5dr. 7 st. SEL	mini				19400	25400	27800
	maxi				22000	28350	30750
m.v. 5dr. 7st. LTD	mini				22250	28550	32550
	maxi				24700	31500	35500
m.v. 5dr. 7st.Sport	mini					22250	24900
	maxi					21500	27800

See page 7 to adapt these figures.

2001 BUICK Parck Avenue

This car is the cream of the crop at GM. They're loaded luxury vehicles and their design is ultra-discrete.

PROS

• **Advanced technical** features, because these front-wheel drive vehicles have independent suspensions and standard ABS.

• **Five passengers** can be comfortably seated in the cabin and the trunk sure holds a lot of luggage.

• **The ride is regal** when you're seated in such plush seats, rocked by the soft suspension and soothed by ultimate quiet.

• **The V6 engines** are adequate and gas consumption is reasonable.

• **The Park Avenue Ultra** engine with supercharger has almost the vim and vigor of the V8 Cadillac engine...

• **If you're looking for space** and comfort at an affordable price, these reliable and durable cars are the answer.

CONS

• **The overly soft** suspension makes for a pretty rock 'n roll ride (except on the Ultra).

• **Brakes** aren't too smooth and they fizzle out with intensive use.

• **Seats are straight** and the lumbar section isn't adjustable.

• **Power steering** is too over-assisted and you don't have a clue as to what the road is like and there's generally poor maneuverability with these cars.

• **High depreciation** of such big cars doesn't make for a good investment.

VERDICT

This model is elegant and it works like a charm if it is properly maintained.

RECALLS

1997   Brake's electronic command module is defective.

1998   Powertrain control module is miscalibrated.

2000   The hydraulic modulator of the ABS system will be inspected and replaced if necessary.

2001   Dealers will replace the windshield wiper motor cover which contains the microprocessor.

01-02   The antitheft device must be reprogrammed.

RELIABILITY PROBLEMS

	1997	1998	1999	2000	2001	2002
Engine:	X	-	X	X	-	-
Transmission:	-	X	X	-	-	-
Suspension:	X	X	X	X	X	-
Steering:	-	-	-	-	-	-
Brakes:	X	X	X	X	X	-
Electricity:	X	X	X	X	X	X
Body:	X	X	X	X	-	-
Accessories:	X	X	X	X	-	-
Fit/finish:	-	-	X	-	-	-

POWERTRAIN

Year	Type/ L/Camshaft/bhp	Drivetrain & gearbox	Acceler. 0/100 sec.	Top. speed km/h	Ave. Fuel consp. l./100 km
97-02	V6/3.8/OHV/170-205	front-A4	9.5	180	13.0
	V6C/3.8/OHV/205-240	front-A4	8.5	200	13.5

SPECIFICATIONS

Model	Wlb. mm	Lght. mm	Cb.wt kg	Brakes fr/rr	Steering type	Standard tires
Park Avenue						
sdn. 4dr.	2891	5253	1714	dc/ABS	pwr.r&p.	225/60R16
sdn. 4dr. Ultra	2891	5253	1762	dc/ABS	pwr.r&p.	225/60R16

PRICES

Model / version		1997	1998	1999	2000	2001	2002
sdn. 4dr. base	mini	9450	12900	17300	21700	25700	28900
	maxi	13650	16800	21300	25200	29900	33600
sdn. 4dr. Ultra	mini	12100	15900	19600	24900	28900	32000
	maxi	15650	18900	23100	28350	33100	36750

See page 7 to adapt these figures.

2001 BUICK Park Avenue

GM E Series

BUICK Riviera

1999 BUICK Riviera

This big coupe has always been prized by a very specific clientele that has dwindled over the years, who are looking for a vehicle of the same look and dimensions as their family yacht.

PROS

• **Four adults** can be comfortably seated in the cabin and the trunk can handle all their luggage.

• **The supercharged** engines are very spirited, but they don't have the guts or gusto of real Sportscars.

• **Driving one** of these cars is like being on cloud nine with the supple suspension, deep, cushy seats and really top-notch soundproofing.

• **The car holds** the road, thanks to well-adjusted shock absorbers.

• **Brakes** are powerful brutes, with or without ABS.

• **The 3.8L V6** engine is quite easy on gas, given the vehicle weight.

• **The instrument panel** on the latest generation models is straightforward and convenient, but some people don't like all the round motifs.

CONS

• **Riviera is a big boat** by today's standards.

• **Steering** is pretty touch and go, and you really have to keep an eye on it if you want to keep on track.

• **Outward visibility** isn't great with the low-slung driver's seat and the relatively high body frame.

• **The electronic instruments** on some models can be terribly distracting for the driver and they cost an arm and a leg to repair.

• **On some models**, trunk capacity has been cut down to accommodate the rear end body design, and it doesn't hold what it should for a vehicle this size.

• **To be improved upon**: rear windows that don't open and the awkward steering column which, even when adjusted, doesn't allow for a comfortable driving position.

VERDICT

These coupes are still quite unique and they don't appeal to everyone. They're rare and if they're in good shape, they're a good investment.

RECALLS

None over this period.

RELIABILITY PROBLEMS

	1997	1998	1999	2000	2001	2002
Engine:	X	X	X			
Transmission:	X	X	-			
Suspension:	X	-	X			
Steering:	-	-	-			
Brakes:	X	X	X			
Electricity:	X	X	X			
Body:	-	-	-			
Accessories:	X	X	-			
Fit/finish:	-	X	X			

POWERTRAIN

Year	Type/ L/Camshaft/bhp	Drivetrain & gearbox
97-98	V6/3.8/OHV/170-205	front-A4
97-99	V6C/3.8/OHV/225-240	front-A4

PERFORMANCE

	Acceler. 0/100 sec.	Top. speed km/h	Ave. Fuel consp. l./100 km
	9.5	190	12.0
	7.8	180	13.5

SPECIFICATIONS

Model Riviera	Wlb. mm	Lght. mm	Cb.wt kg	Brakes fr/rr	Steering type	Standard tires
cpe. 2dr.	2891	5263	1684	dc/ABS	pwr.r&p.	225/60R16

PRICES

Model / version		1997	1998	1999	2000	2001	2002
cpe. 2dr.	mini	10500	11850	15200			
	maxi	14200	16300	19200			

See page 7 to adapt these figures.

1997 BUICK Riviera

GM F Series

2000 CHEVROLET Camaro

The Camaro-Firebird are now in their fifth generation and available as coupes or convertibles.

PROS

- **Their bold** and brassy look appeals to the young and young at heart.
- **You get a lot for your money** and it's a good buy because of reasonably low maintenance bills.
- **Road stability** on the latest generation models is steadier because of the beefed up reinforced body.
- **The V8** engine takes your breath away, but the V6 is a wiser and more economical choice.
- **Passenger safety** is assured with standard ABS and dual airbags.
- **The instrument panel** on the latest model is more practical.
- **The well-designed** convertible top is a breeze.

CONS

- **Driving on curved roads** can be tricky because of excessive weight.
- **The drive can be a drag** with the Jack-in-the-box suspension, stiff seats and high noise level with all engine models.
- **Visibility isn't grea**t with the low-slung driver's seat and the blind spots with the convertible top.
- **Steering is over-assisted** and far too sensitive.
- **Brakes lack grip**, but with ABS, they're more reliable.
- **Gas consumption** is never really economical particularly with a V8 engine.
- **Fit and finish** and trim materials aren't what you'd expect on such a vehicle.
- **The catalytic converter** bump under the front passenger's legs can be quite annoying on long trips.

VERDICT

Only dyed-in-the-wool fanatics will be willing to spend the cash it takes to keep these beasts on the road and these days, there are fewer and fewer takers...

RECALLS

1998   Exhaust gas recirculation valve may fail.
2002   Dealers must install 3 poprivets to secure the welding on the driver's door.

RELIABILITY PROBLEMS

	1997	1998	1999	2000	2001	2002
Engine:	X	X	X	X	X	X
Transmission:	-	-	-	-	-	-
Suspension:	-	X	-	-	-	-
Steering:	X	-	-	-	-	-
Brakes:	X	X	X	X	X	-
Electricity:	X	X	X	X	X	X
Body:	X	-	-	-	X	-
Accessories:	X	X	X	X	X	-
Fit/finish:	X	X	X	X	-	-

POWERTRAIN

Year	Type/ L/Camshaft/bhp	Drivetrain & gearbox	Acceler. 0/100 sec.	Top. speed km/h	Ave. Fuel consp. l./100 km
97-02	V6/3.8/OHV/200	rear-M5	9.0	185	12.2
		rear-A4	9.8	180	12.4
	V8/5.7/OHV/240-320	rear-M5/M6	5.3	230	14.5
		rear-A4	6.0	220	14.0

PERFORMANCE

SPECIFICATIONS

Model	Wlb. mm	Lght. mm	Cb.wt kg	Brakes fr/rr	Steering type	Standard tires
Camaro 97-02						
cpe. 2dr. base	2568	4907	1500	dc/ABS	pwr.r&p.	215/60R16
con. 2dr. base	2568	4907	1588	dc/ABS	pwr.r&p.	215/60R16
cpe. 2dr. Z28	2568	4907	1560	dc/ABS	pwr.r&p.	235/55R16
con. 2dr. Z28	2568	4907	1622	dc/ABS	pwr.r&p.	235/55R16
Firebird 97-02						
cpe. 2dr. base	2568	4910	1507	dc/ABS	pwr.r&p.	215/60R16
con. 2dr. base	2568	4910	1543	dc/ABS	pwr.r&p.	215/60R16
cpe. 2dr. Formula	2568	4910	1515	dc/ABS	pwr.r&p.	245/50ZR16
con. 2dr. Formula	2568	4912	1584	dc/ABS	pwr.r&p.	245/50ZR16
cpe. 2dr. T.A.	2568	4920	1541	dc/ABS	pwr.r&p.	245/50ZR16
con. 2dr. T.A.	2568	4920	1594	dc/ABS	pwr.r&p.	245/50ZR16

PRICES

Model / version		1997	1998	1999	2000	2001	2002
Camaro							
cpe. 2dr. base	mini	7900	10800	13550	16800	19950	21500
	maxi	10900	13650	16600	19950	24150	25700
cpe. 2dr. Z28	mini	12100	14400	17750	22000	24150	27300
	maxi	14700	17650	20700	24150	27800	31500
con. 2dr.	mini	12600	15200	17300	21500		27800
	maxi	15200	18400	19950	24150		32000
con. 2dr. Z28	mini	15200	18900	20700	24700	27300	32000
	maxi	17850	22000	23600	27300	31000	36200
Firebird							
cpe. 2dr.	mini	10000	11200	14700	17000	20500	23600
	maxi	13100	14200	17500	19950	24150	27300
cpe. 2dr. Formula	mini	10500	12900	19950		25700	27800
	maxi	13650	15750	22800		28900	31500
cpe. 2dr.Trans Am	mini	13650	15750	21000	23100	26250	29400
	maxi	16800	18900	23800	26250	29400	33100
con. 2dr.	mini	12600	15400	18900	22000		26800
	maxi	15750	18400	21700	25200		30450
con. 2dr.Trans Am	mini	15200	18400	22000	26800	28900	32000
	maxi	18400	21500	24900	29400	32000	36200
con. 2dr. Formula	mini	12600					
	maxi	16300					

See page 7 to adapt these figures.

GM F/UT Series

2000 CHEVROLET Blazer

These sport utility vehicles are more and more popular since they were put on the market in 1982. They were modified in 1995 and driven by a 4.3L V6 engine. A luxurious version of the Jimmy, the Envoy, is available since 1998.

PROS

• **The 4.3L V6** engine has power and torque to burn, so it can pull a heavy load or head out to explore rough terrain whenever it pleases.

• **These vehicles** are more comfortable with their improved suspension, big tires that don't bounce too much and better-contoured seats.

• **Handling** on the latest generation models is more crisp and clean because of the reinforced frame.

• **These vehicles** are much more reliable, but «we reckon they still have a ways to go» to beat the Ford Explorer...

CONS

• **The manual transmission** shifter is stiff, steering is over-assisted and all over the map.

• **Handling** off-the-road is pretty rough, because of poor shock absorbers and by the less than sturdy body.

• **Brakes** lack grip, lasting power and reliability on sudden stops.

• **These vehicles** are expensive to run, whether it be at the pump, at the insurance company office or at the good local garage.

• **Access** to rear seats is not easy on two-door models.

• **The big tires** make quite a racket, as does the engine at the least acceleration.

• **Storage compartments** are scarce and the split rear hatch door complicates access to the baggage compartment.

VERDICT

The Jimmy-Blazer's sell and resell well for they're more affordable than their main rivals. The reason for this is their less robust build, a less spit and polish finish and lower-quality materials.

RECALLS

1997	Front outboard seatbelt webbing could separate on frontal impact.
1998	The right-hand rear brake may wear itself out.
2000	Some seatbelts doesn't satisfied strenght regulations. Payload informations can be wrong and label replaced.
00-02	Dealers must replaced the hazard lights switch on some vehicles.

RELIABILITY PROBLEMS

	1997	1998	1999	2000	2001	2002
Engine:	X	X	-	X	X	-
Transmission:	X	-	X	X	-	-
Suspension:	-	X	-	-	-	-
Steering:	X	-	-	-	-	-
Brakes:	X	X	X	X	-	-
Electricity:	X	X	X	X	X	X
Body:	X	X	X	X	X	X
Accessories:	X	X	X	X	X	X
Fit/finish:	X	-	X	-	-	-

POWERTRAIN / PERFORMANCE

Year	Type/ L/Camshaft/bhp	Drivetrain & gearbox	Acceler. 0/100 sec.	Top. speed km/h	Ave. Fuel consp. l./100 km
97-02	V6/4.3/OHV/160-190	rear/all-M5	9.6	175	17.2
		rear/all-A4	9.9	185	15.4

SPECIFICATIONS

Model 97-02	Wlb. mm	Lght. mm	Cb.wt kg	Brakes fr/rr	Steering type	Standard tires
Blazer-Jimmy						
wgn. 2dr. 4x2	2553	4491	1596	dc/ABS	pwr.bal.	205/75R15
wgn. 2dr. 4x4	2553	4491	1746	dc/ABS	pwr.bal.	205/75R15
wgn. 4dr. 4x2	2718	4656	1666	dc/ABS	pwr.bal.	205/75R15
wgn. 4dr. 4x4	2718	4656	1837	dc/ABS	pwr.bal.	205/75R15

PRICES

Model / version		1997	1998	1999	2000	2001	2002
Jimmy / Blazer 4x2							
wgn. 2dr.base/SL	mini	8000	10000	11550	13300	17200	22600
	maxi	12100	13850	15200	15200	19400	25400
wgn. 2dr. LS/SLS	mini	8900	11550	13100	14200	18000	23600
	maxi	11200	13650	14700	16400	20500	26250
wgn.4dr. base/SL	mini	10500	13100	14200			
	maxi	13100	15200	16400			
wgn. 4dr. LT/SLT	mini	11850	14200	15750	21500	26250	
	maxi	14200	16300	17850	23800	28750	
wgn. 4dr. LS/SLS	mini	13100	15200	15750	19300	25500	27800
	maxi	15400	17300	17850	21200	27300	31000
wgn. 4dr. SLE	mini				20250	25500	
	maxi				22700	27300	
Jimmy / Blazer 4x4							
wgn. 2dr. base/SL	mini	9000	11200	13100	15200	18800	24150
	maxi	11550	13300	15400	16800	21000	27100
wgn. 2dr. LS/SLS	mini	10000	12800	14700	15750	19600	25200
	maxi	12300	14900	16300	17850	22000	27800
wgn. 4dr.base/SL	mini	11550	14400	15750			
	maxi	14200	16500	17850			
wgn. 4dr. LT/SLT	mini	12900	15400	17300	23100	27800	
	maxi	15200	17500	19400	25400	30350	
wgn. 4dr. LS/SLS	mini	14200	17500	17300	20900	26000	29400
	maxi	16500	18600	19400	22800	28900	32550
wgn. 4dr. Envoy	mini		17850	20700	21950		
	maxi		19950	22700	26000		
wgn. 4dr. TrailBlazer	mini				22600	26250	
	maxi				24900	28900	
wgn. 4dr. SLE	mini				21850	26000	
	maxi				24150	28900	

See page 7 to adapt these figures.

2002 OLDSMOBILE Aurora

The Aurora, a deluxe sedan powered by a V8, was launched in '95 and has been redefined in 2000.

PROS

- **It's competitively** priced in comparison with its smaller and less zippy rivals.
- **Its sleek**, aerodynamic design is just sensational.
- **It's solidly built**, finish is clean and tight, overall design is terrific and trim materials look great.
- **The interior cabin** design is unique and very spiffy.
- **The car handles** well in most situations, but it doesn't have an ounce of Sportscar zoom and zest.
- **Gas consumption** is quite low, given the good power to weight ratio.
- **This is a comfy car** equipped with a smooth suspension, nicely upholstered and contoured seats and excellent soundproofing.
- **There are sufficient storage** compartments, and they're convenient too, which is rare for a GM product!

CONS

- **Brakes** of the first models are inadequate because of vehicle weight and they heat up in no time flat.
- **Steering** is over-assisted and so it's oversensitive, and besides it has a large steer angle diameter and high reduction ratio, which is no picnic when you're at the wheel of such a big car.
- **Visibility** is obstructed by the thick roof supports.
- **Accelerations** and pick-up are only adequate for engine weight is pretty hefty and the engine rarely really puts out 250-bhp.
- **Some equipment** items have been overlooked or botched up, for example, there's no shifter indicator on the instrument panel and seat belt buckles are poorly designed.
- **Getting to the trunk** of the first Aurora isn't easy with such a high, narrow opening.

VERDICT

The Aurora has a overall good reliability record so far, and so we recommend it as a good used car purchase.

RECALLS

2002 Dealers will inspect and replace if necessary the driver's airbags module.

RELIABILITY PROBLEMS

	1997	1998	1999	2000	2001	2002
Engine:	X	-	-		-	-
Transmission:	-	-	-		-	-
Suspension:	-	-	-		-	-
Steering:	-	-	-		-	-
Brakes:	X	X	X		X	-
Electricity:	X	X	X		X	X
Body:	X	X	X		X	-
Accessories:	X	X	X		X	-
Fit/finish:	X	X	X		-	-

POWERTRAIN

Year	Type/ L/Camshaft/bhp	Drivetrain & gearbox
97-99	V8/4.0/DOHC/250	front-A4
01-02	V6/3.5/SOHC/215	front-A4
	V8/4.0/DOHC/250	front-A4

PERFORMANCE

	Acceler. 0/100 sec.	Top. speed km/h	Ave. Fuel consp. l./100 km
	9.0	215	13.5
	8.5	200	13.3
	8.0	215	13.5

SPECIFICATIONS

Model	Wlb. mm	Lght. mm	Cb.wt kg	Brakes fr/rr	Steering type	Standard tires
97-99						
sdn. 4dr.	2891	5217	1799	dc/ABS	pwr.r&p.	235/60R16
01-02						
ber. 4 p. 3.5	2850	5062	1645	dc/ABS	pwr.r.&p.	225/55R17
ber. 4 p. 4.0	2850	5062	1725	dc/ABS	pwr.r.&p.	235/55R17

PRICES

Model / version		1997	1998	1999	2000	2001	2002
sdn. 4dr.	mini	10000	13450	16500			
	maxi	14200	17300	20500			
sdn. 4dr. 3.0	mini					25700	30450
	maxi					29900	34650
sdn. 4dr. 4.0	mini					28350	33100
	maxi					32550	37800

See page 7 to adapt these figures.

1998 OLDSMOBILE Aurora

GM H Series

1998 OLDSMOBILE 88

Introduced in 69 as full-size vehicles, they became pared down front-wheel drive in 86. The unavoidable V6 is the only option available, even on the Pontiac Bonneville SSE and on the Oldsmobile 88 LSS both assisted with a Roots compressor.

PROS
• **Performance** is good, thanks to the reasonable weight/power ratio and the venerable V6 is up to the task assigned to it.
• **Driving pleasure** comes from wide visibility, a well-geared steering system and efficient brakes that are easy to gauge.
• **Comfort** resulting from a smooth suspension and a discreet mechanical system make these cars perfect for long highway journeys.

CONS
• **Lines** on the Bonneville SSE are much too complex.
• **Weight** is way too high and prevents the Bonneville SSE from giving the performance expected from its compressor-powered engine.
• **Interior design** is uninspired, the instrument panel is frustrating, storage spaces are all but nonexistent.
• **Seats** are badly shaped and provide little support, something strange in cars designed primarily for comfort.
• **The base suspension** is excessively smooth and shock absorbers are unable to filter out road surface irregularities; the «Heavy Duty» option is advisable.
• **Steering** is over-assisted and requires a lot of concentration on the part of the driver.

VERDICT
Roomy, easy to maintain and well-equipped, these intermediate sedans are reliable and available at a reasonable price.

RECALLS
1998   Powertrain control module is miscalibrated.
98-99   Defective chrome plated aluminum wheels that might have not been machined properly can separate from the vehicle. Incorrect emission control labels.
1999   Driver's indication "PRNDL" state may differ from the hydraulic state of the transmission due to a loose retaining clip.
2000   The hydraulic modulator of the ABS system will be inspected and replaced if necessary.
2002   Dealers will inspect and replace if necessary the driver's airbags module, and check if the two bolts of the steering box are properly tightened.

RELIABILITY PROBLEMS

	1997	1998	1999	2000	2001	2002
Engine:	X	X	-	-	-	-
Transmission:	-	-	X	-	-	-
Suspension:	-	-	-	-	-	-
Steering:	-	-	-	-	-	-
Brakes:	X	X	X	-	-	-
Electricity:	-	X	X	X	X	X
Body:	X	X	X	X	X	X
Accessories:	X	X	X	X	-	-
Fit/finish:	X	-	-	-	-	-

POWERTRAIN

Year	Type/ L/Camshaft/bhp	Drivetrain & gearbox
97-02	V6/3.8/OHV/165 -205	front-A4
	V6C/3.8/OHV/205-240	front-A4

PERFORMANCE

	Acceler. 0/100 sec.	Top. speed km/h	Ave. Fuel consp. l./100 km
	8.2	180	12.4
	7.7	200	13.3

SPECIFICATIONS

Model	Wlb. mm	Lght. mm	Cb.wt kg	Brakes fr/rr	Steering type	Standard tires
LeSabre 97-02						
sdn. 4dr. Custom	2814	5100	1562	dc/dr/ABS	pwr.r&p.	205/70R15
sdn. 4dr. Limited	2814	5100	1573	dc/dr/ABS	pwr.r&p.	205/70R15
88 97-99						
sdn. 4dr. base	2814	5090	1567	dc/dr/ABS	pwr.r&p.	205/70R15
sdn. 4dr. LS	2814	5090	1569	dc/dr/ABS	pwr.r&p.	215/65R15
sdn. 4dr. LSS	2814	5090	1609	dc/dr/ABS	pwr.r&p.	225/60R16
Bonneville 97-99						
sdn. 4dr. SE-SLE	2814	5093	1563	dc/dr/ABS	crém.ass.	215/65R15
sdn. 4dr. SSEi	2814	5133	1627	dc/dr/ABS	crém.ass.	225/60R16
Bonneville 00-02						
sdn. 4dr. SE-SLE	2850	5146	1628	dc/ABS	pwr.r&p.	225/60R16
sdn. 4dr. SSEi	2850	5146	1695	dc/ABS	pwr.r&p.	235/55R16

PRICES

Model / version		1997	1998	1999	2000	2001	2002
LeSabre							
sdn. 4dr. Custom	mini	8900	11300	13650	15500	18400	20500
	maxi	12000	14700	16600	18900	22000	24150
sdn. 4dr. LTD	mini	10500	13450	15200	17650	19950	22600
	maxi	14200	16800	18600	20700	23600	26250
88							
sdn. 4dr. LS	mini	7350	8900	12100			
	maxi	10500	10500	15000			
sdn. 4dr. LSS	mini	8900	10800	13100			
	maxi	12100	13650	16000			
sdn. 4dr. 50th Ann.	mini			13650			
	maxi			16600			
Bonneville							
sdn. 4dr. SE	mini	8900	11350	13650	16000	19950	21500
	maxi	12000	14300	16500	18900	22600	24150
sdn. 4dr. SSE	mini	10000	12900	15200	18000	21500	23100
	maxi	13000	16300	17850	21000	24150	25700
sdn. 4dr. SSEi	mini	11000	14400	18800	23100	28350	32000
	maxi	14100	17300	21500	26250	30450	34650

See page 7 to adapt these figures.

1998 PONTIAC Sunfire convertible

These compact cars have nothing spectacular about them, but they are economical and reliable. Positioned as the most widely sold in Canada, few vehicles can rival with the Cavalier-Sunbird models.

PROS

• **Model range** is wide, with a chance for everyone to find something within their budget.

• **Performance** with the V6 and the A3 transmission are the best.

• **Price** is affordable and results from the minimal design and mechanical changes made over the years.

• **The passenger compartment** on the sedans and wagons can accommodate five adults and the trunk is large enough for their baggage.

• **The suspension** is firm but counters road defects effectively.

CONS

• **Steering:** the manual is spongy and the power system is over-assisted.

• **Fuel consumption** with the V6 isn't at all economical.

• **The four-cylinder engine** is listless, noisy and vibrates noticeably.

• **The trunk** is tiny on the convertible version and offers few storage capacity.

• **Driving pleasure** on base models is absent because of bad quality tires and shock absorbers.

• **Reliability** is precarious and even the latest generation suffers from mechanical problems and the early onset of rust.

VERDICT

The Cavalier-Sunbird models are good bargains as long as driven kilometers aren't too high. Beware of sports versions that may have suffered abuse at the hands of their previous owners.

RECALLS

1997 Airbag control module must be recalibrated.
Weak rear suspension trailing arm fasteners.
The rim of the spare tire doesn't match the actual size of the tire, which could cause the tire to separate itself from the rim.
Welding might be necessary on side doors.

RELIABILITY PROBLEMS

	1997	1998	1999	2000	2001	2002
Engine:	X	X	X	X	-	-
Transmission:	X	X	X	-	-	-
Suspension:	X	X	X	-	-	-
Steering:	X	X	X	-	-	-
Brakes:	X	X	X	X	X	-
Electricity:	X	X	X	X	X	-
Body:	X	X	X	X	X	X
Accessories:	X	X	-	X	X	-
Fit/finish:	X	X	X	X	-	-

POWERTRAIN / PERFORMANCE

Year	Type/ L/Camshaft/bhp	Drivetrain & gearbox	Acceler. 0/100 sec.	Top speed km/h	Ave. Fuel consp. l./100 km
97-02	L4/2.2/SOHC/95-130	front-M5	10.0	165	9.7
		front-A3/4	11.2	160	10.0
	L4/2.4/DOHC/150	front-M5	8.0	180	10.2
		front-A4	8.8	175	10.7
2002	L4/2.2/DOHC/140	front-M5	9.2	180	11.0

SPECIFICATIONS

Model 97-02	Wlb. mm	Lght. mm	Cb.wt kg	Brakes fr/rr	Steering type	Standard tires
Cavalier						
cpe. 2dr. base	2644	4590	1188	dc/dr/ABS	pwr.r&p.	195/70R14
cpe. 2dr. BS	2644	4590	1191	dc/dr/ABS	pwr.r&p.	195/65R15
cpe. 2dr. Z24	2644	4590	1247	dc/dr/ABS	pwr.r&p.	205/55R16
con. 2dr. Z24	2644	4590	1288	dc/dr/ABS	pwr.r&p.	195/65R15
sdn. 4dr. base	2644	4590	1214	dc/dr/ABS	pwr.r&p.	195/70R14
sdn. 4dr. LS	2644	4590	1235	dc/dr/ABS	pwr.r&p.	195/65R15
Sunfire						
cpe. 2dr. SE	2644	4620	1193	dc/dr/ABS	pwr.r&p.	195/70R14
cpe. 2dr. GT	2644	4620	1280	dc/dr/ABS	pwr.r&p.	205/55R16
sdn. 4dr. SE/GT	2644	4615	1209	dc/dr/ABS	pwr.r&p.	195/70R14

PRICES

Model / version		1997	1998	1999	2000	2001	2002
Cavalier							
cpe. 2dr. base	mini.	4200	5550	6300	8200	10000	
	maxi.	6300	7900	8600	10500	13100	
cpe. 2dr. Z24	mini.	5250	6800	8400	9900	12100	13450
	maxi.	7900	9400	10500	12400	15200	16800
cpe. 2dr. VLX	mini.						10800
	maxi.						13450
cpe. 2dr. VL	mini.						7650
	maxi.						10500
con. 2dr. LS	mini.	5800					
	maxi.	9450					
con. 2dr. Z24	mini.		8700	10700	12100		
	maxi.		10500	13600	15450		
sdn. 4dr.	mini.	4400	5800	6600	8400		
	maxi.	6500	8100	8900	10800		
sdn. 4dr. LS	mini.	4700	8100	8900	9450	11550	12400
	maxi.	6800	8400	9450	11550	14200	15250
sdn. 4dr. VL	mini.					9100	7900
	maxi.					11550	10800
sdn. 4dr. VLX	mini.					12300	11000
	maxi.					13100	13650
sdn. 4dr. Z24	mini.					13950	
	maxi.					17300	
Sunfire							
cpe. 2dr.	mini.					10500	
	maxi.					13100	
cpe. 2dr. SE	mini.	4100	5450	6800	8100		
	maxi.	6300	7650	8900	10500		
cpe. 2dr. GT	mini.	5250	6600	8100	10000	12100	14200
	maxi.	7900	9450	10500	12100	14700	16800
cpe. 2dr. SL	mini.						7850
	maxi.						10500
cpe. 2dr. SLX	mini.						10500
	maxi.						13650
con. 2 dr. SE	mini.	8400	9750				
	maxi.	10500	11550				
con. 2 dr. GT	mini.			11550	13650		
	maxi.			13650	15250		
sdn. 4dr. SE	mini.	4400	5700	7000	8400		
	maxi.	6600	7900	9100	10800		
sdn. 4dr. GTX	mini.					13100	14200
	maxi.					15750	17300
sdn. 4dr. SL	mini.					6800	7850
	maxi.					9450	10900
sdn. 4dr. SLX	mini.					11000	11550
	maxi.					13650	14700

See page 7 to adapt these figures.

GM K Series

2001 CADILLAC DeVille DTS

The DeVille was inaugurated in 1970, the Eldorado in 1968 and the Seville in 1979. These models have come equipped with the famous Northstar engine in 1994 and the DeVille was redesigned in 2000.

PROS
• **These cars easily** accommodate five adults and all their belongings.
• **The V8 Northstar** engine really makes these cars go away fast.
• **The flexible suspension**, thickly cushioned seats and superb soundproofing make for a really comfortable ride.
• **Handling** is predictable with such well-adjusted shock absorbers.
• **Brakes grip** but lack real power, for stops are long due to excessive vehicle weight, but thanks to ABS, stops are nice and stable.
• **Car design** has become more classic and elegant over the years, especially the Seville that has acquired a truly international look.

CONS
• **Maneuvering** the DeVille isn't the best since it got a rejuvenating face-lift...
• **The base model suspension** is really too flexible, so all the swing and sway can make you feel seasick after a while.
• **Seats** aren't too firm and don't provide much support, something you wouldn't expect on luxury cars.
• **Steering** is over-assisted and far too light and it doesn't give you a real feel for the road.

VERDICT
These are nice upper-crust, comfortable American-style cars that are more affordable than their imported counterparts.

RECALLS
1997	Brakes' electronic command module is defective.
	The evaporative emissions harness is misrouted.
1998	Hood hinge pivot bolts may break. (DeVille)
	Faulty windshield wiper motor microprocessor. (Seville)
1999	A rectifier bridge short may develop in the generator even when the engine is off, causing an engine compartment fire.
2000	The ABS hydraulic modulator must be inspected and replaced if it leaks. (DeVille)
	Remplacement of the crankshaft position sensor and verification of the torque of the bolts on the rear link assembly. (Eldorado-Seville)
2002	Dealers will inspect and replace if necessary the driver's airbags module.
	Dealers will inspect and replace if necessary the front seatbelt pretensioner.

RELIABILITY PROBLEMS

	1997	1998	1999	2000	2001	2002
Engine:	X	X	X	X	X	-
Transmission:	X	X	-	-	-	-
Suspension:	X	X	X	X	-	-
Steering:	-	-	-	-	-	-
Brakes:	X	X	X	X	X	-
Electricity:	X	X	X	X	X	X
Body:	X	X	X	X	-	-
Accessories:	X	X	X	X	X	X
Fit/finish:	X	-	X	X	X	-

POWERTRAIN

Year	Type/ L/Camshaft/bhp	Drivetrain & gearbox
97-02	V8/4.6/DOHC/270-300	front-A4

PERFORMANCE

Acceler. 0/100 sec.	Top. speed km/h	Ave. Fuel consp. l./100 km
8.0	240	14.2

SPECIFICATIONS

Model	Wlb. mm	Lght. mm	Cb.wt kg	Brakes fr/rr	Steering type	Standard tires
DeVille 97-99						
sdn. 4dr.	2891	5330	1820	dc/ABS	pwr.r&p.	225/60R16
sdn. 4dr.Concours	2891	5330	1843	dc/ABS	pwr.r&p.	225/60R16
sdn. 4dr.Elegance	2891	5330	1838	dc/ABS	pwr.r&p.	225/60R16
DeVille 00-01						
sdn 4dr.	2929	5270	1820	dc/ABS	pwr.r&p.	225/60R16
sdn. 4dr. DHS	2929	5270	1843	dc/ABS	pwr.r&p.	225/60R16
sdn. 4dr. DTS	2929	5270	1838	dc/ABS	pwr.r&p.	225/60R16
Eldorado/Seville 97-01						
cpe. 2dr.	2743	5095	1743	dc/ABS	pwr.r&p.	225/60R16
sdn. 4dr.	2819	5177	1688	dc/ABS	pwr.r&p.	225/60R16
sdn. 4dr. 98-99	2850	5105	1815	dc/ABS	pwr.r&p.	235/60R16

PRICES

Model / version		1997	1998	1999	2000	2001	2002
CADILLAC DeVille							
sdn. 4dr.	mini	10500	17100	22600	29900	37800	46700
	maxi	14700	20500	26250	34650	41500	50900
sdn. 4dr. Concours	mini	13650	20250	25700	38300	46200	55100
DTS	maxi	18900	23600	29400	42000	49900	59300
sdn. 4dr.D'Elegance	mini	12100	18700	24150	37300	45150	53550
DTS	maxi	17200	22600	27800	40950	48800	57750
Eldorado							
cpe. 2dr.	mini	12600	18700	26800	31500		
	maxi	17850	24700	30650	35700		
cpe. 2dr. Touring	mini	14700	19950	27800	33600	39900	43600
	maxi	19950	25700	33100	37800	45700	49900
cpe. 2dr. Collectors	mini						45700
	maxi						52000
Seville							
sdn. 4dr. STS	mini	14200	20900	25700	32000	39900	47800
	maxi	19950	26800	33100	39900	46700	55100
sdn. 4dr. SLS	mini	13100	18900	26800	31500	38850	46700
	maxi	18900	25700	32000	38850	45700	54100

See page 7 to adapt these figures.

1998 CHEVROLET Malibu

In 1997 the Malibu replaced the Corsica. It's driven by a 2.4L and 3.1L 4 or 6-cylinder engine, providing both the same bhp.

PROS

• **Overall value** for your buck is good, considering the rich equipment, which makes the Malibu highly competitive with some Asian models.

• **The flowing lines** are reminiscent of other slick model designs.

• **The generous cabin and trunk** can really and truly accommodate five passengers and all their luggage.

• **Performance** are a pleasant surprise with both engines that provide zippy accelerations and pick-up, thanks to a favorable power to weight ratio.

• **Ride comfort** is amazing for a popular model. The suspension irons out road faults and seats provide the occupants with effective support.

• **Handling** is crisp and clean even with the iffy-quality original tires. The Malibu takes all kinds of curves with assurance and remains nice and even on emergency maneuvers.

• This car is **passenger-friendly**. There are enough storage compartments, especially for front seat passengers.

CONS

• **A high noise level** is an indication that soundproofing isn't what it should be and it sort of takes the pleasure out of the trip.

• **Brakes** don't dig in when applied, no doubt due to poor-quality linings that you need to keep a close eye on.

• **Some plastic trim components** are of dubious quality and they look rather cheap, especially on the dashboard and inner doors.

• **Some items** need to be improved: not quite enough storage spots, no assist grips in the rear seat area and a missing footrest.

VERDICT

The Malibu represents GM's neat solution that shines in the race against popular Asian cars, for it offers good-level value for the going price and the dealership network is more widespread than is the case for the competition.

RECALLS

2000   The fuel fill fitting may leaks more than standards allowed. The fuel tank must be inspected and replaced if necessary.

2002   Dealers will inspect left low beam headlight and replace it, if it is not satisfactory.

RELIABILITY PROBLEMS

	1997	1998	1999	2000	2001	2002
Engine:	X	X	X	X	-	-
Transmission:	X	X	-	-	-	-
Suspension:	X	X	X	-	-	-
Steering:	X	-	-	-	-	-
Brakes:	X	X	X	X	X	X
Electricity:	X	X	X	X	X	-
Body:	X	X	X	X	-	-
Accessories:	-	X	X	X	X	X
Fit/finish:	X	X	X	X	-	-

POWERTRAIN

Year	Type/ L/Camshaft/bhp	Drivetrain & gearbox	Acceler. 0/100 sec.	Top. speed km/h	Ave. Fuel consp. l./100 km
97-01	L4/2.4/DOHC/150	front-A4	10.0	170	11.3
97-02	V6/3.1/OHV/150-170	front-A4	9.5	180	12.3

SPECIFICATIONS

Model 97-02	Wlb. mm	Lght. mm	Cb.wt kg	Brakes fr/rr	Steering type	Standard tires
sdn. 4dr. base	2718	4836	1384	dc/dr/ABS	pwr.r&p.	215/60R15
sdn. 4dr. LS	2718	4836	1396	dc/dr/ABS	pwr.r&p.	215/60R15

PRICES

Model / version		1997	1998	1999	2000	2001	2002
sdn. 4dr. base	mini	5250	7900	8400	10500	12100	14200
	maxi	7350	11000	12100	13650	15200	17300
sdn. 4dr. LS	mini	6300	8900	9450	11550	13100	15200
	maxi	8400	12100	13100	14700	16300	17850

See page 7 to adapt these figures.

2000 CHEVROLET Malibu

GM M Series

1998 CHEVROLET Metro

Assembled in Canada, the Metro/Sprint/Firefly models are the modern versions of the Chevette/Acadian. They took over in 1985, derived from the Suzuki Forsa frame and, nowadays, they represent the lowest-end products assembled by GM and Suzuki. Throughout the years, this model has been commercialized under different banners bearing multiple body style and powertrains.

PROS
• **Quality** of assembly and finishing is exemplary.
• **Styling** is modern, simple and tasteful. These cars seem to be specifically destined for city driving and the 4-door sedan features original sizing.
• **Handling** is consistent as long as tires and the suspension are in good condition.
• **Fuel consumption** is excellent and one of the lowest on the market.

CONS
• **Comfort** is basic because of an overly firm suspension, poorly padded seats and poor soundproofing.
• **Ride** suffers the effects of side winds and the torque has a strange effect on the steering system during strong accelerations on damp road surfaces. Lastly, gear shifting isn't easy unless the car is well warmed up.
• **Panels** are paper thin, show the scars of even the slightest impacts and fall victim to rust very early on.
• **Roominess** is limited and rear doors are small and limit access.
• **The trunk** on hatchback versions is too small if there are four passengers on board.
• **Storage spaces** are rare and far between on the base model.

VERDICT
The Sprint/Firefly/Metro models are pleasant, economical and practical minicars for city driving but their size makes them unsuitable for longer outings. Parts are expensive and users must be vigilant when it comes to maintenance.

RECALLS
1997 Automatic transmission shifter must be replaced on some models.

RELIABILITY PROBLEMS

	1997	1998	1999	2000	2001	2002
Engine:	X	X	X	X		
Transmission:	-	-	X	-		
Suspension:	-	-	-	-		
Steering:	-	-	-	-		
Brakes:	X	X	X	X		
Electricity:	-	X	X	-		
Body:	-	-	-	-		
Accessories:	X	X	X	X		
Fit/finish:	X	X	X	X		

POWERTRAIN

Year	Type/ L/Camshaft/bhp	Drivetrain & gearbox	Acceler. 0/100 sec.	Top. speed km/h	Ave. Fuel consp. l./100 km
97-00	L3/1.0/SOHC/55	front-M5	14.3	145	5.4
	L4/1.3/SOHC/70-79	front-M5	13.2	160	6.4
		front-A3	14.0	150	7.7

PERFORMANCE

SPECIFICATIONS

Model 97-00	Wlb. mm	Lght. mm	Cb.wt kg	Brakes fr/rr	Steering type	Standard tires
cpe. 3dr.	2365	3795	860	dc/dr	r&p.	155/80R13
sdn. 4dr.	2365	4166	900	dc/dr	r&p.	155/80R13

PRICES

Model / version		1997	1998	1999	2000	2001	2002
Metro/Firefly							
ber. 3dr. & FE	mini	3350	4200	5250	6300		
	maxi	4700	5800	7150	8400		
sdn. 4dr.	mini	4200	5250	6300	7550		
	maxi	5800	6800	8400	9450		
Geo/Chevrolet Metro							
sdn. 3dr.	mini	3700	4600	5800	6600		
	maxi	5250	6100	7350	8700		
sdn. 4dr.	mini	4700	5150	6600	7900		
	maxi	6300	6800	8400	10000		

See page 7 to adapt these figures.

1998 CHEVROLET Metro

GM M-UT Series

1998 GMC Safari

The rear-wheel drive Astro and Safari minivans were first put on the market in 1985 and all-drive models were available in 1990. They were designed along the same lines as the S-10 pickup truck frame and are equipped with a 4.3L V6 engine.

PROS

• **The V6 engine** has the torque and horsepower you need to haul or pull heavy loads.

• **The driver's seat** is high and with the wide rearview mirrors, visibility is just great.

• **Power steering** is smooth, well-calibrated and amazingly clean and crisp.

• **The look** of these minivans has improved with the style modifications on the front end.

• **Noteworthy**: the more functional '95 instrument panel, the Dutch-style hatch and the rear bumper that serves as a step.

CONS

• **These vehicles** are gas-thirsty even when not carrying a load.

• **It's impossible to park** these high-perched vehicles in a garage or inside some public parking spaces.

• **Handling** can be pretty touch and go on the rear-wheel drive models in winter conditions or on slippery roads.

• **The interior** is quite cramped, for it's hard to get around the seats and leg room is tight in the front passenger seat.

• **To be taken into account**: no standard rear defroster or windshield wipers, complicated instrument clusters that are hard to read night or day, rough shifting on the automatic, inconvenient engine access and scarce storage compartments on some models.

VERDICT

In spite of their fancy, dressed-up look, the Astro/Safari minivans are more plain and simple than family-style vans.

RECALLS

None over this period.

RELIABILITY PROBLEMS

	1997	1998	1999	2000	2001	2002
Engine:	X	X	X	X	-	-
Transmission:	X	-	-	-	-	-
Suspension:	X	X	X	X	-	-
Steering:	-	-	-	-	-	-
Brakes:	X	X	X	X	X	-
Electricity:	X	X	X	X	X	X
Body:	X	X	X	X	X	-
Accessories:	X	X	X	X	X	X
Fit/finish:	X	-	X	X	-	-

POWERTRAIN

Year	Type/ L/Camshaft/bhp	Drivetrain & gearbox
97-02	V6/4.3/OHV/150-190	rear-M5
		rear/all-A4

PERFORMANCE

	Acceler. 0/100 sec.	Top. speed km/h	Ave. Fuel consp. l./100 km
	11.0	170	15.0
	11.7	165	15.3

SPECIFICATIONS

Model 4x2	Wlb. mm	Lght. mm	Cb.wt kg	Brakes fr/rr	Steering type	Standard tires
m.v. 4dr. LWB	2825	4821	1903	dc/dr/ABS	pwr.bal.	215/75R15
4x4						
m.v. 4dr. LWB	2825	4821	2015	dc/dr/ABS	pwr.bal.	215/75R15

PRICES

Model / version		1997	1998	1999	2000	2001	2002
m.v. 4dr. Cargo	mini	5800	7900	8900	12100	14600	17300
	maxi	8200	10000	11000	14200	16800	19950
m.v. 4dr. SLX/CS	mini	7750	10100	11150	14200	16400	20500
	maxi	10000	12300	13650	16300	18900	23100
m.v. 4dr. SLE/CL	mini	9750	11150	13100	15200	17650	20500
	maxi	12100	13350	15200	17300	19500	24150
m.v. 4dr. SLT/LT	mini	10800	12600	15200	17850	20250	22600
	maxi	13100	14700	17300	19950	22600	25700
m.v. 4dr. SL	mini					16700	19400
	maxi					19100	22000
m.v. 4dr. SLT/LT	mini	11850	13650	16300	19100	21500	24150
LWB 4x4	maxi	14200	15750	18400	21000	23600	27300

See page 7 to adapt these figures.

GM N Series

1997 BUICK Skylark

These front-wheel drive compact cars were first sold in '85. Both coupes and sedans are powered by either a 2.4L 4-cylinder or a 3.4L V6 engine. In 1999, the Achieva has been replaced by the Alero.

PROS

• **The Alero** is by far the most stunning of these vehicles, followed closely by the Grand Am, which is why it's always been so popular.

• **The V6** engine is a better choice than the QuadFour for any model, especially for the Grand AM, if it was available at that time.

• **The sports models** handle quite well with their stiffer suspension and larger tires.

• **Steering** is sensitive but becomes vague at high speeds.

• **The V6 engine** is more spirited and more fun to run than the 4-cylinder.

• **The latest model** dashboards are nicer looking and are more straightforward and convenient than before.

CONS

• **The cabin** is smaller than that of the competition, especially in the rear seat area of the coupes that is a chore to climb into, and trunk size is skimpy.

• **Comfort** isn't cushy on the sports models because of the rather primitive suspension, firm tires and high noise level.

• **Rearward view** isn't the greatest with the rear panel support and such small rearview mirrors.

• **Assembly** and finish are slipshod and some components, especially the plastic trim, look flimsy and cheap.

• **The manual transmission** is poorly calibrated and the shifter is tricky to use, but the 3-speed automatic is terrible and to be avoided.

• **Brakes are poor**, ABS is pretty rough and rustic, and it takes forever to get any kind of pedal response.

• **Steering** is light and sensitive, because it's over-assisted and the fact that it's so crisp can make some maneuvers difficult.

VERDICT

These cars may look good, but they're not too impressive once you get them on the road. Performance are poor, and overall design and build quality are just as unimpressive. The only exception to this rule remains in the Alero which is manufactured so tight that it clearly indicates that the "small" Olds division at GM is managed better than the larger ones in a very significative and lucrative market segment.

POWERTRAIN

Year	Type/ L/Camshaft/bhp	Drivetrain & gearbox
97-98	L4/2.4/DOHC/150	front-M5
		front-A4
	V6/3.1/OHV/155-160	front-A4
99-01	L4/2.4/DOHC/150	front-A4
2002	L4/2.2/DOHC/138	front-M5
		front-A4
99-02	V6/3.4/OHV/170-175	front-A4

PERFORMANCE

Acceler. 0/100 sec.	Top. speed km/h	Ave. Fuel consp. l./100 km
9.8	180	12.0
10.5	175	10.7
9.0	175	11.8
10.0	175	10.8
8.8	175	11.4
10.4	170	11.2
8.5	180	12.0

SPECIFICATIONS

Model	Wlb. mm	Lght. mm	Cb.wt kg	Brakes fr/rr	Steering type	Standard tires
Buick Skylark 1997						
cpe. 2dr.	2626	4806	1269	dc/dr/ABS	pwr.r&p.	185/75R14
sdn. 4dr.	2626	4788	1354	dc/dr/ABS	pwr.r&p.	195/70R14
cpe. 2dr. GS	2626	4806	1290	dc/dr/ABS	pwr.r&p.	205/55R16
sdn. 4dr. GS	2626	4806	1311	dc/dr/ABS	pwr.r&p.	205/55R16
OLDSMOBILE Achieva 97-98						
cpe. 2dr. S	2627	4773	1292	dc/dr/ABS	pwr.r&p.	185/75R14
sdn. 4dr. S	2627	4773	1223	dc/dr/ABS	pwr.r&p.	185/75R14
cpe. 2dr. SC	2627	4773	1255	dc/dr/ABS	pwr.r&p.	195/70R14
sdn. 4dr. SL	2627	4773	1323	dc/dr/ABS	pwr.r&p.	195/65R15
PONTIAC Grand Am 97-02						
cpe. 2dr. SE	2718	4732	1391	dc/dr/ABS	pwr.r&p.	215/60R15
sdn. 4dr. SE	2718	4732	1413	dc/dr/ABS	pwr.r&p.	215/60R15
cpe. 2dr. GT	2718	4732	1402	dc/ABS	pwr.r&p.	225/50R16
sdn. 4dr. GT	2718	4732	1437	dc/ABS	pwr.r&p.	225/50R16
OLDSMOBILE Alero 99-02						
cpe. 2dr.GX/GL	2718	4742	1372	dc/dr/ABS	pwr.r&p.	215/60R15
sdn. 4dr. GLS	2718	4742	1396	dc/dr/ABS	pwr.r&p.	225/50R16

See prices on the following pages

1998 PONTIAC Grand Am

2001 PONTIAC Grand Am

RECALLS

1997	Evaporative emission canister built incorrectly.
	Protective cover for underhood fuse centre may be missing.
1999	Loose steering wheel retaining nut.
	Defective child rear seat tether anchorages.
2001	Defective automatic transmission locking system (Grand Am).

RELIABILITY PROBLEMS

	1997	1998	1999	2000	2001	2002
Engine:	X	X	X	X	-	-
Transmission:	X	-	-	-	-	-
Suspension:	X	X	X	-	-	-
Steering:	-	X	-	X	-	-
Brakes:	X	X	X	X	X	X
Electricity:	X	X	X	-	-	-
Body:	X	X	X	X	X	X
Accessories:	X	X	X	X	X	X
Fit/finish:	X	X	X	-	-	-

2000 OLDSMOBILE Alero

PRICES

Model / version		1997	1998	1999	2000	2001	2002
BUICK Skylark							
cpe. 2dr.Custom	mini	5800					
	maxi	8900					
sdn. 4dr. Custom	mini	6000	7350				
	maxi	9200	10500				
OLDSMOBILE Achieva							
cpe. 2dr. SC	mini	6000					
	maxi	8900					
sdn. 4dr. SL	mini	6200					
	maxi	9150					
PONTIAC Grand Am							
cpe. 2dr. SE	mini	5800	7650	10000	11550	13650	15000
	maxi	8400	10500	13350	14700	16300	18400
cpe. 2dr. GT	mini	6800	9250	11550	13350	15200	16300
	maxi	11000	12100	14400	16300	17850	19950
cpe. 2dr. GTi	mini					17850	19400
	maxi					20500	22600
cpe. 2dr. SET	mini					14700	16300
	maxi					17300	19400
sdn. 4dr. SE	mini	6000	7900	10200	11850	14000	15200
	maxi	8600	10800	13650	15000	16600	18700
sdn. 4dr. GT	mini	7000	9450	12100	13650	15550	16600
	maxi	11250	12300	14700	16600	18150	20350
sdn. 4dr. SET	mini					15000	16600
	maxi					17650	19950
sdn. 4dr. GTi	mini					18150	19950
	maxi					20800	23100
OLDSMOBILE Alero							
cpe. 2dr. GX	mini			9450	11850	13450	15200
	maxi			12600	14700	16300	18900
cpe. 2dr. GL	mini			11000	13850	14700	17300
	maxi			13850	15950	18150	20500
cpe. 2dr. GLS	mini			12000	14400	16800	18700
	maxi			14900	17000	19950	22000
sdn. 4dr. GX	mini			9650	12000	13650	15550
	maxi			12900	15000	16600	19400
sdn. 4dr. GL	mini			11300	14200	15200	17850
	maxi			14200	16300	18700	21000
sdn. 4dr. GLS	mini			12600	14700	17300	18900
	maxi			15200	17300	20500	22600

See page 7 to adapt these figures.

F/UT GM Series

2002 GMC Envoy

These vehicles are mechanically identical and respectively replace the Blazer, Jimmy and previous-generation Bravada. They are larger than their predecessors and sport a 4.2-liter inline 6 cylinder engine.

PROS

• **The vast cabin** and cargo bay are capable of seating up to seven people and swallowing an impressive amount of baggage.

• **The great ride comfort** stems from the supple suspension and quiet cabin.

• **The inline engine** cranks out interesting performance and ample low-end torque is great for an all-terrain utility vehicle.

• **The efficient brakes** produce short and straight stops despite a spongy pedal that is difficult to modulate and the pads resist well to fade.

• **The reasonable** turning circle of these vehicles translates into interesting maneuverability given their bulk.

• **The hand brake** is conveniently located on the center console, a pleasant surprise for an American vehicle.

CONS

• **The high price** of these vehicles despite a limited list of standard equipment and poor fuel economy command a high budget.

• **The vague handling** results from the overly soft suspension and fuzzy steering that makes it impossible to quickly bring the vehicle back on track.

• **The driving position** is unpleasant because of poorly designed and uncomfortable seats.

• **The steering** is vague and suffers from high gear reduction. This hinders driving precision and forces the driver to constantly resort to the steering wheel to correct trajectories.

• **The suspension** is too soft and generates high body movement as well as numerous jolts on uneven terrain.

• **The body rattles** in the cabin on rough roads point to a certain lack of build quality.

VERDICT

Placed midway between SUVs and minivans, these vehicles have created a new category of utility vehicles which are more comfortable but not as efficient off road.

RECALLS

2002 Dealers must inspect and change if necessary: the module of the driver's side airbag, the fuel filter quick connections, the right and left front lower A arm attachment and reprogrammed the transfer case command module.

RELIABILITY PROBLEMS

	1997	1998	1999	2000	2001	2002
Engine:						-
Transmission:						-
Suspension:						-
Steering:						-
Brakes:						-
Electricity:			Insufficient data			-
Body:						-
Accessories:						-
Fit/finish:						-

POWERTRAIN / PERFORMANCE

Year	Type/ L/Camshaft/bhp	Drivetrain & gearbox	Acceler. 0/100 sec.	Top. speed km/h	Ave. Fuel consp. l./100 km
2002	L6/4.2/DOHC/270	A4-rear./all	9.3	175	15.0

SPECIFICATIONS

Model 2002	Wlb. mm	Lght. mm	Cb.wt kg	Brakes fr/rr	Steering type	Standard tires
Chevrolet Trailblazer						
LS/LT/LTZ	2869	4871	2015	dc/ABS	pwr.r&p.	245/70R16
GMC Envoy						
SLE/SLT	2869	4871	2087	dc/ABS	pwr.r&p.	245/65R17
OLDSMOBILE Bravada						
TI	2869	4871	2099	dc/ABS	pwr.r&p.	255/60R17

PRICES

Model / version		1997	1998	1999	2000	2001	2002
Chevrolet TrailBlazer							
wgn. 4dr. SLE/LS	mini						28350
	maxi						32550
wgn. 4dr. SLT/LTZ	mini						36750
	maxi						40400
wgn. 4dr. LT	mini						32000
	maxi						35200
wgn. 4dr. LT LONG	mini						37000
	maxi						38850
GMC Envoy							
wgn. 4dr. SLE	mini						33600
	maxi						36750
wgn. 4dr.SLT	mini						37800
	maxi						41500
OLDSMOBILE Bravada							
wgn. 4dr.	mini						35700
	maxi						38850

See page 7 to adapt these figures.

GM U Series

2001 PONTIAC Montana

These vehicles are available in two wheelbase versions, equipped with a 3.4L V6 driven by a 4-speed automatic transmission. In 1998, the Oldsmobile Silhouette entered this market segment and in 1999 the Trans Sport has been renamed Montana.

PROS

• **Highway driving** is a joy due to the smooth suspension, nicely shaped and cushy front seats and sure-proof soundproofing.
• **They can accelerate** to 100 kph in about 11 seconds and pick-up is muscular enough to pass on the highway with a good safety margin. Fuel economy is normal achieving around 13L/100 km.
• **The automatic transmission** is a small wonder and you can brake by downshifting while in third or second gear.
• **Handling** is honest in most situations, thanks to vehicle stability, so you can take any curve with assurance and precision.
• **Kudos for:** power sliding door, functional storage compartments, rear bumper that serves as a boarding step, effective wipers that sweep a large section of the windshield in no time flat.

CONS

• **Seats** are quite low, because of tight head room, so they aren't terribly comfortable. Rear seats are flat and hard and the small headrests aren't of much use.
• **Brakes** don't offer enough grip to achieve short stops and the elastic pedal is hard to hit just right.
• **The multi-function** shifter located under the driving wheel is too complicated.
• **The suspension** acts up on rough road surfaces and front wheels bounce a lot because of the low-slung suspension components.
• **Access** to the engine is as tricky as it was on the former model, because the engine is located way back there under the windshield and the dashboard.
• **The bland interior** sure doesn't get spruced up much by the cheap-looking plastic trim.

VERDICT

These three vehicles are more competitive with their 2 wheel-bases and left side sliding door. But the craftsmanship is not the best of all and safety is less than average.

RECALLS

97-98 Locking mechanisms on bench seats are unprotected. Must be inspected for possible brake fluid line damage.
1997 A brake pipe retainer clip must be installed to the underbody.
1998 Shift cable must be inspected and replaced if necessary. Water may seep into the evaporitive emission canister and may cause an engine malfunction.
1999 Defective left and right front lower cradle to suspension insulators and the attaching bolts.
2000 Some seatbelts doesn't satisfied strenght regulations. Fuel tank with inoperative rollover valve will be changed.
2001 Dealers will install a new power sliding door and latch assembly (Montana).
2002 Driver's side airbag module must be inspected and changed if necessary.

RELIABILITY PROBLEMS

	1997	1998	1999	2000	2001	2002
Engine:	-	-	-	-	-	-
Transmission:	-	-	-	-	-	-
Suspension:	X	X	X	-	-	-
Steering:	-	-	-	-	-	-
Brakes:	X	X	X	-	-	-
Electricity:	X	X	X	X	-	-
Body:	X	X	X	X	X	X
Accessories:	X	X	X	X	X	X
Fit/finish:	X	X	X	-	-	-

POWERTRAIN

Year	Type/ L/Camshaft/bhp	Drivetrain & gearbox	Acceler. 0/100 sec	Top speed km/h	Ave. Fuel consp. l/100 km
97-02	V6/3.4/OHV/180-185	front-A4	11.0	170	13.0

SPECIFICATIONS

Model 97-02	Wlb. mm	Lght. mm	Cb.wt kg	Brakes fr/rr	Steering type	Standard tires
m.v. 4dr. short	2845	4760	1699	dc/dr/ABS	pwr.r&p.	205/70R15
m.v. 4dr. long	3048	5116	1788	dc/dr/ABS	pwr.r&p.	215/70R15

PRICES

Model / version		1997	1998	1999	2000	2001	2002
CHEVROLET Venture							
m.v. 4dr. short	mini	6300	8400	10000			
	maxi	8400	10500	12600			
m.v. 5dr. short	mini	7900	10500	12100	15100	17300	21000
	maxi	10500	12800	14700	17550	19950	24150
m.v. 4dr. LWB	mini	7300	10000				
	maxi	9450	11850				
m.v. 5dr. LWB	mini	8900	11550	13650	16000	18300	22000
	maxi	11450	13650	16000	18700	21200	25200
m.v. 5dr. Value	mini				13650	15750	19750
	maxi				16150	18900	21750
m.v. 5dr. short LS	mini				17000	18700	22600
	maxi				18900	21650	25700
m.v. 5dr LWB LS	mini				17100	19300	23100
	maxi				19750	22250	26250
m.v. 5dr. LWB LT	mini				19400	21600	25550
	maxi				22000	24550	28550
m.v. 5dr. W/Bros.	mini					22700	26250
	maxi					27700	29900
PONTIAC Trans Sport / Montana (1999)							
m.v. 4dr. short	mini	7450	9450	12300			
	maxi	10000	11550	14500			
m.v. 5dr. short	mini	9350	11500				
	maxi	11550	12600				
m.v. 4dr. LWB	mini		10250	13100			
	maxi		12600	15450			
m.v. 5dr. LWB	mini	10900	11350	14200			
	maxi	12600	13650	16800			
PONTIAC Montana							
m.v. 5 dr.	mini				15950	19550	24700
	maxi				18500	22000	27700
m.v. 5dr. SE	mini				18400	21900	27300
	maxi				21000	24550	30000
m.v. 5dr. LWB	mini				18300	21400	26800
	maxi				20600	24000	29600
m.v. 5dr. LWB LE	mini				19950	23100	28550
	maxi				20000	25700	31300
m.v. 5dr. short GT	mini					23550	28900
	maxi					26150	32650
m.v. 5dr. LWB GT	mini					24550	30650
	maxi					27200	33600
m.v. 5dr. VISION	mini				21750	25700	32000
	maxi				24000	29100	35200
OLDSMOBILE Silhouette							
m.v. 5dr. GS	mini		12300	15200			
	maxi		13850	17400			
m.v. 5dr. GL LWB	mini		11550	13750	18000	19950	23600
	maxi		13650	16000	20250	22350	25900
m.v. 5dr. GLS LWB	mini		15000	17850	23500	24450	27800
	maxi		17200	19950	25500	27300	31000
m.v. 5dr. Pr. Ed. LWB	mini				24900	26000	29400
	maxi				27100	28900	32550

See page 7 to adapt these figures.

2002 BUICK Rendezvous

The versatile Rendezvous is derived from the Venture/Silhouette/ Montana minivans and available with front- or all-wheel drive.

PROS

• **The original presentation**, although not unanimously accepted, makes the Rendezvous quite distinctive on the road.

• **The versatility** of this vehicle stems from its position midway between an SUV and a minivan.

• **The cabin and cargo bay** are vast and the modular configuration can be adapted to suit the needs of passengers or luggage.

• **The appreciable ride comfort** is ensured by the supple suspension, well-padded seats and quiet highway driving.

• **The fuel consumption** remains reasonable at approximately 13.0 L of regular unleaded per 100 km.

• **The extensive list** of luxury amenities partially justifies the price and status of this luxury model.

• **The access** to the cabin is facilitated by large doors that open wide.

• **The storage spaces** are practical and just as numerous in front as they are in back where the windows descend 90% of their tracks.

• **The quality** of the materials and finish is surprising for a mid-range model.

CONS

• **The average performance** is due to a limited weight-to-power ratio that produces mediocre full-stop and passing acceleration.

• **The overly soft suspension** generates high levels of body motions and high body roll which hampers handling capabilities. The Rendezvous cannot leave the beaten path very far because of inadequate ground clearance.

• **The heavy hatch door** is difficult to use and the fixed rear glass is not very practical.

• **The wind and road noise** hinder ride comfort somewhat.

• **The busy body styling** creates a rather heterogeneous effect in certain colors.

VERDICT

The Rendezvous offers Buick aficionados the combined benefit of all-wheel drive versatility and minivan practicality in a single package. It is the only model in its range to do so.

RECALLS

2002   Dealers must inspect and change if necessary the module of the driver's side airbag.

RELIABILITY PROBLEMS

	1997	1998	1999	2000	2001	2002
Engine:						-
Transmission:						-
Suspension:						-
Steering:						-
Brakes:						-
Electricity:			Insufficient data			-
Body:						-
Accessories:						-
Fit/finish:						-

POWERTRAIN

PERFORMANCE

Year	Type/ L/Camshaft/bhp	Drivetrain & gearbox	Acceler. 0/100 sec.	Top. speed km/h	Ave. Fuel consp. l./100 km
2002	V6/3.4/ACC/185	A4-front./all	12.0	170	13.0

SPECIFICATIONS

Model 2002	Wlb. mm	Lght. mm	Cb.wt kg	Brakes fr/rr	Steering type	Standard tires
Rendezvous	2851	4738	1829	dc/ABS	pwr.r&p.	215/70R16

PRICES

Model / version		1997	1998	1999	2000	2001	2002
wgn. 4dr. CX	mini						24150
	maxi						26800
wgn. 4dr. CX AWD	mini						27300
	maxi						29400
wgn. 4 dr.CLX AWD	mini						29400
	maxi						32550

See page 7 to adapt these figures.

2002 BUICK Rendezvous

2002 PONTIAC Aztek

The Aztek is a hybrid vehicle that fits midway between a minivan and an SUV. Available with 2- or 4-wheel drive, it's based on the Trans Sport's platform and mechanics.

PROS

• **This vehicle is versatile** and features a modular rear-end assembly. It targets active individuals and sports amateurs.

• **Performance** is respectable with the infamous 3.4-liter V6, whose weight-to-power ratio is quite good.

• **The Aztek is comfortable** and relaxing to drive on the highway thanks to its soft suspension and good soundproofing.

• **The 3.4-liter** is reasonable on fuel; in fact, it's a fuel economy champion and makes the competition look shameful.

• **The interior features** an original presentation and youthful styling that's out of the ordinary.

• **The front seats** are well-designed and provide good support. Also, their adequate padding makes them quite comfortable.

• **The climate control** system works as efficiently in warm as in cold weather, no matter where your expeditions take you.

CONS

• **The controversial styling** is far from pleasing everyone, to the point that GM has decided to redesign future models to avoid catastrophic consequences.

• **The mediocre brakes** produce long stopping distances, but ABS nevertheless enables the Aztek to maintain a straight trajectory.

• **The suspension** is too supple and generates important body motions that are as unpleasant as they are dangerous.

• **The two-part hatchback** is heavy and cumbersome, in that its lower half complicates access to the cargo bay.

• **The transmission** shifts with irregularity and often seems to be searching for the right gear. This makes driving frustrating, especially given the lack of any form of compression braking.

• **Rearward visibility** is hindered by the two-part rear window, whose top section is sharply sloped, as well as by the headrests.

• **The instrument panel** does not feature a gear selector reminder for the automatic transmission.

VERDICT

Most of the Aztek's target clientele will continue to shrug it off because of its unusual styling.

RECALLS

None over this period.

RELIABILITY PROBLEMS

	1997	1998	1999	2000	2001	2002
Engine:					X	X
Transmission:					-	-
Suspension:					X	-
Steering:					-	-
Brakes:					X	-
Electricity:					X	-
Body:					-	-
Accessories:					X	-
Fit/finish:					-	-

POWERTRAIN

Year	Type/ L/Camshaft/bhp	Drivetrain & gearbox	Acceler. 0/100 sec.	Top. speed km/h	Ave. Fuel consp. l./100 km
01-02	V6/3.4/OHV/185	FWD front-A4	10.5	170	12.3
		AWD front-A4	11.0	165	12.7

PERFORMANCE

SPECIFICATIONS

Model 01-02	Wlb. mm	Lght. mm	Cb.wt kg	Brakes fr/rr	Steering type	Standard tires
fam. 4 p FWD	2751	4625	1714	dc/dr/ABS	pwr.r.&p.	215/70R16
fam. 4 p. AWD	2751	4625	1834	dc/dr/ABS	pwr.r.&p.	215/70R16

PRICES

Model / version		1997	1998	1999	2000	2001	2002
wgn. 4dr. AWD	mini					19500	22600
	maxi					22000	25400
wgn. 4dr. GT AWD	mini					22450	25700
	maxi					25100	28450

See page 7 to adapt these figures.

2002 PONTIAC Aztek

2000 CADILLAC Catera

The Catera is a 4-door sedan who is sold in a single trim level equipped with a standard 3.0L V6 driven by an automatic. This German-built import has been available since 1997.

PROS

• **This car** has some class, even though it's so quietly elegant that it can go unnoticed. The cabin is very lovely and lush.

• **A lot of goodies** for your money, compared to direct rivals, for example, there are heated seats both up front and in the rear.

• **This German-built** car is sure-proof safe and it's as solid and heavy as an army tank. Visibility is clear in all directions.

• **Sitting** is royal on plush seats that offer perfect support, carried along by a velvety suspension that absorbs every bump in the road. All this in a quiet atmosphere, thanks to superb soundproofing.

• **Handling** is honest, for the Catera is stable in any situation.

• **The engine** achieves Sportscar capabilities, but when it comes to pick-up, it's more sluggish, because of heavy vehicle weight.

• **Brakes** are powerful, well-balanced and tough, so you can make any number of sudden stops without a hitch...

• **Assembly quality**, trim materials and fit and finish are perfect examples of Germanic car standards.

• **The car maneuvers** superbly because of a good steering ratio and its very short turning diameter.

• **Practicality** like the trunk, who can hold a lot of luggage and it can be extended by lowering one or both sections of the split rear seatback.

CONS

• **Anonymous** looks make it hard to identify easily and don't do much to add pizzazz.

• **Driving** isn't quite what you'd expect, for the engine lacks get up and go in some situations when the car is the least bit loaded with passengers or luggage.

• **The instrument** panel is massive and takes up crucial space needed by front-seat passengers.

• **Winter driving** isn't as safe and sure as with a front-wheel drive, and the traction control do its best to keep the car on course...

VERDICT

The small Cadillac is a solid, well-built car that can boast of impressive capabilities, luxurious equipment and cream of the crop comfort.

RECALLS

1997   Defective child seat anchoring.

RELIABILITY PROBLEMS

	1997	1998	1999	2000	2001	2002
Engine:	X	X	X	-	-	
Transmission:	-	X	-	-	-	
Suspension:	-	X	X	X	-	
Steering:	-	-	-	-	-	
Brakes:	X	X	X	X	X	
Electricity:	X	X	X	X	X	
Body:	-	X	X	X	-	
Accessories:	X	X	X	X	X	
Fit/finish:	-	-	-	-	-	

POWERTRAIN

Year	Type/ L/Camshaft/bhp	Drivetrain & gearbox
97-01	V6/3.0/DOHC/200	front-A4

PERFORMANCE

Acceler. 0/100 sec.	Top. speed km/h	Ave. Fuel consp. l./100 km
9.0	200	12.9

SPECIFICATIONS

Model 97-01	Wlb. mm	Lght. mm	Cb.wt kg	Brakes fr/rr	Steering type	Standard tires
sdn. 4dr.	2730	4928	1710	dc/ABS	pwr.bal.	225/55HR16

PRICES

Model / version		1997	1998	1999	2000	2001	2002
sdn. 4dr.	mini	10500	12900	16300	19750	23100	
	maxi	13100	16300	19750	23100	26800	

See page 7 to adapt these figures.

2000 CADILLAC Catera

GM W Series

2001 CHEVROLET Impala

These mid-size front-wheel drive coupes and sedans were first sold in 1989, and the Lumina models were added to the roster in '91. Unfortunately for the people at GM, who wanted these cars to be the flagships of its car fleet, they weren't as popular as hoped. But in '97, the Buick Century came back and one year later the introduction of the Oldsmobile Intrigue has surely helped a lot that platform to get back on track in terms of sales and craftsmanship.

PROS
• **The Pontiac Grand Prix** is by far the most spectacular, with its sensational body design. Although the Intrigue and Regal-Century are charming for they are coated in finesse.

• **Both the 3.4L and 3.8L** engines are quite impressive for they put out more than 200-hp

• **The cabin interior** comfortably accommodates five passengers and the nicely shaped trunk can hold all their luggage.

• **The sports models** handle much better because of their higher performance shock absorbers and sturdier springs.

• **The 4-speed automatic** is one of the best on the market, for the shifter is smooth and right on and it provides really good braking effect in 3rd and 2nd gear.

• **Four-disc brakes** are quite stable, even without ABS (optional on the upper-end models during the first few years).

• **Build and finish quality**, as well as materials used, have vastly improved especially on the latest models, notably on the Intrigue.

CONS
• **Excessive vehicle weight** makes gas bills soar sky high.

• **Low-end models** are more suited for highway driving, for their suspension isn't really too firm.

• **Road stability** on base models isn't the greatest because of the overly flexible suspension that causes quite a bit of swing and sway.

• **Things to consider**: poor visibility on the coupes, scarce storage compartments, weak headlights, ineffective windshield wipers and poor ventilation.

VERDICT
This large family of cars offers many models to choose from, all equipped with virtually the same mechanical features. Whether it be the popular Lumina or the wild and woolly Grand Prix, car choice only really depends on people's tastes and pocketbooks...

POWERTRAIN

Year	Type/ L/Camshaft/bhp	Drivetrain & gearbox	Acceler. 0/100 sec.	Top. speed km/h	Ave. Fuel consp. l./100 km
97-01	V6/3.1/OHV/140-160	front-A4	9.8	165	12.3
	V6/3.8/OHC/170-205	front-M5	8.5	200	12.9
		front-A4	8.3	175	12.4
	V6C/3.8/DOHC/215-240	front-A4	7.2	200	13.2
00-02					
Intrigue	V6/3.5/DOHC/215	front-A4	8.5	190	12.5
	V6/3.4/OHC/180	front-A4	9.6	180	11.8
Impala	V6/3.8/OHC/200 Impala	front-A4	8.5	190	12.5

SPECIFICATIONS

Model	Wlb. mm	Lght. mm	Cb.wt kg	Brakes fr/rr	Steering type	Standard tires
BUICK Century 97-02						
sdn. 4dr.Custom	2769	4943	1521	dc/dr/ABS	pwr.r&p.	205/70R15
sdn. 4dr. LTD	2769	4943	1529	dc/dr/ABS	pwr.r&p.	205/70R15
CHEVROLET Impala 00-02						
sdn. 4dr. base	2807	5080	1537	dc	pwr.r&p.	225/60R16
sdn. 4dr. LS	2807	5080	1572	dc/ABS	pwr.r&p.	225/60R16
CHEVROLET Lumina 97-99						
sdn. 4dr. base	2730	5104	1511	dc/dt/ABS	pwr.r&p.	205/70R15
sdn. 4dr. LS	2730	5104	1531	dc/dt/ABS	pwr.r&p.	225/60R16
sdn. 4dr. LTZ	2730	5104	1551	dc/ABS	pwr.r&p.	225/60R16
CHEVROLET Monte Carlo 97-98						
cpe. 2dr. LS	2730	5098	1470	dc/dt/ABS	pwr.r&p.	205/70R15
cpe. 2dr. Z34	2730	5098	1559	dc/ABS	pwr.r&p.	225/60R16
CHEVROLET Monte Carlo 00-02						
cpe. 2dr. LS	2807	5026	1515	dc/dt/ABS	pwr.r&p.	225/60R16
cpe. 2dr. SS	2807	5026	1538	dc/ABS	pwr.r&p.	225/60R16
OLDSMOBILE Cutlass Supreme 1997						
cpe. 2dr. SL	2730	4926	1489	dc/ABS	pwr.r&p.	205/70R15
sdn. 4dr. S	2730	4921	1537	dc/ABS	pwr.r&p.	215/60R16
sdn. 4dr. SL	2730	4921	1550	dc/ABS	pwr.r&p.	215/60R16
OLDSMOBILE Intrigue 98-02						
sdn. 4dr. base	2769	4976	1555	dc/ABS	pwr.r&p.	225/60R16
sdn. 4dr.GL/GLS	2769	4976	1567	dc/ABS	pwr.r&p.	225/60R16
PONTIAC Grand Prix 1997						
cpe. 2dr. SE	2730	4948	1471	dc/ABS	pwr.r&p.	215/60R16
cpe. 2dr. GTP	2730	4948	1471	dc/ABS	pwr.r&p.	225/60R16
sdn. 4dr. SE	2730	4950	1505	dc/ABS	pwr.r&p.	205/70R15
sdn. 4dr. GT	2730	4950	1505	dc/ABS	pwr.r&p.	225/60R16
PONTIAC Grand Prix 98-02						
sdn. 4dr. SE	2807	4991	1549	dc/ABS	pwr.r&p.	205/70R15
cpe. 2dr. GT	2807	4991	1540	dc/ABS	pwr.r&p.	225/60R16
sdn. 4dr. GT	2807	4991	1549	dc/ABS	pwr.r&p.	225/60R16

GM W Series

1998 BUICK Regal

RELIABILITY PROBLEMS

	1997	1998	1999	2000	2001	2002
Engine:	X	X	X	X	X	-
Transmission:	-	-	-	-	-	-
Suspension:	-	X	X	X	-	-
Steering:	-	-	-	-	-	-
Brakes:	X	X	X	X	-	-
Electricity:	-	X	X	X	X	X
Body:	-	-	-	-	-	-
Accessories:	X	X	X	X	X	X
Fit/finish:	X	X	-	-	-	-

RECALLS

1997   Stress cracks in the center rear seat belt's anchor plate.
Defective spark plug assembly kit causing rough idle and
poor performance.
Wiper's power feed wire may separate.

98-99   Incorrect emission control label.(Lumina-Monte Carlo)

1999   Missing heater hose clip that can cause a coolant leak.
Possible ABS motor short circuit that can result in a fire.

2000   Some PCM (Power Control Module) from 3.1, 3.8
and 3.8 supercharged V6 engines must be recalibrated to
comply emission regulations.
The fuel hose fill neck will be inspected and if necessary
tightened or change to prevent any leaks.

2001   The hydraulic modulator of the ABS system can leak and
must be inspected and if necessary replaced.
Dealers will replace sensing and diagnostic module (Monte
Carlo).

1999 PONTIAC Grand Prix

BUICK Century-Regal
CHEVROLET Lumina-Monte Carlo-Impala
OLDSMOBILE Cutlass Supreme-Intrigue
PONTIAC Grand Prix

W Series GM

RECALLS (continued)

2002 Dealers must inspect and change if necessary the module of the driver's side airbag.

PRICES

Model / version		1997	1998	1999	2000	2001	2002
BUICK Century							
sdn. 4dr. Custom	mini	7900	8900	11550	13950	16300	18700
	maxi	10500	11550	13950	16300	18900	21500
sdn. 4dr. LTD	mini	8400	9450	12100	14500	17300	19400
	maxi	11000	12100	14500	16800	19950	22000
BUICK Regal							
sdn. 4dr. LS	mini	8900	10800	13100	15500	17300	19950
	maxi	13000	15200	17100	18900	21000	23600
sdn. 4dr. GS	mini	11550	13650	15750	18000	19950	22600
	maxi	15750	17850	19600	21500	24700	26250
CHEVROLET Lumina							
sdn. 4dr.	mini	6300	7650	8900			
	maxi	9450	10500	11850			
sdn. 4dr. LS	mini	6800	8400	9450			
	maxi	10000	11000	12600			
sdn. 4dr. LTZ	mini	7900	9450	10500			
	maxi	10500	12100	13450			
CHEVROLET Monte Carlo							
cpe. 2dr. LS	mini	7000	8400	10500	14900	18400	20500
	maxi	10200	11200	13450	17850	21500	23600
cpe. 2dr. Z34	mini	8400	10000	13100	17000	21000	23600
	maxi	11550	12600	15550	19950	24150	26800
CHEVROLET Impala							
sdn. 4dr.	mini				15400	18400	20500
	maxi				18400	21500	23600
sdn. 4dr. LS	mini				18000	21000	23100
	maxi				21000	24150	26250
OLDSMOBILE Cutlass Supreme							
cpe. 2dr.	mini	6800					
	maxi	10000					
sdn. 4dr.	mini	6300					
	maxi	9450					
OLDSMOBILE Intrigue							
sdn 4dr.	mini		8900				
	maxi		11750				
sdn 4dr. GL	mini		10000	13200	14500	17300	17850
	maxi		12600	16000	16800	19950	20500
sdn 4dr. GLS	mini		11350	14900	16300	19950	20500
	maxi		14300	19750	18900	22600	23100
sdn 4dr. GX	mini			11550	13450	16300	16800
	maxi			14500	16300	18900	19400
PONTIAC Grand Prix							
cpe. 2dr. GT	mini	10500	12400	14700	17000	18700	21500
	maxi	13100	14900	17400	19750	21500	24700
cpe. 2dr. GTP	mini			16300	18700	19750	22600
	maxi			19100	21500	23600	25700
sdn. 4dr. SE	mini		7350	9750	12300	14500	16300	18900
	maxi	10500	12700	15000	17300	19400	22000
sdn. 4dr. GT	mini	10700	12600	14900	17100	18900	21850
	maxi	13300	15200	17650	19950	21700	25000
sdn. 4dr. GTP	mini			16500	18900	19950	23100
	maxi			19400	21700	23800	26250

See page 7 to adapt these figures.

2001 CHEVROLET Corvette

The Corvette has become an institution and a legend on four wheels. It celebrated its 30th birthday in '93. It was completely overhauled in '67 and again in '83 and the breathtaking ZR-1 was launched in '89. Since then, it's been successfully remodelled in '98 et the sporty Hard Top trim level has been introduced in '99 and Z06 in 2001.

PROS
• **The** ZR-1 and Z06 performance.
• **Its stunning style** is the stuff that dreams are made of for a lot of fanatics out there.
• **Handling** is just terrific with the firm suspension and very large Z-grade tires.
• **The driver's position** is perfect with all the adjustments and with the firm, contour bucket seats.
• **Steering** is crisp and clean and silky smooth.
• **With the really large disc brakes** and sophisticated ABS, braking this baby is a piece of cake.

CONS
• **Its hefty price** tag has discouraged quite a few potential buyers.
• **Build and finish** quality are sloppy and some trim components are chintzy, which is totally unacceptable on such a pricy car.
• **The V8 engines** drink up a lot of gas, even more so for racy and raucous Sportscar maneuvers.
• **Comfort** isn't a priority, it seems, with such a snug cabin, harsh suspension, poor wheel travel, acrobatic seat access and loud noise that gets on your nerves in no time.
• **Storage compartments** are almost as rare as hen's teeth and what they call the trunk is teeny tiny.
• **Outward view** is iffy with the high body frame, large blind spots caused by the convertible top, the minuscule rearview mirrors and gauges that are impossible to read in direct sunlight.
• **Note:** a windshield display system (Head-Up) iS standard on '99.

VERDICT
Most Corvette owners have made their dream come true, but it can become a real nightmare if the car hasn't been maintained as it should be, for reliability isn't a strong suit for this car.

RECALLS
1997   Torn seal between the fuel tank and unit pump.
         Seat belts may not be effective.
         Rear suspension tie rod may fracture.
2000   Some defective guides which can twisted and jammed
         safety belts will be replaced.

CHEVROLET Corvette — Y Series GM

RELIABILITY PROBLEMS

	1997	1998	1999	2000	2001	2002
Engine:	X	X	X	X	X	X
Transmission:	X	-	-	-	-	-
Suspension:	-	-	-	-	-	-
Steering:	X	-	-	-	-	-
Brakes:	X	X	X	X	X	-
Electricity:	X	X	X	X	X	-
Body:	-	X	-	X	X	X
Accessories:	X	X	X	X	X	-
Fit/finish:	-	-	X	X	-	-

POWERTRAIN

Year	Type/ L/Camshaft/bhp	Drivetrain & gearbox	Acceler. 0/100 sec.	Top. speed km/h	Ave. Fuel consp. l./100 km
97-02	V8/5.7/OHV/245-350	rear-M6	5.0	270	13.7
		rear-A4	5.3	275	14.0

PERFORMANCE

(see table above)

SPECIFICATIONS

Model 1997	Wlb. mm	Lght. mm	Cb.wt kg	Brakes fr/rr	Steering type	Standard tires
cpe. 2dr.	2443	4534	1501	dc/ABS	pwr.r&p.	275/40R17
con. 2dr.	2443	4534	1512	dc/ABS	pwr.r&p.	285/40R17
cpe. 2dr. ZR-1	2443	4534	1590	dc/ABS	pwr.r&p.	275/40R17
98-02						315/35R17
cpe. 2dr.	2655	4566	1472	dc/ABS	pwr.r&p.	245/45R17
cpe. 2dr.Hard top	2655	4566	1430	dc/ABS	pwr.r&p.	245/45R17
con. 2dr.	2655	4566	1473	dc/ABS	pwr.r&p.	275/40R18
cpe. 2dr. Z06	2655	4566	1456	dc/ABS	pwr.r&p.	275/40R18

PRICES

Model / version		1997	1998	1999	2000	2001	2002
cpe. 2dr.	mini	26250	31500	37500	40950	51450	57200
	maxi	30450	34650	40950	46200	55650	60900
cpe. 2dr. Hard top	mini			31500	38850		
	maxi			34650	44100		
cpe. 2dr. Z06HT	mini					56700	58700
	maxi					60900	65600
con. 2dr.	mini		37800	44100	51450	51450	59000
	maxi		40950	47250	55650	55650	66150

See page 7 to adapt these figures.

2000 CHEVROLET Corvette

GM VSU

1998 CHEVROLET Suburban

Stemming from the venerable Suburban, these vehicles truly inaugurated the market for full-size luxury SUVs. They are available as two- and four-wheel drive and were revamped in 2000.

PROS

• **Spacious cabins**: the Tahoe has room for six people, while the Suburban can seat up to nine . . . not to mention their luggage!
• **Performance** akin to those of big passenger cars.
• **The handling** is much more precise than the previous generations' thanks to a more rigid chassis and improved suspension capabilities.
• **Ride comfort** is appreciable at highway cruising speeds, where the suspension and noise level are acceptable.
• **The dashboard** is not a model of ergonomics, but it houses a lot of instruments and storage compartments.
• **These vehicles** boast impressive load and trailering capabilities.
• **The uppercrust** models are luxurious, but buyers must check off a lot of options before having a complete array of equipment.
• **The high driving position**, low frame belt and big mirrors ensure excellent overall visibility.

CONS

• **These models** are nothing short of gas guzzlers.
• **Maneuverability** is hindered by the imposing hulk and wide steer angle diameter of these vehicles.
• **The Escalade's off-road capabilities** are limited by its front and rear cowls.
• **The seat cushions** are too short and do not provide much in terms of lateral support because they are too flat.
• **The rigid rear axle** often slips and slides.
• **Road noise** from the frame builds up over the kilometers.
• **The two rear side-swing doors** block visibility, while the rear door with swing panel makes it difficult to access the luggage compartment.

VERDICT

At long last, these big GMs have fallen into step with their competitors. Their modern engines and much more rigid bodies make them a lot more roadworthy.

RECALLS

1997 A protector will be installed over the recliner mechanism of the front seats.
1998 Rear brake pipe positioning clip will be relocated, brake pipe will be inspected and replaced if necessary.
A pinch bolt will be torqued properly to specification.
99-00 Front right hand brake pipe will be inspected and replaced if necessary.
Dealers will instal a jumper harness that turn on the required lamps when fog lamps are activated.
Inspection will be conducted for loose or missing wheelhouse plug and installed if necessary.
2000 Brake vacuum booster supply hose will be rerouted.
2001 Dealers will inspect for loose or missing wheelhouse plugs and install them back if necessary.
Some vehicles may have an internal component in the 2nd and 3rd row outboard seat retractor that could be cracked.
2002 Dealers will install a protection to prevent squeezing fingers in the headrests of the rear benches.

RELIABILITY PROBLEMS

	1997	1998	1999	2000	2001	2002
Engine:				X	X	-
Transmission:	X	X	X	-	-	-
Suspension:	X	X	X	X	X	-
Steering:	-	-	-	X	X	-
Brakes:	X	X	X	X	-	X
Electricity:	X	X	X	X	X	-
Body:	-	-	-	X	-	-
Accessories:	X	X	X	X	-	X
Finition:	X	X	X	X	-	-

POWERTRAIN

Year	Type/ L/Camshaft/bhp	Drivetrain & gearbox
97-99	V8/5.7/OHC/255	rr./all-A4
	V8TD/6.5/OHC/195	rr./all-A4
	V8/7.4/OHC/290	rr./all-A4
00-02	V8/4.8/OHC/270	rr./all-A4
	V8/5.3/OHC/285	rr./all-A4
	V8/6.0/OHC/300	rr./all-A4

PERFORMANCE

Acceler. 0/100 sec.	Top. speed km/h	Ave. Fuel consp. l./100 km
9.3	175	18.0
13.5	160	16.0
12.0	180	20.0
10.0	175	17.0
9.5	180	18.0
11.0	175	20.0

SPECIFICATIONS

Model	Wlb. mm	Lght. mm	Cb.wt kg	Brakes fr/rr	Steering type	Standard tires
Escalade						
wgn. 4dr. 4x4	2984	5110	2528	dc/dr/ABS	pwr.ball	275/70R16
Yukon-Tahoe						
wgn. 4dr. 4x2	2832	4775	2053	dc/dr/ABS	pwr.ball	235/75R15
wgn. 4dr. 4x4	2985	5070	2119	dc/dr/ABS	pwr.ball	245/75R16
Suburban-Yukon XL						
wgn. 4dr. 4x2	3340	5575	2187	dc/dr/ABS	pwr.ball	235/75R15
wgn. 4dr. 4x4	3340	5575	2390	dc/dr/ABS	pwr.ball	265/70R17

PRIX

Model / version		1997	1998	1999	2000	2001	2002
CADILLAC Escalade							
wgn. 4dr.	mini.			34650	40950		56700
	maxi.			37800	44100		60900
wgn. 4dr. EXT	mini.						54600
	maxi.						58800
CHEVROLET Tahoe/GMC Yukon							
wgn. 2dr. SL/base	mini.	11900	14700	17850			
	maxi.	14200	17300	20500			
wgn. 2dr. SLE/LS	mini.	14400	16800	21000			
	maxi.	16800	18900	23600			
wgn. 2dr. SLT/LT	mini.	15750	17850	23600			
	maxi.	18150	19950	26200			
wgn. 2dr. GT/Sport	mini.	14400	18700	21200			
	maxi.	17400	20800	23600			
wgn. 4dr. SLE/LS	mini.	17000	19000	24150	30650	35700	43000
	maxi.	19400	21000	26550	33100	38500	46200
wgn. 4dr. SLT/LT	mini.	18800	21000	25600	35900	40950	48300
	maxi.	21200	23100	28000	38500	43800	51450
wgn. 4dr. Denau/	mini.			30650	37500	45000	54600
Over	maxi.			33100	40100	47800	57400
wgn. 4dr. Base/SL	mini.				26800	32000	
	maxi.				28350	33600	
wgn. 4dr. Carryover L	mini.				32550		
	maxi.				35200		
CHEVROLET Suburban/GMC Suburban & Yukon XL							
1500 Series							
wgn. 4dr. SL/base	mini.	14800	16000	18600	26900	32100	
	maxi.	17850	19400	21500	29900	35400	
wgn. 4dr. SLE/LS	mixi.	20250	21300	23100	30750	36100	42000
	maxi.	23350	24150	26000	33600	39400	45150
wgn. 4dr. SLT/LT	mini.	22600	23600	25200	35600	40750	46700
	maxi.	25700	26800	28350	38500	44000	49650
wgn. 4dr. Denau	mini.					45450	53000
	maxi.					49350	56200
2500 Series							
wgn. 4dr. SL/base	mini.	15850	16800	18900	27500	32550	
	maxi.	18900	19850	22000	30450	35300	
wgn. 4dr. SLE/LS	mini.	21300	22900	23600	31700	36750	45700
	maxi.	24350	25200	26250	34650	40100	47650
wgn. 4dr. SLT/LT	mini.	23500	24150	25700	36200	41600	50400
	maxi.	26800	27300	28550	39400	44800	53300

See page 7 to adapt these figures.

HONDA   Accord

2000 HONDA Accord

First sold in 1981, the Accord rapidly rose to the top of the sales chart in North America. It was modified in 1985, 89, 91, 94 and in 98.

PROS

• **Its nice size** that is exactly like that of the traditional compact station wagon and its cleaner, more recent design with a stronger, reinforced frame.

• **Resale value** remains high, for demand for this model is only affected by its high initial price tag.

• **The cabin** comfortably seats four adults and the fairly roomy trunk holds all their luggage.

• **The well-adjusted** suspension and super, good-sized original tires make for effective road stability.

• **Engines** have great get up and go, even if the gears are a bit slow to kick in.

• **Gas consumption** is quite low, given the vehicle size.

• **Flawless engineering**, assembly and finish quality.

• **The station wagon** is a good alternative to a minivan.

CONS

• **Some models** aren't too flashy or smart looking.

• **Front wheels** skid in no time flat on slippery roads, which is a real worry in the winter.

• **Rear seat** area on earlier models is quite snug.

• **Steering** is quick but over-assisted, more so at higher speeds.

• **Brakes** lack bite and endurance.

• **Awkward rear seat** access on the two-door coupe and the high trunk opening.

VERDICT

The Honda Accord has been a smashing success for it's the perfect car for a certain segment of the population, and it's become a sort of prize horse. There are lots of them on the market, so it would be a good idea to have a used car checked out thoroughly before purchase.

RECALLS

1997   Air conditioner wiring harness must be inspected and re-routed.

1998   Automatic transmission selection may be defective.
Front suspension lower ball joints may prematurely wear out.

2000   The rear suspension lower control arm could break due to improper welding.

2002   Inspection and replacement, if necessary, of the water pump and timing belt.

Accord   HONDA

RELIABILITY PROBLEMS

	1997	1998	1999	2000	2001	2002
Engine:	X	X	-	-	-	-
Transmission:	-	-	X	X	-	-
Suspension:	-	X	-	-	-	-
Steering:	-	-	-	-	-	-
Brakes:	-	X	X	X	-	-
Electricity:	-	X	X	X	-	-
Body:	-	X	X	X	X	-
Accessories:	X	-	X	X	-	X
Fit/finish:	-	X	X	X	-	-

POWERTRAIN

Year	Type/ L/Camshaft/bhp	Drivetrain & gearbox
1997	L4/2.2/SOHC/125-130	front-M5
		front-A4
	L4/2.2/SOHC/140-145	front-A4
	V62.7/SOHC/170	front-A4
98-02	L4/2.3/SOHC/135-150	front-M5
		front-A4
	V6/3.0/SOHC/200	front-A4

PERFORMANCE

Acceler. 0/100 sec.	Top. speed km/h	Ave. Fuel consp. l./100 km
9.8	195	9.5
11.0	185	10.5
10.0	200	11.0
8.5	200	12.5
9.4	180	9.5
10.0	175	10.5
8.0	200	11.4

SPECIFICATIONS

Model	Wlb. mm	Lght. mm	Cb.wt kg	Brakes fr/rr	Steering type	Standard tires
1997						
cpe. 2dr.	2715	4695	1237	dc/dr	pwr.r&p.	185/70R14
sdn. 4dr.	2715	4695	1253	dc/dr	pwr.r&p.	185/70R14
sdn. 4dr. V6	2715	4745	1480	dc/ABS	pwr.r&p.	205/60R15
sdn. 4dr. EX-R V6	2715	4785	1485	dc/ABS	pwr.r&p.	205/60R15
wgn. 5dr.	2715	4770	1365	dc/dr	pwr.r&p.	195/60R15
98-02						
cpe. 2dr. LX	2670	4745	1345	dc/dr/ABS	pwr.r&p.	195/65R15
cpe. 2dr. EX	2670	4745	1365	dc/ABS	pwr.r&p.	195/65R15
cpe. 2dr. EX-V6	2670	4745	1480	dc/ABS	pwr.r&p.	205/60R16
sdn. 4dr. DX	2715	4796	1305	dc/dr	pwr.r&p.	195/70R14
sdn. 4dr. LX	2715	4796	1350	dc/dr/ABS	pwr.r&p.	195/65R15
sdn. 4dr. EX	2715	4796	1305	dc/ABS	pwr.r&p.	195/65R15
sdn. 4dr. EX-V6	2715	4796	1350	dc/ABS	pwr.r&p.	205/65R16

PRICES

Model / version		1997	1998	1999	2000	2001	2002
cpe. 2dr. LX	mini	8900	10500	11550	13650		
	maxi	11000	12600	13650	15750		
cpe. 2dr. EX	mini		13100	14700	17300	18400	24150
	maxi		15200	16800	19400	21000	28350
cpe. 2dr. EX-R	mini	12500					
	maxi	14500					
cpe. 2dr. EX-V6	mini		16300	17300	20500	21000	24700
	maxi		17850	19400	22000	25200	28350
cpe. 2dr. SE	mini						19950
	maxi						24150
sdn. 4dr. LX	mini	8900	11000	12000	14200	15550	16800
	maxi	11000	13100	14200	16300	18400	21000
sdn. 4dr. EX	mini	11000	13100	15200	17850	21000	23600
	maxi	13100	15200	17300	19950	24150	28350
sdn. 4dr. DX	mini		10000	12000	13100		
	maxi		11550	13100			
sdn. 4dr. SE	mini	11550			15700		19650
	maxi	13650			17850		24150
sdn. 4dr. EX-R	mini	12600					
	maxi	14700					
sdn. 4dr. SE V6	mini						22600
	maxi						27000
sdn. 4dr. LX V6	mini					20500	
	maxi					23600	
sdn. 4dr. EX V6	mini		15200	17300	19950	21500	24700
	maxi		16800	19400	22000	24700	29200
sdn. 4dr. EX-R V6	mini	12600					
	maxi	15750					

See page 7 to adapt these figures.

1999 HONDA Civic

The Civic got an overhaul in 1992 and the new generation models came out in 1996. They still come in sedan or coupe body styles, and are powered by 1.5L or 1.6L 4-cylinder engines. Since 1999, the sporty SiR is available with its 160-bhp engine ready to roar.

PROS
• **Neat-looking and attractive** car over the years, but the latest models tend to have a more conservative look.
• **Late model cars** are more comfortable because of the smoother suspension and they are more spacious and quiet.
• **The 4-door sedan** is just as roomy as a compact car.
• **Well-designed engines** are powerful and quite economical.
• **The model** for young drivers who want to show off like the Sportscar, especially for the SiR with its 15-inch tires, four-disc brakes, CD player and sporty suspension that shouldn't unplease anyone.
• **Clever engineering**, assembly and finish quality put these cars in a class apart.

CONS
• **Bodywork** is still thin and rust-prone.
• **The rear seat** area on the hatchbacks is very cramped and the trunk is very tiny if the rear seatbench isn't folded down.
• **Brakes** could be improved, for the front wheels lock quickly and stops are iffy without ABS.
• **There's a lot of engine** noise due to poor soundproofing on the '94-'95 models.
• **These subcompacts** are really sensitive to high winds and braking effect could be better, even with the manual.

VERDICT
The small Civic's are really economical and a lot of fun to drive. But it's too bad they're so vulnerable to impact.

RECALLS
97-98   Passenger airbag module not assembled properly.
2001   Dealers will check the hose clamps for proper torque and tighten them correctly if necessary.
                Dealers will inspect the fuel pump. If corrosion is found, the pump electric connector will be replaced.
2002   Inspection of the air filter to remove possible plastic debris.

RELIABILITY PROBLEMS

	1997	1998	1999	2000	2001	2002
Engine:	X	-	X	-	-	-
Transmission:	-	-	-	-	-	-
Suspension:	-	-	-	-	X	-
Steering:	-	-	-	-	-	-
Brakes:	-	X	-	-	-	-
Electricity:	-	-	-	-	-	-
Body:	X	X	X	-	-	-
Accessories:	X	-	X	X	X	-
Fit/finish:	-	-	-	-	-	-

Civic   HONDA

POWERTRAIN / PERFORMANCE

Year	Type/ L/Camshaft/bhp	Drivetrain & gearbox	Acceler. 0/100 sec.	Top. speed km/h	Ave. Fuel consp. l./100 km
97-00	L4/1.6/SOHC/106	front-M5	11.0	175	7.5
		front-A4	12.2	170	8.4
	L4/1.6/SOHC/125-127	front-M5	9.0	190	8.1
		front-A4	10.8	180	9.1
99-00	L4/1.6/SOHC/160	front-M5	NA	NA	NA
01-02	L4/1.7/DOHC/115-127	front-M5	9.9	185	7.4

SPECIFICATIONS

Model	Wlb.	Lght.	Cb.wt	Brakes	Steering	Standard
97-00						
cpe. 2dr. DX	2620	4450	1064	dc/dr	pwr.r&p.	185/65R14
cpe. 2dr. Si	2620	4450	1117	dc/dr	pwr.r&p.	185/65R14
sdn. 3dr. CX	2620	4180	1037	dc/dr	crém.	185/65R14
sdn. 4dr. LX-EX	2620	4450	1060	dc/dr	pwr.r&p.	185/65R14
sdn. 4dr. EX-V	2620	4450	1084	dc/dc	pwr.r&p.	185/65R14
99-00						
cpe. 2dr. SiR	2620	4450	1117	dc/dr	pwr.r&p.	195/60R15
2001						
cpe. 2dr. DX	2619	4437	1091	dc/dr	pwr.r&p.	185/70R14
cpe. 2dr. Si	2619	4437	1175	dc/dr	pwr.r&p.	185/65R15
sdn. 4dr. DX-LX	2619	4435	1096	dc/dr	pwr.r&p.	185/70R15

PRICES

Model / version		1997	1998	1999	2000	2001	2002
cpe. 2dr. DX	mini.	7350	8400	10000	11000	12300	13100
	maxi	9450	10500	11550	12900	14700	16300
cpe. 2dr. SI	mini.	9450	10000	11550	14200	16900	17300
	maxi	11550	13100	13650	16300	18400	19400
cpe. 2dr. DX/ABS	mini.	8400					
	maxi	10500					
cpe. 2dr. SI/ABS	mini.	8700					
	maxi	10800					
cpe 2dr. DX-G	mini.			10000	10500	12600	
	maxi			10500	12100	14500	
cpe. 2dr. LX	mini.					14400	15200
	maxi					16800	17300
cpe. 2dr. Si-G	mini.			11550	13100	15200	16800	18400
	maxi			13650	14700	17300	19100	20500
cpe. 2dr. Si-G veloz	mini.						18900
	maxi						21000
cpe. 2dr. Si-R	mini.				14200	16300	
	maxi				16300	18400	
cpe. 2dr. SE	mini.						1550
	maxi						3450
cpe. 3dr. CX	mini.	6300	7350	8900	10500		
	maxi	8400	9450	10500	12400		
cpe. 3dr. DX	mini.		7900	9450	11550		
	maxi		10000	11000	13450		
cpe. 3dr.CX-G	mini.	6800					
	maxi	8900					
cpe. 3dr. SE	mini.			12000			
	maxi			13950			
cpe. 3dr. SI-R	mini.						19400
	maxi						21500
sdn. 4dr. LX	mini.	5800	7900	10000	12000		
	maxi	7900	10000	11550	14200		
sdn. 4dr. EX	mini.	7350	9450	11550	13650		
	maxi	9450	11550	13100	15750		
sdn. 4dr. LX-G	mini.		8900	11000		14700	15750
	maxi		11000	12600		16800	17850
sdn. 4dr. EX-G	mini.		10500	12100	14200		
	maxi		12600	13650	16300		
sdn. 4dr. SE	mini.			10500	14700		
	maxi			12100	14700		
sdn. 4dr. LX ABS	mini.	6800					
	maxi	8900					
sdn. 4dr. EX ABS	mini.	8400					
	maxi	10200					
sdn. 4dr. DX	mini.					13100	14200
	maxi					15550	16300
sdn. 4dr. DXG	mini.					14700	14700
	maxi					17100	16800
sdn. 4dr. LX-G sport	mini.						17300
	maxi						19400

See page 7 to adapt these figures.

HONDA   CR-V

1999 HONDA CR-V

The CR-V is a 4-door all-wheel drive sport utility vehicle built on the Civic platform with an Accord powertrain. Inaugurated in 1997 it was renewed in 2002.

PROS

• **The concept** is quite unique, for it's a mix of several kinds of vehicles. All-wheel drive with seats straight like in a minivan and it behaves just like a car, when it comes to performance, handling and safety.

• **Driving pleasure** derives from smooth and neat-design, familiar-looking controls and excellent visibility.

• **It's a super-practical vehicle** and you can move easily from front seats to the rear. There are plenty of convenient storage compartments and the fold-up writing pad between the front seats and the picnic table that also serves as cargo area floor liner are unique and simply great.

• **The vehicle handles** like a car, since, even with all the wheel travel, it doesn't sway much and it sticks to the road in curves.

• **Performance** are quite good, due to a reasonable power to weight ratio. Accelerations and pick-up are equivalent to those of much brawnier and less fuel-efficient engines.

• **Maneuverability** is amazing with such a short turning diameter, good reduction ratio and clear visibility.

• **The price** is reasonable, considering its rich range of equipment.

• **Fuel economy** is interesting because the CR-V sips around 13 liters per every 100 km.

CONS

• **Steering** is light and it sometimes gets vague and wandering, which can be pretty unpleasant.

• **Brakes** don't bit enough and sudden stops are long to achieve.

• **Noise level** is high, due to the cabin configuration and lack of soundproofing, so engine roar and road noise are annoying travelling companions.

• **The poor protection** engine and mechanical components; you don't really feel like heading straight into the underbrush.

• **To be improved upon**: shifter and hand brake that are a pain and better tires so you can tackle snow-covered or muddy roads.

VERDICT

Honda has just about succeeded in coming up with the perfect vehicle for our era. The CR-V isn't really a true-grit sport utility vehicle, but it's spacious, practical, fun to drive, and safe.

RECALLS

2002 Defective front seatbelt pretensioners.

RELIABILITY PROBLEMS

	1997	1998	1999	2000	2001	2002
Engine:	-	-	-	-	-	-
Transmission:	-	-	-	-	-	-
Suspension:	X	-	-	-	-	-
Steering:	-	-	-	-	-	-
Brakes:	X	-	-	-	-	-
Electricity:	-	X	-	-	-	-
Body:	-	X	X	X	X	-
Accessories:	X	X	-	-	-	-
Fit/finish:	-	-	-	-	-	-

POWERTRAIN

Type/ L/Camshaft/bhp	Drivetrain & gearbox	Acceler. 0/100 sec.	Top. speed km/h	Ave. Fuel consp. l./100 km
97-01 L4/2.0/DOHC/128-146	all-M5	9.5	175	11.5
	all-A4	11.0	170	12.0
2002 L4/2.4/DOHC/160	all-M5	9.7	175	11.0
	all-A4	10.6	170	11.0

PERFORMANCE Year

SPECIFICATIONS

Model	Wlb. mm	Lght. mm	Cb.wt kg	Brakes fr/rr	Steering type	Standard tires
97-01						
wgn. 4dr.	2620	4470	1350	dc/dr/ABS	pwr.r&p.	205/70R15
2002						
wgn. 4dr.	2620	4537	1507	dc/ABS	pwr.r&p.	205/70R15

PRICES

Model / version		1997	1998	1999	2000	2001	2002
wgn. 4dr. LX	mini	12600	14500	16800	18900	21000	24150
	maxi	15200	16300	18900	21000	23800	26900
wgn. 4dr. EX	mini		15750	17850	19950	22700	27700
	maxi		18000	20150	22350	25400	28650
wgn. 4dr. Ltd. Ed.	mini					23750	
	maxi					26250	

See page 7 to adapt these figures.

2002 HONDA CR-V

HONDA   del Sol

1997 HONDA del Sol

This coupe convertible replaced the CRX in 1993. The 1.6L Si model engine puts out 127 bhp and the VTEC engine puts out 160-bhp.

PROS

• **This is a neat car**, combining coupe and convertible features and the idea of storing the top in the trunk is very clever.
• **The VTEC engine** really moves, but it's always at high rpm, that is, at illegal speeds.
• **It's so original** and sharp that you just want to give this toy a whirl.
• **Engines** are economical, even the VTEC that really pumps out the power.
• **The ride** is surprisingly comfy, with such a smooth and civilized suspension.
• **Convertible-style** removable rear window.
• **Original cabin** design that the competition should sit up and take notice of.
• **The price is high**, but the del Sol is a practical and multi-purpose, year-round car.
• **Build quality** and tight fit and finish are superb, but some trim components look chintzy.
• **The trunk is nice** and big, even with top stored inside it.

CONS

• **The frame really shakes**, rattles and rolls, due to inadequate rigidity and the soft suspension on the Si makes driving a bit touch and go.
• **The base engine** is wimpy and a real drag.
• **Brakes on the Si** aren't the greatest without ABS, and sudden stops aren't straight or predictable.
• **Understeering** (Si) is quite a problem and you have to know what you're doing when driving at high speeds on wet pavement.
• **The manual shifter** is sometimes rough upon a cold start.
• **Rearward view** is obstructed at quarterback because of the thick C-pillar.

VERDICT

It's a shame that Honda didn't iron out all the small wrinkles early on, for this vehicle is original and cleverly designed.

RECALLS

None over this period.

del Sol   HONDA

RELIABILITY PROBLEMS

	1997	1998	1999	2000	2001	2002
Engine:	-					
Transmission:	-					
Suspension:	-					
Steering:	-					
Brakes:	X					
Electricity:	-					
Body:	-					
Accessories:	X					
Fit/finish:	-					

POWERTRAIN

Year	Type/ L/Camshaft/bhp	Drivetrain & gearbox	Acceler. 0/100 sec.	Top. speed km/h	Ave. Fuel consp. l./100 km
1997	L4/1.6/SOHC/125-127	front-M5	9.5	190	8.5
		front-A4	10.7	180	9.5
	L4/1.6/DOHC/160	front-M5	8.5	210	9.5

PERFORMANCE

SPECIFICATIONS

Model 1997	Wlb. mm	Lght. mm	Cb.wt kg	Brakes fr/rr	Steering type	Standard tires
cpe. 2dr. Si	2370	4005	1095	dc/dc	pwr.r&p.	185/60R14
cpe. 2dr. VTEC	2370	4005	1144	dc/ABS	pwr.r&p.	195/60R14

PRICES

Model / version		1997	1998	1999	2000	2001	2002
cpe. 2dr. Si	mini	8900					
	maxi	11000					
cpe. 2dr. VTEC	mini	10000					
	maxi	12300					

See page 7 to adapt these figures.

1997 HONDA del Sol

HONDA   Insight

2000 HONDA Insight

To rob Toyota of any eventual claim to the title of manufacturer of North America's first hybrid vehicle, Honda precipitated the launch of its original-design coupe, the environmentally friendly Insight.

PROS

- **The hybrid system** is highly economical, and fuel consumption is minimal in comparison with conventional automobiles.
- **Emissions** are reduced thanks to the closely managed thermal engine.
- **Leading-edge technologies**, such as a lightweight aluminum body, electronic energy management and smaller-sized batteries.
- **The Insight is very maneuverable** and fits anywhere, thanks to its small overall dimensions and tight steer angle diameter.
- **The cabin** has plenty of room for two adults, with ample clearance and long doors that open up wide to facilitate getting in and out of it.
- **The quality** of the design, manufacturing and finish is up to par with what we have come to expect from Honda.

CONS

- **The sale** and resale of this small car are seriously limited by its outrageous price. It has nothing to offer that would justify investing so much money into it, at least for as long as the price of gasoline remains reasonable.
- **Mediocre performance** is the price to pay to benefit from the Insight's parsimonious appetite. Accelerations and pick-up are frustratingly slow.
- **The brakes** perform disappointingly for such a lightweight vehicle, with the ABS system struggling to prevent the wheels from locking.
- **Not a very practical automobile**: it has a minimal amount of storage space and its albeit accessible trunk is way too small.
- **The hard suspension**, flat seats and high noise level due to a lack of soundproofing combine to produce a generally uncomfortable ride.
- **The low driving position**, poor rearward visibility and confusing instrument panel are not very reassuring for drivers.

VERDICT

The Insight is not a very realistic automobile; originality has been given priority over practicality and its high price—combined with the mistrust the public usually has in new technologies—will do little to make the Insight an easy car to sell on the used-car market.

RECALLS

None over this period.

RELIABILITY PROBLEMS

	1997	1998	1999	2000	2001	2002
Engine:						
Transmission:						
Suspension:						
Steering:						
Brakes:			Insufficient data			
Electricity:						
Body:						
Accessories:						
Fit/finish:						

POWERTRAIN

Year	Type/ L/Camshaft/bhp	Drivetrain & gearbox	Acceler. 0/100 sec.	Top. speed km/h	Ave. Fuel consp. l./100 km
00-02	L3/1.0/DOHC/67 +10 kW electric motor	front-M5	15.5	160	5.0

PERFORMANCE

(merged above)

SPECIFICATIONS

Model 00-02	Wlb. mm	Lght. mm	Cb.wt kg	Brakes fr/rr	Steering type	Standard tires
cpe. 3dr.	2400	3940	852	dc/dr/ABS	pwr.r&p	165/65R14

PRICES

Model / version		1997	1998	1999	2000	2001	2002
cpe. 3dr.	mini				17300	19400	22000
	maxi				18900	21500	25200

See page 7 to adapt these figures.

2000 HONDA Insight

HONDA   Odyssey

1998 HONDA Odyssey

The first Odyssey was midway between a minivan and a station wagon. In 1999, it was entirely redesigned as a full-size minivan with double sliding doors and equipped with a 3.5L V6.

PROS

• **Its clean, classic look** and successfull new shape. The older ones hide well the fact that it's a bit narrow.
• **Good cabin design** gives comfortable seating for six passengers.
• **Engine performance** are gutsier than expected, but the V6 could be livelier and smoother.
• **The feel of the vehicle** that handles more like a car than a minivan.
• **A smooth and quiet ride**, with such a good suspension, nicely contoured seats and relatively low noise level.
• **The driver's position** is simply perfect, with such a nice environment and clear outward view.
• **Adequate trunk capacity**, even with six passengers aboard.

CONS

• **It's pretty pricy**, given its run-of-the-mill engines, plain and simple equipment and rather basic cabin design.
• **Maneuverability** is no picnic with such a large steer angle diameter.
• **The spare tire** on the first generation is a real pain for one of the remote rear seatbench passengers.
• **The terribly bleak** cabin design that has become par for the course on Honda models.
• **Tight leg room** in remote rear seatbench.
• **Rear doors** of the first generation can be awkward in tight parking spots, but they do provide relatively easy access. On the latest models, the addition of two sliding doors has corrected the problem.

VERDICT

The Odyssey isn't for everyone. It's geared for Honda fanatics who are looking for a multipurpose car rather than an in and out minivan.

RECALLS

1998 Front suspension lower ball joints may prematurely wear out.
1999 Water in the resonator subchamber can freeze and interfere with the throttle plate's return to the idle position.
Sliding door latches and power lock remote control actuators must be replaced to avoid improper latching.
2000 A wire harness may be damaged by contact with metal pipe. A dash light dimmer circuit may be damaged by heat build-up in the unit.
2002 Inspection and if necessary replacement of the water pump an timing belt.

RELIABILITY PROBLEMS

	1997	1998	1999	2000	2001	2002
Engine:	-	-	X	-	-	-
Transmission:	-	-	X	-	-	-
Suspension:	X	X	-	-	-	-
Steering:	-	-	-	-	-	-
Brakes:	X	X	X	X	X	-
Electricity:	-	X	X	X	X	-
Body:	X	X	-	-	-	-
Accessories:	-	X	X	X	X	X
Fit/finish:	-	-	X	-	-	-

POWERTRAIN

Year	Type/ L/Camshaft/bhp	Drivetrain & gearbox
97-98	L4/2.2/SOHC/140	front-A4
99-02	V6/3.5/SOHC/210	front-A4

PERFORMANCE

	Acceler. 0/100 sec.	Top. speed km/h	Ave. Fuel consp. l./100 km
	10.4	185	12.0
	9.6	190	12.0

SPECIFICATIONS

Model	Wlb. mm	Lght. mm	Cb.wt kg	Brakes fr/rr	Steering type	Standard tires
97-98						
m.v. 4dr.	2830	4755	1565	dc/ABS	pwr.r&p.	205/65R15
99-02						
m.v. 4dr. LX/ EX	3000	5110	1945	dc/dr/ABS	pwr.r&p.	215/65R16

PRICES

Model / version		1997	1998	1999	2000	2001	2002
m.v. 4dr. 6 st.	mini	12300	14000				
	maxi	14700	16000				
m.v. 4dr. 7 st.	mini	12600	14400				
	maxi	15000	16300				
m.v. 4dr. LX	mini			20500	24700	27200	30350
	maxi			22600	26650	29600	32750
m.v. 4dr. EX	mini			23100	27300	29300	32450
	maxi			25000	29300	32000	35200

See page 7 to adapt these figures.

2001 HONDA Odyssey

2000 HONDA Prelude

When the Prelude coupe was upgraded in 1992, variable valve timing gave it the punch and power it needed.

PROS

• **Its slinky look** is a real winner and reflects its Sportscar character.

• **Engine performance** on the SR and SR-V models are much more spirited than before.

• **Handling** on the SR and SH is clean as a whistle but not as much as on the defunct SR-4WS that was way too expensive at its end.

• **Brakes** are more effective and predictable on the ABS-equipped models than on the base model (1996).

• **Upper-end models** have plush equipment and are worth the going price.

• **The VTEC engine** is amazingly economical at normal speeds.

• **The trunk is adequate** and can be extended by lowering the rear seatbench.

• **Interior design** is more refined and the instrument panel more conventional on the post 1996 versions.

CONS

• **Rear seats** are awful, head and leg room is terribly tight and these seats are really only good for storing luggage, since even children would feel cramped.

• **Steering is vague** and sluggish at low speeds, and at high speed, it gets so light that It's jerky and has a mind of its own.

• **The base model** Prelude isn't too powerful and handling is no fun with such narrow tires.

• **The sound system** is horrible and unworthy of such a high-priced car.

VERDICT

The Prelude is a good buy, even with all the technical snags, high-priced tag and expensive insurance premium. But it's a good idea to avoid the nondescript base model that is more of a pain than a pleasure to drive.

RECALLS

None over this period.

RELIABILITY PROBLEMS

	1997	1998	1999	2000	2001	2002
Engine:	X	-	X	-	-	
Transmission:	-	-	-	-	-	
Suspension:	-	-	-	X	-	
Steering:	X	-	X	-	-	
Brakes:	-	X	X	-	-	
Electricity:	-	-	X	X	-	
Body:	-	X	X	-	-	
Accessories:	X	X	X	X	X	
Fit/finish:	-	-	-	X	-	

POWERTRAIN

Year	Type/ L/Camshaft/bhp	Drivetrain & gearbox
97-01	L4/2.2/DOHC/200	front-M5
	L4/2.2/DOHC/190	front-A4

PERFORMANCE

Acceler. 0/100 sec.	Top. speed km/h	Ave. Fuel consp. l./100 km
7.2	220	10.8
8.5	210	10.9

SPECIFICATIONS

Model 97-01	Wlb. mm	Lght. mm	Cb.wt kg	Brakes fr/rr	Steering type	Standard tires
cpe. 2dr.	2585	4520	1340	dc/ABS	pwr.r&p.	205/50R16
cpe. 2dr.SH	2585	4520	1365	dc/ABS	pwr.r&p.	205/50R16

PRICES

Model / version		1997	1998	1999	2000	2001	2002
cpe. 2dr.	mini	12300	15000	16800	18700	21000	
	maxi	15750	18500	20150	22000	24700	
cpe. 2dr. SH	mini	15000	18150	21000	21850		
	maxi	18400	21500	24300	25200		
cpe. 2dr. SE	mini					22000	
	maxi					25700	

See page 7 to adapt these figures.

2000 HONDA Prelude

HONDA   S2000

2000 HONDA S2000

To mark the beginning of the third millennium, Honda designed this 2.0-liter roadster for high-level performance enthusiasts.

PROS

• **The exciting style** is a radical change from the stereotypes of the past.

• **The engine** begs to run fast and sounds a lot like a race car. The small nimble gear shift lever also makes the S2000 feel like a real racer.

• **The quality** of the development, manufacturing and finish is typical of Honda standards.

• **The cockpit** is a model of logic and ergonomics.

• **The wind** is efficiently channelled when the side windows are up and the wind deflector is in place.

• **The air conditioning** was designed to operate with the top down.

• **The bucket seats** provide effective lateral and lumbar support.

CONS

• **The styling** lacks strength and personality.

• **The engine**—whose power and torque are located at very high rpm—is not well suited to North American driving conditions.

• **The convertible top**'s simplistic design is very disappointing, and it is unacceptable that on a car of this price, it has no lining and no glass rear window or electric defroster.

• **Totally impractical**: it has no glove box, no door pockets, a single cup holder and a minuscule central console.

• **The trunk** is minuscule and houses a compact spare wheel.

• **The digital instrument** cluster is not the most attractive and does not look very sporty at all.

• **The steering wheel** cannot be adjusted in any direction, which for some drivers makes it hard to find a comfortable driving position.

• **Visibility** is hindered by the blind spots resulting from the convertible top. A shame!

• **Flaws**: The central tunnel lets it the heat generated by the engine, and the starter button is completely useless.

VERDICT

Designed for an elitist crowd, the S2000 roadster will be hard-pressed to find buyers on the used-car market.

RECALLS

None over this period.

RELIABILITY PROBLEMS

	1997	1998	1999	2000	2001	2002
Engine:				-	-	-
Transmission:				-	-	-
Suspension:				-	-	-
Steering:				-	-	-
Brakes:				X	X	-
Electricity:				-	-	-
Body:				X	X	-
Accessories:				X	X	X
Fit/finish:				-	-	-

POWERTRAIN

Year	Type/ L/Camshaft/bhp	Drivetrain & gearbox	Acceler. 0/100 sec.	Top. speed km/h	Ave. Fuel consp. l./100 km
00-02	L4/2.0/DOHC/240	rear-M6	6.6	235	11.5

PERFORMANCE

(see table above)

SPECIFICATIONS

Model 00-02	Wlb. mm	Lght. mm	Cb.wt kg	Brakes fr/rr	Steering type	Standard tires
con. 2 dr.	2400	4120	1275	dc/ABS	pwr.r&p.	205/55R16 225/50R16

PRICES

Model / version		1997	1998	1999	2000	2001
con. 2dr.	mini			36200	38300	40950
	maxi			38850	41500	44100

See page 7 to adapt these figures.

2000 HONDA S2000

HYUNDAI   Accent

2000 HYUNDAI Accent

The Accent replaced the Excel in 1995. There's a wide model choice, including the GT, GS and GSi hatchback coupes, 3-door coupes and 4-door sedans, that come in L and GL trim levels, all powered by 1.5L or 1.6L 4-cylinder engines.

PROS

• **A competitive price**, but initial price doesn't include some vital equipment like airbags and ABS.
• **The cabin** can accommodate four adults and the trunk holds all their luggage.
• **Its more muscular engine** performance (given the displacement and vehicle weight) with the manual than with the automatic, that downshifts at the least hill or incline and has quite a hard time adjusting.
• **Fuel consumption** is economical, but not as much as that of the competition.
• **Power steering** is great, it's clean and quick and makes for good maneuverability.
• **The smooth suspension** and nicely contoured front seats provide for a cushy ride.
• **Handling** is much better on the GL, GT and GSi models equipped with better-sized tires.
• **Construction quality**, fit and finish and materials are far nicer than on the former Excel.

CONS

• **Manual steering** is slow and vague because it suffers from too high a reduction ratio.
• **Engine performance** are rather poor compared to those of Japanese counterparts.
• **Brakes lack** bite and lasting power, but they're less touchy than those on the Excel.
• **High noise level** is a sign of inadequate soundproofing and noisy as heck engine. And even though the body design is aerodynamic, there's whistling wind noise.

VERDICT

The Accent beefed up sales for this Korean carmaker that was beginning to drag its feet. But overall quality and reliability aren't on at par with Japanese vehicles.

RECALLS

1997	Corrosion from winter road salt may cause the breakage of the lower spring coil.
	Wiper motor operates irregularly.
1999	Defective pressure control solenoid valve seal in the automatic.
	transmission may affect acceleration.
2000	Driving in extremely cold temperature can freeze the inside throttle body.
	The wiper linkage can separate from the motor because a lack of lubrification.
2001	Dealers will install a modified PCV hose and on manual transmission equipped vehicles without air conditioning.

Accent   HYUNDAI

RELIABILITY PROBLEMS

	1997	1998	1999	2000	2001	2002
Engine:	-	X	X	-	-	-
Transmission:	-	X	-	-	-	-
Suspension:	X	X	X	X	-	-
Steering:	-	-	-	-	-	-
Brakes:	X	-	X	X	-	-
Electricity:	X	X	X	X	X	X
Body:	X	-	X	X	-	-
Accessories:	X	-	X	X	X	X
Fit/finish:	X	-	X	X	-	-

POWERTRAIN

Year 97-02	Type/ L/Camshaft/bhp	Drivetrain & gearbox	
GS	L4/1.5/SOHC/92	front-M5	
		front-A4	
GSi/GL	L4/1.6/DOHC/105	front-M5	

PERFORMANCE

	Acceler. 0/100 sec.	Top. speed km/h	Ave. Fuel consp. l./100 km
GS	11.5	175	8.3
	12.8	165	8.8
GSi/GL	11.0	180	8.8

SPECIFICATIONS

Model 97-99	Wlb. mm	Lght. mm	Cb.wt kg	Brakes fr/rr	Steering type	Standard tires
cpe. 3dr. L	2400	4923	953	dc/dr	r&p.	155/80R13
cpe. 3dr. GT	2400	4103	940	dc/dr	r&p.	155/80R13
cpe. 3dr. GL	2400	4103	959	dc/dr	pwr.r&p.	175/70R13
cpe. 3dr. GSi	2400	4923	959	dc/dr	pwr.r&p.	175/70R14
sdn. 4dr. L	2400	4117	955	dc/dr	r&p.	155/80R13
sdn. 4dr. GL	2400	4117	961	dc/dr	pwr.r&p.	175/70R14
00-02						
cpe. 3dr. GS	2440	4200	992	dc/dr	r&p.	155/80R13
cpe. 3dr. GSi	2440	4200	992	dc/dr	pwr.r&p.	185/60R14
sdn. 4dr. GL	2440	4235	1019	dc/dr	pwr.r&p.	175/70R13

PRICES

Model / version		1997	1998	1999	2000	2001	2002
cpe. 3dr. L	mini	3200	4100	5450			
	maxi	4700	5800	6800			
cpe. 3dr. GL	mini	3550					
	maxi	5250					
cpe. 3dr. GS	mini		4700	6500	7150	7900	11000
	maxi		6300	7900	8400	11000	14200
cpe. 3dr. GSi	mini				8400	10000	13100
	maxi				10000	13350	16300
cpe. 3dr. GT	mini	3900					
	maxi	5500					
cpe. 3dr. Sport	mini	4000	4950				
	maxi	5800	6800				
sdn. 4dr. L	mini	3700	4700				
	maxi	5450	6300				
sdn. 4dr. GL	mini	3800	4800	6700	8400	10000	13350
	maxi	5550	7000	8000	10000	13100	16500

See page 7 to adapt these figures.

1998 HYUNDAI Accent

HYUNDAI   *Elantra*

2000 HYUNDAI Elantra

In 1992, the Elantra, a compact sedan midway between the Excel and the Sonata, was put on the market. In 1996, it was redesigned and a station wagon model was also made available, driven by a 1.8L engine. One year later, the Tiburon's 2.0L makes its debut.

PROS

• **Its shapely body** design is nice and clean and not at all overdone.
• **Power steering** is smooth, crisp and benefits from a good reduction ratio.
• **The Alpha and Beta** 1.8L and especially the 2.0L Hyundai engines have really spiffed up the Elantra image.
• **Handling** is safe and sure, due to a simple but effective suspension and 14-inch tires.
• **Driving one** of these cars is a real pleasure because of the cushy suspension and firm seats that provide good support.
• **The GLS model** is loaded and is easier to resell.

CONS

• **The 1.6L engine** is rough and noisy and in fact drinks up as much gas as the 1.8L engine.
• **Brakes lack grip**, which explains why sudden stops are long, and they're unpredictable without ABS.
• **The hard seats** can be a real pain on long trips.
• **Soundproofing** isn't up to snuff, for there's loud road and engine noise.
• **Build quality** is solid, but fit and finish and the look of some trim components aren't what they should be.
• **The big trunk** is convertible, but its small opening makes it impossible to store large items.

VERDICT

With each generation, the Elantra is more technically refined, better built and more comfortable, but there's still room for improvement.

RECALLS

1997	Wiper motor operates irregularly.
1999	Defective pressure control solenoid valve seal in the automatic. transmission may affect acceleration.
99-00	Low speed engine stalling can be caused by a defective MAF (Mass Air Flow) sensor.

Elantra   HYUNDAI

RELIABILITY PROBLEMS

	1997	1998	1999	2000	2001	2002
Engine:	X	X	X	X	X	-
Transmission:	X	-	X	-	-	-
Suspension:	X	-	X	-	-	-
Steering:	X	-	-	-	-	-
Brakes:	-	X	X	X	X	-
Electricity:	-	X	X	X	X	-
Body:	X	-	-	-	-	-
Accessories:	-	X	X	X	X	X
Fit/finish:	-	-	-	-	-	-

POWERTRAIN

Year	Type/ L/Camshaft/bhp	Drivetrain & gearbox
97-98	L4/1.8/DOHC/124-130	front-M5
		front-A4
99-02	L4/2.0/DOHC/140	front-M5
		front-A4

PERFORMANCE

	Acceler. 0/100 sec.	Top. speed km/h	Ave. Fuel consp. l./100 km
	9.5	175	11.0
	11.0	170	10.4
	9.7	175	10.6
	11.0	170	10.5

SPECIFICATIONS

Model 97-00	Wlb. mm	Lght. mm	Cb.wt kg	Brakes fr/rr	Steering type	Standard tires
sdn. 4dr. GL/SE	2550	4420	1144	dc/dr	pwr.r&p.	175/65R14
wgn.4dr. GL/SE	2550	4450	1188	dc/dr	pwr.r&p.	175/65R14
sdn. 4dr. GLS	2550	4420	1173	dc/dr	pwr.r&p.	195/60R14
wgn. 4dr. GLS	2550	4450	1218	dc/dr	pwr.r&p.	195/60R14
01-02						
sdn. 4dr.GL/VE	2610	4495	1217	dc/dr	pwr.r&p.	195/60R15
sdn. 5dr.GT	2610	4495	1241	dc/dr	pwr.r&p.	195/60R15

PRICES

Model / version		1997	1998	1999	2000	2001	2002
sdn. 4dr. GL	mini	3900	4400	5800	7650	10000	10800
	maxi	5800	6300	7900	9450	12100	14200
sdn. 4dr. GLS	mini	5100	6300	7900			
	maxi	6800	8400	10000			
sdn. 4dr. SE	mini	4700	5450	6800			
	maxi	6300	7350	8900			
sdn. 4dr. VE	mini				9150	12100	14200
	maxi				10500	14200	16300
sdn. 5 dr. GT	mini						14700
	maxi						17800
wgn. 4dr. GL	mini	4100	4950	6300	8600		
	maxi	6000	6800	8400	10000		
wgn. 4dr. GLS	mini	5850	6600	8400			
	maxi	7000	8900	10500			
wgn. 4dr. SE	mini	5000	5800	7350			
	maxi	6800	7900	9450			
wgn. 4dr. VE	mini				9250		
	maxi				11000		

See page 7 to adapt these figures.

2001 HYUNDAI Santa Fe

The Santa Fe was introduced to the market in 2000. This all-road vehicle was designed using the Sonata's platform and mechanical components. It is available with front- or all-wheel drive.

PROS

• **The aggressive styling** is sure to please young drivers, especially former owners of a Tiburon coupe.
• With sure handling and low body roll, the Santa Fe drives more like an automobile than a utility vehicle.
• **Ride comfort** is ensured by the soft suspension and generous wheel travel. As for the seats, the front ones provide better support than the flat rear bench.
• **The average weight-to-power ratio** translates into honest performance figures.
• **The cockpit** is well laid out and has personality. However, it's as busy as the sheet metal.
• **The powerful headlights** provide good visibility in all circumstances, both in low- and high-beam positions.
• **Front and rear storage** spaces abound.
• **The well-adapted tires** provide good levels of traction on dry and slippery pavement as well as on slightly hilly terrain.

CONS

• **The exaggerated styling** will turn off older drivers, unless they are looking for a way to show off their youthful spirit.
• **The brakes** stand to be improved because stopping is not always straight and reassuring without ABS.
• **The seats** are too firmly padded to provide optimal comfort levels on long trips.
• **The cheap-looking plastics** tarnish the interior presentation somewhat.
• **The compact spare tire** makes the Santa Fe look ridiculous in the event of a puncture.
• **The radio's controls** will drive even the most stoic music fan crazy.

VERDICT

The Santa Fe is a serious competitor in the all-road versatile vehicle market and offers remarkable quality for the price, a trait that will leave no one indifferent.

RECALLS

None over this period.

RELIABILITY PROBLEMS

	1997	1998	1999	2000	2001	2002
Engine:					-	-
Transmission:					-	-
Suspension:					-	-
Steering:					-	-
Brakes:					-	-
Electricity:					-	-
Body:					X	X
Accessories:					X	X
Fit/finish:					X	-

POWERTRAIN

Year	Type/ L/Camshaft/bhp	Drivetrain & gearbox
01-02		
GL	L4/2.4/DOHC/149	FWD front-M5
GL/GLS	V6/2.7/DOHC/181	FWD front-A4
	V6/2.7/DOHC/181	AWD all-A4

PERFORMANCE

Acceler. 0/100 sec.	Top. speed km/h	Ave. Fuel consp. l./100 km
NA		
11.8	180	12.5
12.0	175	12.6

SPECIFICATIONS

Model 01-02	Wlb. mm	Lght. mm	Cb.wt kg	Brakes fr/rr	Steering type	Standard tires
wgn. 4dr. FWD	2620	4500	1585	dc	pwr.r.&p.	225/70R16
wgn. 4dr. AWD	2620	4500	1687	dc	pwr.r.&p.	225/70R16

PRICES

Model / version		1997	1998	1999	2000	2001	2002
wgn. 4dr. GL .4cyl	mini						17300
FWD	maxi						20150
wgn. 4dr. GL. 6cyl	mini						18800
FWD	maxi						21500
wgn. 4dr. GL. 6cyl	mini					19400	23100
AWD	maxi					22000	25800
wgn. 4dr. GLS6cyl	mini					22600	25200
AWD	maxi					25200	28000

See page 7 to adapt these figures.

2001 HYUNDAI Santa Fe

2002 HYUNDAI Sonata

The Sonata began its career in 1989. This mid-size sedan is powered by a 2.0L 4-cylinder engine or a 3.0L V6. It was revamped in 1999, with a 2.4L L4 and 2.5L V6 engines and in 2002 with a 2.7L V6.

PROS

• **A more affordable price** than the competition, because of fairly unsophisticated technical features and components.

• **Five passengers** and all their belongings can be accommodated in this car.

• **The relatively lively 4-cylinder** engine is quite economical.

• **The two V6 engines** are much more spirited because of a better power to weight ratio.

• **The lavish GLS sedan** comes loaded with all kinds of equipment and the '99 GLS comes standard with four very handy disc brakes.

CONS

• **Low resale value** that is the upshot of customer mistrust both in regard to vehicle reliability and overall quality.

• **The manual shifter** is rough and inaccurate.

• **The poorly designed** and hard seats are tiring on long hauls.

• **Power steering** is smooth and well-calibrated, but is affected by torque on strong accelerations.

• **The rustic suspension** is harsh when it hits road faults.

• **Wind, road and engine noise** roars away in the cabin.

• **Stops are too long** and the front end locks in no time flat.

VERDICT

The Sonata is a good choice if mileage is reasonably low and if it's been meticulously maintained. If in doubt, look elsewhere...

RECALLS

1997	Wiper motor operates irregularly.
	Weak support of frontal shock absorber and headlights.
99-00	Low speed stalling can be caused by a defective Mass Air Flow sensor.

RELIABILITY PROBLEMS

	1997	1998	1999	2000	2001	2002
Engine:	X	X	X	X	X	-
Transmission:	-	-	-	X	X	-
Suspension:	X	-	-	-	-	-
Steering:	-	-	-	-	-	-
Brakes:	X	-	X	X	X	-
Electricity:	-	X	X	X	-	X
Body:	X	-	-	-	-	-
Accessories:	X	X	X	X	-	X
Fit/finish:	X	-	-	-	-	-

POWERTRAIN

Year	Type/ L/Camshaft/bhp	Drivetrain & gearbox	Acceler. 0/100 sec.	Top. speed km/h	Ave. Fuel consp. l./100 km
97-98	L4/2.0/DOHC/126-137	front-M5	10.0	170	10.5
		front-A4	11.0	165	11.0
	V6/3.0/OHV/142	front-A4	9.6	180	12.0
99-01	L4/2.4/DOHC/148	front-A4	11.0	180	11.4
	V6/2.5/DOHC/163	front-A4	10.0	200	11.7
2002	L4/2.4/DOHC/148-149	front-A4	11.0	180	11.4
	V6/2.7/DOHC/181	front-A4	9.5	200	11.8

PERFORMANCE

(see table above)

SPECIFICATIONS

Model	Wlb. mm	Lght. mm	Cb.wt kg	Brakes fr/rr	Steering type	Standard tires
97-98						
sdn. 4dr. GL	2650	4680	1265	dc/dr	pwr.r&p.	185/70R14
99-01						
sdn. 4dr. GL	2700	4710	1409	dc/dr	pwr.r&p.	195/70R14
sdn. 4dr. GLS V6	2700	4710	1409	dc/dc	pwr.r&p.	205/60R15
2002						
sdn. 4dr. GL	2700	4747	1410	dc/dr	pwr.r&p.	205/60R15
sdn. 4dr. GL/GLX	2700	4747	1420	dc/dc	pwr.r&p.	205/60R15

PRICES

Model / version		1997	1998	1999	2000	2001	2002
sdn. 4dr. base	mini	5800	7350				
	maxi	7900	9150				
sdn. 4dr. GL	mini	6300	9000	9500	11350	14500	16800
	maxi	8400	10200	11000	13100	16800	18900
sdn. 4dr. GLS	mini	6800	10200	11550	15950		
	maxi	8900	11250	13650	17850		
sdn. 4dr. GLX	mini					19100	21500
	maxi					21500	23600

See page 7 to adapt these figures.

HYUNDAI   Tiburon

2001 HYUNDAI Tiburon

The Tiburon, built on the Elantra platform, replaces the former Scoupe. It's sold in a base model equipped with a 1.8L 4-cylinder engine or in an FX model powered by a 2.0L.

PROS

• **Its bold and brawny** body that seems to have been honed by the wind, its aggressive airscoop, its streamlined curves that give it an unmistakable shark look.

• **Driving** is quite exhilarating on both models, engines are prim and responsive, the car cuts neatly through curves and the accurate steering really makes for slick moves.

• **The 2.0L engine** feels like a Sportscar powerplant, even if accelerations and pick-up are comparable to those of the Elantra.

• **Road adherence** is quite good, due mostly to the finely adjusted suspension designed with Porsche and good standard tires.

• **Ride comfort** is surprising for this type of car, generous cabin space offers lots of room up front, seats offer excellent support and noise level low at cruising speed.

• **The good value** of the FX who gives a good resale dollar.

• **The interior** reminds you a bit of the first Eagle Talon with its off-center dashboard that lets the driver consult white-on-black analog instruments that are easy to read.

• **Cabin size** is quite spacious for the car category, thanks to a long wheelbase and wide wheel tracks.

• **Commodities** are surprising with lots of handy storage spots in the cabin and the convertible trunk can hold quite a bit of luggage.

CONS

• **The dashboard** isn't terribly ergonomic because the radio and climate controls are opposite to normal position.

• **Rear seats** are really more suited to the small fry rather than to full-fledged adults. Knee and head room is very tight and access is rather dangerous.

• **The base model engine** strains a bit, so it's a good idea to stick with the manual gearbox.

• **The dashboard** really reflects into the windshield and into the instrument panel.

VERDICT

The Tiburon is a nice proposition to young drivers who are searching for a dramatic look and interesting performance at a bargain price.

RECALLS

1997 Wiper motor operate irregularly.
1999 Defective pressure control solenoid valve seal in the automatic.
transmission may affect acceleration.
2000 The daytime running lights doesn't turn off when headlight switch is turned on.

RELIABILITY PROBLEMS

	1997	1998	1999	2000	2001	2002
Engine:	X	X	X	X	X	-
Transmission:	-	-	-	-	-	-
Suspension:	X	-	-	-	-	-
Steering:	-	-	-	-	-	-
Brakes:	X	X	X	-	-	-
Electricity:	X	X	X	X	X	-
Body:	X	X	X	-	-	-
Accessories:	X	X	X	X	X	X
Fit/finish:	-	-	-	-	-	-

POWERTRAIN

Year	Type/ L/Camshaft/bhp	Drivetrain & gearbox	Acceler. 0/100 sec.	Top. speed km/h	Ave. Fuel consp. l./100 km
97-02					
base	1.8/DOHC/130	front-M5	9.2	175	10.5
		front-A4	NA	NA	NA
FX/SE	2.0/DOHC/140	front-M5	8.7	185	10.8
		front-A4	9.5	180	11.3

PERFORMANCE

SPECIFICATIONS

Model 97-02	Wlb. mm	Lght. mm	Cb.wt kg	Brakes fr/rr	Steering type	Standard tires
cpe. 2dr. base	2474	4340	1156	dc/dr	pwr.r&p.	195/60R14
cpe. 2dr. FX/SE	2474	4340	1173	dc/dc	pwr.r&p.	195/55R15

PRICES

Model / version		1997	1998	1999	2000	2001	2002
cpe. 2dr. base	mini	7150	8400	10300	12100	13350	14600
	maxi	9450	10500	12100	13850	16500	17850
cpe. 2dr. FX	mini	8200	8700	11350			
	maxi	10500	10700	12100			
cpe. 2dr. SE	mini		9450	12400	14200	15450	16800
	maxi		11550	14200	16000	18600	20500

See page 7 to adapt these figures.

1999 HYUNDAI Tiburon

HYUNDAI   XG300-350

2002 HYUNDAI XG350

The XG300 became Hyundai's flagship in 2001. It is based on the Korean Dynasty and is equipped with a 3.0-liter V6 mated to a 5-speed automatic transmission. In 2002 the engine is a 3.5L and the car becomes the XG350.

PROS
• **The price/equipment ratio** is unbeatable for a car capable of competing directly against the likes of the Lexus ES 300 and Infiniti I30.
• **The technical content** and extensive equipment make the XG300 an excellent value, at least on paper.
• **The flattering presentation** lacks neither styling nor personality.
• **Performance** is honest as long as the vehicle is not carrying a full load, in which case the V6 seems to run out of breath somewhat.
• **The generous cabin** and extendable trunk provide roominess for up to five normally sized adults.
• **The careful finish** and quality materials set the XG300 apart from Hyundai's other more utilitarian models.
• **The many practical storage** spaces are efficiently laid out through the cabin.

CONS
• **The windshield wipers** are inefficient and too slow to provide safe visibility in pouring rain.
• **The hefty weight** and simplistic suspension combine to hinder performance in tight turns.
• **The cheap-looking instruments** are out of place and reveal their humble origins.
• **The compact spare tire** does not give the XG300 a very flattering look in the event of a puncture.

VERDICT
Hyundai has invested heavily in the affordable luxury-car market by offering a level of value that is sure to entice the competition's clientele.

RECALLS
None over this period.

RELIABILITY PROBLEMS

	1997	1998	1999	2000	2001	2002
Engine:						
Transmission:						
Suspension:						
Steering:						
Brakes:			Insufficient data			
Electricity:						
Body:						
Accessories:						
Fit/finish:						

POWERTRAIN   PERFORMANCE

Year	Type/ L/Camshaft/bhp	Drivetrain & gearbox	Acceler. 0/100 sec.	Top. speed km/h	Ave. Fuel consp. l./100 km
2001	V6/3.0/DOHC/192	front-A5	9.5	200	13.5
2002	V6/3.5/DOHC/194	front-A5	8.5	200	14.0

SPECIFICATIONS

Model 01-02	Wlb. mm	Lght. mm	Cb.wt kg	Brakes fr/rr	Steering type	Standard tires
sdn. 4dr.	2750	4864	1650	dc/ABS	pwr.r.&p.	205/65R15

PRICES

Model / version	1997	1998	1999	2000	2001	2002
XG300						
sdn. 4dr. GLS mini					21000	
maxi					24150	
XG350						
sdn. 4dr. GLS mini						23600
maxi						26800

See page 7 to adapt these figures.

2002 HYUNDAI XG350

INFINITI

G20

2000 INFINITI G20t

The G20 is a lavish compact car with a sporty side that was added to the luxury model range at Nissan in 1991, pulled out in 1997 and reintroduced in 1999 without a lot of major changes.

PROS

• **This solid and sturdy** car really holds to the road.

• **Sportscar handling** is enhanced by the sophisticated suspension and nonslip differential that makes for super wheel function, even on slippery roads.

• **Driving this baby** is a lot of fun, because it's so frisky and gutsy, also because you're comfortable behind the wheel and you have an adequate outward view; besides, steering is crisp and quick as a flash and the brakes have real bite.

• **Solid construction**, tight finish and nice-looking materials, but plain and simple overall design.

• **Longer wheel base**, overall length and height of the latest generation provide the driver and the passengers a lot more leg and elbow room.

• **Standard equipment** is very extensive and compares well with rival European counterparts.

CONS

• **There isn't much choice**, since there's only a single body style and a single engine model, and the different body design «t» model only comes equipped with a different suspension.

• **The rather bland look** of the car doesn't reflect its character, especially in regard to its luxury or performance level.

• **A small service network**, even in large cities, complicates things when it comes to upkeep and repairs.

• **The poorly calibrated** automatic transmission doesn't help you get the most out of the engine.

VERDICT

The G20 is solidly built, well equipped and reliable, but it just doesn't have the looks of its breed, but it's pleasant to drive and it's economical. Yet, depending on where one lives, its upkeep can be a hassle.

RELIABILITY PROBLEMS

	1997	1998	1999	2000	2001	2002
Engine:			-	-	-	-
Transmission:			X	-	-	-
Suspension:			X	X	-	-
Steering:			-	-	-	-
Brakes:			X	X	-	-
Electricity:			X	X	-	-
Body:			-	X	X	X
Accessories:			X	X	-	-
Fit/finish:			-	-	-	-

POWERTRAIN

Year	Type/ L/Camshaft/bhp	Drivetrain & gearbox	Acceler. 0/100 sec.	Top. speed km/h	Ave. Fuel consp. l./100 km
99-02	L4/2.0/DOHC/140	front-M5	9.0	205	10.5
		front-A4	9.6	200	10.3

PERFORMANCE

SPECIFICATIONS

Model	Wlb. mm	Lght. mm	Cb.wt kg	Brakes fr/rr	Steering type	Standard tires
99-02						
sdn. 4dr.	2600	4509	1332	dc/ABS	pwr.r&p.	195/65R15

PRICES

Model / version		1997	1998	1999	2000	2001	2002
sdn. 4dr.Touring	mini			18000	21000	23600	
	maxi			21000	23600	26250	
sdn. 4dr. Luxury	mini			17000	19400	21500	24700
	maxi			19950	22000	24700	26800
sdn. 4dr. Sport	mini						25200
	maxi						28350

See page 7 to adapt these figures.

2000 INFINITI G20t

2001 INFINITI I30

Derived from the Maxima, the I30 was launched in 1996 powered by a 3.0L V6 engine. It was refreshed in 2002 and replaced in 2002 by the I35 with a 3.5L engine.

PROS

• **Its unique** classic look is really very different from the Maxima design.

• **Reliability** is topnotch because of build quality, tight finish and top-quality components.

• **Engines** are fairly powerful and economical, but less spirited than the Maxima engine that benefits from a better power to weight ratio.

• **The "Multilink"** rear suspension enhances comfort, which is cushy smooth, as well as handling, that is already neutral.

• **Brakes** are terrific since stopping distances are below 40 m. Brakes are also stable and really keep a grip on things.

• **Steering is clean**, quick, well assisted and benefits from a good reduction ratio, but it tends to get light at high speeds.

• **Equipment** is more extensive than on the Maxima, for it includes standard heated front seats.

CONS

• **Seats aren't terribly** comfortable, because they're firmly upholstered and their sunken-in shape doesn't make for good support.

• **The instrument panel** isn't too ergonomic and external rearview mirrors are too small.

• **Trunk size** is fair to middling and the only access from the cabin is the ski slot.

• **Things to consider**: no shifter position indicator on the instrument panel and poor rear windshield wipers and defroster.

• **There are no vents** in the rear seat area, which is often the case on cars of this caliber.

VERDICT

Less pricy than the ES300, the I30 is less run-of-the-mill than the Maxima and is just as good a car.

RECALLS

97-98   Damaged alternator diode that could cause the melting of the plastic housing and a possible alternator fire.

RELIABILITY PROBLEMS

	1997	1998	1999	2000	2001	2002
Engine:	X	X	X	X	-	-
Transmission:	-	-	-	-	-	-
Suspension:	-	-	-	-	-	-
Steering:	-	-	-	-	-	-
Brakes:	X	X	X	X	X	-
Electricity:	X	X	X	X	-	-
Body:	-	-	-	-	-	-
Accessories:	X	X	-	X	X	-
Fit/finish:	-	-	-	-	-	-

POWERTRAIN

Year	Type/ L/Camshaft/bhp	Drivetrain & gearbox
97-01	V6/3.0/DOHC/190-227	front-A4
2002	V6/3.5/DOHC/255	front-A4

PERFORMANCE

	Acceler. 0/100 sec.	Top. speed km/h	Ave. Fuel consp. l./100 km
	9.0	200	11.5
	8.8	220	12.0

SPECIFICATIONS

Model 97-99	Wlb. mm	Lght. mm	Cb.wt kg	Brakes fr/rr	Steering type	Standard tires
sdn. 4dr. base	2700	4816	1429	dc/ABS	pwr.r&p.	205/65R15
sdn. 4dr. «t»	2700	4816	1463	dc/ABS	pwr.r&p.	215/55R16
00-01						
sdn. 4dr.	2750	4919	1515	dc/ABS	pwr.r&p.	215/55R16
sdn. 4dr. «t»	2750	4919	1530	dc/ABS	pwr.r&p.	225/50R17
2002						
sdn. 4dr.	2750	4920	1495	dc/ABS	pwr.r&p.	225/50R17

PRICES

Model / version		1997	1998	1999	2000	2001	2002
I30							
sdn. 4dr.	mini	12100	17000	19400			
	maxi	14700	19550	22600			
sdn. 4dr. Touring	mini	12000	18700	21000	24900	27800	
	maxi	16300	22150	24450	28350	31500	
sdn. 4dr. Luxury	mini				23800	26800	
	maxi				27300	30450	
I35							
sdn. 4dr. Sport	mini						32550
	maxi						36200
sdn. 4dr. Luxury	mini						31000
	maxi						34650

See page 7 to adapt these figures.

2001 INFINITI I35

1997 INFINITI J30

Since 1993, the Infiniti J30 has been the main rival of the Lexus GS300. It's a rear-wheel drive vehicle powered by a 3.0L V6 engine designed along the lines of the 300ZX engine.

PROS

• **Its seven-way adjustable** automatic transmission and nonslip differential by viscocoupling make for very impressive road stability and are proof positive that this is a high-tech car.

• **Handling** on the Touring model is more sporty and the car really hugs the road with its four-wheel steering system.

• **Construction quality** and fit and finish are simply perfect.

• **Top-notch comfort** is the result of the ingeniously designed suspension and seats, that are well-contoured, even if not too cushy.

• **The attractive**, ergonomic instrument panel includes all the necessary controls.

• **Equipment is lavish**, but some accessories found on European rivals in the same price range are nowhere to be seen.

CONS

• **Its ovoid design** goes out of style in no time.

• **Engine performance** are pretty wimpy and lack pizzazz.

• **Head and leg** room is very snug in the rear seats and the small doors don't help much when it comes to climbing aboard.

• **ABS system is pretty** rough and ready, causing really serious wheel lock and brakes lack gripping power.

• **Steering** is too light and sensitive because it's over-assisted.

• **The trunk** isn't too big and the opening is too high off the ground.

• **Things to consider**: no on-board computer, tiny rearview mirrors and no heated seats...

• **Low resale value** is a real trap for potential buyers.

VERDICT

The J30 is a mixed bag: it's reliable and luxurious, but it's not too practical all-round and it's really no fun to drive.

RECALLS

None over this period.

RELIABILITY PROBLEMS

	1997	1998	1999	2000	2001	2002
Engine:	-					
Transmission:	-					
Suspension:	-					
Steering:	-					
Brakes:	X					
Electricity:	X					
Body:	-					
Accessories:	X					
Fit/finish:	-					

POWERTRAIN

Year	Type/ L/Camshaft/bhp	Drivetrain & gearbox
1997	V6/3.0/DOHC/210	rear-A4

PERFORMANCE

Acceler. 0/100 sec.	Top. speed km/h	Ave. Fuel consp. l./100 km
8.7	210	12.0

SPECIFICATIONS

Model 1997	Wlb. mm	Lght. mm	Cb.wt kg	Brakes fr/rr	Steering type	Standard tires
sdn. 4dr.	2761	4859	1576	dc/ABS	pwr.r&p.	215/60R15
sdn. 4dr.Touring	2761	4859	1620	dc/ABS	pwr.r&p.	215/60R15

PRICES

Model / version		1997	1998	1999	2000	2001	2002
sdn. 4dr.	Mini	11000					
	maxi	14500					
sdn. 4dr. Touring	mini	12600					
	maxi	16300					

See page 7 to adapt these figures.

1997 INFINITI J30

2001 INFINITI Q45

The Q45 is the flagship of the Infiniti fleet. It was launched in 1990, 1997 and 2002. It is powered by V8 engines.

PROS

• **It's a very plush car** with a wonderfully quiet and spacious cabin, and the ride is really smooth, thanks to its suspension.

• **The silky smooth V8** engine and the technically advanced automatic transmission are a great combination, resulting in terrific performance levels.

• **Driving** this car is really safe because of brakes that have real bite, a sturdy frame and dual airbags.

• **Equipment** is lavish and includes all the gadgetry you'd normally expect on a car of this caliber.

• **Now that there's a real grille** up front, the car looks more stylish.

• **It's amazingly reliable**, given its sophisticated mechanical components, and should light the path for European rivals.

CONS

• **High depreciation** because it's a victim of pretty vicious competition in this market segment.

• **The cabin isn't as luxurious** as that of some rivals, for the imitation wood and synthetic leather trim rob it of all class.

• **Vehicle weight** and size make this car moves well-nigh impossible and really affect maneuverability and agility.

• **Some trim details** are in poor taste, like the coffin-style door handles or the crest up front that looks like a cowboy belt buckle on the earlier models...

VERDICT

The Infiniti has never won the hearts of those it was set out to court. Its low used car price may look like a bargain, but upkeep can be expensive when the car is no longer under warranty.

RECALLS

97-98 Ignition key can be removed when engine is turn off without placing the transmission shift lever in the "Park" position.

RELIABILITY PROBLEMS

	1997	1998	1999	2000	2001	2002
Engine:	X	X	-		-	-
Transmission:	-	X	-		-	-
Suspension:	-	-	-		-	-
Steering:	-	-	-		-	-
Brakes:	X	X	X		-	-
Electricity:	-	-	-		-	-
Body:	-	-	-		-	-
Accessories:	X	X	X		-	-
Fit/finish:	-	-	-		-	-

POWERTRAIN / PERFORMANCE

Year	Type/ L/Camshaft/bhp	Drivetrain & gearbox	Acceler. 0/100 sec.	Top. speed km/h	Ave. Fuel consp. l./100 km
97-01	V8/4.1/DOHC/266	rear-A4	8.0	220	13.4
2002	V8/4.5/DOHC/340	rear-A5	7.3	240	13.6

SPECIFICATIONS

Model	Wlb. mm	Lght. mm	Cb.wt kg	Brakes fr/rr	Steering type	Standard tires
97-01						
sdn. 4dr.	2830	5060	1765	dc/ABS	pwr.r&p.	215/50R17
2002						
sdn. 4dr.	2870	5069	1724	dc/ABS	pwr.r&p.	245/45R17

PRICES

Model / version		1997	1998	1999	2000	2001	2002
sdn. 4dr.	mini	20500	28150				
	maxi	25500	33000				
sdn. 4dr. Touring	mini	21500	30250	34650			
	maxi	26550	35200	39900			
sdn. 4dr. Anni.Ed.	mini					44100	
	maxi					49350	
sdn. 4dr. Luxury	mini						53550
	maxi						58800
sdn. 4dr. Premium	mini						55650
	maxi						61400

See page 7 to adapt these figures.

2002 INFINITI Q45

2001 INFINITI QX4

The QX4 is the near-twin, luxury version of the Nissan Pathfinder in the Infiniti model range.

PROS

• **The high-tech** all-wheel drive, akin to that of a race car, gives the QX4 a highly refined roadability and handling.

• **This lush** utility vehicle's super smooth handling derives from its sturdy body and clean front and rear powertrain guidance.

• **Brakes** are easy to apply as needed and they really dig in, so they can bring this 2.5-ton vehicle to a nice and straight stop.

• **Overall** ride comfort is due to the relatively supple suspensions, thick, cushy seats and effective soundproofing.

• **Build quality**, finish job and trim materials are super, putting this vehicle on a par with its most prestigious rivals.

• **The front end** design is quite fetching and distinguishes the QX4 from the Pathfinder.

CONS

• **Performance** are somewhat sluggish with such a wimpy engine that's unsuited to this type of vehicle; what's needed is the V8 that powers the Q45.

• **Insufficient** ground clearance really hampers this vehicle's off-the-road prowess, so much so that the chassis sometimes gets a scrape on rough terrain.

• **Snug legroom** in the rear seat sure doesn't help boarding and unboarding.

• **Gas consumption** is completely out of zinc with performance and is a good indication of the trouble this engine has to put the muscle on such a heavy vehicle.

• **The overall design** is rather blah and is too much like that of the Pathfinder.

VERDICT

The QX4 is a compact and quite lush vehicle that's pretty reasonably priced. Just what city slickers with an adventurous spirit are looking for.

RECALLS

2001   Defective rear door strut brackets must be replaced.
Ignition lock assembly will be inspected and connecting pins replaced if necessary.

RELIABILITY PROBLEMS

	1997	1998	1999	2000	2001	2002
Engine:	-	-	X	X	-	-
Transmission:	X	-	X	-	-	-
Suspension:	X	-	-	-	-	-
Steering:	-	-	-	-	-	-
Brakes:	-	X	X	-	-	-
Electricity:	X	X	X	X	X	-
Body:	X	X	X	X	-	-
Accessories:	-	X	X	-	X	X
Fit/finish:	X	-	-	X	-	-

POWERTRAIN

Year	Type/ L/Camshaft/bhp	Drivetrain & gearbox
97-02	V6/3.3/SOHC/168	all-A4

PERFORMANCE

Acceler. 0/100 sec.	Top. speed km/h	Ave. Fuel consp. l./100 km
11.2	175	15.7

SPECIFICATIONS

Model 97-02	Wlb. mm	Lght. mm	Cb.wt kg	Brakes fr/rr	Steering type	Standard tires
wgn. 4dr.	2700	4671	1939	dc/dr/ABS	pwr.r&p.	245/70R16

PRICES

Model / version		1997	1998	1999	2000	2001	2002
wgn. 4dr.	mini	19750	23000	25000	30450	36350	43000
	maxi	22000	25600	27800	33400	39900	47000
wgn. 4 dr. (1999.5)	mini			26000			
	maxi			28900			

See page 7 to adapt these figures.

2001 INFINITI QX4

ISUZU   Rodeo

2000 ISUZU Rodeo

Since its introduction back in 1980, the Rodeo has had its ups and downs consequently to its pricing. It is powered by 4 and 6-cylinder engines. Since 1998, the Rodeo has been radically transformed and the luxury version LSE has made its debut in '99.

PROS

• **The cabin interior** is spacious and rear seat access is convenient in spite of high ground clearance, the baggage compartment is quite big and can be extended by lowering the rear bench.

• **Passengers** will be comfortable in this vehicle, because the suspension is fairly flexible on the highway, seats are nicely contoured and noise level is quite low.

• **The 3.2L V6** engine is powerful enough to handle rough terrain or pull a trailer.

• **The cockpit** is great with the nicely located steering wheel, seat and pedals and the driver has good all-round visibility.

• **Very dependable** vehicle, as you'd expect, for construction is solid, finish is tight and trim and components are attractive.

• **A good note** for the new and improved rear hatch that gives a lower and easier access to the luggage compartment.

CONS

• **Fuel consumption** is very high because of excessive vehicle weight, high aerodynamic coefficient and especially because of a poor power to weight ratio.

• **Steering** is too light and suffers from a high reduction ratio, so driving is inaccurate and unpredictable in strong crosswinds and the large steer angle diameter really cripples maneuverability.

• **Seats** aren't too well upholstered and don't provide good lateral support.

• **Equipment** on the base model (S) is very basic indeed and yet this model still doesn't come with a lower price tag!

• **Its low resale** price isn't an asset, since it makes potential buyers really stop and think.

VERDICT

The Rodeo was very appealing at first, but it losts its charm when prices went sky-high and because the carmaker dragged its feet before making any modifications.

Rodeo   ISUZU

RECALLS

1998 The engine wire harness ground connection terminal may fracture due to improper crimping causing an engine stall.

2001 Dealers will inspect fuel return hose date code and replace it if required.

RELIABILITY PROBLEMS

	1997	1998	1999	2000	2001	2002
Engine:	X	-	-	-	-	-
Transmission:	-	X	X	-	-	-
Suspension:	X	X	X	X	X	-
Steering:	-	-	-	-	-	-
Brakes:	-	X	X	X	-	-
Electricity:	X	X	X	X	X	X
Body:	-	-	X	X	X	-
Accessories:	X	X	X	X	-	X
Fit/finish:	X	-	-	-	-	-

POWERTRAIN | PERFORMANCE

Year	Type/ L/Camshaft/bhp	Drivetrain & gearbox	Acceler. 0/100 sec.	Top. speed km/h	Ave. Fuel consp. l./100 km
97-02	V6/3.2/DOHC/175-205	rear/all-M5	9.0	170	14.4
		rear/all-A4	9.7	165	14.0

SPECIFICATIONS

Model 97-02	Wlb. mm	Lght. mm	Cb.wt kg	Brakes fr/rr	Steering type	Standard tires
wgn. 2dr. 4x2	2760	4690	1583	dc/dr	pwr.bal.	225/75R15
wgn. 2dr. 4x4(S)	2702	4658	1748	dc/ABS	pwr.r&p.	235/75R15
wgn. 2dr. 4x4	2702	4658	1782	dc/ABS	pwr.r&p.	245/70R16

PRICES

Model / version		1997	1998	1999	2000	2001	2002
wgn. 4dr. 4x4 S	mini	8700	11550	12400	14300	17000	21000
	maxi	11000	13450	15200	17200	20150	23300
wgn. 4dr. 4x4 SE	mini						23600
	maxi						26450
wgn. 4dr. 4x4 LS	mini	11550	14700	14900	17000	21700	25700
	maxi	13650	17000	18400	20350	24900	28550
wgn. 4dr. 4x4 LSE	mini			17300	21600	27000	30950
	Auto maxi			21000	25100	30150	33400

See page 7 to adapt these figures.

2000 ISUZU Rodeo

ISUZU   Trooper

2000 ISUZU Trooper

The Trooper was renewed in 1992, then it changed format, style, engine and price, which didn't make for good sales.

PROS

• **Its clean**, classic body design really never goes out of style and the asymmetrical dual-section rear doors are quite original.

• **It's really a multipurpose** vehicle with its almost minivan-style cabin interior and all-wheel drive that provides for safe driving on slippery roads.

• **Driving** is pleasant with such a comfortable driver's seat, adequate visibility and smooth, accurate controls.

• **Brakes** are more effective on a cold start than when the engine has been running.

• **Solidly built** and components are attractive and tightly fitted, but some colour shades of trim materials are rather weird.

• **The huge baggage** compartment is convertible and easy to use, and storage compartments are conveniently located throughout the cabin.

CONS

• **Soft suspension**, there's a lot of swing and sway, and if you don't keep an eye on things, you could lose control of the vehicle.

• **The 24-valve V6** engine is more powerful, but it still isn't as muscular as that of the competition.

• **Excessive vehicle** size and weight affect maneuverability, engine performance and fuel consumption.

• **Fuel consumption** is really pretty high, for the engine yield is never less than 16 L/100 km, whether you're driving in the city or over rough terrain.

• **Safety** isn't a sure thing on some models that aren't equipped with airbags.

VERDICT

The Trooper isn't a poor investment, but you have to be willing to put up with its limitations, and a small service network makes for snags when it comes to upkeep and besides, repairs are costly.

RECALLS

1997 Left frontal brake line built too close to the suspension's control arm.
Lock washer and screws missing for bearing adjustement.

1998 Lock nuts of the "Torque-On-Demand" 4WD transfer case might not be staked and that may cause the separation of the propeller shaft.

2001 Dealers will install a revised fuel hose.

RELIABILITY PROBLEMS

	1997	1998	1999	2000	2001	2002
Engine:	X	-	-	-	-	-
Transmission:	X	X	X	X	-	-
Suspension:	-	-	-	-	-	-
Steering:	-	-	-	-	-	-
Brakes:	X	X	X	X	X	-
Electricity:	X	-	X	X	X	-
Body:	-	-	-	-	-	-
Accessories:	-	X	X	X	X	X
Fit/finish:	-	-	-	-	-	-

POWERTRAIN   PERFORMANCE

Year	Type/ L/Camshaft/bhp	Drivetrain & gearbox	Acceler. 0/100 sec.	Top. speed km/h	Ave. Fuel consp. l./100 km
1997	V6/3.2/SOHC/175	rear/all-A4	13.5	160	14.5
98-02	V6/3.5/DOHC/215	rear/all-M5	9.0	180	16.1
		rear/all-A4	9.8	175	15.8

SPECIFICATIONS

Model 97-02	Wlb. mm	Lght. mm	Cb.wt kg	Brakes fr/rr	Steering type	Standard tires
wgn. 4dr. S	2760	4670	1991	dc/ABS	pwr.bal.	245/70R16
wgn. 4dr. LS	2760	4670	1995	dc/ABS	pwr.bal.	245/70R16
wgn. 4dr. LTD	2760	4670	2059	dc/ABS	pwr.bal.	245/70R16

PRICES

Model / version		1997	1998	1999	2000	2001	2002
wgn. 4dr. S	mini	6800	8900	13000	15000	19200	25000
	maxi	9450	11000	15750	17650	22700	27500
wgn. 4dr. LS	mini	10500	13350	17850	19750	24000	29400
	maxi	13100	15750	20150	22350	26250	32150
wgn. 4dr. LTD	mini	15200	17850	18700	22000	26250	32150
	maxi	17850	20500	21300	24800	28350	34000

See page 7 to adapt these figures.

1999 ISUZU Trooper

2000 JAGUAR S-Type

To ensure its presence in market segments that generate higher sales, Jaguar introduced the S-Type to go against the Mercedes-Benz E-Class and BMW 5 Series. It shares its platform and main mechanical components with the Lincoln LS.

PROS

• **The styling** is extremely good and modern. Its powerful lines inevitably conjure up images of the venerable Mark II.

• The S-Type integrates the most **recent technology**: voice-activated systems, Dynamic Stability Control and an adjustable suspension.

• **Driving** this car is a pleasure: the controls are smooth and this model behaves itself as a luxury sedan more than a sportscar.

• **The V6 engine** is already quite spirited, while the V8 cranks out even more invigorating performance.

• **The interior presentation** is typically British, with decorative leather and wood inlays that set Jaguar apart from its rivals.

• **Comfort** is achieved through well-padded seats and a smooth enough suspension, while the noise level is kept to a minimum.

CONS

• **The S-Type's passenger compartment** is not the roomiest, and rear-seat passengers had best not be too tall to fit comfortably in the space provided.

• **The trunk** lacks height and space given the fact that it also houses a full-size emergency spare and a large battery.

• **The V8 engine** is far from economical; it is not unusual to go beyond 18 L/100 km when driving at faster speeds and the level rarely drops below 16 L/100 km under normal conditions.

• **The designers** could have done a lot more in terms of practicality: the glove box is minuscule, the door pockets are too narrow and the rear-seat passengers have to get by with minimal amenities.

VERDICT

The S-Type is a car that is easy to get attached to, but it needs to mature before we are in a position of assessing its reliability and durability.

RECALLS

2001   Belt buckle assembly will be inspected and replaced if necessary.
The front suspension lower balljoint may not have been tightened properly. Its torque will be inspected, tightened or replaced.

RELIABILITY PROBLEMS

	1997	1998	1999	2000	2001	2002
Engine:				X	-	-
Transmission:				X	X	-
Suspension:				X	X	-
Steering:				-	-	-
Brakes:				-	-	-
Electricity:				X	X	X
Body:				X	X	-
Accessories:				X	X	X
Fit/finish:				-	-	-

POWERTRAIN

Year	Type/ L/Camshaft/bhp	Drivetrain & gearbox	Acceler. 0/100 sec.	Top. speed km/h	Ave. Fuel consp. l./100 km
00-02	V6/3.0/DOHC/240	rear-A5	8.5	220	13.0
	V8/4.0/DOHC/281	rear-A5	7.0	240	15.0

SPECIFICATIONS

Model 00-02	Wlb. mm	Lght. mm	Cb.wt kg	Brakes fr/rr	Steering type	Standard tires
sdn. 4dr. 3.0	2909	4860	1656	dc/ABS	pwr.r&p.	225/55R16
sdn. 4dr. 4.0	2909	4860	1710	dc/ABS	pwr.r&p.	225/55R16

PRICES

Model / version		1997	1998	1999	2000	2001	2002
sdn. 4dr. S-Type	mini				31400	40750	48300
3.0	maxi				36000	45700	53550
sdn. 4dr. S-Type	mini				39150	48100	54600
4.0	maxi				44800	53500	59850

See page 7 to adapt these figures.

2000 JAGUAR S-Type

2002 JAGUAR X-Type

The X-Type is Jaguar's entry-level model and enables the make to compete against highly popular models such as the Audi A4 and BMW 3 Series in the luxury sport market segment.

PROS

• **The attractive** base price allows less wealthy individuals to enter Jaguar showrooms through the front door, although the dealer network is limited.

• **The traditional styling** is this model's second advantage. Its round lines are complemented by touches of chrome, leather and wood.

• The all-wheel drive system is a definite advantage in Northern countries to ensure safe winter driving.

• **The 3.0-liter engine** provides a more inspired driving experience because it accelerates and passes more swiftly than the 2.5-liter.

• **The base engine** is quite fuel efficient, averaging between 13.0 and 14.0 L of super unleaded per 100 km.

• **The excellent road handling** is in tune with the British make's reputation. Several electronic aids keep track of trajectories and traction quality.

• **The efficient headlights** provide for hassle-free driving in poor weather conditions.

CONS

• **The tight cabin** corresponds to what you will find in a compact sedan and only individuals of small stature will feel comfortable in it.

• The automatic transmission is slow to react and the J-shaped gate is not very pleasant to use.

• **The 2.5-liter's performance** is adequate for highway driving but generates more noise than driving pleasure in sporty driving.

• **The slow windshield wipers** do not ensure adequate visibility in poor weather.

• **The hard original tires** hamper both ride comfort and handling.

• **The limited height** of the trunk makes it impossible to fit bulky items.

• **The high number of options** boost the attractive base price and there are too few dealers when it comes to maintenance.

VERDICT

Despite the lack of nobility of its mechanical components, the X-Type remains an attractive offering for those who privilege British opulence over the sobriety of German efficiency.

RECALLS

None over this period.

RELIABILITY PROBLEMS

	1997	1998	1999	2000	2001	2002
Engine:						-
Transmission:						-
Suspension:						-
Steering:						-
Brakes:			Insufficient data			-
Electricity:						-
Body:						-
Accessories:						-
Fit/finish:						-

POWERTRAIN   PERFORMANCE

Year	Type/ L/Camshaft/bhp	Drivetrain & gearbox	Acceler. 0/100 sec.	Top. speed km/h	Ave. Fuel consp. l./100 km
2002					
2.5	V6/2.5/DOHC/194	all-A5	9.5	190	13.0
3.0	V6/3.0/DOHC/231	all-A5	8.0	210	14.0

SPECIFICATIONS

Model 2002	Wlb. mm	Lght. mm	Cb.wt kg	Brakes fr/rr	Steering type	Standard tires
sdn. 4dr. 2.5	2710	4672	1555	dc/ABS	pwr.r&p.	205/55R16
sdn. 4dr. 3.0	2710	4672	1595	dc/ABS	pwr.r&p.	205/55R16

PRICES

Model / version		1997	1998	1999	2000	2001	2002
sdn. 4dr. 2.5	mini						33600
	maxi						39400
sdn. 4dr. 3.0	mini						40950
	maxi						45150

See page 7 to adapt these figures.

2002 JAGUAR X-Type

JAGUAR   XJ

2000 JAGUAR XJ8

The XJ6 hit the market in 1986 and was powered by a 3.6L 6-cylinder engine that was replaced by a 4.0L engine in '90. The V12 engine came out in 1994 and the XJR model was available the following year. In '99, two new V8 engines, including a turbo one, replaced the less "environmental-friendly" L6 and V12.

PROS

• **Its very classic look** and pristine design with leather and polished wood are hallmarks of its British origins.
• **With its cushy suspension** and superb soundproofing, it provides comfort that is hard to beat.
• **Top-notch materials**, perfect build craftsmanship and meticulous fit and finish.
• **Handling** is a dream because of the sophisticated suspension.
• **Steering is accurate**, but too over-assisted.
• **The well-calibrated** automatic transmission is great with its mixed shifting.
• **Fuel consumption** with the 4.0L engine is reasonable, considering vehicle weight and high aerodynamic coefficient.
• **A good outward view** and nicely arranged instrument panel make for pleasant driving.

CONS

• **Its high depreciation** that is the result of customer mistrust because of its poor reliability record and astronomical cost of upkeep.
• **The sky-high** fuel consumption of the XJR which can reach 20L/100km.
• **The driver's position** isn't perfect because the front seats don't provide much lumbar support.
• **Things to consider**: some complicated or inconveniently located controls, the noisy and awkward sliding roof and the air conditioner that is just impossible to adjust properly.

VERDICT

Before buying one of these dream cars, have it checked out by an expert and be very careful about making an investment that could cost you your shirt...

RECALLS

1998   Throttle cable may block throttle from opening completely. Potential fine cracks may be present between gear teeth inside the automatic transmission and may cause a "lockup".

RELIABILITY PROBLEMS

	1997	1998	1999	2000	2001	2002
Engine:	X	X	X	-	-	-
Transmission:	-	X	X	X	X	-
Suspension:	X	-	-	-	-	-
Steering:	-	-	-	-	-	-
Brakes:	X	X	X	X	X	X
Electricity:	X	X	X	X	X	X
Body:	-	X	X	-	-	-
Accessories:	X	X	X	X	X	X
Fit/finish:	-	-	-	-	-	-

POWERTRAIN

Year	Type/ L/Camshaft/bhp	Drivetrain & gearbox
97-98	L6/4.0/DOHC/223-290	rear-A4
	L6C/4.0/DOHC/322-370	rear-A4
99-02	V8/4.0/DOHC/290	rear-A5
	V8C/4.0/DOHC/370	rear-A5

PERFORMANCE

Acceler. 0/100 sec.	Top. speed km/h	Ave. Fuel consp. l./100 km
8.0	230	14.0
6.0	240	16.0
7.6	230	13.5
6.0	240	16.0

SPECIFICATIONS

Model 97-02	Wlb. mm	Lght. mm	Cb.wt kg	Brakes fr/rr	Steering type	Standard tires
sdn. 4dr. XJ6/8	2870	5024	1813	dc/ABS	pwr.r&p.	225/60R16
sdn. 4dr. VDP	2995	5149	1836	dc/ABS	pwr.r&p.	225/60R16
sdn. 4dr. XJR	2870	5024	1848	dc/ABS	pwr.r&p.	255/40R18
sdn. 4dr. V12	2870	5024	2005	dc/ABS	pwr.r&p.	225/60R16

PRICES

Model / version		1997	1998	1999	2000	2001	2002
sdn. 4dr. XJ6	mini	15750					
	maxi	21000					
sdn. 4dr. XJR	mini	22000	35200	40600	50400	51450	71900
	maxi	27800	40950	47250	56700	55900	77200
sdn. 4dr. XJ8	mini		26250	32350	38850	64600	59500
	maxi		32000	38500	45150	69600	64600
sdn. 4dr. VDP.	mini	19400	29800	37400	42500	58300	65600
	maxi	25200	35700	43600	48800	63500	70900
sdn. 4dr. VDP.S/C	mini			41500	52500	70350	75600
	maxi			47800	58800	75600	81400

See page 7 to adapt these figures.

2000 JAGUAR XJ8

JAGUAR   XK8

2000 JAGUAR XK8 convertible

The XK8, that replaced the XJS in 1997, is available as a 2+2 coupe and convertible in a single trim level. Both models are equipped with a 4L V8 engine that develops 290-hp and is driven by a 5-speed automatic with dual-mode shifter.

PROS

• **Driving pleasure** is due to the incredibly clean and crisp front and rear powertrain precision, the accurate steering and crisp brakes.

• **The V8 engine** is responsive and oozing with energy, besides being velvety smooth and discreet. It yields truly amazing output, thanks to a comfortable 5.74 kg/hp power to weight ratio.

• **Vehicle craftsmanship** has really come a long way, assembly is more well executed, finish details are very refined, but vehicle quality still isn't on a par with that of German or Japanese rivals. The lined convertible top is exquisitely made and its control mechanism is completely automatic.

•**Handling** is much better than that of the former XJS models. The XK8 exhibit great competence on wide curves and on slalom runs, even with their hefty weight and size.

• **Steering** is silky smooth, direct and precise, so controlling car path is very accurate both on the highway and in city traffic. The car maneuvers quite nicely in city snarls and tight spots.

CONS

• **The absence** of chrome that's so typical of a Jaguar; not a bit of the lovely shiny stuff to be seen either on the wheels, rearview mirrors, rear taillights or bumpers.

• **Outward view** is hampered by the high frame, thick windshield supports and there's a blind spot in rear view at quarterback because of the convertible hood, and the rear window is just too narrow.

• **The dashboard**, like the body itself, lacks accent details, the wooden panels on the dash are thick and massive and lack of ergonomics.

• **The rear seats** are useless, head and leg room are terribly tight and it would have been a neat idea to use this space for luggage storage.

• **To be improved upon**: no rear wiper on the coupe.

VERDICT

The XK8 is a very bright offspring of the former XJS, but it lacks of some nice chrome touches and inlaid work that are so characteristic of the British firm.

RECALLS

1997   The differential output shaft might detach itself.
1998   Throttle cable may block throttle from opening completely.
1999   Fine cracks may occur on the automatic transmission gears.

RELIABILITY PROBLEMS

	1997	1998	1999	2000	2001	2002
Engine:	X	X	X	-	-	-
Transmission:	X	-	X	X	X	-
Suspension:	X	X	-	-	-	-
Steering:	-	-	-	-	-	-
Brakes:	X	X	X	X	X	X
Electricity:	-	X	X	X	X	X
Body:	X	-	-	-	-	-
Accessories:	X	X	X	X	X	X
Fit/finish:	X	X	X	-	-	-

POWERTRAIN

Year	Type/ L/Camshaft/bhp	Drivetrain & gearbox
97-02	V8/4.0/DOHC/290	rear-A5
00-02	V8C/4.0/DOHC/370	rear-A5

PERFORMANCE

	Acceler. 0/100 sec.	Top. speed km/h	Ave. Fuel consp. l./100 km
	6.7	245	13.5
	6.0	240	16.0

SPECIFICATIONS

Model 97-02	Wlb. mm	Lght. mm	Cb.wt kg	Brakes fr/rr	Steering type	Standard tires
cpe. 2dr.	2588	4760	1666	dc/ABS	pwr.r&p.	245/50R17
con. 2dr.	2588	4760	1754	dc/ABS	pwr.r&p.	245/50R17
cpe. 2dr. XKR	2588	4760	1666	dc/ABS	pwr.r&p.	245/50R17
con. 2dr. XKR	2588	4760	1754	dc/ABS	pwr.r&p.	245/50R17

PRICES

Model / version		1997	1998	1999	2000	2001	2002
cpe. 2dr. XK8	mini	26500	33100	39700	43000	58800	76650
	maxi	31500	39500	46200	49400	63850	81900
con. 2dr. XK8	mini	35700	42850	50000	55100	70900	93450
	maxi	40900	49150	55900	61600	75600	98500
cpe. 2dr. XKR	mini				57750	72950	86800
	maxi				64000	78200	92200
con. 2dr. XKR	mini				66150	82950	96100
	maxi				72450	88000	101800

See page 7 to adapt these figures.

1999 JAGUAR XK8 coupe

1998 JEEP Cherokee

This sport utility dates back to 1984 as a 4x4 and as a 4x2 on the following year with a V6 engine which was replaced with an in-line 6-cylinder two years later.

PROS

• **Exceptional wheel function** (4X4) and the ability to get just about anywhere make the Cherokee a truly multipurpose vehicle.

• **It's a comfortable vehicle** with a long wheelbase, well-adjusted suspension and nice and quiet 6-cylinder engine.

• **The 2.5L engine** on the 4X2 is very economical when coupled with a manual transmission, as is the V6 engine achieving high torque that's more suited to an automatic.

• **Wide choice of models**: 2 or 4-door, 4X2 or 4X4, sport utility or luxury trim levels, 2 engine models, 2 transmissions and 3 modes on the 4X4.

CONS

• **Expensive upkeep** and high gas consumption.

• **Poor maneuverability** crippled by a large steer angle diameter and light, sensitive steering that is over-assisted.

• **The cabin interior** is quite snug every which way and rear seat access is awkward with the narrow doors.

• **Driving isn't too pleasant** with a steering column that is too long, poorly designed seats and tiny external rearview mirrors.

• **Fit and finish** as well as build quality aren't what they should be and mechanical components aren't always reliable.

VERDICT

You need to have these vehicles inspected, for many of them have taken a lot of abuse and repairs aren't cheap by any means. Avoid the very frustrating 4-cylinder engine. Overall, a good value for the price.

RECALLS

1997	Fuel level sending unit may degrade.
1998	Power brake booster is defective.
	Safety belt's anchors are defective.
1999	Defective spark plugs.
00-01	Dealers will modify the 4.0L engine exhaust manifold to eliminate the risk of fire.

Cherokee   JEEP

RELIABILITY PROBLEMS

	1997	1998	1999	2000	2001	2002
Engine:	X	X	X	X	-	
Transmission:	X	X	-	-	-	
Suspension:	-	-	X	X	X	
Steering:	-	X	X	-	-	
Brakes:	X	X	X	X	X	
Electricity:	X	X	X	X	-	
Body:	-	X	X	X	-	
Accessories:	X	X	X	X	X	
Fit/finish:	X	X	X	X	-	

POWERTRAIN / PERFORMANCE

Year	Type/ L/Camshaft/bhp	Drivetrain & gearbox	Acceler. 0/100 sec.	Top. speed km/h	Ave. Fuel consp. l./100 km
97-01	L4/2.5/OHV/121-125	rear/all-M4-M5	12.5	150	11.7
		rear/all-A3	13.5	145	13.1
	L6/4.0/OHV/177-190	rear/all-M5	9.0	180	13.3
		rear/all-A4	10.0	175	15.2

SPECIFICATIONS

Model 97-01	Wlb. mm	Lght. mm	Cb.wt kg	Brakes fr/rr	Steering type	Standard tires
wgn. 2dr. 4x2	2576	4254	1369	dc/dr	pwr.bal.	215/75R15
wgn. 4dr. 4x2	2576	4254	1431	dc/dr	pwr.bal.	225/70R15
wgn. 2dr. 4x4	2576	4254	1442	dc/dr	pwr.bal.	215/75R15
wgn. 4dr. 4x4	2576	4254	1521	dc/dr	pwr.bal.	225/75R15

PRICES

Model / version		1997	1998	1999	2000	2001	2002
4X2							
wgn. 2dr. SE	mini	6100	8400	11000			
	maxi	8400	10300	13100			
wgn. 2dr. Sport	mini.	6600	9450	12000	13650	15750	
	maxi	8900	11550	14700	15750	18900	
wgn. 4dr. SE	mini	7650	9000	12200			
	maxi	10000	11000	14200			
wgn. 4dr. Sport	mini	8600	10300	13100	16800	18900	
	maxi	11000	12400	15200	18900	22000	
wgn. 4dr. Country	mini	9650					
	maxi	12100					
4X4							
wgn. 2dr. SE	mini	7150	9650	12600			
	maxi	9450	11550	14700			
wgn. 2dr. Sport	mini	7650	10700	13650	15200	17300	
	maxi	10000	12800	16300	17300	20500	
wgn. 4dr. SE	mini	8700	10300	13650			
	maxi	11000	12700	15700			
wgn. 4dr. Sport	mini	9650	11650	14700	18400	20500	
	maxi	12100	13650	16800	20500	23600	
wgn. 4dr. Country	mini	10700					
	maxi	13100					
wgn. 4dr. Classic	mini		12100	15200	18600		
	maxi		14200	17300	20700		
wgn. 4dr. LTD	mini		14200	15750	18900	21600	
	maxi		15200	18400	21500	24700	

See page 7 to adapt these figures.

JEEP   Grand Cherokee

1999 JEEP Grand Cherokee

The Grand Cherokee, first sold in '92, came equipped with the 4.0L 6-cylinder Cherokee engine and in '93, the 5.2L V8 engine was also available, followed in '98 by a 5.9L. In 1999, Jeep has remodelled its flagship by introducing a new platform, a rounder body design and two new engines: a 4.0L L6 and a 4.7L V8.

PROS
• **The stylish** Grand Cherokee is stunning.
• **Driving comfort** is akin to that of a luxury sedan, for the suspension is super smooth, seats are thickly upholstered and soundproofing is really effective.
• **Its off-the-road** capabilities are awesome with such high ground clearance, short overhang and the spare tire stored in the baggage compartment.
• **The vehicle handles** really well, in spite of a bit of sensitivity to strong crosswinds.
• **Both engine displacements** are exceptionally muscular and really have get up and go, given vehicle size and weight.
• **The cabin interior** is attractive, yet isn't too classy with the imitation wood on the instrument panel and the rather synthetic-looking leather trim.

CONS
• **Very expensive** to buy, insure, drive, keep in good running order and repair.
• **Some components** aren't too reliable, which spoils this vehicle's image, for if it weren't for these snags, this vehicle would be a perfect specimen of its breed.
• **Steering** is over-assisted, so it's inaccurate and vague.
• **Seats** aren't firm enough and don't provide adequate support.
• **You can't store** as much in the baggage compartment because of the spare tire.
• **The instrument panel** isn't ergonomic for controls on the center console are out of the driver's reach.

VERDICT
The Grand Cherokee is popular and in great demand, but it's costly to run, especially if all you really want is to be in style...

RECALLS
1997	Inadvertent airbag deployment may occur.
	Defective fuel gauge indicator.
1998	Power brake booster is defective.
98-99	Defective rear outboard seat belt retractors assemblies.
	Wrong Vehicle Emission Control Information (VECI) label.
1999	Defective spark plugs.
99-00	The adjustable turning loop bolt of the shoulder belt will be replaced by a proper one.

2000	Some fuel tank may have a suspect vent tube welds. They will be inspected and replaced if necessary.
	Some steering gear unit may have missed the heat treat process. They will be inspected and replaced if necessary.
	Some passsenger-side airbag contains an incorrect inflator charge. The suspect module will be replaced.
2001	Steering gear assembly will be replaced on some vehicles.
00-02	Dealers will modify the 4.0L engine exhaust manifold to eliminate the risk of fire.
2002	Possible fuel leak and fire in case of a crash.
	Defective fuel tank on some vehicles.
	Reset of the instrumentation software.

RELIABILITY PROBLEMS

	1997	1998	1999	2000	2001	2002
Engine:	-	-	X	X	-	-
Transmission:	X	X	-	-	-	-
Suspension:	X	-	X	X	X	-
Steering:	X	X	X	-	-	-
Brakes:	X	X	X	X	X	X
Electricity:	X	X	X	X	-	-
Body:	X	X	X	X	X	X
Accessories:	X	X	X	X	X	X
Fit/finish:	X	X	X	-	-	-

POWERTRAIN

PERFORMANCE

Year	Type/ L/Camshaft/bhp	Drivetrain & gearbox	Acceler. 0/100 sec.	Top. speed km/h	Ave. Fuel consp. l./100 km
97-98	L6/4.0/OHV/185	rear/all-M5	9.0	190	15.0
		rear/all-A4	9.5	185	16.0
	V8/5.2/OHV/220	rear/all-A4	8.8	195	17.2
1998	V8/5.9/OHV/245	rear/all-A4	8.0	200	19.0
99-02	L6/4.0/OHV/195	rear/all-A4	9.5	190	15.0
	V8/4.7/SOHC/235	rear/all-A4	8.5	200	17.3

SPECIFICATIONS

Model 97-98	Wlb. mm	Lght. mm	Cb.wt kg	Brakes fr/rr	Steering type	Standard tires
Grand Cherokee						
wgn. 4dr. SE	3690	4501	1637	dc/dr/ABS	pwr.bal.	215/75R15
wgn. 4dr. Lar/LTD	3690	4501	1781	dc/dr/ABS	pwr.bal.	225/70R16
99-02						
wgn. 4dr. Laredo	2691	4610	1696	dc/ABS	pwr.bal.	225/75R16
wgn. 4dr. Limited	2691	4610	1730	dc/ABS	pwr.bal.	245/70R16

PRICES

Model / version		1997	1998	1999	2000	2001	2002
wgn. 4dr. Laredo	mini	10200	13450	21750	23850	27800	33400
	maxi	13100	15750	24150	26150	30450	36000
wgn. 4dr. LTD	mini	14800	19300	24900	25700	29900	35500
	maxi	17300	21750	27500	28450	32850	38300
wgn. 4dr. Orvis	mini	15750					
	maxi	18400					
wgn. 4dr. LTD 5.9	mini		21200				
	maxi		23600				
wgn. 4dr.Overland	mini						38300
	maxi						41500

See page 7 to adapt these figures.

2002 JEEP Liberty

The Jeep Liberty replaces the Cherokee which had a long and glorious career. It is completely redesigned and is driven by either a 2.4-liter L4 or 3.7-liter V6, both brand new.

PROS

• **The great styling** was inspired by Dakar studies and constitutes one of the Liberty's high points. Its cabin is oriented more toward luxury than utility.

• **The format** remains maneuverable despite increased dimensions over the Cherokee, especially in height.

• **The roominess** has been greatly improved in all directions. Thus, the Liberty is more accessible and more comfortable.

• **The off-road capabilities** remain a fundamental quality and well-studied design of Jeep vehicles.

• **The V6 engine** cranks out more energetic performance than the anemic 4-cylinder which is decent only with the manual gearbox.

• **The practicality** is aided by ample storage space and a cargo bay that is easy to transform to transport bulky items.

• **The very sure road handling** is closer to that of a passenger car than a utility vehicle.

CONS

• The Liberty's **less attractive pricing** will prevent it from enjoying the same success as its predecessor.

• **The 2.4-liter's performance** is inadequate given the Liberty's hefty weight.

• **The poor fuel economy** results from a high engine displacement and overall weight.

• **The springy steering** is just as unpleasant on road as it is off road but off-road maneuverability is quite adequate.

• **The mediocre brakes** produce longer than average emergency stopping distances and, without the optional ABS, braking stability is compromised.

• **The power window** switches are poorly placed on the center console and not very practical to use.

• **Certain stingy details** result in a less than generous standard equipment list.

VERDICT

Jeep made a mistake by replacing its Cherokee with the Liberty given its heavy weight and poor fuel economy. The Ford Escape and Mazda Tribute take full advantage of this costly error.

RECALLS

None over this period.

RELIABILITY PROBLEMS

	1997	1998	1999	2000	2001	2002
Engine:						-
Transmission:						-
Suspension:						-
Steering:						-
Brakes:		Insufficient data				-
Electricity:						-
Body:						-
Accessories:						-
Fit/finish:						-

POWERTRAIN

Year	Type/ L/Camshaft/bhp	Drivetrain & gearbox
2002		
Sport	L4/2.4/DOHC/150	rear/all-M5
Limited	V6/3.7/SOHC/210	rear/all-A4

PERFORMANCE

	Acceler. 0/100 sec.	Top. speed km/h	Ave. Fuel consp. l./100 km
	12.5	165	13.0
	10.0	180	15.0

SPECIFICATIONS

Model 2002	Wlb. mm	Lght. mm	Cb.wt kg	Brakes fr/rr	Steering type	Standard tires
wgn. 4dr. 2.5L	2649	4430	1735	dc/dc	pwr.r&p.	215/75R16
wagn. 4dr. 3.7L	2649	4430	1801	dc/dc	pwr.r&p.	235/70R16

PRICES

Model / version		1997	1998	1999	2000	2001	2002
wgn. 4dr.Sport	mini						25200
	maxi						27800
wgn. 4dr.Ltd	mini						27300
	maxi						30100
wgn. 4dr.Renegade	mini						27800
	maxi						30450

See page 7 to adapt these figures.

2002 JEEP Liberty

JEEP   TJ

2001 JEEP TJ

This all-terrain vehicle was redesigned in '86 and was equipped with Cherokee mechanical features, renamed the YJ in Canada, and powered by a 2.5L 4-cylinder or 4.0L 6-cylinder in-line engine.

PROS
• **Its neat-looking** body design is a real winner.
• **Its off-road capabilities** are really awesome when it's equipped with the right tires.
• **Steering** is crisp and smooth, but it's still a bit too sensitive because over-assisted, and you have to keep an eye on it.
• **Brakes** are oversensitive and difficult to gauge with the optional ABS.

CONS
• **Road stability** is still iffy even with the longer wheel base and last designed suspension.
• **Sudden stops** are hazardous, for they're very unstable even with ABS...
• **You're in for a pretty rough ride** with such a soft suspension, poorly designed cabin design and inadequate seats that finally never provided the proper support, even after its '97 face-lift.
• **Off-road maneuverability** is really crippled by the large steer angle diameter, vehicle width and really vulnerable front fenders.
• **Convenience** just isn't a priority on this vehicle, for there's next to no storage space, either inside the cabin or in the baggage compartment, boarding is awkward and opening or lowering the convertible top is a nightmare.
• **Poor fit** and finish and pretty basic trim materials that just don't jive with the hefty price tag.
• **It's an expensive** vehicle for what you don't get for your money, gas consumption is high and repairs cost a mint.
• **Things to consider**: uncomfortable cockpit, limited visibility with the convertible top, poorly shaped external rearview mirrors and tiny windshield wipers.

VERDICT
The Jeep is popular because of its spirited adventurous look. This would explain the fact that it sells so much in spite of its hazardous behaviour, its lack of comfort and its impractical side.

RECALLS
1997   Inadvertent airbag deployment may occur.
97-98   Driver side airbag may become inoperative.
1998   Safety belt's anchors are defective.
            Power brake booster is defective.
1999   Defective spark plugs.
            Instrument wiring ground attachment screws may loosen.

2001	The driver seat belt retractor assembly will be replaced with a new constant force retractor.
00-02	Dealers will modify the 4.0L engine exhaust manifold to eliminate the risk of fire.
01-02	Dealers will install a new ignition switch on some vehicles.

RELIABILITY PROBLEMS

	1997	1998	1999	2000	2001	2002
Engine:	X	X	X	X	-	-
Transmission:	X	X	X	-	-	-
Suspension:	X	-	-	X	X	-
Steering:	X	X	X	-	-	-
Brakes:	X	X	X	-	-	-
Electricity:	X	X	X	X	X	X
Body:	-	X	X	X	-	-
Accessories:	X	X	X	X	-	X
Fit/finish:	X	X	X	X	-	-

POWERTRAIN   PERFORMANCE

Year	Type/ L/Camshaft/bhp	Drivetrain & gearbox	Acceler. 0/100 sec.	Top. speed km/h	Ave. Fuel consp. l./100 km
97-02	L4/2.5/OHV/117-120	rear/all-M5	13.5	140	13.1
		rear/all-A3	14.8	130	14.3
	L6/4.0/OHV/180-185	rear/all-M5	10.5	165	14.1
		rear/all-A3	11.2	160	15.3

SPECIFICATIONS

Model	Wlb. mm	Lght. mm	Cb.wt kg	Brakes fr/rr	Steering type	Standard tires
TJ 97-02						
con. 2dr.SE	2373	3886	1505	dc/dr	pwr.bal.	205/75R15
con. 2dr.Sport	2373	3886	1559	dc/dr	pwr.bal.	215/75R15
con. 2dr.Sahara	2373	3886	1570	dc/dr	pwr.bal.	225/75R15

PRICES

Model / version		1997	1998	1999	2000	2001	2002
con. 2dr. SE	mini	10700	13850	15750	18400	19950	22000
	maxi	13100	15750	18400	19950	22000	24150
con. 2dr.Sahara	mini	14200	17850	19400	21500	23600	27700
	maxi	16500	19850	22000	24150	25700	28150
con. 2dr. Sport	mini	12100	15700	17750	20500	22000	24150
	maxi	15200	17850	20150	22600	24150	26250

See page 7 to adapt these figures.

2000 JEEP TJ

KIA   Magentis

2002 KIA Magentis

For the time being, the Magentis is Kia's high-end luxury sedan. It shares its platform with the Hyundai Sonata, its South Korean competitor.

PROS

• **The advantageous** price/equipment ratio makes the Magentis a great deal.

• **The performance** of both engines is robust and gives these vehicles brisk acceleration and passing capabilities and improved driving pleasure.

• **The quality tires** fitted on the V6 model effectively contribute to road handling.

• **The overall presentation** of the V6 model is flattering for an affordable luxury sedan.

• **The great ride comfort** results from the soft suspension, great front/rear seat contours and extensive soundproofing of the V6 model.

• **The incisive steering** is at once smooth and precise and the short turning radius authorizes good maneuverability.

• **The rigorous build quality** is almost on par with that of well-established Japanese manufacturers.

CONS

• **The brakes** are mediocre in emergency situations. Stopping distances are longer than average and the front wheels lock prematurely on the LX, which is deprived of ABS at the expense of braking stability.

• **The lack of traction control** is questionable on such a recent offering.

• **The overly supple suspension** generates high body roll that hampers the handling of 4-cylinder models whose tires are more modest.

• **The cabin presentation** of LX models is much more utility-grade than that of their V6 counterparts.

• **The overly assisted steering** is at once light and fuzzy as well as sensitive in crosswinds.

• **The Kias' major disadvantage** will remain poor resale value until these models have established their reliability and durability over the medium term.

VERDICT

In base trim, the Magentis is an affordable compact sedan whereas the SE can almost be considered a luxury offering.

RECALLS

None over this period.

RELIABILITY PROBLEMS

	1997	1998	1999	2000	2001	2002
Engine:						
Transmission:						
Suspension:						
Steering:						
Brakes:			Insufficient data			
Electricity:						
Body:						
Accessories:						
Fit/finish:						

POWERTRAIN

PERFORMANCE

Year	Type/ L/Camshaft/bhp	Drivetrain & gearbox	Acceler. 0/100 sec.	Top. speed km/h	Ave. Fuel consp. l./100 km
2002					
base	L4/2.4/DOHC/130	front-M5	NA		
		front-A4	11.0	175	11.0
V6	V6/2.7/DOHC/178	front-A4	9.5	200	12.0

SPECIFICATIONS

Model 2002	Wlb. mm	Lght. mm	Cb.wt kg	Brakes fr/rr	Steering type	Standard tires
sdn. 4dr. LX	2700	4722	1320	dc/dr	pwr.r&p.	195/70R14
sdn. 4dr. LX Spt	2700	4722	1330	dc/dr	pwr.r&p.	205/60R15
sdn. 4dr. LX V6	2700	4722	1400	dc/ABS	pwr.r&p.	205/60R15
sdn. 4dr. SE	2700	4722	1410	dc/ABS	pwr.r&p.	205/60R15

PRICES

Model/version		1997	1998	1999	2000	2001	2002
sdn. 4dr.LX	mini						15200
	maxi						18900
sdn. 4dr. V6	mini						18400
	maxi						22000
sdn. 4dr.Lx.sport	mini						19400
	maxi						23100
sdn. 4dr.Lx.V6 sport	mini						20500
	maxi						24150
sdn. 4dr.SE	mini						22600
	maxi						26800

See page 7 to adapt these figures.

2002 KIA Magentis

KIA   Rio

2001 KIA Rio

Since 2001, the Rio constitutes Kia's base model on the Canadian market. It is based on the former Ford Festiva and Aspire models, that used to be built by this Korean auto maker.

PROS
• **The price/equipment ratio** is competitive. The RS and LS models are well-equipped and offer good value.
• **The brakes** are powerful, stable and easy to gauge even without ABS. However, they produce longer-than-average stopping distances.
• **The powerful headlights** and windshield wipers produce safe driving conditions even in the worst of weather.
• **Handling** is safe and predictable despite the simplistic technical solutions used for the suspension systems.
• **The cabin is roomy**, and the trunk offers a very respectable minimum in terms of space and access.
• **The quality** of the construction and finish are remarkable, approaching the standards set by the Japanese.
• **The presentation** is pleasing to the eye both inside and out. There is an obvious attention to esthetics and the materials look quite honestly good.

CONS
• **The 1.5-liter engine** cranks out timid performance levels. Its weight-to-power ratio works to its disadvantage, but the manual transmission nevertheless makes the most out of what's available.
• **The cabin** exudes a strong chemical smell when the car is new that persists for a long time.
• **The mediocre tires** do not provide very good grip on slippery surfaces and they are also quite noisy.
• **The inadequate soundproofing** results in a high noise level, punctuated by a symphony of engine, road and wind noise beyond 100 kph.
• **The weak shocks** combined with the soft springs and ample wheel travel make the car jumpy over undulated pavement.
• **The narrow trunk** opening makes it impossible to fit anything large.

VERDICT
The Rio is a good means of economical transportation. Most of its drawbacks could be easily corrected. However, its long-term reliability has yet to be demonstrated.

RECALLS
None over this period.

Rio KIA

RELIABILITY PROBLEMS

	1997	1998	1999	2000	2001	2002
Engine:						
Transmission:						
Suspension:						
Steering:						
Brakes:			Insufficient data			
Electricity:						
Body:						
Accessories:						
Fit/finish:						

POWERTRAIN   PERFORMANCE

Year	Type/ L/Camshaft/bhp	Drivetrain & gearbox	Acceler. 0/100 sec.	Top. speed km/h	Ave. Fuel consp. l./100 km
01-02	L4/1.5/SOHC/96	front-M5	12.4	165	8.8
		front-A4	13.5	160	9.2

SPECIFICATIONS

Model 01-02	Wlb. mm	Lght. mm	Cb.wt kg	Brakes fr/rr	Steering type	Standard tires
sdn. 4dr. base	2410	4215	944	dc/dr	r.&p.	175/70R13
sdn. 4dr. RS/LS	2410	4215	944	dc/dr	pwr.r.&p.	175/70R13
wag. 4dr. RX-V	2410	4215	1021	dc/dr	pwr.r.&p.	175/65R14

PRICES

Model / version		1997	1998	1999	2000	2001	2002
sdn. 4dr. 5 speed	mini					7000	9450
	maxi					9650	11550
sdn. 4dr. RS	mini					8100	11000
	maxi					10200	13450
sdn. 4dr. LS	mini					9150	
	maxi					11250	
wgn. 4dr. RX-V	mini						11350
	maxi						12100
wgn. 4dr.RX-V Sport	mini						12100
	maxi						14200

See page 7 to adapt these figures.

2002 KIA Rio RX-V

KIA   Sedona

2002 KIA Sedona

The Sedona is the only South Korean minivan sold on the Canadian market. This midsize offering is powered by a 3.5-liter V6.

PROS

• **The driving pleasure** of this medium-wheelbase model results from the performance of its large-displacement V6.

• **The dashboard** is well presented and ergonomic. Its shift lever is housed in a carriage like certain European vehicles.

• **The seriousness** of the build quality is reflected by tight assembly tolerances and the hefty overall weight resulting from the addition of numerous reinforcements.

• **The finish** is polished despite certain plastics that look utility-grade.

• The powerful headlights are a rare feature on this type of vehicle.

CONS

• **The poor fuel economy** is the price to pay for the high weight and above-average performance capabilities.

• **The high weight** results from the rigidified body to meet current safety and handling standards.

• **The standard tires** are of mediocre quality.

• **The lack** of rear-wheel disc brakes and traction control partially explain the attractive pricing of these vehicles.

• **The cabin presentation** is bland and certain trim materials look dull despite the use of simulated woodgrain in the De Luxe version.

• **The slow windshield wipers** are not conducive to worry-free driving in bad weather.

• **The average maneuverability** results for the most part from the wide turning circle whereas the steering is vague on center.

VERDICT

The Sedona competes against a host of models already on the market, most of which are of North American origin. Its advantages are rigorous build quality and engine performance, at the expense however of fuel economy.

RECALLS

None over this period.

RELIABILITY PROBLEMS

	1997	1998	1999	2000	2001	2002
Engine:						
Transmission:						
Suspension:						
Steering:						
Brakes:		Insufficient data				
Electricity:						
Body:						
Accessories:						
Fit/finish:						

POWERTRAIN

Year	Type/ L/Camshaft/bhp	Drivetrain & gearbox
2002		
base	V6/3.5/DOHC/195	avant-A5

PERFORMANCE

Acceler. 0/100 sec.	Top. speed km/h	Ave. Fuel consp. l/100 km
10.0	180	16.0

SPECIFICATIONS

Model 2002	Wlb. mm	Lght. mm	Cb.wt kg	Brakes fr/rr	Steering type	Standard tires
wgn. 4dr. LX	2910	4930	2136	ds/dr	pwr.r&p.	215/70R15
wgn. 4dr. EX	2910	4930	2138	dc/dr/ABS	pwr.r&p.	215/70R15
wgn. 4dr. EXDL	2910	4930	2140	dc/dr/ABS	pwr.r&p.	215/70R15

PRICES

Model / version		1997	1998	1999	2000	2001	2002
wgn.4dr.EX	mini						16800
	maxi						19400
wgn.4dr.LX	mini						19400
	maxi						22000
wgn.4dr.LX Luxe	mini						23600
	maxi						25700

See page 7 to adapt these figures.

2002 KIA Sedona

KIA   Sephia/Spectra

2000 KIA Sephia

The arrival of a new Korean manufacturer to the Canadian market opens up opportunities for new entry-level models. The Sephia is a 4-door sedan powered by a 1.8-liter engine. It was replaced by the Spectra in 2002.

PROS

• **Price** is the Sephia's strongest attraction, with the LS version representing the best value.

• **The 1.8-liter engine** inherited from the Protegé ensures interesting acceleration and pick-up, even with the automatic transmission.

• **The Sephia is relatively economical** in terms of fuel consumption, even though it does travel fewer kilometers per tank than some of its more modern competitors.

• **Careful fit and finish**, but the fabrics and plastics used are a throwback to another era.

• **The cabin can seat five occupants**, including three in the rear seat depending on their size.

• **The interior** is conservative and logical, with a well-organized dashboard and sufficient storage space up front.

CONS

• **The design** does date back some ten years, which explains the questionable presentation and mushy suspension and steering systems.

• **Braking** is mediocre and stopping distances are long, but the brakes' biggest drawbacks are their lack of stability and wheels that lock in emergency situations.

• **Reliability** remains to be proven given the questionable quality of some components.

• **The Sephia is far from quiet**, and a lot of engine and road noise seeps into the cabin. Furthermore, the seats are thinly padded and the suspension is stiff.

• **The trunk** is smaller than average for this category, and its floor is some 15 cm (6 inches) lower than the bumper.

• **Depreciation** will be higher than average as long as the model's reputation has not been clearly established.

• **The lack of storage space** in the rear, very small sideview mirrors and the lack of a gear indicator with the automatic transmission are some other flaws.

VERDICT

The Sephia will have earned the right to its billing as a good, cost-effective mode of transportation when it proves its reliability and when the efficiency of its manufacturer is demonstrated beyond a shadow of a doubt.

RECALLS

2000   A bilingual adhesive label will be fixed in compliance of the regulations.

RELIABILITY PROBLEMS

	1997	1998	1999	2000	2001	2002
Engine:						
Transmission:						
Suspension:						
Steering:						
Brakes:			Insufficient data			
Electricity:						
Body:						
Accessories:						
Fit/finish:						

POWERTRAIN

Year	Type/ L/Camshaft/bhp	Drivetrain & gearbox	Acceler. 0/100 sec.	Top. speed km/h	Ave. Fuel consp. l./100 km
00-02	L4/1.8/DOHC/125	front-M5	11.5	170	11.5
		front-A4	12.8	165	12.0

PERFORMANCE

(see PERFORMANCE columns in POWERTRAIN table above)

SPECIFICATIONS

Model	Wlb. mm	Lght. mm	Cb.wt kg	Brakes fr/rr	Steering type	Standard tires
Sephia 00-01						
sdn. 4dr. base	2560	4430	1124	dc/dr	pwr.r&p.	185/65R14
sdn. 4dr. LS	2560	4430	1157	dc/dr	pwr.r&p.	185/65R14
Sephia 2002						
sdn. 4dr. base	2560	4510	1207	dc/dr	pwr.r&p.	185/65R14
sdn. 4dr. LS	2560	4510	1232	dc/dr	pwr.r&p.	185/65R14
sdn. 4dr.GX-S	2560	4510	1248	dc/dr	pwr.r&p.	185/65R14

PRICES

Model / version		1997	1998	1999	2000	2001	2002
sdn. 4dr.	mini				7900		
	maxi				10000		
sdn. 4dr. L	mini					9450	
	maxi					12100	
sdn. 4dr. LS	mini				8900	10500	
	maxi				11000	12600	
Spectra							
sdn. 4dr.	mini						12600
	maxi						15200
sdn. 4dr. GSX	mini						12800
	maxi						15200
sdn. 4dr. LS	mini						13350
	maxi						15750

See page 7 to adapt these figures.

2002 KIA Spectra

1999 KIA Sportage

The Sportage arrived at the same time as the Lada Niva bowed out and thus took over the title of the least expensive 4x4 sold on the market. It is a 4-door extended cab version powered by a 2.0-liter engine.

PROS

• **The competitive price** of this 4x4 makes it one of the least expensive vehicles in its class.

• **The sympathetic** styling and rounded lines please the eye.

• **Versatility** comes at a relatively economical price, and the Sportage is perfectly at home on both city and country roads.

• **There is enough room** on board for four adults and their luggage, and accessing the passenger and baggage compartments is relatively easy.

• **The soft suspension** is surprisingly comfortable and the seats are well-padded.

• **The brakes** are stable and resist well, but do not pack much bite.

• **The Sportage is remarkably maneuverable** in spite of its low-geared steering system.

• **For a vehicle sold at this price**, the Kia is consistent and provides good value.

• **Kudos** for the airbag designed to protect the driver's knees.

CONS

• **The poor weight/power ratio** translates into mediocre performance levels.

• **The brakes** are not very efficient, given the long distances required to make panic stops.

• **The recirculating ball** steering is a throwback to another era and is very mushy on centre.

• **The very high noise level** points to a serious lack of soundproofing.

• **The low ground clearance** limits off-road capabilities and makes the Sportage an all-road rather than all-terrain vehicle.

• **Oversights**: The spare tire hinders rear visibility, the hatch is hard to open in a hurry or in bad weather, and the windshield wipers are painfully slow.

VERDICT

The Sportage is by far the Kia model that offers the highest value for the moment, as long as it proves to be reliable.

RECALLS

None over this period.

RELIABILITY PROBLEMS

	1997	1998	1999	2000	2001	2002
Engine:						
Transmission:						
Suspension:						
Steering:						
Brakes:			Insufficient data			
Electricity:						
Body:						
Accessories:						
Fit/finish:						

POWERTRAIN

PERFORMANCE

Year	Type/ L/Camshaft/bhp	Drivetrain & gearbox	Acceler. 0/100 sec.	Top. speed km/h	Ave. Fuel consp. l./100 km
00-02	L4/2.0/DOHC/130	rr./all-M5	11.8	165	11.5
		rr.-all-A4	12.0	170	12.5

SPECIFICATIONS

Model 00-02	Wlb. mm	Lght. mm	Cb.wt kg	Brakes fr/rr	Steering type	Standard tires
wgn. 4dr. X	2649	4128	1520	dc/dr	pwr.ball	205/75R15
wgn. 4dr. EX	2649	4128	1540	dc/dr	pwr.ball	205/75R15

PRICES

Model / version		1997	1998	1999	2000	2001	2002
wgn. 4dr. X	mini				11850	14200	17300
	maxi				13650	16300	19400
wgn. 4dr. EX	mini				14900	17850	20500
	maxi				16800	19950	22800
wgn.4dr.LTD	mini					18600	
	maxi					20800	

See page 7 to adapt these figures.

2001 KIA Sportage

LADA   Niva

1997 LADA Niva

Imported from Russia since 1980, this all-terrain vehicle is powered by a 1.6L 4-cylinder engine. In 1995, it got a 1.7L fuel-injected engine and full-height rear hatch.

PROS

• **Its very competitive price** makes it the least expensive all-terrain vehicle on the market.

• **It's cleverly designed**, because it has effective Porsche suspension and transmission, it's the perfect shape and it's very practical, given the small vehicle size.

• **Its off-road capabilities** are even better than for Jeep vehicles because it's really much more maneuverable.

• **Convenience** has definitely not been overlooked, for the Niva provides comfortable seating for four, the trunk is adequate and there are enough storage compartments in the cabin.

• **It's sturdy and solidly built**, so it's a low-upkeep vehicle.

• **Handling** is safer compared to that of its rivals, thanks to permanent all-wheel drive, a well-adjusted suspension, relatively stable brakes without ABS and its good resistance to crosswinds. But tire quality is crucial, for it can definitely affect how it handles.

• **The 1.7L** fuel-injection engine performance are equivalent to those of the competition.

CONS

• **It's not the most comfortable** vehicle with its bouncy suspension, vinyl-trimmed seats with short back section (before '95) and shake, rattle and roll that assails passengers due to bad soundproofing.

• **Some poor-quality components**, slipshod build and fit and finish.

• **The bodywork is rust-prone** and the very poor-quality paint peels off prematurely.

• **The small gas tank** and high gas consumption limit road autonomy.

• **This old-design engine** is rough, noisy and shaky.

• **Brakes** are only fair to middling, but they're more stable than before.

VERDICT

The Niva is an excellent and sturdy vehicle, powerful and economic to use. That must be why they're so rare on the used car market.

RECALLS

None over this period.

RELIABILITY PROBLEMS

	1997	1998	1999	2000	2001	2002
Engine:	-	-				
Transmission:	-	-				
Suspension:	-	-				
Steering:	-	-				
Brakes:	X	X				
Electricity:	X	X				
Body:	X	X				
Accessories:	X	X				
Fit/finish:	X	X				

POWERTRAIN

Year	Type/ L/Camshaft/bhp	Drivetrain & gearbox
97-98	L4/1.7/SOHC/80	all-M5

PERFORMANCE

Acceler. 0/100 sec.	Top. speed km/h	Ave. Fuel consp. l./100 km
15.0	140	11.0

SPECIFICATIONS

Model 97-98	Wlb. mm	Lght. mm	Cb.wt kg	Brakes fr/rr	Steering type	Standard tires
wgn. 2dr. base	2200	3720	1100	dc/dr	w&r.	175/80R16
wgn. 2dr. Cossack	2200	3720	1150	dc/dr	w&r.	195/75R15
wgn. 2dr. SE	2200	3720	1150	dc/dr	w&r.	175/80R16

PRICES

Model / version		1997	1998	1999	2000	2001	2002
wgn. 2dr. base	mini	1600	2600				
	maxi	3150	4200				
wgn. 2dr. Cossack	mini	2100	3150				
	maxi	3700	4700				
wgn. 2dr. SE	mini		4400				
	maxi		5800				

See page 7 to adapt these figures.

1997 LADA Niva Cossack

LADA   Samara

1997 LADA Samara Sagona

These compact cars hail back to 1986. They come in a 3-door sedan model equipped with a 1.3L engine, a 5-door sedan model with 1.5L engine since '89 and a 4-door as well as the Sagona since 1993.

PROS

• **These very affordable** cars are the least expensive models on the Canadian market.

• **Driving** is safe and sure because of good wheel travel, firm shock absorbers, stable brakes and clean, crisp steering in spite of a high reduction ratio. Yet good-quality tires are a must.

• **The 1.5L fuel-injected engine** (GM) who is more powerful and quite economical, allows pleasant driving.

• **The cabin** is roomy and well-designed, the trunk is practical and there are some nice items, such as adjustable headlights, front and rear windshield wipers and headlight wipers.

• **It's quite comfortable** for such a low price car, since there isn't much vibration because of good tires, effective shock absorbers and comfortable seats.

• **High ground clearance** allows for hassle-free driving on bumpy roads.

CONS

• **The body design** isn't quite in style these days and overall design is bland and basic.

• **Reliability** isn't guaranteed with such sloppy build quality, loose fit and finish and some components that are problematic.

• **The 1.3L engine** is wimpy and it drinks up as much gas as the 1.5L engine.

• **The shifter layout** is confusing and you can easily mix up reverse with first gear.

• **Seats are quite** straight and there's a lot of noise, which is a sure sign of inadequate soundproofing.

VERDICT

Used Samara's are more reliable than brand new models, which explains why there are so few of them on the used car market and why they're so cheap.

RECALLS

None over this period.

RELIABILITY PROBLEMS

	1997	1998	1999	2000	2001	2002
Engine:	X	X				
Transmission:	-	-				
Suspension:	-	-				
Steering:	-	-				
Brakes:	X	-				
Electricity:	X	X				
Body:	X	X				
Accessories:	X	X				
Fit/finish:	X	X				

POWERTRAIN

Year	Type/ L/Camshaft/bhp	Drivetrain & gearbox	Acceler. 0/100 sec.	Top. speed km/h	Ave. Fuel consp. l./100 km
97-98	L4/1.3/SOHC/65	front-M5	15.0	145	7.5
	L4/1.5/SOHC/67-79	front-M5	13.5	160	8.2

PERFORMANCE

SPECIFICATIONS

Model 97-98	Wlb. mm	Lght. mm	Cb.wt kg	Brakes fr/rr	Steering type	Standard tires
sdn. 3dr. 1.3L	2460	4006	900	dc/dr	r&p.	165/70R13
sdn. 3dr. 1.5L	2460	4006	930	dc/dr	r&p.	165/70R14
sdn. 4dr. 1.5L	2460	4210	975	dc/dr	r&p.	165/70R14
sdn. 5dr. 1.5L	2460	4115	950	dc/dr	r&p.	165/70R14

PRICES

Model / version		1997	1998	1999	2000	2001	2020
sdn. 3dr. 1.5L	mini	1300	1800				
	maxi	3050	3700				
sdn. 3dr. Sport	mini	1600	2100				
	maxi	3050	4200				
sdn. 4dr. 1.5L	mini	1600	2100				
	maxi	3150	4200				
sdn. 4dr. Sagona	mini	1900	2100				
	maxi	3550	4750				
sdn. 5dr. 1.5L	mini	1550	2100				
	maxi	3150	4200				

Note: Vehicles sold in 1998 were 1997 model year.

See page 7 to adapt these figures.

1997 LADA Samara

LEXUS   ES

2000 LEXUS ES 300

The ES 300 was first sold in '92 and replaced the Lexus entry-model ES 250. Like its predecessor, this car was also inspired by the Toyota Camry. Its last generation was introduced in 1997 while the performance of its V6 was brought up to 210-bhp in '99, at the same time of the VVT-I (Variable Valve Timing) unveiling.

PROS

• **Reliability** and durability are outstanding which makes it a great buy!

• **The cabin interior** is quite spacious and can hold five adults and the trunk can accommodate them adequately.

• **The suspension** is smooth, seats are nicely shaped and uphol-stered and there's low noise level at cruising speed.

• **Driving** is pleasant with such well-calibrated controls and power and engine performance are exceptional.

• **Equipment** is quite extensive and plush, yet not quite as refined as that of some European cars.

• **Construction** quality, fit and finish and trim materials are definitely topnotch, but the car is blah and lacks personality.

CONS

• **The body design** isn't distinctive enough to make it stand out from other Japanese counterparts.

• **Steering** is vague because it's over-assisted, which makes it light and sensitive.

• **The initial price** is too expensive compared to that of the Camry V6 that tended to be as effective and almost as luxurious.

VERDICT

The ES 300 has been really very popular and it's become a sort of prize horse in this very competitive and high demand car category.

RECALLS

1997   Brake booster vacuum hose might freeze.

2002   Dealers will inspect the front brake line and replace it if necessary.

Dealers will replace the driver's airbag module.

RELIABILITY PROBLEMS

	1997	1998	1999	2000	2001	2002
Engine:	X	-	-	-	-	-
Transmission:	X	-	-	-	-	-
Suspension:	-	-	X	-	-	-
Steering:	-	-	-	-	-	-
Brakes:	X	-	X	-	-	-
Electricity:	X	X	X	-	-	-
Body:	X	X	X	X	X	X
Accessories:	X	X	X	X	-	-
Fit/finish:	-	-	-	-	-	-

POWERTRAIN

Year	Type/ L/Camshaft/bhp	Drivetrain & gearbox
97-02	V6/3.0/DOHC/185-210	front-A4

PERFORMANCE

Acceler. 0/100 sec.	Top. speed km/h	Ave. Fuel consp. l./100 km
8.3	225	12.3

SPECIFICATIONS

Model	Wlb. mm	Lght. mm	Cb.wt kg	Brakes fr/rr	Steering type	Standard tires
97-02						
sdn. 4dr.	2670	4831	1532	dc/ABS	pwr.r&p.	206/65VR15

PRICES

Model / version		1997	1998	1999	2000	2001	2002
sdn. 4dr.	mini	16300	19950	24150	26250	29900	34650
	maxi	19950	24150	27300	29900	32550	38300

See page 7 to adapt these figures.

2000 LEXUS ES 300

LEXUS   GS

2000 LEXUS GS 400

Midway between the ES 300 and the LS 400, the Lexus GS 300 is a rear-wheel drive luxury sedan that was first sold in '93 and was renewed in 1998 where the 400's V8 was added to the 6-cylinder in-line engine of the 300.

PROS
• **Its look** is more stylish than that of the ES 300.
• **The engine purrs quietly**, controls work like a charm, the instrument panel is ergonomic, there's good visibility and the cockpit is comfy.
• **Performance** of the GS 400's V8 engine run alongside exotic models such as the BMW 540i.
• **You feel like** you're virtually being transported in a bubble with such top-notch shock absorbers, cushy seats and low noise and vibration.
• **Construction quality**, tight fit and finish and spiffy materials are what you've come to expect in a Toyota.
• **Safety is guaranteed** with the really rigid body, dual airbags and 4-disc brakes that come with standard ABS and anti-skid system.
• **The car is neutral**, even if the suspension is more geared to comfort and the GS models are quite frisky on curved roads.
• **The cabin interior** is nice and trim, but not as lavish as that of European rivals and the equipment is complete but there are no gadgets.

CONS
• **Resale value** of the 300 plummets because this car doesn't sell too well, either as a new or used car.
• **Engine performance** of the 300 are crippled by a definitely poor power to weight ratio, so driving is devoid of all zip and zoom.
• **The interior** isn't too roomy because only four passengers can be comfortably accommodated and the trunk capacity is limited.

VERDICT
Avoid this model because it isn't a good investment, unless of course, the price is a real steal...

RECALLS
1997   Inadequate lubrication of the front suspension lower ball joints. (GS 300)
1998   A new electronic command module must be installed. Defective speed sensor.

RELIABILITY PROBLEMS

	1997	1998	1999	2000	2001	2002
Engine:	X	X	X	-	-	-
Transmission:	-	-	-	-	-	-
Suspension:	X	X	X	-	-	-
Steering:	-	-	-	-	-	-
Brakes:	X	X	X	-	-	-
Electricity:	X	X	X	X	-	-
Body:	X	X	X	X	X	-
Accessories:	-	X	X	X	X	-
Fit/finish:	-	-	-	-	-	-

POWERTRAIN

Year	Type/ L/Camshaft/bhp	Drivetrain & gearbox
97-02	L6/3.0/DOHC/220-225	rear-A5
98-01	V8/4.0/DOHC/300	rear-A5
01-02	V8/4.3/DOHC/300	rear-A5

PERFORMANCE

Acceler. 0/100 sec.	Top. speed km/h	Ave. Fuel consp. l./100 km
8.0	220	12.1
6.8	240	13.7
6.5	240	12.9

SPECIFICATIONS

Model	Wlb. mm	Lght. mm	Cb.wt kg	Brakes fr/rr	Steering type	Standard tires
1997						
sdn. 4dr. 300	2779	4950	1660	dc/ABS	pwr.r&p.	215/60VR16
98-02						
sdn. 4dr. 300	2799	4800	1649	dc/ABS	pwr.r&p.	215/60VR16
sdn. 4dr. 400	2799	4800	1674	dc/ABS	pwr.r&p.	225/55VR16 235/45ZR17

PRICES

Model / version		1997	1998	1999	2000	2001	2002
sdn. 4dr. 300	mini	22000	26800	28900	32000	37300	43000
	maxi	23600	29900	32000	35700	41500	47250
sdn. 4dr. 400	mini		32550	35700	40900		
	maxi		36750	40400	45150		
sdn. 4dr. 430	mini					45150	48800
	maxi					48900	53550

See page 7 to adapt these figures.

2000 LEXUS GS 400

LEXUS   LS

1999 LEXUS LS 400

The LS 400, first available in 1991, is the jewel of the Lexus model range. It becomes the LS 430 in 2002 with the new 4.3L V8 engine.

PROS

• **The body design** is reminiscent of the lush Mercedes look, but the coupe is much more original and dashing, it's sporty but very classy.

• **The cabin** can comfortably seat five passengers, but the coupe can only accommodate four passengers. The thick seats provide topnotch support and noise and vibration are barely felt at all, which makes for a pretty plush ride.

• **The V8 engine** is very muscular and whoops quite a torque, yet it runs so smoothly that you have to look at the instrument gauges to be sure it's really running.

• **Handling** is great with the power traction control. Yet handling is cleaner on the coupe with its stiffer suspension.

• **Trim finish** and build quality are simply perfect, equipment is extensive and sophisticated and overall design is superb. Moreover, these cars are extremely reliable and durable.

CONS

• **The short cushion** on the rear bench has obviously been designed to provide more leg room.

• **The small trunk** volume compare to this car's format.

• **The rear suspension** on the sedan is too soft and produces quite a sway on tight curves.

• **A small service network** can make upkeep and repairs problematic.

• **The very slow** windshield wipers.

VERDICT

The lavish Lexus LS is equipped with both straightforward and sophisticated features. Prices have jumped over the last years, compared with German rivals, and it makes you really wonder if the carmaker is offering these products at a fair price.

RECALLS

1997 Magnetic switch of the starter motor must be replaced.
1998 A new electronic command module must be installed.

RELIABILITY PROBLEMS

	1997	1998	1999	2000	2001	2002
Engine:	X	-	-	X	-	-
Transmission:	-	X	X	-	-	-
Suspension:	X	-	X	X	X	-
Steering:	-	-	-	-	-	-
Brakes:	X	-	-	-	-	-
Electricity:	X	X	X	-	-	-
Body:	-	-	X	-	-	-
Accessories:	X	X	-	X	X	X
Fit/finish:	-	-	-	-	-	-

POWERTRAIN

Year	Type/ L/Camshaft/bhp	Drivetrain & gearbox
97-00	V8/4.0/DOHC/250-290	rear-A5
01-02	V8/4.3/DOHC/290	rear-A5

PERFORMANCE

	Acceler. 0/100 sec.	Top. speed km/h	Ave. Fuel consp. l./100 km
	7.2	230	12.7
	7.5	240	12.8

SPECIFICATIONS

Model	Wlb. mm	Lght. mm	Cb.wt kg	Brakes fr/rr	Steering type	Standard tires
LS 400 97-00						
sdn.4dr. LS400	2850	4996	1765	dc/ABS	pwr.r&p.	225/60R16
LS 430 01-02						
sdn. 4dr. LS430	2925	4995	1795	dc/ABS	pwr.r&p.	225/55R17

PRICES

Model / version		1997	1998	1999	2000	2001	2002
sdn. 4dr. LS400	mini	26250	32000	38300	45700		
	maxi	31500	37300	43000	50400		
sdn. 4dr. LS430	mini					58800	64000
	maxi					65600	71400

See page 7 to adapt these figures.

2001 LEXUS LS 430

2001 LEXUS LX 470

The LX 450 is a dressed-to-kill Land Cruiser introduced in 1996 and sporting a 4.5L L6 engine. It was renewed in 1998 as LX 470, sporting the 4.7L V8.

PROS

• **Impressive terrain** tackling capabilities and traction control make of the LX 450 a true off-roader.

• **The cabin** is quite versatile and can accommodate five to eight passengers depending on whether the optional bench is installed.

• **The cargo area** holds heaps of stuff, but loading luggage isn't a treat with the awkward rear hatch design and high door. The baggage compartment can be extended by folding the middle bench, but it's pretty skimpy with the third rear bench in there.

• **Getting aboard** is great with the running boards and handy handle-grips, but it's tough getting way back to the third bench.

• **The ride** is quite comfy, even with the two rigid-axle suspension, but even off-road bumps and ruts are a breeze with such good wheel travel. The suspension is soft as velvet on smooth highways.

• **Handling** is quite good with permanent all-wheel drive and with a more civilized suspension than the original Land Cruiser.

• **Engine response** is quite good, considering the 2,300 kg vehicle weight. Accelerations are zippier than pick-up, especially with a full load, but the big 6-cylinder engine has impressive torque, for standard trailering capacity is 2,250 kg.

• **The cockpit** is neat with the huge dashboard that houses most controls under a big visor. The driver is comfortable, but the seat doesn't offer much lateral support.

CONS

• **It's outrageously** priced and the greedy engine can guzzle up to 20 l/100 km on tough terrain.

• **Maneuverability** is not marvellous either in city traffic or out in the bush. This vehicle can be pretty clumsy at times.

• **Rear seat access** is no fun with those narrow doors and tight maneuvering room between the seats.

• **Steering** is smooth, but a high reduction ratio (3.4 turns) and large steer angle diameter make quick lane changes pretty hazardous.

VERDICT

The LX is like a Japanese-made Range Rover, meaning that adding to its purposeful side is reliability and durability.

RECALLS

98-99 Defective towing wire harness converter may cause the failure of the trailer and vehicle's rear lights.

RELIABILITY PROBLEMS

	1997	1998	1999	2000	2001	2002
Engine:	X	X	-	-	-	-
Transmission:	X	-	X	-	-	-
Suspension:	X	X	X	X	X	-
Steering:	-	-	-	-	-	-
Brakes:	X	X	-	X	X	-
Electricity:	-	X	X	X	-	-
Body:	-	X	X	X	-	-
Accessories:	X	X	X	X	X	-
Fit/finish:	X	-	-	-	-	-

POWERTRAIN

Year	Type/ L/Camshaft/bhp	Drivetrain & gearbox
97-98	L6/4.5/DOHC/212	rear/all-A4
99-02	V8/4.7/DOHC/230	rear/all-A4

PERFORMANCE

	Acceler. 0/100 sec.	Top. speed km/h	Ave. Fuel consp. l./100 km
	11.4	175	18.4
	10.5	175	18.4

SPECIFICATIONS

Model 97-98	Wlb. mm	Lght. mm	Cb.wt kg	Brakes fr/rr	Steering type	Standard tires
wgn. 4dr. 450	2850	4821	2255	dc/ABS	pwr.bal.	275/70R16
99-02						
wgn. 4dr. 470	2850	4890	2450	dc/ABS	pwr.r&p.	275/70R16

PRICES

Model / version		1997	1998	1999	2000	2001	2002
wgn. 4dr. 450	mini	29700					
	maxi	33600					
wgn. 4dr. 470	mini		37400	49350	55100	65100	70350
	maxi		41500	53000	58400	69100	74550

See page 7 to adapt these figures.

1999 LEXUS LX 470

1999 LEXUS RX 300

The RX 300 is a compact SUV derived from the Camry platform and it's powered by the Camry's 3.0L V6.

PROS

• **Such elegant style** is a definite plus in the horde of rather plain-looking vehicles of this type.

• **Performance** are more car-like than SUV-ilk, since you can go from 0 to 100 km/h in about 10 seconds.

• **The ride** on smooth roads is wonderful with such a velvety suspension and thickly upholstered seats make for fatigue-free trips.

• **The cargo hold** is easy to get to and can be easily extended, there's lots of storage space and the air conditioner works like a charm.

• **The overall quality** of this vehicle surpasses that of its main rivals since build craftsmanship, finish job and trim materials are beyond reproach.

CONS

• **The overly soft suspension**, hard tires and insufficient wheel travel limit the RX 300 to road travel since even on the highway there's quite a bit of sway, so you're in for some unpleasant demeanor.

• **Brakes** aren't terrific, not with sudden stops that stretch to kingdom come and wishy-washy follow-through, even with ABS.

• **Maneuverability** is less smooth than that of the bulky LX 470, due to a wide steer angle diameter and visibility hampered by thick B- and C-pillars.

• **The instrument panel** is overdone with its massive wood appliques and the screen that indicates ambient air readings (when there isn't a GPS system) is hard to decipher.

• **Noise interference** is high, a bit of a surprise for a vehicle of this breeding, and rear seat access is tricky with the narrow doors.

VERDICT

The RX 300 appeals to folks who'd like to own a 4X4, but who really don't need one...

RECALLS

1999   Defective automatic light control system that may not activate the headlights and the tail lights in low ambient light.

RELIABILITY PROBLEMS

	1997	1998	1999	2000	2001	2002
Engine:			-	-	-	-
Transmission:			-	-	-	-
Suspension:			-	-	-	-
Steering:			-	-	-	-
Brakes:			X	X	X	-
Electricity:			X	-	-	-
Body:			X	-	-	-
Accessories:			X	X	-	-
Fit/finish:			-	-	-	-

POWERTRAIN

Year	Type/ L/Camshaft/bhp	Drivetrain & gearbox
99-02	V6/3.0/DOHC/220	front/all-A4

PERFORMANCE

Acceler. 0/100 sec.	Top. speed km/h	Ave. Fuel consp. l./100 km
10.4	180	13.0

SPECIFICATIONS

Model 99-02	Wlb. mm	Lght. mm	Cb.wt kg	Brakes fr/rr	Steering type	Standard tires
wgn. 4dr.	2616	4575	1769	dc/ABS	pwr.r&p.	225/70R16

PRICES

Model / version		1997	1998	1999	2000	2001	2002
wgn. 4dr.	mini			31500	35700	39900	42520
	maxi			34650	38850	44600	47250

See page 7 to adapt these figures.

1999 LEXUS RX 300

2002 LEXUS SC 430

The SC was initially introduced as a coupe derived from the LS 400 sedan. In 2001, a coupe-convertible derived from the LS 430 was introduced with most of the latter's mechanical components.

PROS

• **The coupe-convertible** format has more than one advantage, namely to enable owners to drive it during a greater number of months throughout the year.

• **The extraordinary build** quality can easily be compared to that of German rivals with the added bonus of improved reliability.

• **The cabin presentation** is warm and refined thanks to the addition of fine leather and wood trim.

• **The discrete** yet efficient V8 engine cranks out spicy and smooth performance. Acceleration and passing times are lightning fast without the slightest racket.

• **The efficient tires** and headlights increase the driver's confidence in all weather conditions.

• **The excellent audio** system will meet the expectations of the most demanding audiophiles and it is very user-friendly.

• **The fuel consumption** is reasonable given the vehicle's weight and engine's displacement and rarely goes beyond 13.0 L of super unleaded per 100 km.

• **The ingeniously** designed articulated roof cleverly folds down into the trunk but does have the disadvantage of taking up precious luggage space.

CONS

• **The space** taken up by the useless rear seats could be more efficiently used if they were replaced by a luggage shelf, given the limited trunk capacity.

• **The rough ride** resulting from non-adjustable shock absorbers is disappointing in this price range.

• **The trunk space** is extremely limited when the top is folded down.

• **The handling** is delicate in rainy conditions, despite the use of dynamic control devices designed to ensure vehicle stability.

• **The windshield wipers** operate too slowly for a vehicle capable of such performance and will do nothing to reassure the driver in bad weather.

• The limited dealership network complicates maintenance and has a limiting effect on sales outside of large urban areas.

VERDICT

The SC 430 will interest those in search of a prestigious, practical and reliable coupe.

RECALLS

None over this period.

RELIABILITY PROBLEMS

	1997	1998	1999	2000	2001	2002
Engine:						
Transmission:						
Suspension:						
Steering:						
Brakes:		Insufficient data				
Electricity:						
Body:						
Accessories:						
Fit/finish:						

POWERTRAIN / PERFORMANCE

Year	Type/ L/Camshaft/bhp	Drivetrain & gearbox	Acceler. 0/100 sec.	Top. speed km/h	Ave. Fuel consp. l./100 km
97-00	V8/4.0/DOHC/250-290	rear-A5	7.2	230	12.7
2002	V8/4.3/DOHC/290	rear-A5	7.5	240	13.0

SPECIFICATIONS

Model	Wlb. mm	Lght. mm	Cb.wt kg	Brakes fr/rr	Steering type	Standard tires
1997						
cpe.2dr. SC400	2690	4890	1635	dc/ABS	pwr.r&p.	225/55R16
2002						
cpe.2dr. SC430	2620	4515	1742	dc/ABS	pwr.r&p.	245/40R18

PRICES

Model / version		1997	1998	1999	2000	2001	2002
cpe. 2dr. SC400	mini	30450					
	maxi	35700					
cpe. 2dr. SC430	mini						73500
	maxi						78750

See page 7 to adapt these figures.

2002 LEXUS SC 430

LINCOLN   Continental

1998 LINCOLN Continental

This luxury sedan became a front-wheel drive in 87, featuring a 3.8L V6 and a pneumatic suspension and was completely revamped in 95 with a 4.6L V8 and rear-wheel drive and then again in 1998.

PROS

• **Comfort** is excellent due to the air suspension, which makes even the roughest roads pleasant to drive on. The passenger compartment is noise-free.

• **Styling** is sober, in keeping with the tradition set by these prestige automobiles.

• **Steering** is precise, providing surprisingly good maneuvrability in spite of its low-gearing and a barely acceptable turning diameter.

• **Performance** of the V8 has enough power and torque to accelerate and pass safely.

• **Braking** is responsive and well-balanced, however it is a little difficult to control and the pedal should be approached with some caution.

• **Finishing** is rigorous and standard equipment is detailed.

CONS

• **The suspension** is too soft and causes left-to-right roll on curves and front-to-back rocking during acceleration and braking.

• **Seats** are spongy and don't provide enough support.

• **Steering** suffers from overgearing.

• **Interior design** is unworthy of a luxury car, there's a lot of plastic to be seen, the instrument panel is dull and the false inlaid wood looks dreadful.

VERDICT

A nice, well-behaved and conservative sedan, too American to compete effectively with its German cousins. With a V8 engine and a more international interior, things could change.

RECALLS

1998 Defective fuel rail may leak and in the presence of an ignition source, a fire could result.

2000 In some vehicles lap and shoulder belts have an incorrect pin.

Continental   LINCOLN

RELIABILITY PROBLEMS

	1997	1998	1999	2000	2001	2002
Engine:	X	X	X	X	X	-
Transmission:	X	X	-	-	-	-
Suspension:	X	-	X	-	-	-
Steering:	-	-	-	-	-	-
Brakes:	X	X	X	X	X	-
Electricity:	X	X	X	X	X	X
Body:	-	X	X	X	X	-
Accessories:	X	X	X	X	X	X
Fit/finish:	X	X	-	-	-	-

POWERTRAIN

Year	Type/ L/Camshaft/bhp	Drivetrain & gearbox
97-02	V8/4.6/DOHC/260-275	front-A4

PERFORMANCE

Acceler. 0/100 sec.	Top. speed km/h	Ave. Fuel consp. l./100 km
8.3	200	13.9

SPECIFICATIONS

Model	Wlb.	Lght.	Cb.wt	Brakes	Steering	Standard
1997						
sdn. 4dr.	2769	5240	1774	dc/ABS	pwr.r&p.	225/60R16
98-02						
sdn. 4dr.	2769	5296	1755	dc/ABS	pwr.r&p.	225/60R16

PRICES

Model / version		1997	1998	1999	2000	2001	2002
sdn. 4dr.	mini	10500	14500	19400	26200	27300	34650
	maxi	14700	18900	23600	30450	34100	38850
sdn. 4dr. DSS	mini						35700
	maxi						39900
sdn. 4dr. Luxe	mini						36750
	maxi						40950

See page 7 to adapt these figures.

1998 LINCOLN Continental

LINCOLN   LS

2000 LINCOLN LS

Before extending its market to the mid-size luxury niche, Lincoln created the LS to compete more aggressively against its Japanese and European rivals who have held a monopoly on this category since the dawn of the automotive era.

PROS

• **The original styling** leaves the beaten path and has character.
• **In terms of size**, the LS fits in between the Infiniti I30 and Lexus ES 300.
• **Ample comfort** is derived from the smooth suspension and well-padded seats that provide adequate lateral and lumbar support.
• **Both engines** produce adequate performance levels for this category.
• **The LS handles** with surprising assurance; it is well-balanced and has just enough bite to satisfy the Sportscar enthusiast.
• **The trunk** is large enough and can be extended into the cabin by folding down the rear 60/40 split bench.
• **The moisture-sensitive windshield wipers** do a good job and they position themselves automatically.

CONS

• **The interior presentation** is boring and was obviously inspired by the Lexus' lifeless centre console.
• **The materials** look cheap, and this is especially true of the fake wood inlays above the glove box.
• **The suspension** jumps a lot over poor road surfaces, which in turn affects the occupants' comfort.
• **Access** to the cabin is hindered by the narrow door openings, especially in the rear where the doors are not as long as in front.
• **Designers** could have done more in terms of practicality: storage spaces are ridiculously minuscule in front, while the back seat is practically devoid of any storage space at all.
• **The automatic transmission** makes its presence brutally known when changing gears.
• **It is impossible to adjust the front seat** while the vehicle is moving; there is simply not enough space to fit a hand in between the seat and the door.
• **The over-assisted steering** feels very light, which complicates certain maneuvres.

VERDICT

The Lincoln LS is the first Lincoln ever with an international flavour to it, which gives it an honest chance of being sold around the world.

RECALLS

2000 The output voltage of 9.6 volts the Daytime Running Lamps results in a brightness exceeding the requirements of the regulations. Dealers will install a revised EMF module.
2001 The front suspension lower ball joint may not have been tightened properly. It must be check, tightened or replaced.

RELIABILITY PROBLEMS

	1997	1998	1999	2000	2001	2002
Engine:				-	-	-
Transmission:				X	-	-
Suspension:				X	-	-
Steering:				-	-	-
Brakes:				-	-	-
Electricity:				X	X	X
Body:				X	-	-
Accessories:				X	X	-
Fit/finish:				X	-	-

POWERTRAIN

Year	Type/ L/Camshaft/bhp	Drivetrain & gearbox	Acceler. 0/100 sec.	Top. speed km/h	Ave. Fuel consp. l./100 km
00-02					
LS6	V6/3.0/DOHC/210	rear-M5	8.5	200	12.5
		rear-A5	9.0	190	13.2
LS8	V8/4.0/DOHC/252	rear-M5	8.0	210	14.0

SPECIFICATIONS

Model 00-02	Wlb. mm	Lght. mm	Cb.wt kg	Brakes fr/rr	Steering type	Standard tires
sdn. 4dr. LS6	2908	4952	1632	dcABS	pwr.r&p.	215/60HR16
sed. 4dr. LS8	2908	4952	1675	dc/ABS	pwr.r&p.	215/60HR16

PRICES

Model / version		1997	1998	1999	2000	2001	2002
sdn. 4dr. V6 SP	mini				21000	25700	32550
	maxi				25200	29900	36750
sdn. 4dr. V6 AT	mini				24150	27800	33600
	maxi				28350	34100	37800
sdn. 4dr. V8 At	mini				26250	29900	35700
	maxi				30450	34100	39900

See page 7 to adapt these figures.

2001 LINCOLN LS

LINCOLN   Mark VIII

1998 LINCOLN Mark VIII

The Mark VIII coupe replaced the venerable Mark VII in '93 and the engine model went from a 5.0L V8 to a more technically advanced 4.6L engine.

PROS

• **The Mark VIII 4.6L engine** is much more muscular than the former 5.0L, which was anyway quite sprightly.

• **There's more stable** handling with the stiff suspension and crisper steering on the LSC.

• **Comfort** in this hefty car is a sure thing because of the highly sophisticated suspension.

• **The Mark VIII** is a safer car because its body structure has been beefed up and because it comes equipped with standard dual airbags.

• **Cabin design** and rear seat access have definitely improved on the latest generation models.

• **These cars** are quite stunning and do not go unnoticed.

• **Brakes** are powerful and stable on sudden stops, given the vehicle weight.

CONS

• **Poor construction** quality, slipshod fit and finish and some chintzy trim materials aren't at all what you'd expect on this caliber car and, consequently, the cabin design isn't too great.

• **The base model Mark VIII** suspension is too soft and causes a lot of swing and sway and it doesn't handle bumps and such in a civilized fashion.

• **Roof supports** are too wide and obstruct rearward view at quarterback.

• **It's too bad the spare tire** is stored in the trunk, which cuts down on luggage capacity and inside the cabin, storage compartments are few and far between.

• **Rear seat access** on the Mark VIII is a real chore and the low roof makes long trips uncomfortable.

• **The instrument panel** on the Mark VIII is high and massive.

VERDICT

Sport utility vehicles have stolen the show, so sports coupes are no longer in as great demand, and the same applies to the used car market.

RECALLS

None over this period.

RELIABILITY PROBLEMS

	1997	1998	1999	2000	2001	2002
Engine:	X	X				
Transmission:	-	-				
Suspension:	X	-				
Steering:	-	-				
Brakes:	-	X				
Electricity:	-	X				
Body:	X	X				
Accessories:	X	X				
Fit/finish:	-	-				

POWERTRAIN

Year	Type/ L/Camshaft/bhp	Drivetrain & gearbox
97-98	V8/4.6/DOHC/280-290	rear-A4

PERFORMANCE

Acceler. 0/100 sec.	Top. speed km/h	Ave. Fuel consp. l./100 km
7.5	200	13.4

SPECIFICATIONS

Model 97-98	Wlb. mm	Lght. mm	Cb.wt kg	Brakes fr/rr	Steering type	Standard tires
cpe. 2dr. Mk VIII	2870	5255	1709	dc/ABS	pwr.r&p.	225/60R16
cpe. 2dr. LSC	2870	5265	1714	dc/ABS	pwr.r&p.	225/60R16

PRICES

Model / version		1997	1998	1999	2000	2001	2002
cpe. 2dr. Mk VIII	mini	10500	18900				
	maxi	15750	23100				
cpe. 2dr. LSC	mini	12600	21000				
	maxi	17300	25200				

See page 7 to adapt these figures.

1998 LINCOLN Mark VIII

1998 LINCOLN Navigator

The Navigator, the deluxe, top-of-the-line version of the Expedition, is animated by a standard 5.4L V8 which has seen its output being boosted to 300-bhp in '99.

PROS

• **Cabin size** is awesome since up to seven passengers can be accommodated with the three rows of seats.

• **The lavish interior** is equivalent to what Lincoln limos offer. The rear bucket seats make you feel like you're travelling inside a private jet.

• **General ride comfort** is a cut above that of other vehicles of this type, due to a well-honed suspension that's silky smooth, plush seat upholstery and super soundproofing.

• **Driving** is a dream with such a gutsy engine that yields zippy accelerations, albeit more impressive than on pick-up, for a vehicle that weighs in at nearly 3 tons when at full load capacity.

• **This bulky beast's** maneuverability is amazing, thanks to the steer angle diameter that's akin to that of a 4X4 compact...

• **The rear hatch** is really handy since it has a window that opens and rear seat passengers have loads of spacious spots to store stuff.

CONS

• **The Navigator** is a big brute of a vehicle, so it isn't a champion when it comes to getting around in city traffic and parking and such can be awkward.

• **Brakes** don't bite in as they should. Actually, only locomotive brakes could bring this heavyweight to a sudden stop...

• **Fuel bills** are high, especially for travel on rough terrain or when hauling a heavy trailer.

• **Getting aboard** is no picnic even with the running boards, since they're narrow and slippery.

• **The third seatbench** is tough to get to and is pretty snug, so it's really only suited to accommodate small children.

VERDICT

The Navigator is the all-round favorite with SUV customers. Sales have been a real surprise for everyone, even for the manufacturer, and resale value is currently a sure thing.

RECALLS

1999 Missing or partially installed retainer clip that holds the master cylinder pushrod to the brake pedal arm.
17-inch chrome steel wheels can separate from the vehicle due to insufficient wheel contact area with the hub and lack of lug nuts torque.

2000 The bolts of the trailer hitch assembly can become loose and the trailer hitch can potentialy separate from the vehicle.

RELIABILITY PROBLEMS

	1997	1998	1999	2000	2001	2002
Engine:		X	X	X	X	X
Transmission:		X	-	-	-	-
Suspension:		X	X	X	X	-
Steering:		X	-	-	-	-
Brakes:		X	X	-	-	-
Electricity:		X	X	X	X	-
Body:		-	-	X	X	X
Accessories:		X	X	X	X	-
Fit/finish:		X	X	-	-	-

POWERTRAIN

Year	Type/ L/Camshaft/bhp	Drivetrain & gearbox
98-02	V8/5.4/SOHC/230-300	rear-A4
		rear/all-A4

PERFORMANCE

	Acceler. 0/100 sec.	Top. speed km/h	Ave. Fuel consp. l./100 km
	10.5	175	17.0
	11.0	170	18.2

SPECIFICATIONS

Model 98-01	Wlb. mm	Lght. mm	Cb.wt kg	Brakes fr/rr	Steering type	Standard tires
wgn. 4dr. 4x2	3025	5202	NA	dc/ABS	pwr.bal.	245/75R16
wgn. 4dr. 4x4	3025	5202	2444	dc/ABS	pwr.bal.	245/75R16

PRICES

Model / version		1997	1998	1999	2000	2001	2002
wgn. 4dr. 4x2	mini		27300	30150	36750		
	maxi		31500	35200	39400		
wgn. 4dr. 4x4	mini		29000	32000	39850	42000	47250
	maxi		33100	36750	41500	46700	51650

See page 7 to adapt these figures.

1999 LINCOLN Navigator

LINCOLN   Town Car

2001 LINCOLN Town Car

This big rear-wheel drive sedan, powered by a V8 engine, was upgraded in 1990. In '98, when Cadillac pulled its counterparts off the market, it monopolized the limousine market segment.

PROS

• **Its prestigious look** has become a symbol of the American luxury car.

• **Highway driving** is a dream with such a smooth suspension that gently rocks you as you sit in the superbly quiet cabin.

• **The big and spacious** cabin comfortably seats six passengers and holds their luggage.

• **Handling** on the latest generation models is much better because of the suspension that benefits from electronic ride control, thus controlling sway and nose-dive.

• **Equipment** is plush and includes scads of power assists and a very powerful climate control system.

• **The 4.6L engine** is almost economical with a 14 L/100 km yield.

• **The sensational climate control**, sound system, power assists and headlights.

CONS

• **Handling** isn't the greatest with such excessive vehicle weight, overly long wheelbase and steering that suffers from too high a reduction ratio.

• **The soft suspension** can really jostle passengers when it hits road faults.

• **The trunk** with it's sinuous design makes it hard to take advantage of and the lack of space impairs on its usefulness.

• **Seats** are poorly designed and don't provide adequate support.

• **The instrument clusters** are simplistic and insufficient in number, and the only storage compartment is the tiny glove compartment.

VERDICT

The Town Car is the favorite vehicle of limousine service companies and elderly car buyers, who consider it to be the best built car of its kind...

RECALLS

97-99 Eventual cracking of the lower control arm ball joints. (Limo)

2000 Belt buckle assembly may not comply with standard and must be inspected and replaced if necessary.

Town Car   LINCOLN

RELIABILITY PROBLEMS

	1997	1998	1999	2000	2001	2002
Engine:	X	X	X	-	-	-
Transmission:	-	X	-	-	-	-
Suspension:	-	X	X	X	X	-
Steering:	-	-	-	-	-	-
Brakes:	X	X	X	X	X	-
Electricity:	X	X	X	X	X	X
Body:	X	-	-	X	-	-
Accessories:	X	X	X	X	X	X
Fit/finish:	X	X	X	-	-	-

POWERTRAIN

Year	Type/ L/Camshaft/bhp	Drivetrain & gearbox
97-02	V8/4.6/SOHC/190-235	rear-A4

PERFORMANCE

Acceler. 0/100 sec.	Top. speed km/h	Ave. Fuel consp. l./100 km
9.5	180	13.9

SPECIFICATIONS

Model 1997	Wlb. mm	Lght. mm	Cb.wt kg	Brakes fr/rr	Steering type	Standard tires
sdn. 4dr. Exec.	2982	5560	1828	dc/ABS	pwr.bal.	215/70R15
sdn. 4dr. Sign.	2982	5560	1837	dc/ABS	pwr.bal.	215/70R15
sdn. 4dr. Cartier	2982	5560	1847	dc/ABS	pwr.bal.	225/60R16
98-02						
sdn. 4dr. Exec.	2990	5469	1805	dc/ABS	pwr.bal.	225/60R16
sdn. 4dr. Sign.	2990	5469	1821	dc/ABS	pwr.bal.	225/60R16
sdn. 4dr. Cartier	2990	5469	1835	dc/ABS	pwr.bal.	225/70R16

PRICES

Model / version		1997	1998	1999	2000	2001	2002
sdn. 4dr. Executive	mini	10000	14500	19950	26250	31000	36750
	maxi	13650	18400	24150	30450	35200	40960
sdn. 4dr. Executive L	mini					32000	37800
	maxi					36200	42000
sdn. 4dr. Signature	mini	12600	17650	23100	28350	33100	38850
	maxi	16800	21500	27300	32550	37300	43000
sdn. 4dr. Designer	mini	13650	18700	24150	30450	34100	39900
	maxi	17850	23600	28350	34650	39400	43000
sdn. 4dr. Cartier L	mini					36200	42500
	maxi					40400	47250

See page 7 to adapt these figures.

2001 LINCOLN Town Car

2001 MAZDA Miata

Mazda had a bright idea when they launched the Miata convertible in 1989. In 1994, the 1.6L engine was replaced by the 1.8L engine that is much more spirited. In '99, its body style has dramatically changed for its headlights that are now part of the front grille.

PROS

• **Its design**, reminiscent of those legendary British Sportscars of the sixties, was a smashing success.

• **Handling** is a dream with such crisp, frisky engines, transmission and steering.

• **Engines really unleash** a lot of power and make for a thrilling ride, even if they seem to be going faster than they really are.

• **The soft top** and the optional hard top handle easily and are very waterproof.

• **The 1.8L engine** is more muscular and smoother and gas consumption isn't any greater than for the former 1.6L engine.

• **Running this car** is quite economical because it's reliable, durable and upkeep is pretty straightforward.

CONS

• **The price of the Miata** is climbing, especially in good weather when you have to cough up more cash to buy one that's in good shape. Don't forget that some replacement parts are expensive...

• **Its Spartan comfort** level won't discourage the young at heart.

• **Cabin and trunk space** are at a minimum, so if you're bulky or hulky or have a lot of luggage, this car isn't the one for you.

• **There aren't too many storage** compartments in the cabin and the dashboard reflects into the windshield.

• **Things to consider**: poor rearward visibility at quarterback with either the soft top or the hard top, external rearview mirrors located too far back and not power-assisted, poor defrosting on side windows in cold weather.

VERDICT

In spite of its more upper-crust European rivals, the Miata is still the best small convertible Sportscar around.

RECALLS

1997   Injector harness may be damaged and should be replaced.

RELIABILITY PROBLEMS

	1997	1998	1999	2000	2001	2002
Engine:	X		X	X	X	-
Transmission:	-		-	X	-	-
Suspension:	-		-	-	-	-
Steering:	-		-	-	-	-
Brakes:	X		X	X	-	-
Electricity:	X		X	-	-	-
Body:	-		X	X	-	-
Accessories:	X		X	X	X	X
Fit/finish:	X		-	-	-	-

POWERTRAIN

Year	Type/ L/Camshaft/bhp	Drivetrain & gearbox	Acceler. 0/100 sec.	Top. speed km/h	Ave. Fuel consp. l./100 km
1997	L4/1.8/DOHC/128-133	rear-M5	9.0	190	10.8
		rear-A4	10.4	180	10.8
99-02	L4/1.8/DOHC/140-142	rear-M5-M6	8.2	200	11.4
		rear-A4	9.5	185	10.6

PERFORMANCE

SPECIFICATIONS

Model 1997	Wlb. mm	Lght. mm	Cb.wt kg	Brakes fr/rr	Steering type	Standard tires
con. Soft top	2266	3948	1014	dc/dc	r&p.	185/60R14
con. Hard top	2266	3948	1070	dc/dc	pwr.r&p.	185/60R14
99-02						
con. base	2265	3945	1032	dc/dc	pwr.r&p.	185/60R14
con. leather	2265	3945	1035	dc/ABS	pwr.r&p.	205/45R16

PRICES

Model / version		1997	1998	1999	2000	2001	2002
con. 2dr.	mini	12400		16000	18900	21500	24150
	maxi	14700		18400	21000	23600	26800
con. 2dr. 10th Ann.	mini			22000			
	maxi			24150			
con. 2dr. SE	mini				23600		28900
	maxi				25700		31500
con. 3dr. 6 speed	mini					22600	25200
	maxi					24700	27800

See page 7 to adapt these figures.

2001 MAZDA Miata

MAZDA   Millenia

2001 MAZDA Millenia S

The Millenia is the ultimate, top-end model of the Mazda choice range. It's available in the base model, powered by a 2.5L V6 borrowed to the 626, or S models driven by a Miller cycle engine.

PROS
• **The classic and elegant** body design that is also aerodynamic.
• **Engine performance** with the Miller cycle engine are sensational, considering displacement and engine weight.
• **The suspension** on the base model is smoother than on the S model.
• **Seats** are well-designed and soundproofing is effective.
• **Handling** is good, so there isn't much body movement and steering is quick, crisp and benefits from a good reduction ratio.
• **Equipment** is more than complete, for the only options are leather trim seats and sunroof.
• **The unusually deep trunk** is huge, but it can't be extended because the rear bench doesn't fold down.

CONS
• **This is a pricy car**, insurance isn't cheap and gas consumption isn't really economical.
• **The 2.5L V6 engine** from the 626 model isn't too frisky, for it has to carry an extra 216 kg, which affects power to weight ratio.
• **Brakes** aren't powerful enough for such muscular engines, and stops are longer than average.
• **The front suspension** on the S model is stiff and is crippled by poor wheel travel.
• **The futuristic cabin** interior design doesn't quite jive with the classic body design.
• **Rear seats** are tight, there isn't much head room or leg room and a third passenger would be pretty uncomfortable (and unwelcome).
• **There really** isn't enough storage space in the cabin, for the glove compartment has been replaced by the center console compartment.

VERDICT
Only the later Millenias are recommended as used cars, as long as mileage is low, and it's a good idea to avoid the engine on the 626 because it's less pleasant to drive.

RECALLS
None over this period.

RELIABILITY PROBLEMS

	1997	1998	1999	2000	2001	2002
Engine:	X	X	X	-	-	-
Transmission:	-	-	-	-	-	-
Suspension:	X	X	X	X	-	-
Steering:	-	-	X	-	-	-
Brakes:	X	X	X	-	-	-
Electricity:	-	X	X	X	X	X
Body:	-	X	X	-	-	-
Accessories:	-	X	X	X	X	-
Fit/finish:	-	X	-	-	-	-

POWERTRAIN

Year	Type/ L/Camshaft/bhp	Drivetrain & gearbox
97-02	V6/2.5/DOHC/170	front-A4
	V6C/2.3/DOHC/210	front-A4

PERFORMANCE

	Acceler. 0/100 sec.	Top. speed km/h	Ave. Fuel consp. l./100 km
	10.2	200	12.2
	8.2	220	12.2

SPECIFICATIONS

Model 97-02	Wlb. mm	Lght. mm	Cb.wt kg	Brakes fr/rr	Steering type	Standard tires
sdn. 4dr. base	2750	4820	1470	dc/ABS	pwr.r&p.	215/55R16
sdn. 4dr. S/ED	2750	4820	1522	dc/ABS	pwr.r&p.	215/50R17

PRICES

Model / version		1997	1998	1999	2000	2001	2002
sdn. 4dr. base	mini	10500	13100	16300	20700		
	maxi	13650	15750	19100	23600		
sdn. 4dr. S	mini	11550	14500	17850		30450	31000
	maxi	14700	17300	20700		33600	34100
sdn. 4dr. Mill. Ed.	mini				22000		
	maxi				25200		

See page 7 to adapt these figures.

2001 MAZDA Millenia S

MAZDA   MPV rwd

1998 MAZDA MPV RWD

The Mazda MPV 2WD made its debut in 1988 and one year later, the all-wheel drive came out of the factory. They're powered until '95 by a 2.6L 4-cylinder engine or a 3.0L V8. The MPV has not been actively commercialized in 1999 because its expected front wheel-drive replacement with dual sliding doors only hit the market very late in the season and is considered a 2000 model.

PROS

• **Its body design** is more that of a station wagon than a sport utility vehicle. It's too bad the latest model design was ruined with all those weird add-ons.

• **The suspension** is smoother than that of the competition for it provides for handling akin to that of a car.

• **The cockpit** is well designed, the instrument panel is straightforward, visibility is great and the automatic shifter is easy to control.

• **Construction quality** explains the excessive weight and fit. The finish is meticulous, even if some trim components look rather plain.

• **Practical touches**: the fourth door on the latest models, the numerous storage compartments and the rear windows that can be lowered.

CONS

• **For winter driving**, the all-wheel drive model is safer than the less predictable rear-wheel drive model.

• **Brakes** don't have enough grip, for stops are too long and they aren't predictable without ABS.

• **Gas consumption** is sky-high, especially on the 4X4, especially given that engine performance aren't anything out of the ordinary.

• **The side door** doesn't slide open and takes up more room.

• **Maneuverability** is crippled by too high a reduction ratio and too big a steer angle diameter.

• **These cars** aren't too reliable and repairs can be quite pricy.

• **Seats are hard** and don't provide much support, the armrests aren't adjustable height-wise up front. The main and rear benches are hard to handle.

VERDICT

The MPV is more of a station wagon than a minivan and isn't the best used car to buy.

RECALLS

None over this period.

RELIABILITY PROBLEMS

	1997	1998	1999	2000	2001	2002
Engine:	X	X				
Transmission:	-	-				
Suspension:	X	-				
Steering:	X	-				
Brakes:	-	X				
Electricity:	X	X				
Body:	-	-				
Accessories:	-	-				
Fit/finish:	X	X				

POWERTRAIN

Year	Type/ L/Camshaft/bhp	Drivetrain & gearbox	Acceler. 0/100 sec.	Top. speed km/h	Ave. Fuel consp. l./100 km
97-98	V6/3.0/SOHC/150-155	rear-A4	11.0	170	14.7
		rear/all-A4	11.8	165	17.0

PERFORMANCE

SPECIFICATIONS

Model 97-98	Wlb. mm	Lght. mm	Cb.wt kg	Brakes fr/rr	Steering type	Standard tires
m.v. 4dr. base	2805	4660	1692	dc/ABS	pwr.r&p.	195/75R15
m.v. 4dr. LX	2805	4660	1719	dc/ABS	pwr.r&p.	215/65R15
m.v. 4dr. LX 4RM	2805	4660	1842	dc/ABS	pwr.r&p.	225/70R15

PRICES

Model / version		1997	1998	1999	2000	2001	2002
m.v. 4dr. 7 st. V6	mini	6700	8900				
	maxi	8900	10700				
m.v. 4dr. 7 st. LX	mini	8700	10900				
	maxi	11000	12800				
m.v. 4dr. 7 st. V6	mini	11550	13650				
LX 4WD	maxi	13000	15750				

See page 7 to adapt these figures.

1998 MAZDA MPV RWD

MAZDA MPV FWD

2000 MAZDA MPV

It took Mazda quite some time to replace its rear-wheel drive MPV with a front-wheel drive model. The last MPV is more modern and was first powered by a 2.5L V6 engine and by a 3.0L since 2002.

PROS

• **The styling** is exciting and in keeping with the philosophy recently adopted by Mazda.

• **Passenger room** has increased, the seats are roomy and passengers do not feel cramped.

• **Performance** are better with the 3.0L V6 developing 200-hp.

• **The dashboard** is simple, highly functional and its ergonomic design is remarkable, because all controls are within easy reach.

• **The seat organization** is very clever: the rear bench folds into the floor where it can be used as a storage bin. Also, the middle seats slide to the sides to form a bench and can be moved to the rear to nestle passengers under the hatch.

• **The ride** is pleasant thanks to the excellent position of the steering wheel, good visibility and the very practical handbrake.

• **The power windows** on the sliding doors are a rare feature in the minivan world.

CONS

• **The poor weight/power ratio** translates into inadequate performance levels with the 2.5L V6.

• **The firmly padded** and relatively flat seats are uncomfortable and offer very little in terms of support.

• **Access** to the cabin is hindered by front doors that do not open up wide enough and sliding doors that are too narrow.

• **The engine** consumes as much fuel as a larger V6.

• **The base model** takes the bare-bones approach, which may make it difficult to resell.

• **Flaws**: the high rear ratio, the impractical gear shift lever, the fixed hatch window and the minimal number of storage spaces available to middle-seat passengers.

VERDICT

The latest MPV is more universal than its predecessor, but its engine is marginal (2.5L) or and its seats are uncomfortable.

RECALLS

2000 The tire pressure information is incorrect on the label and the tires too. Both will be replaced on some vehicles.
On some vehicles the Powertrain Control Module will be reprogrammed.
The rear-door childproof locking doesn't work properly and will be modified.
The lower intake manifold doesn't match the fuel injectors and will be replaced.

RELIABILITY PROBLEMS

	1997	1998	1999	2000	2001	2002
Engine:				X	X	-
Transmission:				-	-	-
Suspension:				X	-	-
Steering:				-	-	-
Brakes:				X	-	-
Electricity:				X	X	X
Body:				-	-	-
Accessories:				X	X	-
Fit/finish:				-	-	-

POWERTRAIN

Year	Type/ L/Camshaft/bhp	Drivetrain & gearbox
00-01	V6/2.5/DOHC/170	front-A4
2002	V6/3.0/DOHC/200	front-A5

PERFORMANCE

	Acceler. 0/100 sec.	Top. speed km/h	Ave. Fuel consp. l./100 km
	12.0	180	13.5
	11.5	175	14.0

SPECIFICATIONS

Model 00-02	Wlb. mm	Lght. mm	Cb.wt kg	Brakes fr/rr	Steering type	Standard tires
m.v. 4dr.	2840	4750	1665	dc/dr	pwr.r&p.	205/65R15

PRICES

Model / version		1997	1998	1999	2000	2001	2002
m.v. 4dr. 7st. DX	mini				14700	18500	23000
	maxi				17200	21400	25850
m.v. 4dr. 7st. LX	mini				17850	21650	26150
	maxi				23400	24550	29000
m.v. 4dr. 7st. ES	mini				21400	24800	29300
	maxi				23750	27700	32150

See page 7 to adapt these figures.

2000 MAZDA MPV FWD

MAZDA   Protegé

2000 MAZDA Protegé

These small front-wheel drive subcompact and compact cars replaced the GLC models in 1989 and got a face-lift in 1995. In 1999, Mazda has completely revamped its body design and the Protegé5 entered the market in 2002 with a new 2.0L L4 engine.

PROS

• **Vehicle size** is well distributed, for the cabin is one of the most spacious in this car category.

• **Handling** is clean with such a long wheel base, good-quality tires and shock absorbers. Handling on the Protegé LX is even more stable on curves because of a stiffer suspension.

• **Engines** are powerful and run smoothly, especially the last generation DOHC engines which are quite economical.

• **The Protegé5** model is very attractive because it is at the same time a practical station wagon and a sportscar.

• **The shifter** is well-calibrated, especially on the sports models, and it's clean and smooth.

• **Really comfortable** cars with nicely contoured, thick seats and smooth suspension.

• **Wide choice** of car sizes, finish levels, engines and transmissions.

• **Remarkably reliable**, but bodywork is prone to rust.

CONS

• **Brakes** lack grip on sudden stops, that are long (except on the models equipped with 4-disc brakes) and without ABS, there's almost immediate wheel lock.

• **There's a lot** of constant noise, for the body is poorly soundproofed and the engines are very boisterous.

• **The cabin interior** is terribly bleak for everything is a dreary gray.

• **The rear bench** on base model is flat and hard and very uncomfortable.

VERDICT

The Protegé are practical and fun to drive and they're quite economical to run and they're both elegant and dependable.

RECALLS

1999   Possible short circuit in the audio system.

Protegé   MAZDA

RELIABILITY PROBLEMS

	1997	1998	1999	2000	2001	2002
Engine:	X	X	-	-	-	-
Transmission:	-	-	-	X	-	-
Suspension:	-	-	-	-	-	-
Steering:	-	-	-	-	-	-
Brakes:	X	X	X	X	-	-
Electricity:	-	-	X	-	-	-
Body:	X	-	X	X	-	-
Accessories:	-	-	X	X	X	-
Fit/finish:	-	-	-	-	-	-

POWERTRAIN / PERFORMANCE

Year	Type/ L/Camshaft/bhp	Drivetrain & gearbox	Acceler. 0/100 sec.	Top. speed km/h	Ave. Fuel consp. l./100 km
97-98	L4/1.5/DOHC/92	front-M5	11.0	165	7.7
		front-A4	12.3	160	9.1
	L4/1.8/DOHC/122-125	front-M5	8.5	190	10.5
99-02	L4/1.6/DOHC/103	front-M5	11.6	175	8.5
		front-A4	13.5	165	9.3
99-01	L4/1.8/DOHC/122-130	front-M5	10.5	190	8.9
		front-A4	12.6	175	9.7
2002	L4/2.0/DOHC/130	front-M5	11.0	180	9.6
		front-A4	11.8	175	9.9

SPECIFICATIONS

Model	Wlb.	Lght.	Cb.wt	Brakes	Steering	Standard
Protegé 97-98						
sdn. 4dr. SE/S	2605	4440	1145	dc/dc	pwr.r&p.	185/65R14
sdn. 4dr. LX	2605	4440	1145	dc/dc	pwr.r&p.	185/65R14
Protegé 99-01						
sdn. 4dr.DX/LX/SE	2610	4420	1105	dc/dr	pwr.r&p.	185/65R14
wgn. 4dr. 5	2610	4431	1231	dc/dc	pwr.r&p.	195/50R16

PRICES

Model / version		1997	1998	1999	2000	2001	2002
sdn. 4dr. DX	mini			9450	11350		
	maxi			11350	13100		
sdn. 4dr. LX	mini	6850	8950	11000	13450	14200	16800
	maxi	8400	10500	12900	15200	16300	18900
sdn. 4dr. SE	mini	6300	7900	10000	12400	13100	15750
	maxi	8400	9450	11850	13650	15200	17850
sdn. 4dr. ES	mini					15200	17300
	maxi					17300	19400
sdn. 5dr. 5ES	mini						17650
	maxi						19400

See page 7 to adapt these figures.

MAZDA   626 / MX-6

2000 MAZDA 626

First launched in 1988, they got a face-lift in '93 and a new 2.5L V6 engine, and   in 1998.

PROS

• **Wide choice** of body designs, mechanical features and trim levels for both the sedans and the coupes.
• **All engines are powerful**, whether it be the conventional 4-cylinder model or the V6 which is undoubtedly one of the best in its generation.
• **The slick rear suspension** eliminates sway and provides for neutral road stability.
• **The cabin** is nice and roomy, seats are comfy (except on the DX) and noise level is very tolerable at cruising speed.
• **Fit and finish** are clean as a whistle and construction quality is really topnotch.

CONS

• **The anonymous body design** which does not stand out compared to its rivals.
• **Older models** aren't too reliable and must be thoroughly inspected before purchase.
• **The unsettling performance** of the 4-cylinder engine loses its appeal with the automatic transmission.
• **Brakes** aren't wonderful and gas consumption with the V6 on the latest generation is terribly high.
• **The stiff suspension** on the 626 and MX-6 is harsh when it hits bumps.
• **Cabin design** is bland, controls are inconveniently located and equipment is pretty plain and simple on base models.

VERDICT

The Mazda 626 and MX-6 models are good cars, they're nice and stable on the road, but they're terribly unreliable, which is a real problem.

RECALLS

1997 Minor undercarriage impacts can result in unnecessary airbag deployment.
Defective fuel cap that allows fuel vapor to leak from the pipe.
Engine may stall if a spring in the tensioner breaks.
1998 Powertrain control module is not properly programmed.
1999 Possible condensation entering the audio unit and causing a short circuit. Aluminum tape must be affixed over the audio unit to prevent water from entering.
2000 The brake master cylinder cap doesn't have ventilation hole.

RELIABILITY PROBLEMS

	1997	1998	1999	2000	2001	2002
Engine:	X	X	X	-	-	-
Transmission:	-	X	X	X	-	-
Suspension:	X	X	X	-	-	-
Steering:	X	X	X	-	-	-
Brakes:	-	X	X	X	X	X
Electricity:	X	-	-	X	X	-
Body:	X	X	X	X	-	-
Accessories:	-	-	X	X	-	-
Fit/finish:	X	X	-	-	-	-

POWERTRAIN

Year	Type/ L/Camshaft/bhp	Drivetrain & gearbox
97-02	L4/2.0/DOHC/114-125	front-M5
		front-A4
	V6/2.5/DOHC/165	front-M5
		front-A4

PERFORMANCE

	Acceler. 0/100 sec.	Top. speed km/h	Ave. Fuel consp. l./100 km
	10.0	180	9.0
	12.2	175	10.7
	8.0	210	11.7
	10.4	200	12.2

SPECIFICATIONS

Model	Wlb. mm	Lght. mm	Cb.wt kg	Brakes fr/rr	Steering type	Standard tires
626 1997						
sdn. 4dr. SE	2610	4685	1247	dc/dr	pwr.r&p.	195/70SR14
sdn. 4dr. ES	2610	4685	1315	dc/ABS	pwr.r&p.	205/55VR15
MX-6 1997						
cpe. 2dr. RS	2610	4615	1190	dc/dr	pwr.r&p.	195/65R14
cpe. 2dr. LS	2610	4615	1270	dc/dc	pwr.r&p.	205/55R15
98-02						
sdn. 4dr. DX/LX	2670	4760	1299	dc/dr	pwr.r&p.	185/70R14
sdn. 4dr. ES	2670	4760	1409	dc/ABS	pwr.r&p.	205/55R16

PRICES

Model / version		1997	1998	1999	2000	2001	2002
626							
sdn. 4dr. DX	mini	5800	7350	9750			
	maxi	8400	10000	12100			
sdn. 4dr. LX	mini	6800	8400	10800	12600	14700	18400
	maxi	9450	11000	13100	14700	17300	21000
sdn. 4dr. ES V6	mini	8100	8900	12400	14700	16800	20500
	maxi	10500	11550	14700	16800	19400	23100
sdn. 4dr. LX V6	mini	9450	10500	14500	16800	19950	23600
	maxi	12100	13100	16800	18900	22600	26250
MX-6							
cpe. 2dr. RS	mini	10500					
	maxi	12600					
cpe. 2dr. LS V6	mini	12300					
	maxi	14700					

See page 7 to adapt these figures.

2000 MAZDA 626

MAZDA   Tribute

2001 MAZDA Tribute

The Tribute is the Ford Escape's twin brother. They differ only with respect to a few presentation and equipment details.

PROS

• **The compact size** is current and practical, and the youthful styling is highly successful within the otherwise very conservative lineup.

• **The Tribute handles** as safely as a car, to the great delight of female drivers.

• **The overall comfort** level is quite adequate for a utility vehicle, thanks to efficient seats and soundproofing.

• **The brakes** are powerful and easy to modulate. Stops are short and straight, even without ABS.

• **The V6** cranks out honorable performance levels, and output is quite reasonable under load.

• The simple and efficient **all-wheel traction system** requires no driver intervention.

• **The Tribute's off-road capabilities** are adequate to allow it to travel over quite hilly terrain, but it's not a real 4x4.

• **The powerful headlights** provide good visibility even in poor weather.

CONS

• **The 4-cylinder's** limited performance is adequate only with front-wheel drive and the manual transmission.

• **Rear-seat roominess** is limited. Indeed, rear accessibility and legroom are at a premium.

• **The standard tires** are of poor quality because their provide mediocre grip even on dry roads.

• **The suspension** reacts harshly on poor roads where the occupants get jostled around without mercy.

• **Ford's plastics look very cheap** and give the dashboard a very utilitarian look to it.

• **The windshield wipers** operate too slowly to ensure adequate visibility in rainy conditions.

VERDICT

The Tribute is a more luxurious version of the Ford Escape, which explains its popularity with female buyers.

RECALLS

None over this period.

RELIABILITY PROBLEMS

	1997	1998	1999	2000	2001	2002
Engine:					X	-
Transmission:					-	-
Suspension:					-	-
Steering:					-	-
Brakes:					-	-
Electricity:					X	-
Body:					X	X
Accessories:					-	-
Fit/finish:					-	-

POWERTRAIN

Year	Type/ L/Camshaft/bhp	Drivetrain & gearbox	Acceler. 0/100 sec.	Top. speed km/h	Ave. Fuel consp. l./100 km
01-02	L4/2.0/SOHC/125	ft./all-M5	12.0	160	10.0
	V6/3.0/OHV/200	ft./all-A4	10.0	175	13.0

PERFORMANCE

SPECIFICATIONS

Model 01-02	Wlb. mm	Lght. mm	Cb.wt kg	Brakes fr/rr	Steering type	Standard tires
wgn. 4dr. FWD	2620	4395	1402	dc/dr	pwr.r.&p.	225/70R15
wgn. 4dr. AWD	2620	4395	1567	dc/dr	pwr.r.&p.	235/70R15

PRICES

Model / version		1997	1998	1999	2000	2001	2002
wgn. 4dr. DX L4	mini					18600	21850
	AWD maxi					21000	24350
wgn. 4dr. DX V6	mini					19650	22900
	AWD maxi					22000	25400
wgn. 4dr. LX V6	mini					22600	26000
	AWD maxi					25200	28550
wgn. 4dr. ES V6	mini					27700	29200
	AWD maxi					28350	31700

See page 7 to adapt these figures.

2001 MAZDA Tribute

MERCEDES-BENZ   C Class

1999 MERCEDES-BENZ C-Class

The C-Class was first sold in 1984 and is the entry-level Mercedes model range. The sedan were renewed in 2001 and a coupe, a station wagon and an AMG sedan were added in 2002.

PROS

• **Good resale value** because they're solidly built, fit and finish are clean, and trim components are attractive.
• **C-Class cars handle** beautifully and are quite insensitive to crosswinds, because they come equipped with very sophisticated suspensions that stabilize the vehicles in most situations.
• **The 6-cylinder** engine is more skittish and is more economical because of a better power to weight ratio and because of smoother functioning. Engine performance on the C36 and the C43 with its V8 are like those of a big, exotic touring car.
• **Brakes** are smooth and effective, achieving short, straight stops.
• **The cockpit** is adequate in spite of the large steering wheel which still isn't adjustable.
• **Steering** is smooth and precise and makes for superb maneuverability, even with a slightly high reduction ratio.
• **The instrument panel** is well-designed, gauges are easy to read, controls are within easy reach, though a few of them are unusual and outward view is simply perfect.
• **The suspension** handles bumps and such smoothly and the seats provide adequate support.

CONS

• **This is an expensive** car, it costs a bundle, insurance premiums aren't cheap and running and maintaining this baby can be pretty costly...
• **Gas consumption** is high.
• **The rear seat area** is cramped, there isn't much leg room and access isn't great with the narrow doors.
• **Trunk size** is good, but it's impossible to store large items because of its small opening.

VERDICT

C-Class Mercedes cars are fun to drive, they're reliable, luxurious and comfy, but they take a bit out of your pocketbook. Nevertheless, they're a blue chip investment.

RECALLS

2001   Headlamp function will be checked and incorrect Signal Acquisition Active Module unit will be replaced.

RELIABILITY PROBLEMS

	1997	1998	1999	2000	2001	2002
Engine:	X	-	-	X	X	X
Transmission:	-	X	X	X	-	X
Suspension:	-	-	-	-	-	-
Steering:	-	-	-	-	-	-
Brakes:	X	X	X	X	X	-
Electricity:	-	X	X	X	-	X
Body:	-	-	-	X	X	X
Accessories:	X	X	X	X	X	X
Fit/finish:	-	-	-	-	-	-

POWERTRAIN

Year	Type/ L/Camshaft/bhp	Drivetrain & gearbox	Acceler. 0/100 sec.	Top. speed km/h	Ave. Fuel consp. l./100 km
97-00	L4/2.2/DOHC/147	rear-A4	10.5	210	11.0
	L6/2.8/DOHC/162	rear-A4	9.0	230	12.0
1997	L6/3.6/DOHC/268	rear-A4	7.0	250	13.3
1998	V6/2.8/SOHC/194	rear-A5	8.2	210	11.8
99-01	L4C/2.3/DOHC/185	rear-A5	NA	NA	NA
	V6/2.8/SOHC/194	rear-A5	8.2	210	11.8
	V8/4.3/SOHC/302	rear-A5	NA	NA	NA
01-02	L4C/2.3/DOHC/185	rear-A5	NA	NA	NA
	V6/2.6/SOHC/168	rear-A5	10.7	220	12.3
	V6/3.2/SOHC/215	rear-A5	8.2	220	12.9
AMG	V6C/3.2/DOHC/349	rear-A5	NA	NA	NA

SPECIFICATIONS

Model 97-00	Wlb. mm	Lght. mm	Cb.wt kg	Brakes fr/rr	Steering type	Standard tires
sdn. 4dr. Diesel	2665	4447	1345	dc/dc	pwr.bal.	185/65R15
sdn. 4dr. 2.2	2665	4447	1315	dc/ABS	pwr.bal.	185/65R15
sdn. 4dr. 2.6	2665	4447	1370	dc/ABS	pwr.bal.	185/65R15
sdn. 4dr. 2.2/2.3	2690	4507	1474	dc/ABS	pwr.bal.	205/60R15
sdn. 4dr. 2.8	2690	4507	1504	dc/ABS	pwr.bal.	205/60R15
sdn. 4dr. 3.6/4.3	2690	4507	1610	dc/ABS	pwr.bal.	225/45ZR17 245/40ZR17
01-02						
sdn. 4dr. C240	2715	4528	1524	dc/ABS	pwr.r.&p.	205/55R16
sdn. 4dr. C320	2715	4528	1585	dc/ABS	pwr.r.&p.	205/55R16
2002						
cpe. 2dr. C230	2715	4346	1515	dc/ABS	pwr.r.&p.	205/55R16
sdn. 4dr. AMG	2715	4544	1585	dc/ABS	pwr.r.&p.	245/40R17
wgn. 4dr. C320	2715	4544	1585	dc/ABS	pwr.r.&p.	205/55R16

PRICES

Model / version		1997	1998	1999	2000	2001	2002
cpe. 2dr. CL230	mini						23100
	maxi						27300
sdn. 4dr. C280	mini		25200	31000	36750		
Sport	maxi		28750	34650	40200		
sdn. 4dr. C230	mini			27300	30750		
Sport	maxi			30450	34100		
sdn. 4dr. C280	mini	22150	24150	32000	35700		
	maxi	25700	27700	35400	38850		
sdn. 4dr. C36	mini	34545					
	maxi	38650					
sdn. 4dr. 230 SE	mini	13250					
	maxi	16800					
sdn. 4dr. 230	mini	17900					
	maxi	22000					
sdn. 4dr. Classic	mini		17200	21000	25800		
C230	maxi		20600	24700	29300		
sdn. 4dr. Elegance	mini		21750	26200	30450		
C230	maxi		25200	29400	34100		
sdn. 4dr. C43 AMG	mini			40650			
	maxi			44100			
sdn. 4dr. CLS240	mini					31400	32950
	maxi					35000	36750
sdn. 4dr. C240	mini					35000	36200
ELG	maxi					38850	39900
sdn. 4dr. C240	mini					38200	40950
	maxi					42000	46200
sdn. 4dr. C320	mini					40850	43000
	maxi					44500	49250
sdn. 4dr. 320	mini					44000	47250
Sport	maxi					47250	52500
sdn. 4dr. C32.AMG	mini						54600
	maxi						60900
wgn. 4dr. C320.S	mini						43000
	maxi						49350
wgn. 4dr. C320Sport	mini						49350
	maxi						54600

See page 7 to adapt these figures.

2000 MERCEDES-BENZ CLK-Class

The CLK coupe is a spin-off of the C-Class platform. It was launched in 1997 and is equipped with a 3.2L V6 engine. Later in 1999, it got the brand new 4.3L V8 to inspire a newcomer in the serie, the CLK 430. Since 1999, the CLK is available in two body style, a 2-door coupe and convertible.

PROS

• **The car's gorgeous style** is proof that a car can be elegant and compact as well.

• **The overall value** for your buck makes it an interesting alternative to some coupes that are a lot pricier.

• **Active and passive** safety features are the feather in the cap of this car manufacturer.

• **Zippy performance** with the initial V6 that had never been put on the market by the builder yield awesome accelerations and pick-up without overly straining mechanical components.

• **Driving pleasure** derives from super overall balanced demeanor and from this coupe's dual personality that can be comfy or sporty, depending on the driver's whim.

• **The trunk** is unusually spacious for a model of this type. Besides, it can be extended towards the cabin and includes a ski-sized passthrough.

CONS

• **The constantly** pervasive high noise level doesn't jive with the lavish character of this model and exhaust noise isn't anything to write home about.

• **Steering** suffers from a poor reduction ratio, so lively, moves are tricky due to lack of accuracy in this department.

• **The rear seats** aren't any more roomy than inside the C-Class and upholstery is really too firm.

• **Vehicle stability** is sometimes jeopardized by wind and road surface conditions, so the awful sway effect can only be due to poor tire quality.

• **Storage spots** are few and far between and the glove and console compartments are tiny.

• **Power windows** are annoyingly slow to function and headlights are less than up to par on low beam.

VERDICT

The CLK coupe has assets that will convince parents whose children have left home to exchange their minivan for this toys that will put new zest into their life...

RECALLS

1998   Front seat belt shoulder anchor bolts must be reinforced.

RELIABILITY PROBLEMS

	1997	1998	1999	2000	2001	2002
Engine:		X	X	X	X	X
Transmission:		-	-	-	-	-
Suspension:		-	-	-	-	-
Steering:		X	-	-	-	-
Brakes:		X	X	X	-	-
Electricity:		X	X	X	X	X
Body:		-	-	X	X	X
Accessories:		X	X	X	X	X
Fit/finish:		-	-	-	-	-

POWERTRAIN

Year	Type/ L/Camshaft/bhp	Drivetrain & gearbox
98-01	V6/3.2/SOHC/215	rear-A5
99-02	V8/4.3/SOHC/275	rear-A5
01=02	V8/5.5/SOHC/342 AMG	rear-A5

PERFORMANCE

	Acceler. 0/100 sec.	Top. speed km/h	Ave. Fuel consp. l./100 km
	7.8	210	11.2
	7.0	210	11.0
	6.0	250	13.5

SPECIFICATIONS

Model 98-02	Wlb. mm	Lght. mm	Cb.wt kg	Brakes fr/rr	Steering type	Standard tires
cpe. 2dr. (320)	2690	4577	1470	dc/ABS	pwr.bal.	205/55R16
99-02						
con. 2dr.	2690	4577	1618	dc/ABS	pwr.bal.	205/55R16
cpe. 2dr. (430)	2690	4577	1525	dc/ABS	pwr.bal.	225/45ZR17
01-02						245/40ZR17
cpe. 2dr. 55AMG	2690	4577	1562	dc/ABS	pwr.bal.	225/45R17
						245/45R17

PRICES

Model / version		1997	1998	1999	2000	2001	2002
cpe. 2dr. 320	mini.		28000	34650	39900	47150	
	maxi		32550	39050	44100	52000	
cpe. 2dr. 430	mini.			42400	47800	55500	
	maxi			47250	52200	60400	
cpe. 2dr. C55	mini.					72450	
	maxi					77200	
cpe. 2dr. C55AMG	mini.						84000
	maxi						91350
con. 2dr. 320	mini.			41500	46700	57650	63000
	maxi			45700	51150	62500	69300
con. 2dr. 430	mini.				53550	66000	74550
	maxi				57750	70900	78250
con. 2dr.C55AMG	mini.						92400
	maxi						95500

See page 7 to adapt these figures.

2000 MERCEDES-BENZ CLK-Class

MERCEDES-BENZ   E Class

1999 MERCEDES-BENZ E-Class

The E-Class sedan hails back to 1984, the TD station wagon came out in 86, all-wheel drive models in 90 and V8 engines in 92. The latest generation cars were first available in 1996 and the AMG version appeared in 2001.

PROS

• **Construction quality**, components and fit and finish are among the best in this car category.

• **Handling** is a cut above, for these cars are stable, neutral and very safe at all times.

• **Gas engine** performance is terrific, allowing for Sportscar zip and zoom.

• **Steering** is almost perfect, even with the huge steering wheel.

• **The appealing body** design of the latest models is also quite aerodynamically efficient.

• **The instrument panel** is loaded and gauges are very easy to read, and outward view is just great.

• **Power brakes** are muscular, well-calibrated and smooth, but they're quite over-assisted.

• **The cabin is spacious** and comfortable, the suspension is well-adjusted and noise level is low at cruising speed.

• **There are lots of storage** compartments in the cabin interior and there's easy access to the huge trunk.

CONS

• **These cars** don't come cheap, they're expensive to buy and upkeep, and fuel consumption on gas engine models are costly.

• **The Diesel engine** is economical but not worth the hassles (wimpy power, noise and a lot of shake, rattle and roll).

• **Some items** need to be improved on older models, for example, the non-adjustable steering column and some inconveniently located controls.

• **Rearward view** at quarterback isn't great because of the thickness of the C-pillar.

VERDICT

The E-Class is without a doubt the most practical Mercedes model range, both for size and for overall performance.

RECALLS

1999   Defective window bag that may not fully deploy in the event of a side impact collision.

RELIABILITY PROBLEMS

	1997	1998	1999	2000	2001	2002
Engine:	X	X	X	-	-	-
Transmission:	X	X	X	-	-	-
Suspension:	X	X	X	X	X	-
Steering:	-	-	-	-	-	-
Brakes:	-	-	-	-	-	-
Electricity:	X	X	X	X	X	X
Body:	-	-	-	-	-	-
Accessories:	X	X	X	X	X	X
Fit/finish:	-	-	-	-	-	-

POWERTRAIN / PERFORMANCE

Year	Type/ L/Camshaft/bhp	Drivetrain & gearbox	Acceler. 0/100 sec.	Top. speed km/h	Ave. Fuel consp. l./100 km
97-98	L6D/3.0/DOHC/134	rear-A4	12.5	205	8.5
	L6/3.2/DOHC/217	rear-A4	8.2	210	12.4
	V8/4.2/DOHC/275	rear-A4	7.5	210	13.3
99-01	L6TD/3.0/DOHC/174	rear-A5	9.0	210	8.9
99-02	V6/3.2/SOHC/221	rear-A5	7.5	210	11.3
		all-A5	7.8	210	11.8
	V8/4.3/DOHC/275	rear-A5	6.5	210	15.2
01-02	V8/5.5/DOHC/349 AMG	rear-A5	6.0	250	13.6

SPECIFICATIONS

Model 97-02	Wlb.	Lght.	Cb.wt	Brakes	Steering	Standard
sdn. 4dr. E300D	2833	4810	1605	dc/ABS	pwr.r&p.	215/55R16
sdn. 4dr. E320	2833	4810	1570	dc/ABS	pwr.r&p.	215/55R16
wag.4dr. E320 AWD	2833	4825	1755	dc/ABS	pwr.r&p.	215/55R16
sdn.4dr. E320/ 430	2833	4810	1715	dc/ABS	pwr.r&p.	215/55R16
ber. 4 p. 55 AMG	2833	4810	1649	d/ABS	crém.ass.	275/35R18

PRICES

Model / version		1997	1998	1999	2000	2001	2002
sdn. 4dr. E320	mini	24900					
	maxi	32250					
sdn. 4dr. 300D	mini	21600					
	maxi	25700					
sdn. 4dr. E420	mini	35300					
	maxi	38550					
sdn. 4dr. 300 TD	mini		25700	29900			
	maxi		29400	33600			
sdn. 4dr. 320W	mini		31200	34350	42000	50200	59800
	maxi		35200	38300	46100	53950	64000
sdn. 4dr. 4Matic	mini		33300	37500	45150	53350	63000
	maxi		37300	41500	49250	57100	68200
sdn. 4dr. E430W	mini		38100	43350	51150	54400	68200
	maxi		42000	47250	55100	58300	72400
sdn. 4dr.E430	mini					56700	70300
4Matic	maxi					60900	74500
sdn. 4dr. E55AMG	mini						89200
	maxi						94500
sdn. 4dr. E55	mini			55100	63500	74500	
	maxi			58800	67200	78750	
wgn. 4dr. E320 S	mini		31200	35400	43000	53000	61900
	maxi		35200	39400	47150	57200	67200
wgn. 4dr. 4Matic	mini		35350	38500	46200	56200	63000
	maxi		38300	42500	50200	60400	68200

See page 7 to adapt these figures.

MERCEDES-BENZ   M Class

2002 MERCEDES-BENZ M-Class

In 1998, Mercedes-Benz introduced the ML320 powered by a 3.2L V6, the 430, the 55 AMG and the 500 powered by V8 engines. All-wheel drive is achieved by electronically controlled locking differentials.

PROS
• **The social status** associated with owning an affordable vehicle sporting the Stuttgart star made this model as rare as hen's teeth, at least in the first production years.
• **The style** mid-way between that of a 4X4 and a minivan created a whole new breed and the body's aerodynamic efficiency is the reason behind such economic fuel consumption for a heavy vehicle.
• **The ML320**'s appealing value explains why new or used models are hard to come by and they don't come cheap either.
• **This model** behaves very much like a car, so it's unique and quite different from its rivals, due to sophisticated, state-of-the-art technical applications.
• **The vehicle format** is really neat, since it offers really airy cabin space yet it's quite compact.
• **Performance** is comparable to those of much bigger and brawnier engines, in spite of vehicle weight, namely more than 2 tons when at full load capacity. Of course, the performance of the V8 is even better and its towing capacities are way above average. The ML55 AMG is a real sports truck.
• **Ride comfort** is terrific due to the well-honed suspension, nicely contoured seats and reasonable noise interference at cruising speed.
• **Headlights** provide safe driving and the luggage cover design is really clever.

CONS
• **Some trim materials** such as the plastic components aren't up to snuff, considering the German automaker's reputation, which explains in part the fairly affordable price.
• **This vehicle** is load-sensitive and the all-wheel drive function seemed taxed on the first models.
• **The rear seatbench** is tough to get to due to the narrow doors and the complicated seat removal device is hard to decipher, in short, a real nightmare.
• **Weird features:** the control for cruise control, the location of the CD player inside the cargo, hold and missing shifter position indicator on the dashboard.

VERDICT
Mercedes-Benz came onto the SUV stage with great assurance and poise, since the ML320 and ML 430 are equipped with some innovative handling and ride comfort features.

RECALLS
None over this period.

RELIABILITY PROBLEMS

	1997	1998	1999	2000	2001	2002
Engine:		X	X	X	X	X
Transmission:		X	X	-	-	-
Suspension:		-	X	X	-	-
Steering:		-	-	-	-	-
Brakes:		X	X	X	-	-
Electricity:		-	X	X	X	X
Body:		X	X	X	X	-
Accessories:		X	X	X	X	-
Fit/finish:		X	X	X	-	-

POWERTRAIN

Year	Type/ L/Camshaft/bhp	Drivetrain & gearbox	Acceler. 0/100 sec.	Top. speed km/h	Ave. Fuel consp. l/100 km
98-02	V6/3.2/SOHC/215 (320)	rear/all-A5	9.0	180	14.0
99-01	V6/4.3/SOHC/288 (430)	rear/all-A5	7.5	200	16.0
00-02	V8/5.5/SOHC/342 (AMG)	rear/all-A5	6.0	240	20.0
2002	V8/5.0/SOHC/288 (500)	rear/all-A5	8.0	180	15.0

(PERFORMANCE columns: Acceler. 0/100 sec., Top. speed km/h, Ave. Fuel consp. l/100 km)

SPECIFICATIONS

Model	Wlb. mm	Lght. mm	Cb.wt kg	Brakes fr/rr	Steering type	Standard tires
99-01						
wgn. 4dr.ML430	2820	4683	2010	dc/ABS	pwr.r&p.	275/55R17
98-02						
wgn. 4dr.CLassic	2820	4683	1905	dc/ABS	pwr.r&p.	255/65R16
wgn. 4dr.Elegance	2820	4683	1922	dc/ABS	pwr.r&p.	255/65R16
wgn. 4dr.M55AMG	2820	4683	2110	dc/ABS	pwr.r&p.	285/50R18
2002						
wgn 4dr. ML500	2820	4683	2150	dc/ABS	pwr.r&p.	275/55R17

PRICES

Model / version		1997	1998	1999	2000	2001	2002
wgn. 4dr. 320	mini		24700	27300	31500	37800	42000
Classic	maxi		28150	31300	35200	40900	46200
wgn. 4dr. 320	mini		30450	34100	39400	43600	43600
Elegance	maxi		34100	37800	42800	44600	47000
wgn. 4dr. 430	mini			37300	42500	46200	
	maxi			40900	46000	49900	
wgn. 4dr. 500	mini						56700
	maxi						61900
wgn. 4dr. 55 AMG	mini				57200	69300	
	maxi				60700	73500	

See page 7 to adapt these figures.

1999 MERCEDES-BENZ M-Class

MERCEDES-BENZ

S Class Sedans

2001 MERCEDES-BENZ S-Class

The last S-Class cars replaced the former models in 2000 are available on two wheel base, and are powered by V8 and V12-cylinder gas engines.

PROS

• **State-of-the-art gadgetry,** and such, on these cars that are among the most technically advanced vehicles on the market.

• **Safety** is more than guaranteed with such a very robust and rigid body, and dual frontal and side-mounted airbags, so you feel very safe indeed behind the wheel of such a car.

• **The V8 and V12** engines really unleash the power, considering hefty vehicle size and weight.

• **Handling** is a dream because of the sophisticated suspension, muscular brakes, clean steering and impressive road stability that really only sheer vehicle weight can sometimes affect.

• **Construction quality**, fit and finish and trim components are among the best in the world.

• **Comfort** is assured with such an airy, spacious cabin and trunk, adjustable suspension, better-designed seats and efficient sound-proofing that is enhanced by the dual-pane windows, luxurious controls and accessories.

CONS

• **You're so comfy** inside this car that you can lose a feel for the road and the outside world, for that matter, so you have to remember to be careful on slippery roads.

• **This is an expensive**, upper-crust car that costs a mint and the subsequent price of insurance premium, gas, upkeep and repairs can be astronomical.

• **The 6-cylinder** engines are much less lively than the others.

• **Maneuverability and quick moves** are crippled by excessive vehicle weight and size.

• **Driving** is less fun with all the power assists and self-adjusting systems.

VERDICT

Mercedes S Class cars are the nec plus ultra as far as automobile technology is concerned, but they're just too plush and really too out-of-sight costly.

S Class Sedans　　MERCEDES-BENZ

RELIABILITY PROBLEMS

	1997	1998	1999	2000	2001	2002
Engine:	X	X	X	X	X	-
Transmission:	-	-	-	-	-	-
Suspension:	X	-	-	-	-	-
Steering:	-	-	-	-	-	-
Brakes:	X	X	X	X	X	-
Electricity:	X	-	X	X	X	X
Body:	X	X	X	-	-	-
Accessories:	X	X	X	X	X	X
Fit/finish:	-	-	-	-	-	-

POWERTRAIN

Year	Type/ L/Camshaft/bhp	Drivetrain & gearbox	Acceler. 0/100 sec.	Top. speed km/h	Ave. Fuel consp. l./100 km
97-98	L6TD/3.5/SOHC/148	rear-A4-A5	13.6	180	11.0
97-99	L6/3.2/DOHC/228	rear-A4-A5	9.3	210	13.0
	V8/4.2/DOHC/275	rear-A4-A5	8.5	210	15.3
	V8/5.0/DOHC/315	rear-A4-A5	7.8	210	15.9
	V12/6.0/DOHC/389	rear-A4-A5	7.0	250	18.5
00-02	V8/4.3/SOHC/275 (430)	rear-A5	7.0	210	15.2
	V8/5.0/SOHC/302 (500)	rear-A5	6.5	210	16.0
2002	V8/5.4/SOHC/354 (AMG)	rear-A5	6.0	250	17.0
	V12/5.8/SOHC/362 (600)	rear-A5	NA		

SPECIFICATIONS

Model 97-99	Wlb. mm	Lght. mm	Cb.wt kg	Brakes fr/rr	Steering type	Standard tires
S320/ 320V/ S350D	3040	5113	2090	dc/ABS	pwr.bal.	225/60R16
S420 / 400V	3140	5113	2150	dc/ABS	pwr.bal.	235/60R16
S500 / 500V	3140	5213	2190	dc/ABS	pwr.bal.	235/60R16
S600 / 600V	3140	5213	2310	dc/ABS	pwr.bal.	235/60R16
00-02						
sdn. 4dr. S430	2965	5038	1855	dc/ABS	pwr.r&p.	225/60R16
sdn. 4dr. S430L	3085	5158	1875	dc/ABS	pwr.r&p.	225/60R16
sdn. 4dr. S500L	3085	5158	1875	dc/ABS	pwr.r&p.	225/60R16
sdn. 4 p. S55	3086	5159	1899	dc/ABS	pwr.r&p.	275/40R18
sdn. 4 p. S600	3086	5159	2036	dc/ABS	pwr.r&p.	225/55R17

PRICES

Model / version		1997	1998	1999	2000	2001	2002
sdn. 4dr. S320	mini	34200					
	maxi	38800					
sdn. 4dr. 320V	mini	35300	36750	43600			
	maxi	39900	40900	47700			
sdn. 4dr. 320W	mini		36450	42000			
	maxi		40400	46200			
sdn. 4dr. S420	mini	39000					
	maxi	45150					
sdn. 4dr. 420V	mini		42000	52200			
	maxi		47200	57200			
sdn. 4dr. 430V	mini				64000	76600	84000
	maxi				69700	83000	94500
snd. 4dr. S430L	mini				59800	74400	89200
	maxi				65100	79700	95500
sdn. 4dr. S500	mini	45150					
	maxi	51000					
sdn. 4dr. 500V	mini		51900	60400	67200	88000	101800
	maxi		57200	65600	73000	93400	109200
sdn. 4dr. S55	mini					113400	
	maxi					118600	
sdn. 4dr. S55AMG	mini						122800
	maxi						131200
sdn. 4dr. S600	mini	65700					
	maxi	71900					
sdn. 4dr. 600V	mini		71000	82400		114300	155400
	maxi		76600	87600		119600	161700

See page 7 to adapt these figures.

MERCEDES-BENZ   CL-SL

1999 MERCEDES-BENZ CL-Class

The upper-crust SL convertible was first sold in 1990. Inspired by the S-Class model range, it's powered by a 6, 8 and 12-cylinder engine.

PROS
• **High-tech vehicle** in many respects, it's equipped with sophisticated safety features and everything is electronic when it comes to mechanical components. Safety is topnotch with such a solid structure, front and side-mounted airbags and all the electronic assists.
• **The V8 engine** and especially the V12 have incredible get up and gusto, given the outrageously excessive vehicle weight (two tons!).
• **Handling** is very safe and sure, thanks to an elaborately designed suspension, good tires and various systems, such as ABS and anti-skid system, that will keep even the worst driver from going off the road...
• **Steering** is accurate and brakes are powerful and smooth, which makes for zoomy, zesty driving.
• **Build quality**, tight finish and very spiffy trim components are what you'd expect for such an expensive car.

CONS
• **The preposterously** high price, upkeep and repairs for such a car, even used.
• **Excessive weight** really affects maneuverability and ease on curved roads and all the electronic gizmos can be frustrating for keen Sportscar drivers.
• **Pick-up** is anemic on the 320SL with its much poorer power to weight ratio than that of the 500SL, 600SL and AMG models.

VERDICT
The Mercedes SL convertible is the symbol par excellence of social status and so it appeals to people who place social standing above all else. So it's perfectly normal that such a ritzy car is expensive.

RECALLS
2000 The blower motor regulator of the climate control system can be defective and replaced.
2001 Heated windshield washer bottle hose will be replaced on some vehicles.

RELIABILITY PROBLEMS

	1997	1998	1999	2000	2001	2002
Engine:	X	X	X	X	X	-
Transmission:	-	-	-	-	-	-
Suspension:	-	-	-	-	-	-
Steering:	-	X	-	-	-	-
Brakes:	X	X	X	-	-	-
Electricity:	-	X	X	X	X	X
Body:	X	X	X	-	-	-
Accessories:	X	X	X	X	X	X
Fit/finish:	X	-	-	-	-	-

POWERTRAIN

Year	Type/ L/Camshaft/bhp	Drivetrain & gearbox	Acceler. 0/100 sec.	Top. speed km/h	Ave. Fuel consp. l./100 km
97-98	L6/3.2/DOHC/228	rear-A4-A5	9.5	220	15.0
96-99	V8/5.0/DOHC/315-322	rear-A4-A5	7.1	230	16.0
	V12/6.0/DOHC/389	rear-A4-A5	6.5	240	18.0
2000	V8/5.0/SOHC/339 AMG	rear-A5	6.0	240	17.0
01-02	V8/5.0/SOHC/302	rear-A5	6.8	240	14.5
	V8/5.4/SOHC/355 AMG	rear-A5	6.0	250	15.0
	V12/5.8/SOHC/362	rear-A5	5.8	250	15.2

PERFORMANCE

SPECIFICATIONS

Model	Wlb. mm	Lght. mm	Cb.wt kg	Brakes fr/rr	Steering type	Standard tires
97-99						
con. 2dr.SL 320	2515	4470	1820	dc/ABS	pwr.bal.	225/55R16
con. 2dr.SL 500	2515	4499	1889	dc/ABS	pwr.bal.	245/45R17
con. 2dr.SL 600	2515	4599	2021	dc/ABS	pwr.bal.	245/40R18
98-00						
cpe. 2dr.CL500	2945	5065	2130	dc/ABS	pwr.bal.	235/60R16
cpe. 2dr.CL600	2945	5065	2250	dc/ABS	pwr.bal.	235/60R16
01-02						
cpe. 2dr.CL500	2885	4994	1846	dc/ABS	pwr.r.&p.	225/55R17
cpe. 2dr.CL55	2885	4994	1851	dc/ABS	pwr.r.&p.	245/45R18 275/40R18
cpe. 2dr.CL600	2885	4994	1950	dc/ABS	pwr.r.&p.	225/55R17

PRICES

Model / version		1997	1998	1999	2000	2001	2002
con. 2dr. SL 320	mini	40800					
	maxi	45900					
con. 2dr. SL 500	mini	48800	54600				
	maxi	54100	60000				
con. 2dr. SL 600	mini	60400	73220				
	maxi	65600	78700				
cpe. 2dr. SL500	mini	48800					
	maxi	54300					
cpe. 2dr. CL500	mini		53800	61600	70300	116500	124000
	maxi		61400	67200	76100	135400	132000
cpe. 2dr. CL 55	mini					135400	156400
	maxi					147000	163800
cpe. 2dr. SL 600	mini	69700					
	maxi	75300					
cpe. 2dr. CL 55AMG	mini						135400
	maxi						142800
cpe. 2dr. CL600C	mini		71600	84500		136500	
	maxi		75600	90300		142000	

See page 7 to adapt these figures.

1999 MERCEDES-BENZ SL-Class

MERCEDES-BENZ   SLK

1999 MERCEDES-BENZ SLK-Class

The SLK coupe was first sold in 1997 and is Mercedes-Benz's contender against the BMW Z3. But it's unique with its removable hard top and supercharged 2.3L engine, which was replaced by a 3.2L V6 normally aspirated or supercharged (AMG).

PROS

• **This versatile model** is useful for longer periods during the year than it is the case for a conventional convertible.

• **It's a real eye-catcher**, since the swish and original body design is a real beauty.

• **The cleverly** designed top is this vehicle's main drawing card and lowering or raising the hard top always attracts a throng of admirers.

• **The engine** musters really impressive power and pick-up even if the supercharger is a bit slow to kick in.

• **This car handles** beautifully, thanks to the well-calibrated suspension, accurate steering and brakes, so everything is always under full control.

• **This car** is really safe to drive with its roll bar and four airbags.

• **Overall craftsmanship** is flawless and partly justifies the retail price.

• **Nice features:** great headlights, wipers, climate control and rear defroster.

CONS

• **The driver** won't be terribly comfy when seated behind the wheel and the poorly suited engine seems to strain and sputter.

• **The trunk** is snug and awkward to get to when the top is folded down.

• **Rear visibility** isn't the greatest with the headrests and wind deflector that obstruct the driver's view in the main mirror range and lateral mirrors are too tiny.

• **The complicated mechanism** that controls the hard top may cause potential buyers to ask themselves if it's really dependable and upkeep for this gorgeous gadget may be more expensive than usual.

• **Some practical items** like the skimpy-sized sun visors.

VERDICT

The SLK is a good buy for it's a rather rare bird and so is in great demand, especially during the summertime.

RECALLS

00-02 Dealers will provide owners headlight adjustment instructions.

RELIABILITY PROBLEMS

	1997	1998	1999	2000	2001	2002
Engine:		X	X	X	X	-
Transmission:		X	-	-	-	-
Suspension:		-	-	-	-	-
Steering:		-	-	-	-	-
Brakes:		X				
Electricity:		X	X	X	X	X
Body:		X	X	X	-	-
Accessories:		X	X	X	X	X
Fit/finish:		X	X	X	-	-

POWERTRAIN

Year	Type/ L/Camshaft/bhp	Drivetrain & gearbox	Acceler. 0/100 sec.	Top. speed km/h	Ave. Fuel consp. l./100 km
98-99	L4C/2.3/DOHC/185	rear-A5	7.8	230	10.8
99-00		rear-M5	NA	NA	11.2
2001	V6/3.2/SOHC/215	rear-A5	7.2	225	11.4
		rear-M6	NA	NA	13.0
2002	V6C/3.2/SOHC/349 AMG	rear-A5	5.5	240	13.5

PERFORMANCE

SPECIFICATIONS

Model	Wlb. mm	Lght. mm	Cb.wt kg	Brakes fr/rr	Steering type	Standard tires
98-00						
cpe. 2dr. 230	2400	3995	1377	dc/ABS	pwr.bal.	fr.205/55R16
01-02						rr. 225/50R16
cpe. 2dr. 230	2400	4010	1406	dc/ABS	pwr.bal.	ft.205/55R16
						rr.225/50R16
cpe. 2dr. 320	2400	4010	1430	dc/ABS	pwr.bal.	ft.205/55R16
2002						rr.225/50R16
cpe 2dr.32AMG	2400	4010	1460	dc/ABS	pwr.bal.	ft.225/45R17
						rr.245/40R17

PRICES

Model / version		1997	1998	1999	2000	2001	2002
cpe. 2dr.	mini		28300	34600	37700		
	maxi		33000	38800	41500		
cpe. 2dr. 230	mini					45100	49350
	maxi					49300	53550
cpe. 3dr. 320	mini					50400	54600
	maxi					54600	58800
cpe. 3dr. 320AMG	mini						68200
	maxi						74500

See page 7 to adapt these figures.

1999 MERCEDES-BENZ SLK-Class

1999 NISSAN Altima

The Altima replaced the Stanza in 1993. Powered by a L4 engine it has been renewed in '1998 and 2002 where it received a 3.5L V6.

PROS

• **It's very stylish** and has a lavish luxury car look.
• **The L4 engine** is quite lively and steering is quick and right on.
• **The SE and GLE** models handle better because of the sturdier suspension, while the soft suspension on the XE and GXE models causes more swing and sway.
• **The sportier performance** of the 3.5L V6, inherited from the Maxima.
• **The car is quite comfy**, for the suspension is never harsh, the seats provide good support, soundproofing is effective at cruising speed and the cabin is roomier on the latest version.
• **This is a solidly built** vehicle, with an immaculate fit and finish and attractive trim components and the cabin interior is well-designed and quite spiffy.

CONS

• **Built with such a sturdy frame,** the Altima is heavy, which affects engine efficiency, of course. There's a poorer power to weight ratio and higher fuel consumption than is the case for the competition.
• **Pick-up** is less lively than accelerations, because first and second gears are too closely spaced on the manual transmission.
• **The manual transmission** can be a hassle to operate because of its lack of precision and sluggish feedback.
• **The cabin** on 96-97 models aren't as roomy as that of some rivals.
• **Brakes** are effective, but they heat up with intensive use, and stops are unpredictable, so ABS is a real must.
• **Some controls** are awkwardly located and rearward view at quarterback isn't perfect.

VERDICT

The Altima and the Maxima share the compact market segment that is beating the pants off luxury and Sportscars, as far as sales go. A nice niche that attracts a lot of buyers.

RECALLS

None over this period.

RELIABILITY PROBLEMS

	1997	1998	1999	2000	2001	2002
Engine:	X	X	X	-	-	-
Transmission:	X	-	-	-	-	-
Suspension:	X	X	X	X	X	-
Steering:	-	-	-	-	-	-
Brakes:	-	X	X	X	-	-
Electricity:	X	X	X	X	-	-
Body:	X	X	X	X	X	X
Accessories:	X	X	X	X	X	X
Fit/finish:	X	X	X	-	-	-

POWERTRAIN

Year	Type/L/Camshaft/bhp gearbox	Drivetrain	Acceler. 0/100 sec.	Top speed km/h	Ave. consp. l./100 km	Fuel
97-01	L4/2.4/DOHC/150	front-M5	9.0	190	9.7	
		front-A4	10.2	180	10.6	
2002	L4/2.5/DOHC/175	front-M5	8.0	200	10.5	
		front-A4	8.8	190	11.0	
	V6/3.5/DOHC/240	front-M5	7.3	220	11.0	
		front-A4	7.8	210	12.0	

SPECIFICATIONS

Model	Wlb. mm	Lght. mm	Cb.wt kg	Brakes fr/rr	Steering type	Standard tires
1997						
sdn. 4dr. XE	2620	4585	1283	dc/dr	pwr.r&p.	205/65R15
sdn. 4dr. GXE	2620	4585	1333	dc/dr	pwr.r&p.	205/65R15
sdn. 4dr. SE	2620	4585	1373	dc/ABS	pwr.r&p.	205/65R15
sdn. 4dr. GLE	2620	4585	1403	dc/ABS	pwr.r&p.	205/65R15
98-01						
sdn. 4dr. XE	2619	4661	1304	dc/dr	pwr.r&p.	195/65R15
sdn. 4dr. GXE	2619	4661	1324	dc/dr	pwr.r&p.	195/65R15
sdn. 4dr. SE	2619	4661	1325	dc/dc	pwr.r&p.	205/60R15
sdn. 4dr. GLE	2619	4661	1335	dc/dr	pwr.r&p.	195/65R15
2002						
sdn. 4dr. S	2799	4864	1377	dc/dc	pwr.r&p.	205/65R16
sdn. 4dr. SE	2799	4864	1449	dc/dc	pwr.r&p.	215/55R17

PRICES

Model / version		1997	1998	1999	2000	2001	2002
sdn. 4dr. XE	mini	6300	8600	11000	13850	15200	
	maxi	8400	10500	12900	15750	15750	
sdn. 4dr. GXE	mini	7350	9450	11950	14500	14500	
	maxi	9450	11500	13850	16800	16800	
sdn. 4dr. SE	mini	8400	10500	14900	14900	14900	
	maxi	10500	12600	17300	17300	17300	
sdn. 4dr. GLE	mini		11950	13850	15950	15950	
	maxi		13650	15950	17850	17850	
sdn. 4dr. S	mini						19400
	maxi						22600
sdn. 4dr. 2.5	mini						22600
	maxi						25200
sdn. 4dr. 3.5 SE	mini						25700
	maxi						28900

See page 7 to adapt these figures.

2002 NISSAN Altima SE

NISSAN   Maxima

2000 NISSAN Maxima

Inaugurated in 1984 (front-wheel drive), the Maxima was up-graded in '86, '89 and in '95 and it's powered by a V6 engine. The addition in 1999 of the EuroSport (ES) version won't go unno-ticed, for that trim level will only be available in Canada. Moreo-ver, the anti-skid control system will become standard on model equipped with the automatic transmission and anti-lock brakes. The 3.5L V6 arrived in 2002.

PROS
• **The frisky and fiery V6** engine is thrilling, especially on the lighter-weight base model.
• **The GXE** model is less expensive than its rivals, the Accord, 626 and Camry.
• **The sleek,** classy look of the latest models.
• **The better-adjusted suspension** has improved handling on the SE model that is more agile than the GXE.
• **Maneuverability** is good because of smooth, accurate, quick as a flash steering.
• **The rear "Multilink"** suspension makes for superb road stability on curves and quite a smooth ride.
• **The powerful V6** is the most economical engine in its category, thanks to a good power to weight ratio.
• **Construction quality** and fit and finish are definitely topnotch but the overall look is plain and not at all plush.

CONS
• **The cabin interior** on the GXE is terribly chintzy-looking.
• **Poorly designed seats** don't provide adequate support because they're so sunken-in and they're hard with such firm upholstery.
• **The manual shifter** on the SE isn't at all in keeping with the character of this model, for it's inaccurate and stubborn.
• **The instrument panel** isn't too ergonomic, for the controls located on the center console aren't within easy reach for the driver.
• **There aren't too many storage** compartments and there are no niceties that you find on rival models.
• **Just unbelievable**: no automatic shifter indicator on the instrument panel, crummy windshield wiper and washer system and horrible rear defroster.

VERDICT
The Maxima is a sturdy and reliable car that is comfortable to drive and fun to put through its paces.

RECALLS
2002   Dealers will replaced the front lower A-arm and installed a new stopper on the gas pedal of some vehicles.

RELIABILITY PROBLEMS

	1997	1998	1999	2000	2001	2002
Engine:	X	X	X	X	-	-
Transmission:	X	-	-	-	-	-
Suspension:	X	X	X	-	-	-
Steering:	X	-	-	-	-	-
Brakes:		X	X	X	X	X
Electricity:	X	X	X	X	X	X
Body:	X	X	-	X	X	-
Accessories:	X	X	X	X	-	-
Fit/finish:	X	X	X	-	-	-

POWERTRAIN

Year	Type/ L/Camshaft/bhp	Drivetrain & gearbox	Acceler. 0/100 sec.	Top. speed km/h	Ave. Fuel consp. l./100 km
97-01	V6/3.0/DOHC/190-222	front-M5	8.0	220	10.9
		front-A4	8.5	210	11.3
2002	V6/3.5/DOHC/255	front-M6	7.4	220	11.0
		front/A4	8.0	210	12.0

PERFORMANCE

SPECIFICATIONS

Model 97-99	Wlb. mm	Lght. mm	Cb.wt kg	Brakes fr/rr	Steering type	Standard tires
sdn. 4dr. GXE	2700	4810	1369	dc/dc	pwr.r&p.	205/65R15
sdn. 4dr. SE/ES	2700	4810	1396	dc/ABS	pwr.r&p.	215/55R16
sdn. 4dr. GLE	2700	4810	1399	dc/ABS	pwr.r&p.	205/65R15
00-02						
sdn. 4dr. GXE	2751	4864	1450	dc/ABS	pwr.r&p.	205/65R15
sdn. 4dr. SE	2751	4864	1448	dc/ABS	pwr.r&p.	225/50R17
sdn. 4dr. GLE	2751	4864	1496	dc/ABS	pwr.r&p.	215/55R16

PRICES

Model / version		1997	1998	1999	2000	2001	2002
sdn. 4dr. GXE	mini	9450	12400	14700	21500	23600	25700
	maxi	13100	15750	18000	23600	26250	28350
sdn. 4dr. SE	mini	12900	15950	19400	23600		28350
	maxi	16500	19400	23850	26800		31000
sdn. 4dr. GLE	mini	13100	16000	19400	23600	25700	28900
	maxi	16800	17550	23600	27000	28900	31500
sdn. 4dr. ES	mini			16800			
	maxi			20250			
sdn. 4dr. SE Ann.	mini					26800	
	maxi					29400	

See page 7 to adapt these figures.

1998 NISSAN Maxima

NISSAN   Pathfinder

1998 NISSAN Pathfinder

The Pathfinder has been on the market since 1986. It was originally powered by a 2.4L 4-cylinder engine. The 3.0L V6 engine
came out in '87 and the vehicle was revamped in 1996. It's
interesting to know that the Chilkoot trim level is exclusively sold
in Canada.

PROS
- **The bold body style** of the 95 models was a real crowd pleaser.
- **Highway driving** is very smooth and comfy.
- **The cabin is very spacious**, especially in the rear seat area with its
more generous leg room than the competition.
- **Handling** is safe and sure for there's only moderate sway and the
combined springs and shock absorbers are well-calibrated.
- **Brakes** have become very muscular, balanced and easy to adjust
and

smooth power steering provides good maneuverability.
- **The instrument panel** is simple, straightforward and ergonomic.
- **Construction quality** and finish details are good and equipment is
complete.

CONS
- **The look** of the latest model has disappointed a lot of fans because
it isn't as brassy and virile as before.
- **Engine performance** has improved, but not enough to make for
really fun driving, for the V6 still lacks torque.
- **The gears** aren't well-calibrated, especially on the automatic whose
electronic unit should be readjusted.
- **Side view** is obstructed by the spare tire mounted on the rear blocks
rearward view.
- **Seats** on older models are hard because they're thinly upholstered
and they're poorly designed so they don't provide adequate lateral or
lumbar support.
- **Fuel consumption** is never economical, especially off-the-road.
- **Ground clearance** on the latest models is lower with the smaller
tires, which can be a real pain on rough terrain.

VERDICT
This all-terrain vehicle is reliable and quite nice-looking, but its overall
design is beginning to look dusty and needs sprucing up.

RECALLS
None over this period.

RELIABILITY PROBLEMS

	1997	1998	1999	2000	2001	2002
Engine:	X	X	X	X	-	-
Transmission:	X	X	X	-	-	-
Suspension:	-	X	X	X	X	-
Steering:	-	-	-	-	-	-
Brakes:	-	-	-	-	-	-
Electricity:	X	X	X	X	-	-
Body:	X	X	X	X	X	-
Accessories:	-	X	X	X	X	-
Fit/finish:	X	X	X	X	-	-

POWERTRAIN

Year	Type/ L/Camshaft/bhp	Drivetrain & gearbox
97-00	V6/3.3/SOHC/168	rear/all-M5
		rear/all-A4
01-02	V6/3.5/SOHC/250	rr./all-M5
		rr./all-A4

PERFORMANCE

Acceler. 0/100 sec.	Top. speed km/h	Ave. Fuel consp. l./100 km
10.3	165	14.7
11.6	160	15.4
9.5	180	14.7
10.2	175	15.6

SPECIFICATIONS

Model	Wlb.	Lght.	Cb.wt	Brakes	Steering	Standard
97-98 4x2						
wgn. 5dr. XE	2700	4529	1667	dc/ABS	pwr.r&p.	235/70R15
wgn. 5dr. SE	2700	4529	1712	dc/ABS	pwr.r&p.	235/70R15
97-01 4x4						
wgn. 5dr. XE	2700	4641	1803	dc/dr/ABS	pwr.r&p.	265/70R15
wgn. 5dr. SE	2700	4641	1844	dc/dr/ABS	pwr.r&p.	265/70R15
wgn. 5dr. LE	2700	4641	1830	dc/dr/ABS	pwr.r&p.	235/70R15

PRICES

Model / version		1997	1998	1999	2000	2001	2002
wgn. 5dr. XE	mini	11550	13350	15100	19950	22900	26250
	maxi	13650	15450	17300	22000	25200	29100
wgn. 5dr. SE	mini	17850	19950	21500	26150	29800	33100
	maxi	20350	22000	24000	28250	32000	35900
wgn. 5dr. LE	mini	18400	20500	22800	27300	30350	35700
	maxi	21000	22600	24900	29400	32550	38550
wgn. 4dr. Klondike	mini	14700					
	maxi	17200					
wgn. 4dr. Chilkoot	mini		15750	17850			26250
	maxi		17850	24500			29300
1999.5							
wgn. 5dr. XE	mini			16500			
	maxi			18500			
wgn. 5dr. SE	mini			23850			
	maxi			26000			
wgn. 5dr. LE	mini			24150			
	maxi			26250			

See page 7 to adapt these figures.

2001 NISSAN Pathfinder

NISSAN   Quest

1999 NISSAN Quest

The Quest is identical to the Mercury Villager and was first sold in 1993. It's built on the former Maxima platform and is equipped with the Maxima 3.0L V6 engine. In '99, the Quest has been over-hauled and it now offers a second sliding door and a new 3.3L V6 engine.

PROS
• **The modern**, shapely body design is very appealing and the cabin interior design is attractive as well.
• **Modular rear seats** can be modified according to 14 different arrangements and are really surprisingly easy to manipulate.
• **Good wheel travel** and well-adjusted shock absorbers on the rear end enhance driving comfort.
• **The vehicle** is neutral even if the suspension and rear end are of simple, rather rustic design.
• **The GXE** is a safe vehicle with its robust frame, dual airbags, standard headrests on every seat and ABS brakes. This equipment comes standard as well as on all models built after '99.
• **Spiffy trim components**, construction quality and tight finish are typical of Japanese products.

CONS
• **Excessive vehicle weight** affects performance and fuel consumption.
• **The disc-drum brakes** on the XE lack grip and lasting power, so vehicle path is unpredictable.
• **The rear seat** area and baggage compartment are limited with seven adults on board.
• **Maneuverability** isn't the greatest with such a large steer angle diameter and steering is vague at the center and a bit over-assisted.
• **Better soundproofing** would sure make for a more pleasant ride.
• **Some storage compartments** and controls aren't very convenient.
• **Road, engine and wind noise** is almost deafening.

VERDICT
The Quest is more of a station wagon than a minivan, for its hefty weight is more suited to travel than to real work, and buyers who prefer cars to minivans won't be disappointed.

RECALLS
1998 Battery could be defective.
99-00 The retaining bolts for the steering rack mounting may not have been torqued to the proper specifications.
The seatblet buckle assembly are defective and must be replaced.

RELIABILITY PROBLEMS

	1997	1998	1999	2000	2001	2002
Engine:	X	X	X	X	X	
Transmission:	X	X	X	-	-	
Suspension:	X	X	-	-	-	
Steering:	-	-	-	-	-	
Brakes:	X	X	X	X	-	
Electricity:	X	X	X	X	X	
Body:	X	X	-	X	X	
Accessories:	X	X	X	X	X	
Fit/finish:	X	X	X	-	-	

POWERTRAIN

Year	Type/ L/Camshaft/bhp	Drivetrain & gearbox
97-98	V6/3.0/SOHC/151	front-A4
99-01	V6/3.3/SOHC/170	front-A4

PERFORMANCE

	Acceler. 0/100 sec.	Top. speed km/h	Ave. Fuel consp. l/100 km
	13.3	160	12.5
	11.0	180	13.8

SPECIFICATIONS

Model 97-01	Wlb. mm	Lght. mm	Cb.wt kg	Brakes fr/rr	Steering type	Standard tires
m.v. 4dr. GXE	2850	4948	1798	dc/dr/ABS	pwr.r&p.	215/70R15
m.v. 4dr. SE	2850	4948	1756	dc/dr/ABS	pwr.r&p.	225/60R15
m.v. 4dr. GLE	2850	4948	1798	dc/dr/ABS	pwr.r&p.	215/70R15

PRICES

Model / version		1997	1998	1999	2000	2001	2002
m.v. 4dr. XE	mini	10200	12100	13650			
	maxi	12300	14000	15750			
m.v. 4dr. GXE	mini	13650	15750		19950	21500	
	maxi	15750	17850		21600	24000	
m.v. 4dr. SE	mini			16300	22800	24700	
	maxi			18500	25100	27200	
m.v. 4dr. GLE	mini			18900			
	maxi			21600			

See page 7 to adapt these figures.

2000 NISSAN Quest

NISSAN   Sentra/200SX 1998

1999 NISSAN Sentra

Inspired by the former generation, the Sentra was redesigned in 1995 and 2000. A new SE version was introduced in '99 with a 140-bhp 2.0L. SE-R and SE-R Spec V were inaugurated in 2002 with a 2.5L engine.

PROS
• **These cars aren't unattractive**, but they're terribly ordinary.
• **Handling** has improved for there's less swing and sway, but the base model tires are too narrow to be as effective as those that equip the more elaborate models.
• **Power steering** is more pleasant to use than the manual that is sluggish and inaccurate, because it suffers from too high a reduction ratio.
• **The 1.6L and 1.8L engines** are livelier than before, but the 2.0L and 2.5L engine are far more powerful.
• **The ride is quite comfortable** with the upgraded suspension, more spacious cabin interior, better contoured seats and lower noise level.
• **Equipment** and fit and finish are adequate for such economical cars and only the instrument panel seems to be really lacking.

CONS
• **Rear seats** on the Sentra are narrow and hard to get into and only children will be comfortably seated in them.
• **The spongy brake** pedal makes it difficult to control stops with any accuracy.
• **Mediocre** quality tires.

VERDICT
The Sentra and 200 SX models don't have a look that makes you sit up and take notice, but they're solid, reliable cars and, depending on the engine model, they're fun to drive.

RECALLS
1997   Moisture may penetrate into throttle chamber and freeze.
       Light bulbs are not bright enough for brake signal.
       Vehicle identification number might be incorrect.
97-98   Mechanism of the windshield wipers must be inspected and replaced if necessary.
2001   Dealers will replace the lower control arm attachment bolts.
       Odometer that record in miles will be replaced with ones that record in kilometers.
       Dealers will inspect for cracks and replace the faulty wheels.
01-02   Dealers will install a safe protector on the headlamp adjusting screws.
2002   Inspection and replacement if necessary of the two front mats.

Sentra/200SX 1998   NISSAN

RELIABILITY PROBLEMS

	1997	1998	1999	2000	2001	2002
Engine:	X	X	X		-	
Transmission:	-	-	-		-	-
Suspension:	-	-	-		-	-
Steering:	-	-	-		-	-
Brakes:	X	X	X		-	
Electricity:	X	X	X		X	X
Body:	-	X	X		X	X
Accessories:	X	X	-		X	-
Fit/finish:	-	-	X		-	

POWERTRAIN

Year	Type/ L/Camshaft/bhp	Drivetrain & gearbox	Acceler. 0/100 sec.	Top. speed km/h	Ave. Fuel consp. l./100 km
97-01	L4/1.6/DOHC/110-115	front-M5	10.0	165	8.0
		front-A4	11.5	160	8.8
99-01	L4/2.0/DOHC/140 (SE)	front-M5	9.0	180	9.0
		front-A4	NA	NA	NA
01-02	L4/1.8/DOHC/126	front-M5	10.5	170	8.8
		front-A4	11.4	165	9.0
	L4/2.5/DOHC/165	front-M5	8.5	180	10.5
	L4/2.5/DOHC/175	front-M6	8.0	190	11.0

PERFORMANCE

SPECIFICATIONS

Model	Wlb. mm	Lght. mm	Cb.wt kg	Brakes fr/rr	Steering type	Standard tires
Sentra 97-98						
cpe. 2dr.	2430	4326	1064	dc/dr	r&p.	155/80R13
sdn. 4dr.	2430	4326	1090	dc/dr	pwr.r&p.	175/70R13
Sentra 99-02						
sdn. 4dr. base	2535	4509	1050	dc/dr	r&p.	185/65R14
sdn. 4dr. XE/GXE	2535	4509	1080	dc/dr	pwr.r&p.	185/65R14
sdn. 4dr. SE	2535	4509	1188	dc/ABS	pwr.r&p.	185/65R14
sdn. 4dr. SE-R	2535	4509	1238	dc/ABS	pwr.r&p.	195/55R16
sdn. 4dr. Spec V	2535	4509	1244	dc/ABS	pwr.r&p.	215/45ZR17
200SX 97-98						
cpe. 2dr. base	2535	4321	1065	dc/dr	pwr.r&p.	175/70R13
cpe. 2dr. SE	2535	4321	1145	dc/dc	pwr.r&p.	175/65R14
cpe. 2dr. SE-R	2535	4321	1175	dc/dc	pwr.r&p.	195/55R15

PRICES

Model / version		1997	1998	1999	2000	2001	2002
Sentra 97-99							
sdn. 4dr. XE	mini	6800	8400	8900		12400	14200
	maxi	8900	10000	11000		14200	16300
sdn. 4dr. GXE	mini	6800	10000	10000		13850	15750
	maxi	10000	11550	11750		14700	17850
sdn. 4dr. GLE	mini	8400					
	maxi	10500					
sdn. 4 dr. SE	mini			12100		16300	
	maxi			13850		17850	
sdn. 4dr. 5 speed	mini	5250	6300				
	maxi	7350	7900				
sdn. 4dr. SE-R	mini						17850
	maxi						19950
sdn. 4dr. SE-R Spec V	mini						19950
	maxi						22000
200SX 97-98							
cpe. 2dr. SE	mini		7900				
	maxi		9450				
cpe. 2dr. SE-R	mini		10000				
	maxi		11550				

See page 7 to adapt these figures.

2000 NISSAN Xterra

Nissan derived its Xterra from the Pathfinder's chassis and mechanical components to create a smaller SUV with more youthful styling. In 2000, a single version was introduced with a 3.3-liter V6 engine, in 2001 the choice grew to three models and a supercharged version was introduced in 2002.

PROS
• **The large tubular roof rack** adds to the original styling.
• **The Xterra is surprisingly roomy** for such a compact vehicle, especially in the spacious rear seats.
• **The cargo bay** is roomy and features a modular configuration.
• The Xterra is surprisingly **maneuverable** for an SUV.
• **Performance levels** of the two engines are honorable despite a gross weight close of to 2 tons.
• **The brakes are easy to gauge**, which makes for pleasant everyday driving.
• **The numerous front storage spaces** as well as running boards and roof rack emphasize this vehicle's practical side.

CONS
• **The rustic suspension** is uncomfortable on poor roads where it becomes very jumpy partially because of the large bouncy tires.
• **The high center of gravity** makes the Xterra unstable in curves where moderation must be exercised at all times.
• **This vehicle's large engine** requires more fuel than the average.
• **The brakes** are not powerful enough, and stopping distances are above-average.
• **Access** to the rear seats and cargo bay is hindered by the high ground clearance.
• **The headlights** are too dim to be efficient in poor weather conditions.
• **The overassisted steering** feels light and vague on center. This hinders driving precision.

VERDICT
The Xterra is experiencing a good level of commercial success because of the way it defines itself as well as its great looks.

RECALLS
None over this period.

RELIABILITY PROBLEMS

	1997	1998	1999	2000	2001	2002
Engine:				-	-	-
Transmission:						-
Suspension:						-
Steering:				-		-
Brakes:				-	-	-
Electricity:				X	-	-
Body:				X	X	-
Accessories:				X	X	-
Fit/finish:				-	-	-

POWERTRAIN

Year	Type/ L/Camshaft/bhp	Drivetrain & gearbox	Acceler. 0/100 sec.	Top. speed km/h	Ave. Fuel consp. l./100 km
00-02	V6/3.3/SOHC/170	rear/all-M5	11.0	175	14.3
		rear/all-A4	11.8	170	15.2
2002	V6C/SOHC/210	rear/all-M5	10.0	180	16.0
		rear/all-A4	10.8	175	16.0

PERFORMANCE

SPECIFICATIONS

Model 00-02	Wlb. mm	Lght. mm	Cb.wt kg	Brakes fr/rr	Steering type	Standard tires
wgn. 5dr.	2649	4521	1841	dc/dr/ABS	pwr.bal.	265/70R15
wgn. 5dr. XE	2649	4521	1860	dc/dr/ABS	pwr.bal.	265/70R16
wgn. 5dr. SE	2649	4521	1897	dc/dr/ABS	pwr.bal.	265/65R17
2002						
wgn. 5dr. SC	2649	4521	1918	dc/dr/ABS	pwr.bal.	265/65R17

PRICES

Model / version		1997	1998	1999	2000	2001	2002
wgn. 5dr.	mini				20500		
	maxi				24150		
wgn. 5dr. XE	mini					23300	25200
	maxi					26250	28350
wgn. 5dr. SE	mini					24900	26800
	maxi					28000	30000
wgn. 5dr. SE-R S/C	mini						27700
	maxi						30850

See page 7 to adapt these figures.

2000 NISSAN Xterra

1997 NISSAN 240SX

This **rear-wheel drive sports** coupe replaced the 200SX in 1989 and is available in 2 or 3-door models driven by a 2.4L engine. It has been redesigned in 1995 and disappeared in 1999.

PROS

• **This model is stylish** either with or without the rear hatch.

• **The cockpit is comfy**, instrument gauges are easy to read, but who really needs the Eyecue head-up display on the windshield?

• **Road stability** is good, thanks to the rear end that really sticks to the road. But the front end tends to get light at high speeds.

• **Brakes** are muscular, but there's almost immediate rear wheel lock, so ABS is an absolute must.

• **The trunk** isn't very spacious, but it offers an easy access.

• **The LE** is more fun to drive with its good visibility, greater stability and lower noise level.

CONS

• **The 2.4L engine** isn't too hot and it seems to sputter and strain, especially with the automatic transmission that saps its power even more.

• **The stiff rear axle** jumps a lot and seats are poorly designed, so comfort isn't what it should be.

• **Outward view** is obstructed by the thick roof support and the low-angled rear window on the hatchback that gets murky at the first raindrop that falls.

• **Cabin size** is cut down by the huge tunnel that runs down the middle.

• **The insufficiently rigid** frame on the SE cracks a lot.

VERDICT

The 240SX coupe is economical and fun for Sportscar driving fans, but all in all, engine performance isn't too much out of the ordinary.

RECALLS

None over this period.

RELIABILITY PROBLEMS

	1997	1998	1999	2000	2001	2002
Engine:	-	-				
Transmission:	-	-				
Suspension:	-	-				
Steering:	X	-				
Brakes:	X	-				
Electricity:	-	X				
Body:	-	-				
Accessories:	X	X				
Fit/finish:	-	-				

POWERTRAIN

Year	Type/ L/Camshaft/bhp	Drivetrain & gearbox
97-98	L4/2.4/DOHC/155	rear-M5
		rear-A4

PERFORMANCE

Acceler. 0/100 sec.	Top. speed km/h	Ave. Fuel consp. l./100 km
8.6	200	10.7
9.8	195	11.4

SPECIFICATIONS

Model 97-98	Wlb. mm	Lght. mm	Cb.wt kg	Brakes fr/rr	Steering type	Standard tires
cpe. 2dr. base	2525	4501	1270	dc/dc	pwr.r&p.	195/60R15
cpe. 2dr. SE	2525	4501	1276	dc/dc	pwr.r&p.	205/55R16
cpe. 2dr. LE	2525	4501	1304	dc/ABS	pwr.r&p.	205/55R16

PRICES

Model / version		1997	1998	1999	2000	2001	2002
cpe. 2dr. base	mini	7550	9450				
	maxi	10000	11550				
cpe. 2dr. SE	mini	8900	11000				
	maxi	11000	13100				
cpe. 2dr. LE	mini	10000	13100				
	maxi	12600	14200				

See page 7 to adapt these figures.

1997 NISSAN 240SX

SAAB 900-9³

2000 SAAB 9³

This Swedish front-wheel drive car was first sold way back in 1969. It was upgraded in 1978, in '84 (Turbo), in '85 (convertible) and redesigned in 1993 when a V6 engine was also available, along with the traditional 4-cylinder engine. Its name change to 9³ in '99 and it is a good reason for Saab to "clean the house" in terms of engine.

PROS
• **The Turbo and V6** engines are more muscular and economical.
• **The cockpit** and instrument panel are nicely designed.
• **Handling** is good in most situations, but there's oversteering when car is pushed to the limit.
• **Brakes** are strong and reliable.
• **This car has a nice personality**, it's well-built and fitted, it's well equipped and the Turbo has real character.
• **The huge trunk** may be extended or modified as needed.

CONS
• **The body design** is getting a bit dusty and dingy-looking, the convertible could be more robust, the rear end is stiff and it's an overhang engine system.
• **Engine performance** isn't too hot on the base model even with its good power to weight ratio and aerodynamic efficiency.
• **Gears are more** tailored to economy than to performance.
• **The cabin interior** is cramped because rear seats are very tight and the front wheel wells take up a lot of room.
• **Comfort isn't great** with such hard seats, harsh suspension, high noise level, especially on the poorly soundproofed convertible model.
• **Things to consider**: brake pads wear out in no time, rear wheels lock almost immediately without ABS and the engine tends to overheat.

VERDICT
In spite of modifications and a more modern design, the 900 and the 9³ hasn't broken any sales records, because they are too expensive.

RECALLS
1997 Throttle control lever bushings may corrode.
1998 Missing instructions regarding the setting of the headlights.
2002 Dealers will inspect and replace if necessary the brake calipers.

POWERTRAIN

Year	Type/ L/Camshaft/bhp	Drivetrain & gearbox
97-98	L4/2.0/DOHC/185	front-M5
	L4/2.3/DOHC/150	front-A4
	V6/2.5/DOHC/170	front-M5
		front-A4
99-01	L4/2.0/DOHC/185	front-M5
		front-A4
99-02	L4T/2.0/DOHC/200-205	front-M5
		front-A4
Viggen	L4T/2.3/DOHC/200-230	front-M5

PERFORMANCE

Acceler. 0/100 sec.	Top. speed km/h	Ave. Fuel consp. l./100 km
7.5	220	11.0
11.0	180	11.5
8.5	190	11.0
9.2	185	12.0
10.2	205	11.9
11.0	200	12.4
7.5	220	12.2
8.3	210	13.6
7.5	220	12.2

SPECIFICATIONS

Model	Wlb. mm	Lght. mm	Cb.wt kg	Brakes fr/rr	Steering type	Standard tires
900 97-99						
con. 2dr. S	2600	4637	1415	dc/ABS	pwr.r&p.	195/60R15
cpe. 2dr. S	2600	4637	1356	dc/ABS	pwr.r&p.	195/60R15
sdn. 5dr. S	2600	4637	1335	dc/ABS	pwr.r&p.	195/60R15
sdn. 5dr. SE	2600	4637	1495	dc/ABS	pwr.r&p.	195/60R15
9³ 99-02						
con. 2dr. S	2605	4629	1450	dc/ABS	pwr.r&p.	195/60R15
cpe. 3dr. S	2605	4629	1355	dc/ABS	pwr.r&p.	205/50R16
cpe. 3dr.Viggen	2605	4629	1355	dc/ABS	pwr.r&p.	205/50R16
sdn. 5dr. S	2605	4629	1375	dc/ABS	pwr.r&p.	195/60R16
con. 2dr. SE	2605	4629	1450	dc/ABS	pwr.r&p.	205/50R16
sdn. 5dr. SE	2605	4629	1375	dc/ABS	pwr.r&p.	205/50R16
sdn. 5dr.Viggen	2605	4629	1375	dc/ABS	pwr.r&p.	205/50R16

PRICES

Model / version		1997	1998	1999	2000	2001	2002
900							
con. 2dr. S	mini	13600	18400				
	maxi	17000	21750				
con. 2dr. Turbo SE	mini	19200	24150				
	maxi	22800	27800				
con. 2dr. SE V6	mini	18150					
	maxi	21500					
sdn. 3dr. S	mini	6300	7750				
	maxi	8900	10500				
sdn. 3dr. SE Turbo	mini	11550	12300				
	maxi	14200	14700				
sdn. 3dr. S Turbo	mini	7750	8700				
	maxi	11000	11550				
sdn. 5dr. S	mini	6500	8000				
	maxi	9150	10700				
sdn. 5dr. SE V6	mini	11950					
	maxi	14700					
sdn. 5dr. SE Tbo	mini	11750	12800				
	maxi	14500	15450				
9³							
sdn. 3dr.	mini			13550	15750	19950	
	maxi			15750	18400	22600	
sdn. 3dr. Viggen	mini				29400	34650	44100
	maxi				32000	36650	47250
con. 2dr.	mini			21750	28900	32550	45150
	maxi			25200	31200	35200	48300
con. 2dr. SE	mini			26250	33400	37800	51450
	maxi			28900	35900	40300	55100
con. 2dr. Viggen	mini				40600	44600	49000
	maxi				43000	47150	52000
sdn. 5dr.	mini			13750	17100	21400	24100
	maxi			16950	19400	24150	27300
sdn. 5dr. SE	mini			18000	21500	25200	30450
	maxi			20700	31400	27700	36200
sdn. 5dr. SE Tbo	mini						27300
	maxi						31000
sdn. 5dr. Viggen	mini				30450	34650	36550
	maxi				33000	37150	41500

See page 7 to adapt these figures.

SAAB 9000-9⁵

2000 SAAB 9⁵

The 9000 is a top-of-the-line sports sedan that began its career in 1984 and was powered by a Turbo 16 engine. The multi-valve S model came out in '85 and the 9000 SPG sports model hit the market in '88. Engine models include the 4-cylinder, conventional or Turbo, or the V6. And then Saab decided in 1999 to call it the 9⁵ and tried to make it look a little more modern in 2002.

PROS

• **Its classic and elegant body** design, like that of the model with separate trunk, is more attractive than that of the hatchback.

• **The Turbo** engine really moves this car and puts it through its paces without a hitch, especially with the new V6 Turbo.

• **Handling** is quite safe and stable but the car tends to go into understeering and there's frequent loss of wheel function.

• **Visibility** is just great, the instrument panel is well-designed and steering is quick and accurate.

• **Brakes** are effective and stable with ABS, but they're hard to control with the stiff pedal.

• **The cabin interior** is nice and spacious, and easy to climb into.

• **The suspension** is effective, but a bit stiff, so the ride isn't always silky smooth. Fabric trim on the seats is preferable to leather seats.

• **Construction quality**, finish and trim components are impeccable and equipment is very extensive.

CONS

• **Conventional engines** coupled with the automatic are less frisky and feisty and they suffer from a poor power to weight ratio.

• **The Turbo engine** is a real gas-guzzler.

• **On Turbo models**, torque affects steering on strong accelerations.

• **These cars are expensive** to buy, and upkeep is costly because of a small service network, so resale value isn't great.

• **The manual transmission** is poorly calibrated and there's a gap between 3rd and 4th gear.

VERDICT

The Saab 9000 and the 9⁵ are outstanding cars, but you shouldn't buy one used unless you're absolutely sure of what shape it's in, for maintenance and any major repairs can really deplete your bank account.

RECALLS

2002 Inspection and replacement, if necessary, of the steering spindle.

RELIABILITY PROBLEMS

	1997	1998	1999	2000	2001	2002
Transmission:	X	X	X	X	X	-
Suspension:	-	-	X	-	-	-
Steering:	-	-	-	-	-	-
Brakes:	X	X	X	X	-	-
Electricity:	-	X	X	X	X	X
Body:	X	-	X	X	X	-
Accessories:	X	X	X	X	-	-
Fit/finish:	-	-	-	-	-	-

POWERTRAIN / PERFORMANCE

Year	Type/ L/Camshaft/bhp	Drivetrain & gearbox	Acceler. 0/100 sec.	Top. speed km/h	Ave. Fuel consp. l./100 km
97-98	L4/2.3/DOHC/150-170	front-M5	9.9	210	10.5
		front-A4	11.0	200	11.5
	L4T/2.3/DOHC/200-225	front-M5	8.5	225	11.5
		front-A4	9.2	215	12.5
	V6/3.0/OHV/210	front-A4	9.0	220	13.0
99-02	L4T/2.3/DOHC/170	front-M5	10.6	220	11.9
		front-A4	11.7	210	11.5
	L4T/2.3/DOHC/230	front-M5	8.5	225	11.5
	V6/3.0/DOHC/200	front-A4	9.4	220	12.8

SPECIFICATIONS

Model 9000	Wlb. mm	Lght. mm	Cb.wt kg	Brakes fr/rr	Steering type	Standard tires
sdn. 5dr. S	2672	4620	1410	dc/ABS	pwr.r&p.	195/65R15
sdn. 5dr. Turbo	2672	4761	1420	dc/ABS	pwr.r&p.	205/60R15
sdn. 5dr. CSE	2672	4761	1440	dc/ABS	pwr.r&p.	205/60R15
9⁵						
sdn. 4dr. base	2703	4808	1490	dc/ABS	pwr.r&p.	215/55R16
sdn. 5dr. SE	2703	4808	1615	dc/ABS	pwr.r&p.	215/55R16
sdn. 4dr. Aero	2703	4805	1565	dc/ABS	pwr.r&p.	225/45ZR17
wgn. 4dr.	2703	4808	1705	dc/ABS	pwr.r&p.	215/55R16

PRICES

Model / version		1997	1998	1999	2000	2001	2002
9000							
sdn. 4dr. CDE	mini	13540					
	maxi	17100					
sdn. 5dr. CS	mini	10400					
	maxi	13450					
sdn. 5dr. CS Aero	mini	15750					
	maxi	19650					
sdn. 4dr. CSE An.	mini	14900	16800				
	maxi	18400	19950				
9⁵							
sdn. 4dr. 2.3	mini			17300	23300	27100	
	maxi			20150	26250	29900	
sdn. 4dr. 3.0	mini			18400	24700	28750	
	maxi			21500	27800	31500	
sdn. 4dr. 2.3 SE	mini			23100			
	maxi			26250			
sdn. 4dr. 3.0 SE	mini			24150	31000	36200	
	maxi			27300	33600	38850	
sdn. 4dr. Aero	mini				31000	36550	44850
	maxi				35200	39400	47800
sdn. 4dr. Arc	mini						39600
	maxi						42500
sdn. 4dr. Inear	mini						33300
	maxi						36200
wgn. 4dr. Arc	mini						41500
	maxi						44600
wgn. 4dr. Inear	mini						35400
	maxi						38300
wgn. 4dr. 2.3	mini				23950	27000	
	maxi				27100	29900	
wgn. 4dr. 3.0	mini				26800	30350	
	maxi				29900	33000	
wgn. 4dr. Aero	mini					33100	46200
	maxi					35700	49350

See page 7 to adapt these figures.

SATURN   L

2001 SATURN LS

To widen its market, Saturn has decided to compete with Honda Accord and Toyota Camry. The L models are available as 4-door sedans and wagons animated by 4- and 6-cylinder engines.

PROS

• **Styling is plain**, but it does have the advantage of making these models immediately identifiable as members of the Saturn family.

• **The principle** of a structure supporting body panels, including side polymer panels is a good one.

• **Suspension** is an excellent compromise between comfort and handling. Smooth but not soft, it's relatively neutral when cornering at average speeds and it provides a comfortable ride.

• **Performance** level is very respectable with both engines, the 3.0L and 2.2L and manual transmission.

• **Brakes** are reliable, efficient and consistent.

• **Trunk** is roomy in all directions and the rear seat folds down for extra space.

• **The careful assembly** and nice-looking materials provide a solid feel and look for both the body and the passenger compartment.

CONS

• **Noise level** is strangely high because of engine and tire noise and wind that leaks in around the top of the windshield.

• **The 4-cylinder engine** is weak when teamed with the automatic transmission and doesn't justify its fuel consumption.

• **Maneuverability** is mediocre and some parking maneuvers are painful.

• **Wagon cargo space** can barely take on as much as the sedan's trunk, because its height is limited by the glasses design.

• **Storage spaces** are limited to the minimum in front and rear.

• **The Firestone Affinity tires** aren't the best choice for these models - they lack grip and generate noise.

• **Forgotten:** front seats armrests, shifter indicator for the automatic transmission and dummy pedal for the driver's comfort.

VERDICT

The Saturn L haven't encountered a big success and those who take the risk will soon discover that the resale value is low and resale time fairly long.

RECALLS

2001   Dealers will inspect the shift cable retainer clip, verify proper installation and if necessary replace the cable.

RELIABILITY PROBLEMS

	1997	1998	1999	2000	2001	2002
Engine:				X	X	-
Transmission:				-	-	-
Suspension:				-	-	-
Steering:				-	-	-
Brakes:				-	-	-
Electricity:				X	X	-
Body:				X	X	-
Accessories:				X	X	-
Fit/finish:				X	-	-

POWERTRAIN   PERFORMANCE

Year	Type/ L/Camshaft/bhp	Drivetrain & gearbox	Acceler. 0/100 sec.	Top. speed km/h	Ave. Fuel consp. l./100 km
00-02	L4/2.2/DOHC/135	front-M5	10.0	175	10.0
		front-A4	11.0	170	10.5
	V6/3.0/DOHC/182	front-A4	8.8	180	12.0

SPECIFICATIONS

Model 00-02	Wlb. mm	Lght. mm	Cb.wt kg	Brakes fr/rr	Steering type	Standard tires
sdn. 4dr. LS	2705	4836	1320	dc/dr	pwr.r&p.	195/65R15
sdn. 4dr. LS1	2705	4836	1369	dc/dr	pwr.r&p.	195/65R15
sdn. 4dr. LS2	2705	4836	1430	dc/dc	pwr.r&p.	205/65R15
wgn. 4dr. LW1	2705	4836	1395	dc/dr	pwr.r&p.	195/65R15
wgn. 4dr. LW2	2705	4836	1465	dc/dc	pwr.r&p.	205/65R15

PRICES

Model / version		1997	1998	1999	2000	2001	2002
sdn. 4dr. LS	mini				12100	13100	
	maxi				13650	15200	
sdn. 4dr. LS1	mini				13100	14200	
	maxi				14700	16300	
sdn. 4dr. LS2	mini				14200	15200	
	maxi				15200	17300	
sdn. 4dr. L 100	mini						15200
	maxi						17300
sdn. 4dr. L 200	mini						16300
	maxi						18400
sdn. 4dr. L 300	mini						17300
	maxi						19400
wgn. 4dr. LW1	mini				13100	14700	
	maxi				14700	17300	
wgn. 4dr. LW2	mini				14200	15750	
	maxi				15700	17850	
wgn. 4dr. LW200	mini						16800
	maxi						18900
wgn. 4dr. LW300	mini						17850
	maxi						19950

See page 7 to adapt these figures.

2001 SATURN SW

Under GM's wing, Saturn has developed pretty awesome products and amazing P.R. with customers. These sedans and station wagons were first sold in 1991 and were freshened up in '1996 and 1999.

PROS
• **A distinctive style** that is unmistakably that of a Saturn.
• **An original design** with a metallic cage structure on which are mounted polymer panels that are rust-proof and resistant to light impacts.
• **Dealership service** is second to none and makes up for the occasional reliability problems.
• **Handling** is clean with such a well-adjusted suspension.
• **Power brakes** and steering are smooth, so the car moves all of a piece and emergency stops are safe and sure.
• **Build and finish** quality is quite good, but still doesn't compare with that of upper-end Japanese cars.

CONS
• **The snug sedan** cabin only seats four adults, and the tiny seatbench on the coupe isn't too comfortable.
• **Engines** are noisy and rough around the edges and gears on the manual transmission are poorly calibrated.
• **Braking** could have more grip and power, for stopping distances are longer than average.
• **Performance** are by no means sensational, even with the more muscular engines that seem to sputter and strain.
• **There's a heck** of a racket during strong accelerations, but the noise level is more tolerable at cruising speed.
• **The trunk** as well as the baggage compartment on the station wagon aren't roomy, because of the large suspension wells. Luckily the rear seatbench folds down and both can be extended.
• **The plastic trim** in the cabin is far from chic.

VERDICT
The Saturns are good used cars, for they're quite stylish and are durable with their straightforward mechanical components.

RECALLS
1997   Correction to the owner's manual about headlamps adjusting.
        Defective passenger and front passenger seat belts.
        Pinion bearing cage is defective on manual steering.
        Key could be removed while in the "Run" position.
        Defective horn assembly that could generate a fire.

2001 Dealers will check the automatic transaxle park lock cable assembly operation and if necessary adjust the cable. Inspection and if necessary replacement the fuel tank.

2002 Inspection and replacement, if necessary, of the brake pedal and reinforcement of the center pillar on the driver's side.

RELIABILITY PROBLEMS

	1997	1998	1999	2000	2001	2002
Engine:	X	X	X	X	X	-
Transmission:	X	-	X	-	-	-
Suspension:	X	X	-	X	-	-
Steering:	-	-	-	-	-	-
Brakes:	X	X	X	-	-	-
Electricity:	X	X	X	X	-	-
Body:	X	X	X	X	X	X
Accessories:	X	X	X	X	X	-
Fit/finish:	-	-	-	X	-	-

POWERTRAIN

Year	Type/ L/Camshaft/bhp	Drivetrain & gearbox	Acceler. 0/100 sec.	Top. speed km/h	Ave. Fuel consp. l./100 km
97-02	L4/1.9/SOHC/85-100	front-M5	11.0	165	8.0
		front-A4	12.2	160	8.5
	L4/1.9/DOHC/124	front-M5	8.7	185	8.5
		front-A4	9.8	180	9.5

PERFORMANCE

SPECIFICATIONS

Model 97-02	Wlb. mm	Lght. mm	Cb.wt kg	Brakes fr/rr	Steering type	Standard tires
cpe. 2dr. SC1	2520	4400	1035	dc/dr	pwr.r&p.	175/70R14
cpe. 2dr. SC2	2520	4434	1084	dc/dr	pwr.r&p.	195/60R15
cpe. 3dr. SC1/2	2601	4574	1052	dc/dr	pwr.r&p.	195/60R15
sdn. 4dr. SL/SL1	2601	4493	1055	dc/dr	r&p.	175/70R14
sdn. 4dr. SL2	2601	4493	1084	dc/dr	pwr.r&p.	185/65R15
wgn. 4dr. SW1	2601	4493	1085	dc/dr	pwr.r&p.	175/70R14
wgn. 4dr. SW2	2601	4493	1111	dc/dr	pwr.r&p.	185/65R15

PRICES

Model / version		1997	1998	1999	2000	2001	2002
cpe. 2dr. SC1	mini	6300	7350	8400			
	maxi	8400	9450	10500			
cpe. 2dr. SC2	mini	7350	8400	8950			
	maxi	9450	10500	11000			
cpe. 3dr. SC1	mini			9450	10000	12100	14200
	maxi			11550	12100	14200	16300
cpe. 3dr. SC2	mini			10000	11550	13150	15250
	maxi			12100	13100	15200	17350
sdn. 4dr. SL	mini	3150	3700	5300	6500	8400	10500
	maxi	5300	6300	7350	8400	10500	12600
sdn. 4dr. SL1	mini	4750	5800	7350	9450	11000	13100
	maxi	6850	7900	9450	11000	13150	15200
sdn. 4dr. SL2	mini	5800	6850	8400	11000	11550	13650
	maxi	7350	8950	10500	12600	13650	15750
wgn. 4dr. SW1	mini	6300	7350	8950			
	maxi	8400	9450	11000			
wgn. 4dr. SW2	mini	6850	7900	9450	10500	12600	
	maxi	8950	10000	11550	12300	14700	

See page 7 to adapt these figures.

SATURN   Vue

2002 SATURN Vue

Intent on joining the SUV bandwagon, Saturn concocted the Vue using the L Series platform and main mechanical components to which it added all-wheel drive on certain versions.

PROS

• **The modern styling** is original as is the steel frame and polymer panel design.

• **The V6 engine's** performance is most conducive to driving pleasure. Its full-stop and passing acceleration capabilities are livelier than with the anemic 4-cylinder which just barely gets the job done on the FWD version.

• **The brakes** are efficient and stable even without ABS and inspire confidence although mastering threshold braking requires some practice.

• **The handling** is stable in most cases despite the simplistic suspension design which sometimes reacts strangely.

• **The fuel consumption** remains reasonable even with the V6 on board and rarely increase above 13.0 L of regular unleaded per 100 km.

• **The modular** seat configuration increases the versatility of the cabin and cargo bay and makes it possible to suit various needs.

CONS

• **The ride comfort** could be improved given the suspension does not always effectively handle road defects.

• **The consistently high noise** level points to inadequate soundproofing and there is a considerable number of suspicious body rattles.

• **The unflattering dashboard** uses very utility-grade plastics that create a very unseductive look.

• **The electronically** assisted steering system is strange and sometimes varies between high and low assistance levels without the slightest transition.

• **The limited storage** space is shameful for a utility vehicle which, by nature, is supposed to be practical.

• **The windshield wipers** are too slow to adequately clear the windshield in heavy rain.

VERDICT

The Vue will need to undergo some slight design changes before being able to compete effectively against the segment's leading models.

RECALLS

None over this period.

RELIABILITY PROBLEMS

	1997	1998	1999	2000	2001	2002
Engine:						-
Transmission:						-
Suspension:						-
Steering:						-
Brakes:		Insufficient data				-
Electricity:						-
Body:						-
Accessories:						-
Fit/finish:						-

POWERTRAIN   PERFORMANCE

Year	Type/ L/Camshaft/bhp	Drivetrain & gearbox	Acceler. 0/100 sec.	Top. speed km/h	Ave. Fuel consp. l./100 km
2002					
FWD	L4/2.2/DOHC/143	front-M5	12.0	150	11.0
AWD	L4/2.2/DOHC/143	all-ACV	12.0	150	11.3
FWD	V6/3.0/DOHC/181	front-A5	8.7	165	12.0
AWD	V6/3.0/DOHC/181	all-A5	9.0	160	13.0

SPECIFICATIONS

Model 2002	Wlb. mm	Lght. mm	Cb.wt kg	Brakes fr/rr	Steering type	Standard tires
FWD 2.2	2707	4605	1445	dc/dr	crém.ass.	215/70R16
AWD 2.2	2707	4605	1528	dc/dr	crém.ass.	235/65R16
FWD 3.0	2707	4605	1500	dc/dr	crém.ass.	235/65R16
AWD 3.0	2707	4605	1587	dc/dr	crém.ass.	235/65R16

PRICES

Model / version		1997	1998	1999	2000	2001	2002
wgn. 4dr.FWD 4 cyl.	mini						15200
	maxi						19400
wgn. 4dr.AWD 4 cyl.	mini						16800
	maxi						21000
wgn. 4dr.AWD 6 cyl.	mini						22000
	maxi						25800

See page 7 to adapt these figures.

2002 SATURN Vue

SUBARU   Forester

2000 SUBARU Forester

The Forester is built on the Impreza platform and shares its mechanical features. It was first available in 1998.

PROS
- **The automatic all-wheel drive** makes for smooth moves in all kinds of weather and on dirt roads in the middle of... the forest.
- **The vehicle** handles well in spite of high ground clearance. Cornering into curves is no problem at all and demeanor is neutral at normal speeds.
- **Maneuverability** is great due to a tight steer angle diameter and trim overall size.
- **The cargo hold** is spacious and easy to get to with the rear hatch that opens nice and wide and lowers to just the right loading level.
- **Long trips** are fatigue-free with such a civilized suspension, nicely shaped front seats and relatively low noise interference.
- **Nice feature:** storage spots for front seat travelers and luggage cover.

CONS
- **Off-road rambles** are no picnic, a reminder that the Forester is more of a high-perched car than a true grit 4X4.
- **Accelerations** are nothing to rave about with the automatic transmission and pick-up is strained with a full load.
- **The manual transmission** is sensitive to cold conditions and the shifter grinds and isn't always reliable.
- **The engine** is raucous, gets the shakes and yields only average power and torque even with its impressive displacement.
- **Rear seat** passengers don't have enough leg and elbowroom and boarding is tricky with such slim doors.
- **Seats** are terribly firm, especially the rear seatbench that's flat as blazes and offers only a short seat cushion.
- **Some dashboard trim materials** look rather chintzy and don't jive with the overall cabin look.
- **Tires** are poorly suited to this vehicle, so they're disappointing both on the highway and on less traveled roads.
- **To be mentioned:** lack of storage spots in the rear seat area, really awful radio with terribly low-slung dials.

VERDICT
The Forester isn't a true 4X4, but the all-wheel drive feature provides safe travel and the vehicle is right in fashion...

RECALLS
1998   A reinforcement bar had to be installed behind the front bumper.
Oil leaks on the exhaust manifold.
98-99   Defective brake master cylinder on vehicles equipped with ABS.

RELIABILITY PROBLEMS

	1997	1998	1999	2000	2001	2002
Engine:		-	-	X	X	X
Transmission:		X	X	-	-	-
Suspension:		-	-	-	-	-
Steering:		X	X	-	-	-
Brakes:		X	X	X	-	-
Electricity:		X	X	X	-	-
Body:		X	X	-	-	-
Accessories:		X	X	X	X	-
Fit/finish:		X	X	-	-	-

POWERTRAIN

Year	Type/ L/Camshaft/bhp	Drivetrain & gearbox
98-02	H4/2.5/DOHC/165	all-M5
		all-A4

PERFORMANCE

	Acceler. 0/100 sec.	Top. speed km/h	Ave. Fuel consp. l./100 km
	9.2	165	11.5
	10.4	160	11.5

SPECIFICATIONS

Model 98-02	Wlb. mm	Lght. mm	Cb.wt kg	Brakes fr/rr	Steering type	Standard tires
wgn. 4dr. L	2525	4450	1379	dc/dr/ABS	pwr.r&p.	205/70R15
wgn. 4dr. S	2525	4450	1379	dc/ABS	pwr.r&p.	215/60R16

PRICES

Model / version		1997	1998	1999	2000	2001	2002
wgn. 4dr. L	mini		14700	16500	18400	21000	24150
	maxi		16600	18300	19950	22600	26250
wgn. 4dr. S	mini		15750	18400	21650	24700	28350
	maxi		17650	20150	23100	26800	29900
wgn. 4dr. LTD	mini			19950	22600	26200	29400
	maxi			21850	24450	28350	31500
wgn. 4dr. Spe.Ed.	mini					22000	
	maxi					24150	
wgn. 4dr. Sport	mini						25200
	maxi						27300

See page 7 to adapt these figures.

2001 SUBARU Forester

SUBARU   Impreza

2000 SUBARU Impreza

The Impreza replaced the Loyale in 1993. It was available in various body styles: coupes, sedans and station wagons, in 2- and 4-door models, FWD and AWD powered by either a 1.8L, 2.2L or a 2.5L 4-cylinder engine. It was redesign in 1998 and the WRX version launched in 2002.

PROS

• **Its unusual design**, especially the shapely lines of the station wagon that resembles the Pacer.

• **Driving** is enhanced by a muscular engine that whoops quite a torque, by well-calibrated gears and safe all-wheel drive.

• **Handling** on the all-wheel drive model is more impressive than the model equipped with front-wheel drive whose softer suspension causes more swing and sway.

• **Solid build** and clean finish.

• **Steering** is smooth and benefits from a good reduction ratio, which allows for excellent maneuverability, thanks to a small steer angle diameter.

• **The suspension** provides a smooth ride and is less primitive than previously.

• **Brakes** are effective and stable, even without the optional ABS.

• **Standard equipment** is quite adequate and includes an airbag and an AM/FM radio/cassette.

CONS

• **Cabin space** is quite snug, especially in the rear seats and they aren't easy to climb into because of tight leg room.

• **The base engine** coupled with all-wheel drive is anemic and accelerations and pick-up are pretty sluggish and frustrating.

• **The trunk** on the sedan and the baggage compartment on the station wagon are smaller than average for this car category.

• **The center console** isn't too ergonomic with controls out of the driver's reach.

• **Interior trim** is very synthetic looking and some shades are weird.

VERDICT

The Impreza is only really to be commanded in the all-wheel drive model, for the front-wheel drive model has a lot of rivals that are far more competent.

RECALLS

None over this period.

Impreza   SUBARU

RELIABILITY PROBLEMS

	1997	1998	1999	2000	2001	2002
Engine:	X	X	-	-	-	-
Transmission:	X	X	-	-	-	-
Suspension:	-	-	-	-	-	-
Steering:	-	X	-	-	-	-
Brakes:	X	X	X	X	X	-
Electricity:	X	X	X	X	X	-
Body:	-	X	X	X	-	X
Accessories:	-	X	X	X	X	-
Fit/finish:	-	X	X	X	-	-

POWERTRAIN / PERFORMANCE

Year	Type/ L/Camshaft/bhp	Drivetrain & gearbox	Acceler. 0/100 sec.	Top. speed km/h	Ave. Fuel consp. l./100 km
97-01	H4/2.2/SOHC/135-137	all-M5	10.0	170	10.5
		all-A4	11.4	160	10.8
98-01	H4/2.5/DOHC/165 (RS)	all-M5	9.0	175	11.5
2002	H4T/2.0/DOHC/227wRx	all-M5	7.6	220	11.6

SPECIFICATIONS

Model 97-01	Wlb. mm	Lght. mm	Cb.wt kg	Brakes fr/rr	Steering type	Standard tires
cpe. 2dr. AWD	2520	4374	1281	dc/ABS	pwr.r&p.	205/55R16
sdn. 4dr. AWD	2525	4405	1220	dc/dr	pwr.r&p.	195/60R15
wgn.5dr. AWD	2525	4405	1286	dc/dr	pwr.r&p.	175/70R14
sdn. 4dr. AWD	2525	4405	1134	dc/dr/ABS	pwr.r&p.	205/60R15
sdn. 4dr. RS	2525	4405	1150	dc/ABS	pqw.r&p.	205/55R16
wgn.5dr.Outback	2525	4405	1286	dc/ABS	pwr.r&p.	205/55R16
2002						
sdn. 4dr. WRX	2525	4405	1420	dc/ABS	pwr.r&p.	205/55R16
wag. 5dr. WRX	2525	4405	1436	dc/ABS	pwr.r&p.	205/55R16

PRICES

Model / version		1997	1998	1999	2000	2001	2002
cpe. 2dr. RS	mini		13450	15750	18000	20500	
	maxi		15200	17650	19950	25600	
cpe. 2dr. L AWD	mini	7450					
	maxi	9450					
sdn. 4dr. L AWD	mini	7900	9750				
	maxi	10000	11550				
sdn. 4dr. TS	mini			11550	14400	16800	
	maxi			13100	16300	18900	
sdn. 4dr. RS	mini				17550	19950	22600
	maxi				19400	22000	24700
sdn. 4dr. WRXAWD	mini						30350
	maxi						32550
sdn. 4dr. Sport TS	mini						18900
	maxi						21000
sdn. 4dr. WRXAWD	mini						29400
	maxi						31500
wgn. 4dr. L AWD	mini	9450					
	maxi	11550					
wgn. 4dr. Brighton	mini	5350	7350	8900	11750	14200	
	maxi	7900	8900	10800	13650	16300	
wgn. 4dr. Outback	mini	10800	14700	16300	19100	21500	22600
	maxi	13100	16300	18150	21500	23100	24150

See page 7 to adapt these figures.

SUBARU   Legacy

2000 SUBARU Legacy

The Legacy came on the market in 1990 and was refreshed in 1995 and 2000. It is powered by 2.2L, 2.5L and 3.0L H4 and H6 engines

PROS

• **All-wheel drive** is the first drawing card of a Subaru vehicle for it makes for safe driving all year round.
• **Handling** is clean and stable with such a robust frame, competent suspension and optimal wheel function, no matter what the road conditions.
• **Fuel consumption** is a bit more economical with the 2.5L engine that benefits from a better power to weight ratio, especially on the front-wheel drive model.
• **The cabin is roomy**, as is the trunk; four adults and all their luggage can be accommodated by this car.
• **Steering is accurate**, smooth and even with its slightly high reduction ratio, it provides for good maneuverability, thanks to its small steer angle diameter.

CONS

• **Brakes** aren't too hot for they don't really grip as they should and even the 4-disc brakes are tough to control with such a soft pedal.
• **Excessive** vehicle weight cripples the 2.2L engine that really has to puff and strain on the all-wheel drive models.
• **Driving** would be more pleasant if the frame design wasn't so high and if the driver wasn't seated so low.
• **Steering** is too light, because it's over-assisted.
• **Equipment** is very Spartan on base models and every little nicety comes as an option.
• **Noise level** is chronic and loud with such a boisterous engine, road noise and wind whistling around the cabin.

VERDICT

The Legacy is the best choice at Subaru, because of its practical size and its more refined mechanical features.

RECALLS

1997   Front transverse links may break and must be inspected.
The hazard light switch might be defective.
Bearing in throttle assembly may be missing.
1998   Automatic shift lever assembly may fail.
Defective oil filter.
98-99 Defective brake master cylinder on vehicles equipped with ABS.
2000   The bolts of the transverse link will be retorqued.
The low beam bulbs will be reequipped with DOT marked units.
2001   Suspect inner-front seat rails will be replaced.
Vehicles will be inspected and all fuel hoses under lot number 0804 and 0806 will be replaced.
Affected right front bearing housings will be replaced.
Alla beige coloured rear center lap/shoulder belts with lot number 0171 will be replaced.
2002   Dealers will replace the brake master cylinder on some cars.

Legacy — SUBARU

RELIABILITY PROBLEMS

	1997	1998	1999	2000	2001	2002
Engine:	X	X	X	-	-	-
Transmission:	-	-	-	-	-	-
Suspension:	-	X	X	-	-	-
Steering:	-	-	-	-	-	-
Brakes:	-	X	X	-	-	-
Electricity:	X	X	X	X	X	-
Body:	-	-	-	-	-	-
Accessories:	X	X	X	X	X	-
Fit/finish:	-	-	-	X	-	-

POWERTRAIN / PERFORMANCE

Year	Type/ L/Camshaft/bhp	Drivetrain & gearbox	Acceler. 0/100 sec.	Top. speed km/h	Ave. Fuel consp. l./100 km
97-00	H4/2.2/SOHC/130-137	front/all-M5	11.0	180	10.5
97-02	H4/2.5/DOHC/155-165	front/all-A4	12.2	175	10.1
		front/all-M5	10.0	190	11.5
		front/all-A4	NA	NA	NA
01-02	H6/3.0/SOHC/212	front/all-A4	8.8	200	11.6

SPECIFICATIONS

Model	Wlb. mm	Lght. mm	Cb.wt kg	Brakes fr/rr	Steering type	Standard tires
97-99						
sdn. 4dr. Brighton	2629	4686	1318	dc/dr	pwr.r&p.	185/70R14
sdn. 4dr. L	2629	4610	1309	dc/ABS	pwr.r&p.	185/70R14
wgn. 4dr. L	2629	4686	1349	dc/ABS	pwr.r&p.	185/70R14
sdn. 4dr. GT	2629	4610	1402	dc/ABS	pwr.r&p.	205/55R16
wgn. 4dr. GT	2629	4686	1442	dc/ABS	pwr.r&p.	205/55R16
wgn. 4dr. Outback	2629	4719	1431	dc/ABS	pwr.r&p.	205/70R15

PRICES

Model / version		1997	1998	1999	2000	2001	2002
sdn. 4dr. L	mini.				16800	19400	20500
	maxi				19400	22000	23650
sdn. 4dr. L AWD	mini.	11000	13450				
	maxi						
sdn. 4dr. LS AWD	mini.	13600	15750				
	maxi	15100					
sdn. 4dr. LSi AWD	mini.	14700					
	maxi	15750					
sdn. 4dr. GT AWD	mini.	14200	17650	18900	21000	23600	27800
	maxi	16800	19950	21200	23600	26250	31000
sdn. 4dr. L Ann. AWD	mini.			18000			
	maxi			21200			
sdn. 4dr. GT LTD	mini.		19750	22600	24700	26800	27800
	maxi		22000	25200	27300	29800	31000
sdn. 4dr. Outback LTD	mini.			18900	21500	24150	25700
	maxi			21500	24150	25700	28350
sdn. 4dr. L Spec Ed.	mini.						29350
	maxi						29850
sdn. 4dr. H6 3.0 Outback Voc	mini.						33650
	maxi						34850
wgn. 4dr. L	mini.				17850	20500	21500
	maxi				20500	23100	24700
wgn. 4dr. Ann.	Mini.			15750			
	maxi			17850			
wgn. 4dr. L Spec Ed.	mini.						21500
	maxi						24150
wgn. 4dr. L AWD	mini.	11550	13950				
	maxi	14200	16300				
wgn. 4dr. LS AWD	mini.	12600					
	maxi	6850	9250	11000	13650	15750	18400
wgn. 4dr. Bri. AWD	mini.	9450	11550	13650	16300	18400	21500
wgn. 4dr. Bri.S AWD	mini.		10800	13100			
	maxi		13100	15750			
wgn. 4dr. LSi AWD	mini.	15200					
	maxi	17800					
wgn. 4dr. GT AWD	mini.	16800	18150	19950	22000	24700	25700
	maxi		20500	22600	24600	24150	28900
wgn. 4dr. Out.	Mini.			20600	23700	26800	28350
	maxi			23500	24150	27600	28800
wgn. 4dr. Out. Ltd	mini.			24150	27300	27600	29900
wgn. 4dr. Outback AWD	mini.	13650	17100				
	maxi	16800	18950				
wgn. 4dr. Out LTD AWD	mini.	18900	21500				
wgn. 4dr. H6 3.0	mini.					32000	34100
	maxi					35600	37300
wgn. 4dr. H6 3.0 VOC	mini.					34850	36550
	maxi					37800	39900

See page 7 to adapt these figures.

SUZUKI   Esteem

2001 SUZUKI Esteem

In 1996, Suzuki introduced a model inspired by the Swift, but bigger, sturdier and driven by a 1.6L 4-cylinder engine. For its '99 harvest, Suzuki has presented a more muscular GLX powered by a 1.8L engine.

PROS

• **A surprisingly spacious** cabin interior, considering the overall trim size of the car. There's generous head and leg room, and according to exact measurements, the Esteem boasts of a larger interior than its main rivals.

• **Controls** are silky smooth and responses are rarely harsh.

• **The well-adjusted suspension**, nicely designed seats and effective soundproofing make for a comfy ride.

• **The GLX** is a better buy than the competition, considering the equipment you get for the going price.

• **Assembly is solid**, fit and finish are meticulous and trim components look just great.

• **As far as convenience goes**, there's a practical and convertible trunk and sufficient storage compartments throughout the cabin interior.

CONS

• **Driving is vague** because of the rear end that is hard to control and slides off track. The Esteem is very sensitive to crosswinds, road ruts and quick lane changes.

• **The original tires** are undersized and they squeal on the slightest curve taken at higher speed.

• **Its plain** and simple body design isn't at all spectacular but some people find it attractive.

• **The manual shifter** is inaccurate and sluggish and the automatic shifter is rough.

• **Aerodynamic efficiency** can't be the greatest (unpublished), for there's constant wind noise whistling around the windshield.

• **Rear seat** access isn't a piece of cake for heftier individuals, because the narrow doors don't open too wide.

VERDICT

The Esteem isn't recommended as a used car, because its real value is an unknown factor, given that sales are confidential.

RECALLS

1998   Defective accessory engine block heater that may experience an electrical short circuit.

Esteem   SUZUKI

RELIABILITY PROBLEMS

	1997	1998	1999	2000	2001	2002
Engine:	X	X	X	X	X	X
Transmission:	-	-	-	-	-	-
Suspension:	-	-	-	-	-	-
Steering:	-	X	X	-	-	-
Brakes:	X	X	X	X	-	-
Electricity:	X	X	X	X	-	-
Body:	-	X	X	X	X	X
Accessories:	X	X	X	X	X	X
Fit/finish:	-	-	-	-	-	-

POWERTRAIN / PERFORMANCE

Year	Type/ L/Camshaft/bhp	Drivetrain & gearbox	Acceler. 0/100 sec.	Top. speed km/h	Ave. Fuel consp. l./100 km
97-01	L4/1.6/SOHC/98	front-M5	11.0	160	7.7
		front-A4	12.2	150	8.5
99-02	L4/1.8/DOHC/122	front-M5	10.5	180	8.3
		front-A4	11.5	175	9.0

SPECIFICATIONS

Model 97-02	Wlb. mm	Lght. mm	Cb.wt kg	Brakes fr/rr	Steering type	Standard tires
sdn. 4dr. GL	2480	4195	990	dc/dr	pwr.r&p.	185/60R14
sdn. 4dr. GLX	2480	4195	1016	dc/dr	pwr.r&p.	195/55R15
wgn. 4dr. GL	2480	4375	1095	dc/dr	pwr.r&p.	185/60R14
wgn. 4dr. GLX	2480	4375	1140	dc/dr	pwr.r&p.	195/55R15

PRICES

Model / version		1997	1998	1999	2000	2001	2002
sdn. 4dr. GL	mini	4200	5250	6500	7550	8900	
	maxi	5250	6800	8200	9450	11000	
sdn. 4dr. GLX	mini	4800	6900	7550	9100	11000	
	maxi	6800	8000	9250	11000	13100	
wgn. 4dr. GL 1.6	mini		5550	6800			
	maxi		7350	8700			
wgn. 4dr. GLX 1.6	mini		6600	7900			
	maxi		8400	9750			
wgn. 4dr. GL 1.8	mini				8600	10500	12600
	maxi				10500	12600	14700
wgn. 4dr. GLX 1.8	mini			8400	10700	12100	14200
	maxi			10300	12600	14200	16300

See page 7 to adapt these figures.

2001 SUZUKI Esteem

SUZUKI-GEO-PONTIAC

2001 CHEVROLET Tracker

The Tracker and the Sidekick werw available as a convertible and 2-door sedan in 1989, the 4-door station wagon came out in '91 and the DOHC engine in '92.

PROS

• **Its fun body style** is playful and the interior design is very spiffy.
• **There's a wide choice** of models, trim levels and mechanical features.
• **Handling** is better than that of the former Samurai because of the independent suspension up front, wider wheel tracks, more accurate steering and because the leaf springs have been replaced by coil springs.
• **The 1.8L engine** has more gusto and good manners than the base 1.6L engine and gears on the manual transmission are nicely calibrated.
• **Nice practical items**: the folding seatbench and the handy to use soft top.

CONS

• **Brakes** aren't great with such long and unpredictable stops, due to almost immediate wheel lock.
• **With the automatic**, engine performance are anemic and gears aren't as well spaced as on the manual.
• **High sensitivity** to crosswinds on the 4-door model.
• **Thin bodywork** is vulnerable to impact and to corrosion.
• **Low ground clearance** cripples performance on rough terrain.
• **Engine roar**, tire thump, hum and whistling wind sure make for a tiring ride.
• **The trunk holds** next to nothing when the rear seats are occupied on the 2-door.
• **Some trim components** look flimsy and bodywork is fragile and rust-prone.

VERDICT

These minivans are legion and prices vary with the shape they're in, so it's a good idea to check the vehicle over and really think things over carefully.

RECALLS

1999 Steering column shaft coupling could break resulting in loss of steering control. (Tracker)
Miscalibration of the powertrain control module could result in a no-start condition in cold weather.

PONTIAC-GEO-SUZUKI

RELIABILITY PROBLEMS

	1997	1998	1999	2000	2001	2002
Engine:	X	-	X	X	X	X
Transmission:	-	-	-	-	-	-
Suspension:	X	X	X	-	-	-
Steering:	-	-	X	-	-	-
Brakes:	X	X	X	-	-	-
Electricity:	X	X	X	X	X	-
Body:	X	X	-	X	X	-
Accessories:	X	X	X	X	X	X
Fit/finish:	-	-	-	-	-	-

POWERTRAIN / PERFORMANCE

Year	Type/ L/Camshaft/bhp	Drivetrain & gearbox	Acceler. 0/100 sec.	Top. speed km/h	Ave. Fuel consp. l./100 km
97-01	L4/1.6/SOHC/80-97	rear/all-M5	12.2	165	10.5
		rear/all-A3/A4	16.3	135	9.5
97-98	L4 1.8/DOHC/120	rear/all-M5	12.8	155	10.5
		rear/all-A4	14.4	155	10.7
99-02	L4/2.0/DOHC/127	rear/all-M5	11.7	160	10.5
		rear/all-A4	12.8	155	11.5

SPECIFICATIONS

Model 97-01	Wlb. mm	Lght. mm	Cb.wt kg	Brakes fr/rr	Steering type	Standard tires
con. 2dr.	2200	3650	1085	dc/dr	bal.	205/75R15
sdn. 3dr.	2200	3650	1100	dc/dr	bal.	205/75R15
wgn. 5dr.	2480	4030	1240	dc/dr	pwr.bal.	215/65R16

PRICES

Model / version	1997	1998	1999	2000	2001	2002
SUZUKI Sidekick						
con. 2dr. JA 4x4 mini	3150	4700				
maxi	5250	6300				
con. 2dr. JX 4x4 mini	4200	6300				
maxi	6300	8200				
wgn. 4dr. JX 4x4 mini	5250					
maxi	7350					
wgn. 4dr. JX Sport mini	6800	9450				
4x4 maxi	9100	10500				
wgn. 4dr.JLX Sport mini	8900	11000				
4x4 maxi	11550	13100				

GEO/CHEVROLET Tracker - PONTIAC Sunrunner

Model / version	1997	1998	1999	2000	2001	2002
con. 2dr. 4x2 Sunr mini	3900					
maxi	6000					
con. 2dr. 4x4 Sunr mini	4800					
maxi	7000					
con. 2dr. 4x2 Track mini	5800					
maxi	7900					
con. 2dr. 4x4 Track mini	4600	8400	10300	11550	14600	16300
maxi	6800	10500	12400	13650	17000	18900
wgn. 2dr. 4X4 Track mini	6800					
maxi	8900					
wgn. 2dr. LSi 4X4 mini	7350	9100	11000	12600	15750	17300
Track maxi	9650	11350	13100	14700	18200	20150

See page 7 to adapt these figures.

SUZUKI   Swift

2001 SUZUKI Swift

The Swift was first sold in 1989 as a 3 and 5-door sedan, then as a 4-door in '92. It's powered by a 1.6L 4-cylinder engine. It was redesigned and upgraded in '95 and the DLX, a 3-door sedan, is the only trim level available since then.

PROS

• **These small city slicker** cars are attractive.

• **Four adults** can be accommodated in the cabin, in spite of the small vehicle size.

• **The engine** is more efficient with the manual transmission.

• **The car handles well**, for there isn't much sway and understeering is easy to control.

• **It's quite a comfortable car**, for the suspension is quite smooth and the noise level is reasonable at cruising speed.

CONS

• **Brakes** just don't do their job on sudden stops, because almost immediate wheel lock stretches stopping distances to the limit.

• **Steering** is vague and with such a light vehicle, it's hard to stay on track in crosswinds and on rough roads, especially with the small tires that put up a fuss when they hit road ruts.

• **The 3-speed automatic transmission** saps the power of the engines.

• **On the hatchback**, the trunk is teeny tiny, but it can be extended by lowering the rear seatbench.

• **Thin bodywork** is vulnerable to impact and to rust.

VERDICT

These small cars are practical and fun to drive in the city, but they're not quite at home on the highway. They don't hold up too well over time and replacement parts are expensive.

RECALLS

1997   Defective shifter assembly that allows automatic transmission to be moved from the Park position without the use of the key, transmission lever detent button, or depressing the brakes.

Swift   SUZUKI

RELIABILITY PROBLEMS

	1997	1998	1999	2000	2001	2002
Engine:	X	X	X	X	-	
Transmission:	X	-	-	-	-	
Suspension:	-	-	-	-	-	
Steering:	-	X	X	X	-	
Brakes:	X	X	X	-	-	
Electricity:	X	X	X	-	-	
Body:	X	X	X	X	X	
Accessories:	X	X	X	X	X	
Fit/finish:	-	-	-	-	-	

POWERTRAIN

Year	Type/ L/Camshaft/bhp	Drivetrain & gearbox	Acceler. 0/100 sec.	Top. speed km/h	Ave. Fuel consp. l./100 km
97-98	L4/1.0/SOHC/55	front-M5	13.8	145	5.4
97-01	L4/1.3/SOHC/70-79	front-M5	12.8	160	6.1
		front-A3	14.0	150	7.9

SPECIFICATIONS

Model 97-01	Wlb. mm	Lght. mm	Cb.wt kg	Brakes fr/rr	Steering type	Standard tires
sdn. 3dr.	2365	3795	860	dc/dr	r&p.	155/80R13

PRICES

Model / version		1997	1998	1999	2000	2001	2002
sdn. 3dr. DLX	mini	3150	4200	5250	6800	8400	
	maxi	4700	5250	6800	8900	10500	

See page 7 to adapt these figures.

2000 SUZUKI Swift

SUZUKI   Vitara-Grand Vitara-XL7

2001 SUZUKI XL-7

The Vitara and Grand Vitara have replaced the Sidekicks, driven by a 2.0L 4-cylinder engine or 2.5L V6. The stretch version XL7 appears in 2001 powered by a 2.7-liter V6.

PROS

• **Space cabin** is roomier because they're longer and wider, mostly in the XL7 which offers a 3rd row of seats.
• **Affordable prices**, explain why they aren't loaded with equipment. But it's nice to buy a convertible or station wagon without wincing.
• **The V6 engines**, gives the JLX station wagon and XL7 better performance than the 2.0L engine.
• **Handling** is a lot more competent with the more rigid platform and more accurate rack-and-pinion steering.
•**The rack-and-pinion steering** has cut down on the steer angle diameter for both vehicles, so they offer better maneuverability.
• **The inside presentation** has a modern and functional new look; it feels more like a car than a SUV.
• **Well-planned storage** compartments and the baggage compartment on the 4-door wagon can be extended by lowering the rear bench.

CONS

• **Stability** still really depends on the road surface, wind and tire grip. The convertible can reserve some surprises...
•**The fuel economy** is disappointing because these engines are not strong enough to hoist these vehicles to decent performance levels.
• **Off-the-road capabilities** is questionable because entrance and exit angles as well as ground clearance have been reduced.
• **The ride** is far from comfy with such a suspension that reacts badly to the least road flaw, seat upholstery is pretty hard and sound dampening is next to nil.
• **The brakes** are still not up to par, yielding the same long stretches on sudden stops. But vehicle path is more predictable with standard ABS assistance.
• **Access** to the rear seats is limited inside the convertible because of lack of space and missing running boards.
• **The convertible** suffers its very jittery suspension, the near-stingy heater, the cramped rear seat and inadequate luggage compartment, and some trim material still looks a bit cheap...

VERDICT

Attractive bodies seek skilled engines to power two very thirsty vehicles.

RECALLS

2000 Correct label regarding GAWR will replace the wrong one.

Vitara-Grand Vitara -XL7   SUZUKI

RELIABILITY PROBLEMS

	1997	1998	1999	2000	2001	2002
Engine:			X	X	X	-
Transmission:			X	-	-	-
Suspension:			X	-	-	-
Steering:			-	-	-	-
Brakes:			X	X	X	-
Electricity:			X	X	-	-
Body:			X	X	X	X
Accessories:			X	X	X	-
Fit/finish:			-	-	-	-

POWERTRAIN / PERFORMANCE

Year	Type/ L/Camshaft/bhp	Drivetrain & gearbox	Acceler. 0/100 sec.	Top. speed km/h	Ave. Fuel consp. l./100 km
99-02	L4/2.0/DOHC/127	rear/all-M5	NA	NA	10.5
		rear/all-A4	NA	NA	10.5
	V6/2.5/DOHC/155	rear/all-M5	NA	NA	12.3
		rear/all-A4	NA	NA	12.6
01-02	V6/2.7DOHC/183	rear.all-A4	10.7	170	13.8

SPECIFICATIONS

Model 99-02	Wlb. mm	Lght. mm	Cb.wt kg	Brakes fr/rr	Steering type	Standard tires
Vitara						
con. 2dr.	2200	3855	1235	dc/dr	pwr.bal.	205/75R15
wgn. 4dr.	2480	4135	1355	dc/dr	pwr.bal.	215/65R16
Grand Vitara						
wgn. 4dr.	2480	4180	1450	dc/dr	pwr.bal.	235/60R16
01-02						
wgn. 4dr. XL7	2800	4665	1680	dc/dr	pwr.bal.	235/60R16

PRICES

Model / version		1997	1998	1999	2000	2001	2002
Vitara							
con. 2dr. JA 1.6	mini			8100	9650	12600	14200
	maxi			9900	11650	15200	16800
con. 2dr. JA 2.0	mini			10200			
	maxi			11750			
con. 2dr. JX 2.0	mini				11750	13650	15200
	maxi				13750	15950	17850
con. 2dr. JLX 2.0	mini				12600		
	maxi				14600		
wgn. 2dr. JX H.T.	mini			10400	12700	15200	16300
	maxi			12300	14700	17500	18900
Grand Vitara							
wgn. 4dr. JX H.T.	mini			13450	15200	17850	19100
	maxi			15400	17300	20500	21500
wgn. 4dr. JLX H.T.	mini			15750	17300	19950	21200
	maxi			17850	19400	22600	23600
wgn. 4dr. Ltd H.T.	mini				19950	22600	24350
Aut.	maxi				22000	25200	26800
XL7							
wgn. 4dr. Base	mini					24150	23600
	maxi					26800	26250
wgn. 4dr. Plus	mini					25200	
	maxi					27800	
wgn. 4dr. JX	mini						25200
	maxi						27800
wgn. 4dr. JLX	mini						26800
	maxi						29400
wgn. 4dr. Touring	mini						27800
	maxi						30450
wgn. 4dr. Ltd	mini						29400
	maxi						32000

See page 7 to adapt these figures.

1998 SUZUKI X-90

The X-90 hit the market in 1996, and no one blinked an eye. It is based on the body design and powertrain of the defunct Sidekick.

PROS

• **This is an innovative**, fun vehicle, combining all-terrain capabilities with those of a year-round roadster.

• **The X-90** is just loaded with equipment, but costs much less than the Miata that has fewer bells and whistles.

• **Road stability** is quite reasonable, but it's not a good idea to make quick lane changes with steering that suffers from a higher than average reduction ratio. And the X-90 is sensitive to crosswinds, road ruts and extension joints.

• **This small vehicle** is amazingly adaptable, for it can go off the highway and head happily for the open fields, beaches and mountains, in good weather or bad.

• **It maneuvers marvelously** well, for it combines a really short wheel base with quick as a flash steering, so it can get to any spot it pleases.

• **It's convenient too**, for there are lots of storage compartments in the interior and the trunk is practical and easy to get to.

CONS

• **Excessive vehicle weight** affects engine performance, for the Sidekick engine has to strain to pull the extra 250 kg.

• **Brakes** aren't great, achieving stops that are far too long, even if they're nice and predictable with ABS.

• **This vehicle is appealing**, but it's a mixed bag as far as body design goes and looks a bit weird.

• **Comfort** is non-existent, for the suspension jumps around every which way and there's quite a bit of noise and roar.

• **The engine** isn't economical, for mileage stays around 11L/100 km.

• **The cockpit** isn't too comfortable with such a low seat, non-adjustable steering wheel, inaccurate steering and lack of a foot rest.

VERDICT

The X-90 is an innovative concept, but driving isn't fun because the deficient engine and suspension don't optimize the full potential of the vehicle.

RECALLS

None over this period.

RELIABILITY PROBLEMS

	1997	1998	1999	2000	2001	2002
Engine:	X	X				
Transmission:	X	X				
Suspension:	-	-				
Steering:	-	-				
Brakes:	X	-				
Electricity:	-	-				
Body:	-	-				
Accessories:	X	X				
Fit/finish:	X	-				

POWERTRAIN   PERFORMANCE

Year	Type/ L/Camshaft/bhp	Drivetrain & gearbox	Acceler. 0/100 sec.	Top. speed km/h	Ave. Fuel consp. l./100 km
97-98	L4/1.6/SOHC/95	rear/all-M5	NA	NA	NA
		rear/all-A4	15.0	140	9.9

SPECIFICATIONS

Model	Wlb. mm	Lght. mm	Cb.wt kg	Brakes fr/rr	Steering type	Standard tires
cpe. 2dr.	base	2200	3710	dc/dr/ABS	pwr.bal.	195/65R15

PRICES

Model / version		1997	1998	1999	2000	2001	2002
cpe. 2dr.	mini	3150	4200				
	maxi	5250	6300				

See page 7 to adapt these figures.

1998 SUZUKI X-90

TOYOTA   Avalon

1998 TOYOTA Avalon

The Avalon replaced the Cressida in 1995 and had been renewed in 2000. It's built on the Camry platform and shares its 3.0L V6 engine.

PROS
• **The engine** is spectacular for it can accelerate from 0 to 100 km/h in 8.5 seconds with the automatic.
• **The cabin** can comfortably seat five passengers, not six, which is the number of occupants according to Toyota.
• **Brakes** are effective, stable, long-lasting and easy to adjust.
• **The ride** is exceedingly comfortable because of the smooth suspension, nicely contoured, thick seats that provide good support.
• **Assembly, fit and finish** and main trim components are top-notch, but the overall look isn't really lavish.
• **Equipment** is extensive, since ABS is now standard on the XL base model.

CONS
• **Its plain body design** that isn't in keeping with such advanced technical features or such a high price tag.
• **This upper-end** Camry is very pricy indeed, which proves that the renowned Toyota quality and dependability don't come cheap.
• **The six-passenger** model with the shifter located on the steering wheel is a caricature of the big American car, for you can't even seat a child in the middle of the rearbench up front because of the ever so tight leg room.
• **Fuel consumption** is a bit higher than average for equal displacement engines.
• **Steering** is devoid of character, it gets vague at times and you have to keep an eye on it in crosswinds.
• **The noise level** is strangely higher than on counterpart vehicles, especially road noise.
• **Not too convenient**: no storage compartment in the center console, trunk release button inside the glove compartment.

VERDICT
This is a nice car, but it isn't terribly popular. It's a good buy all-round, but you have to be willing to put up the cash to own one.

RECALLS
1997 Moisture may seep and freeze in the brake booster vacuum hose and disable the brakes altogether.
2000 Rear axle hub will be inspected and replaced if necessary.

RELIABILITY PROBLEMS

	1997	1998	1999	2000	2001	2002
Engine:	X	-	-	-	-	-
Transmission:	-	-	-	-	-	-
Suspension:	X	X	X	X	-	-
Steering:	-	-	-	-	-	-
Brakes:	-	-	-	-	-	-
Electricity:	X	X	X	-	-	-
Body:	-	-	X	X	X	-
Accessories:	-	X	-	X	X	-
Fit/finish:	X	X	X	-	-	-

POWERTRAIN

Year	Type/ L/Camshaft/bhp	Drivetrain & gearbox
97-02	V6/3.0/DOHC/192-210	front-A4

PERFORMANCE

Acceler. 0/100 sec.	Top. speed km/h	Ave. Fuel consp. l./100 km
8.5	200	11.2

SPECIFICATIONS

Model 97-99	Wlb. mm	Lght. mm	Cb.wt kg	Brakes fr/rr	Steering type	Standard tires
sdn. 4dr. XL	2720	4875	1560	dc/ABS	pwr.r&p.	205/65R15
sdn. 4dr. XLS	2720	4875	1560	dc/ABS	pwr.r&p.	205/65R15
00-02						
sdn. 4dr. XL	2720	4874	1560	dc/ABS	pwr.r&p.	205/65R15
sdn. 4dr. XLS	2720	4874	1570	dc/ABS	pwr.r&p.	205/60R16

PRICES

Model / version		1997	1998	1999	2000	2001	2002
sdn. 4dr. XL	mini	12100	14700	17850	22000	25700	29400
	maxi	15750	18400	21500	25200	29400	32500
sdn. 4dr. XLS	mini	14200	17100	19950	24700	28400	33600
	maxi	17850	20500	23100	28350	32550	36750

See page 7 to adapt these figures.

2002 TOYOTA Avalon

1998 TOYOTA Camry

The Camry has replaced the Corona in 1983 and was redesigned in 1992, 1997 and 2002. These cars are powered by a L4 or a V6 engines. The Solara coupe join the club in 1999 and the convertible one year later.

PROS

• **The larger cabin** and trunk can accommodate five passengers and their luggage.

• **The suspension** provides a super blend of plush, Germanic comfort and neutral, stable handling at normal speeds.

• **The cockpit boasts** of a nicely designed instrument panel, provides adequate visibility and driving is great with such clean, crisp, just right steering.

• **Solidly built**, neatly assembled and very spiffy, but the overall design lacks character and imagination.

• **The 4-cylinder engine** runs smoothly and is easy on the gas, but the V6 is more popular with its whopping 194-bhp.

• **Steering** is accurate, visibility is good and the instrument panel is super ergonomic, so driving is pleasant.

CONS

• **Brakes** aren't the best with such long stops with or without ABS, but this feature at least stabilizes vehicle path on V6 models that are equipped with standard ABS.

• **The coupe** isn't terribly comfy with its hard seats, harsh suspension and chronically high noise level.

• **Both engines** aren't too efficient because of excessive vehicle weight.

• **The hard seats** are uncomfortable and they're poorly designed and don't provide adequate support.

• **The interior design** is blah and bland.

VERDICT

The Camry is a good buy either as a new or used car and it's become the most sought-after, reliable family car in North America.

RECALLS

1997 Moisture may seep and freeze in the brake booster vacuum hose and disable the brakes altogether.
Ignition module is defective resulting in a possibility that the key could be removed while the car is in "Drive".

2002 Dealers will replace the driver's airbag module on some vehicles.

RELIABILITY PROBLEMS

	1997	1998	1999	2000	2001	2002
Engine:	X	X	-	-	-	-
Transmission:	X	-	-	-	-	-
Suspension:	X	X	X	X	-	-
Steering:	-	-	-	-	-	-
Brakes:	X	X	X	X	-	-
Electricity:	X	X	X	X	X	-
Body:	-	-	-	-	-	-
Accessories:	X	X	X	X	-	-
Fit/finish:	-	-	-	-	-	-

POWERTRAIN

Year	Type/ L/Camshaft/bhp	Drivetrain & gearbox	Acceler. 0/100 sec.	Top. speed km/h	Ave. Fuel consp. l./100 km
97-02	L4/2.2/DOHC/125-157	front-M5	10.5	180	10.0
		front-A4	11.8	175	10.4
	V6/3.0/DOHC/185-192	front-M5	8.4	210	11.4
		front-A4	8.7	200	12.3

PERFORMANCE
(column headers: Acceler. 0/100 sec., Top. speed km/h, Ave. Fuel consp. l./100 km)

SPECIFICATIONS

Model	Wlb. mm	Lght. mm	Cb.wt kg	Brakes fr/rr	Steering type	Standard tires
97-01						
sdn. 4dr. CE	2670	4785	1360	dc/dr	pwr.r&p.	195/70R14
sdn. 4dr. CE V6	2670	4785	1415	dc/ABS	pwr.r&p.	205/65R15
sdn. 4dr. LE	2670	4785	1415	dc/dr/ABS	pwr.r&p.	195/70R14
sdn. 4dr.XLE V6	2670	4785	1475	dc/ABS	pwr.r&p.	205/65R15
99-02						
cpe. 2dr. Solara	2670	4825	1440	dc/dr/ABS	pwr.r&p.	205/65R15
cpe. 2dr. Sol.V6	2670	4825	1465	dc/ABS	pwr.r&p.	205/60R16
2002						
sdn. 4dr. LE	2720	4805	1435	dc/dr	pwr.r&p.	205/65R15
sdn. 4dr. XLEV6	2720	4805	1525	dc/ABS	pwr.r&p.	215/60R16
sdn. 4dr. SE V6	2720	4805	1545	dc/ABS	pwr.r&p.	215/60R16

PRICES

Model / version		1997	1998	1999	2000	2001	2002
cpe. 2 dr. Solara	mini			14200	16800	19400	21500
SE	maxi			16333	18900	22000	24150
cpe. 2 dr. Solara	mini			15750	19950	21000	23100
SE V6	maxi			17850	22000	23100	25700
cpe. 2 dr. Solara	mini						24150
SLE V6	maxi						26800
con. 2dr. Solara	mini				27800	29400	32550
SLE V6	maxi				29900	32550	35200
sdn. 4dr. LE	mini	10200	11850	14200	15750	18400	21000
	maxi	13100	14700	16300	17850	21000	23600
sdn. 4dr. XLE	mini						24150
	maxi						26800
sdn. 4dr. CE	mini	9250	10800	13100	14700	17300	
	maxi	12100	13650	16300	16800	19950	
sdn. 4dr. CE V6	mini	10700	12400	15750	17300	19400	
	maxi	13650	15200	17850	19400	22000	
sdn. 4dr. SE V6	mini						23100
	maxi						25700
sdn. 4dr. LE V6	mini						22000
	maxi						24700
sdn. 4dr. XLE V6	mini	12700	14500	17300	18900	20500	25700
	maxi	15750	17300	19400	21000	21000	28350

See page 7 to adapt these figures.

TOYOTA   **Celica**

2000 TOYOTA Celica

The Celica was first sold in 1970, underwent modifications in '77, '81 and '85, the year it was first equipped with front-wheel drive. The all-wheel drive model was on the market in '89 and the more recent model came out in 2000.

PROS

• **The unusual Celica look** appeals to some and not to others, year after year. But the latest model seems to be the most popular.

• **Handling** is just super with the cushy independent suspension, especially on the GT-S model.

• **The GT** model is really zoomy, but because of its cohesive overall design, the GT-S seems to be a better choice.

• **The really nice** cockpit and variable assist power steering make for very pleasant driving.

• **Fuel consumption** is economical, no matter the transmission type.

• **The front seats** on the GT-S model are incredibly ergonomic with the side cushions and lumbar sections.

CONS

• **Torque effects** on some models on strong accelerations.

• **Brakes** are inadequate and on sudden stops, they're unpredictable. Only the brakes on the latest GT-S generation are really effective.

• **The 2.2L engine** isn't too hot, for it only unleashes its power at high rpm, that is, at illegal speeds.

• **The cabin interior** is cramped in the rear seat area and boarding is tricky.

• **Gauges** are hard to read and the instrument panel is plain and unattractive.

• **The suspension** on the GT-S model is firm, that is, it's very stiff.

• **The trunk** doesn't hold much and luggage handling is inconvenient with such a high opening.

• **Some models** are pretty sensitive to crosswinds.

VERDICT

The Celica coupe is really solidly built, well equipped and affordable. But it doesn't have a real Sportscar character as far as looks go.

RECALLS

None over this period.

Celica   TOYOTA

RELIABILITY PROBLEMS

	1997	1998	1999	2000	2001	2002
Engine:	X	-	-	-	-	-
Transmission:	-	-	-	-	-	-
Suspension:	-	-	-	-	-	-
Steering:	-	-	-	-	-	-
Brakes:	X	X	X	-	-	-
Electricity:	X	X	X	X	-	-
Body:	-	X	X	X	-	-
Accessories:	X	X	X	X	-	-
Fit/finish:	-	-	X	-	-	-

POWERTRAIN

Year	Type/ L/Camshaft/bhp	Drivetrain & gearbox
97-99	L4/2.2/DOHC/130 GTS	front-M5
		front-A4
00-02	L4/1.8/DOHC/140 GT	front-M5
		front-A4
	L4/1.8/DOHC/180 GTS	front-M5

PERFORMANCE

Acceler. 0/100 sec.	Top. speed km/h	Ave. Fuel consp. l./100 km
9.0	200	10.8
10.2	190	10.6
8.8	175	9.0
11.0	170	9.5
8.0	185	10.5

SPECIFICATIONS

Model	Wlb. mm	Lght. mm	Cb.wt kg	Brakes fr/rr	Steering type	Standard tires
97-99						
cpe. 3dr. GT	2540	4425	1100	dc/dr/ABS	pwr.r&p.	185/70R14
cpe. 3dr. GT-S	2540	4425	1170	dc/ABS	pwr.r&p.	205/55R15
00-02						
cpe. 3dr. GT	2540	4430	1095	d/t/ABS	pwr.r&p.	185/70R14
cpe. 3dr. GT-S	2540	4430	1170	d/ABS	pwr.r&p.	205/55R15

PRICES

Model / version		1997	1998	1999	2000	2001	2002
cpe. 3dr. GT	mini	11250			17850	19950	22600
	maxi	14200			24500	22600	24700
cpe. 3dr. GT-S	mini		13650	16500	21000	23100	25700
	maxi		16300	19400	23600	25800	27800

See page 7 to adapt these figures.

2000 TOYOTA Celica

TOYOTA   Corolla

2000 TOYOTA Corolla

This front-wheel compact was launched in 66 and modified in 70, 74, 79, 83, 88, 93 and 98. It truly represents the Toyota bread and butter, for it's the most global modern car, being built in such a huge quantity throughout the most impressive number of countries simultaneously.

PROS
• **Choice** is extensive in this range, which offers a wide selection of body styles and trims, two engines and transmission types, depending on the model year.
• **Comfort** improved drastically in 98, with the introduction of new suspensions.
• **Safety** has been enhanced on the latest edition, with a more rigid body shell, a driver's airbag and more powerful braking.
• **Roominess** and trunk size is good on sedans and wagons, but rear seats on some of these are narrower than average and not easily accessible.

CONS
• **Interior design** is depressing and trims are obviously very inexpensive.
• **The 1.6L engine** has always been timid when coupled with an automatic transmission.
• **Multi-valve engines** last longer if the valves are adjusted on a regular basis.
• **Braking** lacks bite and stopping distances are long.
• **Comfort** would be superior if seats were not as hard and if soundproofing was better on simpler versions.
• **Steering** is imprecise at the center and the driver must compensate constantly to maintain a straight trajectory.
• **Road adherence** on the old base model Corolla is average, but although marked, the roll is rarely dangerous.

VERDICT
The Corolla models boast enviable reliability and their handling and appearance have improved noticeably over the years. They are good buys in the used car market, but are available at higher than average prices.

RECALLS
1997 Airbag computer may be defective.

Corolla   TOYOTA

RELIABILITY PROBLEMS

	1997	1998	1999	2000	2001	2002
Engine:	X	X	-	-	-	-
Transmission:	X	-	-	-	-	-
Suspension:	-	X	X	X	-	-
Steering:	X	-	-	-	-	-
Brakes :	-	X	X	X	X	-
Electricity:	X	X	X	X	X	-
Body:	X	X	X	X	-	-
Accessories:	X	X	X	-	-	-
Fit/finish:	-	-	-	-	-	-

POWERTRAIN

Year	Type/ L/Camshaft/bhp	Drivetrain & gearbox	Acceler. 0/100 sec.	Top. speed km/h	Ave. Fuel consp. l./100 km
1997	L4/1.6/DOHC/90-105	front-M5	11.8	170	9.0
		front-A4	12.5	165	10.0
97-02	L4/1.8/DOHC/105-120	front-M5	9.5	185	7.7
		front-A4	11.2	180	8.3

SPECIFICATIONS

Model 1997	Wlb. mm	Lght. mm	Cb.wt kg	Brakes fr/rr	Steering type	Standard tires
sdn. 4dr. SD	2465	4369	1055	dc/dr	pwr.r&p.	175/65R14
sdn. 4dr. DX	2465	4369	1085	dc/dr	pwr.r&p.	185/65R14
wgn. 4dr. SD/DX	2465	4369	1100	dc/dr	pwr.r&p.	185/65R14
98-02						
sdn. 4dr. VE	2465	4420	1095	dc/dr	pwr.r&p.	175/65R14
sdn. 4dr. CE	2465	4420	1110	dc/dr	pwr.r&p.	175/65R14
sdn. 4dr. LE	2465	4420	1145	dc/dr	pwr.r&p.	185/65R14

PRICES

Model / version		1997	1998	1999	2000	2001	2002
sdn. 4dr. DX 1.8	mini	7900					
	maxi	10000					
sdn. 4dr. DX	mini	7350					
	maxi	9450					
sdn. 4dr. LE	mini		10000	11000	13100	14200	15750
	maxi		12600	13650	15200	16300	17850
sdn. 4dr. SD	mini	6850					
	maxi	8900					
sdn. 4dr. VE	mini		7900	8950	11000		
	maxi		10500	11550	13100		
sdn. 4dr. CE	mini		8950	10000	12100	12600	15200
	maxi		11550	12600	14200	14700	16300
sdn. 4dr. Sport	mini					13100	14700
	maxi					15200	16800

See page 7 to adapt these figures.

2001 TOYOTA Echo

In 2000, the Echo replaced the Tercel as Toyota's low-end model in North America. The Echo comes with 2 or 4 doors and a 1.5-liter 4-cylinder engine.

PROS

• **The styling**, inspired by the Prius' lines, is refreshing and features bold lines and oversized headlights.

• **The passenger compartment** and trunk are unusually roomy for a model in this category.

• **The Echo's good weight-power ratio** (9.9 kg/hp) makes it fun to drive, even when equipped with the automatic transmission.

• **Good fuel economy** considering its performance capabilities.

• The Echo offers **better value** than its predecessor, for its equipment list is much more extensive.

• **A lot of storage space**, located mainly in the front, including two adjacent glove boxes.

• **Comfort** is surprisingly good for a car of this size. The suspension never reacts brutally, the seats are well-upholstered and the noise level is reasonable at cruising speeds.

• **The instrument panel** is resolutely modern and distinctive because of its instrument cluster positioned dead centre and at the foot of the windshield.

• **The rear windows** roll down all the way, much to the joy of kids who enjoy feeling the wind on their faces.

• **The windshield wipers** are efficient; their rhythm and reach keep the windshield clean even in pouring rain.

CONS

• **The rear seats** are more difficult to access because of the narrower rear doors that do not open up as widely as in the front.

• **The radio** and air-conditioning controls are inverted.

• **The optional 14-inch** tires provide better handling than the standard 13-inchers.

• **The trunk's presentation** could be improved. The trim fabric is flimsy and clumsily attached to the bench's seatback.

VERDICT

Toyota is convinced that young buyers will be the ones to revive the small-car market. It is undoubtedly right on the money.

RECALLS

2000 The vacuum port of the PCV valve will be repaired on some vehicles.

01-02 Dealers will replace rear rigid brake line on some models.

RELIABILITY PROBLEMS

	1997	1998	1999	2000	2001	2002
Engine:				-	-	-
Transmission:				-	-	-
Suspension:				-	-	-
Steering:				-	-	-
Brakes:				-	-	-
Electricity:				-	-	-
Body:				X	X	-
Accessories:				X	-	-
Fit/finish:				-	-	-

POWERTRAIN

Year	Type/ L/Camshaft/bhp	Drivetrain & gearbox
00-02	L4/1.5/DOHC/108	front-M5
		front-A4

PERFORMANCE

	Acceler. 0/100 sec.	Top. speed km/h	Ave. Fuel consp. l./100 km
front-M5	10.0	165	7.5
front-A4	11.5	160	8.5

SPECIFICATIONS

Model 00-02	Wlb. mm	Lght. mm	Cb.wt kg	Brakes fr/rr	Steering type	Standard tires
sdn. 2dr.	2370	4145	1077	dc/dr	pwr.r&p.	155/80R13
sdn. 4dr.	2370	4145	1090	dc/dr	pwr.r&p.	155/80R13

PRICES

Model / version		1997	1998	1999	2000	2001	2002
sdn. 2dr.	mini				9450	10500	12100
	maxi				11000	12600	14200
sdn. 4dr.	mini				10000	11000	12600
	maxi				11550	13100	14700

See page 7 to adapt these figures.

2000 TOYOTA Echo

2001 TOYOTA Highlander

To keep up with the SUV market, Toyota came up with the Highlander, based on the platform and mechanics of the Lexus RX 300, itself derived from the Camry. The Highlander comes with a 2.2-liter L4 and 2-wheel drive or a 3.0-liter V6 with 4-wheel drive. Only an automatic transmission is available.

PROS
• **The interesting midsize format** provides a practical amount of space and uses powerful yet economical mechanics.
• **Rear-seat roominess** is surprising given the amount of available legroom. Access is facilitated by a reasonable level of ground clearance as well as large doors that open wide.
• **The relatively low center of gravity** is conducive to safe handling, and the Highlander handles more like an automobile than a utility vehicle thanks to its suspension design.
• **The brakes** are powerful in both normal situations and emergency stops. Decelerations are quick and straight.
• **The body's reasonable dimensions** and the short turning radius make the Highlander extremely maneuverable.
• **The vast trunk** and practical storage spaces will make daily life easier for the typical young family.
• **The powerful headlights** produce great visibility in all conditions.
• The overall **attention to quality** is reminiscent more of what can be found in a Lexus than a Toyota. This is especially true of the high-end model equipped with leather trim.

CONS
• **The stiff suspension** reacts harshly on poor pavement.
• **Road defects** pass easily through the steering column all the way to the driver. This is quite rare to be worthy of mention.
• **The windshield wipers** are not the most efficient out there. There are rather slow and clear only 75% of the windshield's surface.
• **The massive dashboard** is borrowed straight from the Lexus RX 300, and the gear shift lever is rather impractical.

VERDICT
The Highlander is undoubtedly one of the best buys in its category, and chances are it will make for a rare and expensive find on the used-car market.

RECALLS
01-02 Possible fuel leak at the fuel tank recycling fuel vapor assembly in case of a crash.

RELIABILITY PROBLEMS

	1997	1998	1999	2000	2001	2002
Engine:					X	-
Transmission:					-	-
Suspension:					-	-
Steering:					-	-
Brakes:					-	-
Electricity:					-	-
Body:					X	-
Accessories:					X	-
Fit/finish:					-	-

POWERTRAIN

Year	Type/ L/Camshaft/bhp	Drivetrain & gearbox	Acceler. 0/100 sec.	Top. speed km/h	Ave. Fuel consp. l./100 km
01-02	L4/2.4DOHC/155	2WD front-A4	NA		
	V6/3.0/SOHC/220	AWD front/all-A4	10.1	175	13.0

PERFORMANCE

SPECIFICATIONS

Model 01-02	Wlb. mm	Lght. mm	Cb.wt kg	Brakes fr/rr	Steering type	Standard tires
wgn. 4dr. FWD	2715	4685	1580	dc/ABS	pwr.r.&p.	225/70R16
wgn. 4dr. AWD	2715	4685	1760	dc/ABS	pwr.r.&p.	225/70R16

PRICES

Model / version		1997	1998	1999	2000	2001	2002
wgn. 4dr. 2WD	mini					24950	29900
	maxi					28550	33100
wgn. 4dr. AWD	mini					28900	32550
	maxi					31200	35700

See page 7 to adapt these figures.

2001 TOYOTA Highlander

TOYOTA   Previa

1997 TOYOTA Previa

Introduced in '91, the Previa is offered in two trims, base or LE and is powered by a 2.4L 4-cylinder engine which is also available with a turbo compressor, coupled on a 2- or 4-wheel drive transmission, depending on the model year and trim level.

PROS
• **Futuristic lines** give the Previa a very special personality.
• **The engine** is supple enough when equipped with a manual transmission; an automatic transmission is the better alternative on the 4x4.
• **The passenger compartment** is very roomy, easily accessible and well laid out. The baggage compartment is big enough to store luggage for seven passengers.
• **A high driving position** provides excellent visibility.
• **Maneuverability** is enhanced by a short wheelbase and a reduced turning radius.
• **Steering** is well-balanced although imprecise at center.
• **Fuel consumption** is reasonable despite very ordinary engine performance.
• **The 4WD** is very efficient and its stability is above-average.
• **Handling** is safer on the 4WD in winter driving conditions than on the rear-wheel drive, which is quite unstable on icy roads.
• **The instrument panel** on the Previa suffers from wretched excess, but is nevertheless very functional.

CONS
• **The mechanical system** is oddly positioned underneath the front seats.
• **Outrageous selling prices** don't make them very appealing, either as a used vehicle or brand new, while other modern realizations don't suffer from this handicap.
• **Sensitivity** to cross winds, evident on these vehicles, calls for cautious driving and a lot of foresight.
• **Braking** is not efficient enough, but is stable and shows endurance.
• **A V6 engine** would be a welcome feature on the Previa, where the clanking noises of the 4-cylinder engine are a major drawback at cruising speed. The addition in '95 of the turbo compressor doesn't make it punchier than what it would be on any typical V6.
• **The large windows** seriously reduces the effectiveness of the air-conditioning unit in summer time.

VERDICT
The Previa is a good vehicle, but its special mechanical system, cabin and price are incompatible with market requirements.

RECALLS
1997 An oil leak might occur at the air breather plug at highway speeds.

RELIABILITY PROBLEMS

	1997	1998	1999	2000	2001	2002
Engine:	-					
Transmission:	X					
Suspension:	X					
Steering:	-					
Brakes:	-					
Electricity:	-					
Body:	-					
Accessories:	-					
Fit/finish:	-					

POWERTRAIN

PERFORMANCE

Year	Type/ L/Camshaft/bhp	Drivetrain & gearbox	Acceler. 0/100 sec.	Top. speed km/h	Ave. Fuel consp. l./100 km
1997	L4C/2.4/DOHC/161	rear/all-A4	12.1	170	13.5

SPECIFICATIONS

Model 1997	Wlb. mm	Lght. mm	Cb.wt kg	Brakes fr/rr	Steering type	Standard tires
m.v. 4dr.	2865	4750	1703	dc/dr	pwr.r&p.	205/75R14
m.v. 4dr.AWD	2865	4750	1857	dc/dr	pwr.r&p.	215/65R15

PRICES

Model / version		1997	1998	1999	2000	2001	2002
m.v. 4dr. S/C	mini	7900					
	maxi	9900					
m.v. 4dr. S/C LE	mini	8600					
	maxi	10900					
m.v. 4dr. S/C AWD	mini	10200					
	maxi	12600					

See page 7 to adapt these figures.

1997 TOYOTA Previa SC

TOYOTA   Prius

2000 TOYOTA Prius

The Prius was the second hybrid vehicle to be sold in Canada after the Insight. It is equipped with a thermal engine that produces the electricity required to recharge the batteries which in turn enables the electric motor to provide traction in various modes.

PROS
• **State-of-the-art technology** becomes less of a cause for concern when it's marketed by Japanese auto makers, especially Toyota whose models are renowned for being reliable.
• **The excellent fuel economy** and ultra-low emissions are the two main advantages of this avant-garde model.
• **The ride is comfortable** given the soft suspension and well-contoured and padded seats.
• **The Prius is practical** and maneuverable given its compact dimensions, but is nevertheless capable of seating up to 5 people.
• **The modern dashboard** reflects the out-of-the-ordinary spirit of this model.
• **Overall quality** is excellent, whether it be with respect to the solid construction, rigorous finish or simple yet elegant presentation of certain details.

CONS
• The Prius is so **technically complex** that the average small-town mechanic will not be able to assist you in the event of a failure.
• **New and therefore rare technology** comes with a high price tag. Nevertheless, certain environmentalists will undoubtedly make the effort to help reduce emissions of pollutant gases.
• **Performance** is timid when compared to that of a diesel engine, although the Prius has the advantage of being less noisy and smelly.
• **Handling** is average due to the narrow tires used to reduce rolling resistance. Furthermore, the supple suspension encourages body motions in curves.
• **The dashboard's** ergonomics leave to be desired because some elements were designed with right-side driving in mind.
• **There are not enough practical storage spaces**. The existing space is limited to a console bin and a small glove box.

VERDICT
The Prius is a realistic vehicle that is fun to drive. And it's a much better buy that the Insight whose capacities are limited. Calling out to all Martians . . .

RECALLS
None over this period.

Prius   TOYOTA

RELIABILITY PROBLEMS

	1997	1998	1999	2000	2001	2002
Engine:					-	-
Transmission:					-	-
Suspension:					X	-
Steering:					-	-
Brakes:					-	-
Electricity:					X	X
Body:					-	-
Accessories:					-	-
Fit/finish:					-	-

POWERTRAIN

Year	Type/ L/Camshaft/bhp	Drivetrain & gearbox	Acceler. 0/100 sec.	Top. speed km/h	Ave. Fuel consp. l./100 km
01-02	L4/1.5+elec.mot./70	CVT	13.8	160	4.5

SPECIFICATIONS

Model 01-02	Wlb. mm	Lght. mm	Cb.wt kg	Brakes fr/rr	Steering type	Standard tires
sdn. 4dr.	2550	4305	1640	dc/dr/ABS	pwr.r.&p.	175/65R14

PRICES

Model / version		1997	1998	1999	2000	2001	2002
sdn. 4dr.	mini					18400	22600
	maxi					21500	25200

See page 7 to adapt these figures.

2001 TOYOTA Prius

TOYOTA   RAV4

1998 TOYOTA RAV4

The RAV4 is available in either a short wheelbase 2-door model or in a long wheelbase 4-door model, as front-wheel or all-wheel drive, equipped with a 16-valve 2.0L DOHC 4-cylinder engine. Since 1999, only the AWD is available due to the poor demand on the front-wheel drive. It was redefined in 2001 on the same mechanical basis.

PROS
• **Performance** is very much like a car, thanks to a good power to weight ratio of 9.5 kg/hp and the smooth engine yields pretty gutsy pick-up at low rpm, even with the automatic gearbox.
• **Behind the wheel**, you're sitting nice and high, so you can see in all directions. The dashboard is logical and controls are easy to reach.
• **Roadhandling** is competent even on the short model that flits about like a little car, but you do have to be careful negotiating tight curves at zippy speeds.
• **Ride comfort** is more cushy on the 4-door model than is the case for some competitors, that are rustic and old-fashioned by comparison.
• **Pepier engine** provides a more fun to drive (since 2001).
• **Build quality** is Toyota standards. Assembly and fit and finish are superior, and trim components aren't at all plain.
• **Very convenient,** there are loads of storage spots everywhere and the trunk can be extended.

CONS
• **This fun-loving vehicle** isn't cheap, and a good old brawny Cherokee looks like a bargain beside the RAV4.
• **The transfer box** is sorely missed when tackling tough terrain that's ridden with major obstacles, for adherence is very iffy.
• **Equipment** isn't as extensive as on some other same-ilk vehicles and you have to check out the options to butter things up a bit.
• **The ride** isn't too great for long hauls, since seating doesn't offer much support and the Jolly Jumper suspension gets pretty tiring,
• **The retractable roofs** will never give you the free, let-your-hair-down feeling you get in a Jeep or a Sidekick.
• **Rearward view** is poor because of the spare tire and headrests.
• **To be improved upon:** the rear hatch that opens the wrong way from the sidewalk, because in Japan, people drive on the left side of the road...

VERDICT
The RAV4 is a treat to drive, but it's a pretty expensive toy for what you get, for it's neither a comfy car nor a tough, let-me-at-it 4X4.

RECALLS
None over this period.

RAV4   TOYOTA

RELIABILITY PROBLEMS

	1997	1998	1999	2000	2001	2002
Engine:	-	X	X	X	X	-
Transmission:	-	X	-	-	-	-
Suspension:	-	-	-	-	-	-
Steering:	-	-	-	-	-	-
Brakes:	-	X	X	X	X	-
Electricity:	X	-	-	X	-	-
Body:	-	-	X	X	X	X
Accessories:	-	-	X	X	X	-
Fit/finish:	X	-	-	-	-	-

POWERTRAIN

Year	Type/ L/Camshaft/bhp	Drivetrain & gearbox	Acceler. 0/100 sec.	Top. speed km/h	Ave. Fuel consp. l./100 km
97-02	L4/2.0/DOHC/120-148	front/all-M5	11.5	165	10.7
		front/all-A4	13.0	160	10.8

SPECIFICATIONS

Model	Wlb. mm	Lght. mm	Cb.wt kg	Brakes fr/rr	Steering type	Standard tires
97-98 4x2						
wgn. 2dr.	2200	3749	1145	dc/dr	pwr.r&p.	215/70R16
wgn. 4dr.	2410	4150	1210	dc/dr	pwr.r&p.	215/70R16
97-00 4x4						
wgn. 2dr.	2200	3749	1225	dc/dr	pwr.r&p.	235/60R16
wgn. 4dr.	2410	4161	1290	dc/ABS	pwr.r&p.	235/60R16
01-02 4x4						
wgn. 4dr.	2490	4195	1310	dc/dr	pwr.r&p.	215/70R16

PRICES

Model / version		1997	1998	1999	2000	2001	2002
con. 2dr. FWD	mini		11000	14200			
	maxi		13100	15950			
wgn. 2dr. FWD	mini	6300	8950				
	maxi	8950	11000				
wgn. 4dr. FWD	mini	7350	10300				
	maxi	9450	12600				
wgn. 2dr. AWD	mini		11350	14700	16800		
	maxi		13550	15750	19850		
wgn. 4dr. AWD	mini	9450	12200	15750	18600	21500	23600
	maxi	12100	14700	18400	21000	24150	26250

See page 7 to adapt these figures.

2001 TOYOTA RAV4

2001 TOYOTA Sequoia

The Sequoia is the largest SUV available in Toyota's line-up. It borrows the Tundra pick-up's chassis and mechanical components as well as the front end of its body. It's driven by a 4.7-liter V8 engine.

PROS

• **The immense cabin and cargo bay** are roomy enough to carry up to 7 individuals and their luggage.
• **The muscular V8 engine** provides this behemoth with acceleration and pick-up worthy of an automobile's.
• **The ride comfort** is appreciable on the highway, where the suspension and seats combine to produce a comfortable ride.
• **The Sequoia's off-road capabilities** are surprising for a vehicle of this size. In fact, its size is its only limit.
• **Fuel consumption** is relatively reasonable given the overall weight and large engine displacement.
• **The large fuel tank** gives the Sequoia a good travelling range, especially useful when leaving the beaten path.
• **The grab handles** and numerous storage spaces of this vehicle are testimony to Toyota's attention to detail.

CONS

• **The Sequoia** is bland to drive and devoid of sensationalism.
• The center console controls are not very practical because they out of the reach of the driver's and passenger's hands.
• **The high weight** and large size limit the Sequoia's ability to access tight spots.
• **The long stopping distances** are a result of the hefty weight. Trajectories can sometimes be unpredictable and fade resistance is average.
• **The interior** has a distinctively utilitarian look to it given the price, especially when you consider that the presentation of certain competitive models rivals that of a Cadillac.
• **The overhead console**, with its numerous bins, is a little ridiculous.

VERDICT

The Sequoia is the equivalent of the Land Cruiser, which was never sold in Canada during its first years. It's a serious competitor to the large SUVs offered by the domestic auto makers.

RECALLS

None over this period.

RELIABILITY PROBLEMS

	1997	1998	1999	2000	2001	2002
Engine:					-	-
Transmission:					-	-
Suspension:					-	-
Steering:					-	-
Brakes:					-	-
Electricity:					-	-
Body:					X	-
Accessories:					-	-
Fit/finish:					-	-

POWERTRAIN

Year	Type/ L/Camshaft/bhp	Drivetrain & gearbox
01-02	V8/4.7/SOHC/240	rr./all-A4

PERFORMANCE

Acceler. 0/100 sec.	Top. speed km/h	Ave. Fuel consp. l./100 km
10.0	175	17.4

SPECIFICATIONS

Model 01-02	Wlb. mm	Lght. mm	Cb.wt kg	Brakes fr/rr	Steering type	Standard tires
wgn. 4dr. SR5	3000	5180	2390	dc/ABS	pwr.ball.	265/70R16
wgn. 4dr.Limited	3000	5180	2402	dc/ABS	pwr.ball.	265/70R16

PRICES

Model / version		1997	1998	1999	2000	2001	2002
wgn. 4dr SR5 V8	mini					35700	41000
	maxi					39400	43800
wgn. 4dr. Ltd V6	mini					46200	51000
	maxi					49900	54300

See page 7 to adapt these figures.

2001 TOYOTA Sequoia

TOYOTA   Sienna

2002 TOYOTA Sienna

The Sienna replaced the Previa in 1998. It has a more conventional shape and build, is based on the Camry platform and is powered by a 3.0L V6.

PROS
• **Ride comfort** derives from well-adjusted suspensions and nicely soundproofed, sturdy body.
• **Performance** is pretty impressive due to a good power to weight ratio, so accelerations and pick-up are on a par with those achieved by a station wagon.
• **This vehicle** is nicely priced for such a good equipment array, even the entry-level CE version that's perfectly acceptable.
• **Cabin space** is better adapted to accommodating seven passengers than is the case for short wheelbase rivals, yet the Sienna doesn't have rigidity problems that often affect and afflict extended models.
• **Roadability** is competent; the vehicle stays on the straight and narrow normal runs and on curves or tight bends taken at a good clip.
• **Steering** is responsive, precise and gradual, so there isn't torque fallout on strong accelerations.

CONS
• **The plain design** is too similar to that of the former Villager-Quest and the slide-rail for the sliding doors isn't as neatly integrated as on other models.
• **Choice** is limited to a single overall and wheelbase length.
• **Seats** are quite flat, hard and thinly upholstered and the rear bench is hard to get to.
• **The parking brake** is the most awkward on the market.
• **Visibility** is hindered at rear quarterback due to the bulky C-pillar, slim rear window shape and rear headrests.
• **The overly cushy** suspension generates a lot of swish and sway, so you have to slow down and the front end bottoms out when travelling on less than perfect pavement.
• **Maneuverability** suffers from a wide steer angle diameter.
• **Brakes** are stable, but take forever to bring the vehicle to a full stop.
• **The cabin design** is pretty plain with the shiny finish on some plastic parts that look more trashy than classy.
• **Tires** are pretty crummy when it comes to grip and a smooth ride.
• **The instrument panel** isn't too ergonomic. The center console is really low and some accessories are poorly located.

VERDICT
The Sienna is more humdrum when it comes to looks, but it's also more run-of-the-mill than the Previa that it replaced and model choice is too limited.

RECALLS
None over this period.

Sienna   TOYOTA

RELIABILITY PROBLEMS

	1997	1998	1999	2000	2001	2002
Engine:		-	-	-	-	-
Transmission:		-	-	X	-	-
Suspension:		X	X	-	-	-
Steering:		-	-	-	-	-
Brakes:		-	X	-	-	-
Electricity:		X	X	X	X	-
Body:		X	X	X	X	-
Accessories:		X	X	X	X	X
Fit/finish:		X	X	X	-	-

POWERTRAIN

Year	Type/ L/Camshaft/bhp	Drivetrain & gearbox	Acceler. 0/100 sec.	Top. speed km/h	Ave. Fuel consp. l./100 km
98-02	V6/3.0/DOHC/194-210	front-A4	10.5	180	12.9

PERFORMANCE

(merged above)

SPECIFICATIONS

Model 98-02	Wlb. mm	Lght. mm	Cb.wt kg	Brakes fr/rr	Steering type	Standard tires
m.v. 3/4dr. CE	2900	4915	1705	dc/dr/ABS	pwr.r&p.	205/70R15
m.v. 3/4dr. LE	2900	4915	1765	dc/dr/ABS	pwr.r&p.	205/70R15

PRICES

Model / version		1997	1998	1999	2000	2001	2002
wgn. 3dr. Cargo	mini		8900	11350			
	maxi		11550	13100			
wgn. 3dr. CE	mini		12600	13650	17850		
	maxi		14400	15750	19950		
wgn. 3dr. LE	mini		14200				
	maxi		16500				
wgn. 4dr. CE	mini		13100	14200	18900	22000	23600
	maxi		15450	16300	21000	24700	26800
wgn. 4dr. LE	mini		15100	17100	19950	23600	25200
	maxi		17550	19400	22350	26250	28350
wgn. 4dr. XLE	mini		16150	18400	21500	24150	27300
	maxi		18600	20900	23950	25700	30450
wgn. 4dr. XLE LTD	mini						28350
	maxi						32000

See page 7 to adapt these figures.

2002 TOYOTA Sienna

TOYOTA   Supra

1997 TOYOTA Supra

Unveiled in 1978, the GT Supra coupe was built on the Celica platform and was equipped with Cressida mechanical features. It became a model in its own right in '85 and was upgraded in '90 and again in '94.

PROS
• **The Sportscar** character and look of the latest generation.
• **The turbo engine** musters up impressive power given the excessive vehicle weight and it achieves stunning accelerations and pick-up worthy of a true blue Sportscar.
• **Handling is great**, no matter what the situation. Only road faults and vehicle weight can affect road stability.
• **The engine keeps** its Sportscar zip with the manual transmission, but the automatic saps it of such capabilities.
• **Power steering** is accurate and quick on the draw and the cockpit is super, even though the seat is a bit low-slung.
• **Gas consumption** is reasonable, considering engine power and vehicle weight.
• **Build and finish** details are very topnotch.
• **The out-of-ordinary look** of the rear spoiler, for its muscular size and shape that will for sure not go unnoticed.

CONS
• **Excessive vehicle weight** really kills all spontaneity and agility on curved roads.
• **The cabin interior** is blah and just too synthetic-looking to have any real class, yet it's well-designed.
• **Major blind spots** reduce outward view towards the rear and sides.
• **Brakes** are powerful and smooth, making for straight stops, but with ABS, sudden stops take longer to achieve.
• **The poorly designed** seats don't provide adequate lateral and lumbar support.
• **Rear seats** are almost non-functional and this space is more suited for storing excess baggage.
• **Storage compartments** are skimpy and few and far between.

CONCLUSION
The Supra coupe has come a long way and is now a high-caliber car that can boast of stunning performance. Its price is definitely less popular nowadays, now that personal and social values have changed, which explains why sales are so dismally low.

RECALLS
None over this period.

RELIABILITY PROBLEMS

	1997	1998	1999	2000	2001	2002
Engine:						
Transmission:						
Suspension:						
Steering:						
Brakes:		Insufficient data				
Electricity:						
Body:						
Accessories:						
Fit/finish:						

POWERTRAIN

PERFORMANCE

Year	Type/ L/Camshaft/bhp	Drivetrain & gearbox	Acceler. 0/100 sec.	Top. speed km/h	Ave. Fuel consp. l./100 km
1997	L6T/3.0/DOHC/320	rear-M5	5.0	250	13.6
		rear-A4	5.7	250	12.8

SPECIFICATIONS

Model	Wlb. mm	Lght. mm	Cb.wt kg	Brakes fr/rr	Steering type	Standard tires
1997						
cpe. 2dr. Turbo	2550	4515	1594	dc/ABS	pwr.r&p.	235/45R17 255/40R17

PRICES

Model / version		1997	1998	1999	2000	2001	2002
cpe. 2dr. Turbo	mini	27300					
	maxi	30450					

See page 7 to adapt these figures.

1997 TOYOTA Supra

1998 TOYOTA Paseo

The tiny Tercel hails back to 1978. It was redesigned in '82 and '87 and upgraded in '91 and in '95. The Paseo coupe, which is an offshoot of the Tercel, was launched in 1992 and got a face-lift in 1996.

PROS

• **The Tercel is reliable** and inexpensive to run, which explains why there aren't many on the used car market and resale value is so high.

• **The Paseo design** appeals mainly to the ladies.

• **The 1.5L engine** is quite efficient, for it performs adequately and doesn't burn too much gas.

• **Handling** is sure and predictable, except on the base model equipped with small tires. The car hugs the road quite well, but it's sensitive to road faults and to crosswinds.

• **The roomy cabin** on the sedan can comfortably accommodate four adults and there's room for their luggage as well.

• **The driver's seat** is firm and high, providing good outward view.

• **Power steering** is a better choice for city driving.

• **The cabin** and trunk are bigger since 1995.

CONS

• **Brakes** aren't too effective, for sudden stops are long to achieve.

• **The narrow tires** that equip the base model don't grip well on slippery roads.

• **Manual steering** is stiff at slow speed and inaccurate at higher speed because of too high a reduction ratio.

• **The suspension** can be very harsh and bumpy on bad roads, the seats are hard and soundproofing is poor, all of which affect overall comfort.

• **Rear seats** on the Paseo are next to non-existent and are really only serve as extra storage space when the trunk is extended.

• **The instrument panel** is terribly plain and the cabin interior isn't really too attractive.

VERDICT

The Tercel started out as a simple means of transportation, but it has become quite a classy little car, and the Paseo coupe has added good looks to its list of winning traits.

RECALLS

None over this period.

RELIABILITY PROBLEMS

	1997	1998	1999	2000	2001	2002
Engine:	-	-	-			
Transmission:	X	X	X			
Suspension:	-	-	-			
Steering:	X	-	-			
Brakes:	-	-	-			
Electricity:	-	-	-			
Body:	-	-	-			
Accessories:	-	-	-			
Fit/finish:	X	X	X			

POWERTRAIN

Year	Type/ L/Camshaft/bhp	Drivetrain & gearbox	Acceler. 0/100 sec.	Top. speed km/h	Ave. Fuel consp. l./100 km
97-99	L4/1.5/DOHC/93(Tercel)	front-M5	11.0	165	7.2
		front-A4	13.5	165	8.4
	L4/1.5/DOHC/100	front-M5	10.5	160	7.8
		front-A3-A4	11.8	165	8.7

PERFORMANCE

SPECIFICATIONS

Model 97-99	Wlb.	Lght.	Cb.wt	Brakes	Steering	Standard
sdn. 2dr. base	2380	4110	889	dc/dr	r&p.	155/80R14
sdn. 2dr. DX-CE	2380	4110	912	dc/dr	pwr.r&p.	155/80R14
sdn. 4dr. DX-CE	2380	4110	923	dc/dr	pwr.r&p.	155/80R13
cpe. 3dr. Paseo	2380	4155	986	dc/dr	pwr.r&p.	185/60R14

PRICES

Model / version		1997	1998	1999	2000	2001	2002
Tercel							
sdn. 2dr. CE	mini	4750	6300	7350			
	maxi	7350	8400	9450			
sdn. 4dr. CE	mini	5800	6850	7900			
	maxi	7900	8950	10000			
Paseo							
cpe. 3dr.	mini	6300	7350	8400			
	maxi	7900	8950	10000			

See page 7 to adapt these figures.

1998 TOYOTA Tercel

TOYOTA   4Runner

1998 TOYOTA 4Runner

This sport utility vehicle was introduced in 1985 as a 3-door model driven by a 4-cylinder engine and it got a V6 in 1988 and a 5-door body style in '90. Revamped in 1995, it was given in '99 a bunch of small improvements, and especially a vitamin shot that the 4Runner was lacking of to sustain the strong competition in this market segment.

PROS

• **The vehicle is neutral** on the road and well-balanced on rough terrain and out in the rough, it can get just about anywhere with such high ground clearance.

• **The V6 engine** is more muscular but it lacks torque at low rpm in some situations. The 4-cylinder engine has less vim and vitality, but it does its job in a nice, hassle-free way.

• **Construction quality** is very good, for the vehicle is solid and finish is tight and clean.

• **It's a very practical vehicle**, because it's midway between a station wagon and a pick-up truck, and it comes equipped with all-wheel drive.

• **Driving comfort** is really above average, with such well-contoured front seats, smooth and civilized suspension and reasonable noise level with the V6, even though there is some wind noise.

CONS

• **The 4Runner is reliable** and durable, which explains its high price tag and why these models are hard to find on the used vehicle market.

• **Boarding** this vehicle with such a high ground clearance is difficult without a step to climb onto.

• **The V6 engine** really guzzles the gas, especially when carrying a heavy load or going over rough terrain.

• **Steering** is light because it's overassisted. This may be an advantage on rough terrain, but it sure complicates things on the highway when there are crosswinds.

• **The overall look** is very basic and plain before 1997, even on the luxurious upper-end SR5. The Limited edition has truly corrected this annoying situation.

VERDICT

The 4Runner is a good, all-purpose vehicle that's reliable and efficient. The only disadvantage is how much it costs to keep it on the road, so its attributes may be impressive, but there's a hefty price tag attached.

RECALLS

None over this period.

RELIABILITY PROBLEMS

	1997	1998	1999	2000	2001	2002
Engine:	X	-	-	X	-	-
Transmission:	-	X	-	-	-	-
Suspension:	X	X	X	X	-	-
Steering:	-	-	X	-	-	-
Brakes:	X	X	X	X	-	-
Electricity:	X	-	X	X	-	-
Body:	X	X	X	X	-	-
Accessories:	X	X	X	X	-	-
Fit/finish:	-	-	X	-	-	-

POWERTRAIN / PERFORMANCE

Year	Type/ L/Camshaft/bhp	Drivetrain & gearbox	Acceler. 0/100 sec.	Top. speed km/h	Ave. Fuel consp. l./100 km
97-02	L4/2.7/DOHC/150	rear/all-M5	NA	NA	13.7
		rear/all-A4	NA	NA	12.6
	V6/3.4/DOHC/183	rear/all-M5	10.0	165	14.4
		rear/all-A4	11.5	160	14.1

SPECIFICATIONS

Model	Wlb. mm	Lght. mm	Cb.wt kg	Brakes fr/rr	Steering type	Standard tires
97-02						
wgn. 4dr. SR5	2675	4540	1690	dc/dr	pwr.r&p.	225/75R15
wgn. 4dr. V6	2675	4540	1762	dc/dr/ABS	pwr.r&p.	265/70R16
wgn. 4dr. LTD	2675	4540	1803	dc/dr/ABS	pwr.r&p.	265/70R16

PRICES

Model / version		1997	1998	1999	2000	2001	2002
wgn. 4dr. 4x4 V6	mini					27300	30000
	maxi					30300	32750
wgn. 4dr. 4x4 SR5	mini	14500	16800	20500			
	maxi	16800	19100	22600			
wgn. 4dr. 4x4 V6	mini	18250	19950	23100	25600	30150	32000
SR5	maxi	19650	22000	25200	27800	32250	34850
wgn. 4dr. 4x4 V6	mini	22800	25200	27800	31500	36450	38850
LTD	maxi	25500	27300	31000	34650	39000	41700

See page 7 to adapt these figures.

2000 TOYOTA 4Runner

VOLKSWAGEN   Eurovan

2001 VOLKSWAGEN Eurovan

The Eurovan replaced the Vanagon in 1992. It became a front-wheel drive vehicle driven by a 2.5L 5-cylinder gas engine, or a Diesel engine since '93 and a camper model is still available. In '99, the Eurovan has been reintroduced after a year spent at the fountain of Youth and shows up with a VR6 engine and a 4 speed automatic transmission that can haul a mere 2,000kg ! Offered in three different trim levels, including a practical camper, the Eurovan is surely a phoenix of its own.

PROS
• **The cabin interior** is absolutely huge, even on the shorter model and there's unusually generous space every which way which makes for exceptional freedom of movement and access.
• **Handling** is outstanding for a vehicle of this type, for the independent suspension stabilizes and balances the van to a remarkable degree, controlling sway and vehicle path.
• **Build quality**, finish and trim components are flawless, but the overall design is rather plain and simple.
• **Equipment** is more extensive on the more attractive GL and GLS.
• **The cockpit** is perfect, for it provides excellent visibility and good vehicle control.
• **The side door** is light and easy to open and close and rear windows slide open.
• **The very practical baggage** compartment is huge and it opens nice and low, storage compartments are well distributed throughout the cabin and there are headrests for all seats.
• **The economical yield** of the Diesel engine.

CONS
• **The Eurovan looks** more like a van than a real family vehicle.
• **Both Audi L5 engines** are anemic because of a poor power to weight ratio, that 's why VW has brought in the VR6.
• **Gas consumption** on the gas fed L5 engine is comparable to that of a 3.0L V6, without the muscle or torque.
• **The brake pedal** is really soft and makes it hard to slow down with any accuracy and stops are a long time coming.
• **Steering** is vague and doesn't go back to center on its own and needs to be constantly readjusted in crosswinds, for the Eurovan sure doesn't like wind.

VERDICT
The old Eurovan weren't powered by the right engine before '99, which is too bad, for it's a superbly designed, very practical vehicle.

RECALLS
None over this period.

RELIABILITY PROBLEMS

	1997	1998	1999	2000	2001	2002
Engine:						
Transmission:						
Suspension:						
Steering:						
Brakes:			Insufficient data			
Electricity:						
Body:						
Accessories:						
Fit/finish:						

POWERTRAIN   PERFORMANCE

Year	Type/ L/Camshaft/bhp	Drivetrain & gearbox	Acceler. 0/100 sec.	Top. speed km/h	Ave. Fuel consp. l./100 km
1997	L5/2.5/SOHC/110	front-M5	14.5	160	12.5
		front-A4	15.5	155	13.0
	L5D/2.4/SOHC/77	front-M5	18.5	140	8.0
99-02	V6/2.8/DOHC/140	front-A4	12.5	175	14.7

SPECIFICATIONS

Model 1997	Wlb. mm	Lght. mm	Cb.wt kg	Brakes fr/rr	Steering type	Standard tires
m.v. 4dr. CL	2920	4740	1730	dc/dr	pwr.r&p.	205/65R15
m.v. 4dr. GL	2920	4740	1780	dc/dr	pwr.r&p.	205/65R15
m.v. 4dr. CV	2920	4740	1890	dc/dr	pwr.r&p.	205/65R15
99-02						
m.v. 4dr. GLS	2920	4789	1914	dc/ABS	pwr.r&p.	205/65R15
m.v. 4dr. MV	2920	4789	1972	dc/ABS	pwr.r&p.	205/65R15
m.v. 4dr. Camper	3320	5189	2375	dc/ABS	pwr.r&p.	205/65R15

PRICES

Model / version		1997	1998	1999	2000	2001	2002
m.v. 4dr. CV	mini	18600					
	maxi	22450					
m.v. 4dr.GLS Auto	mini			21000	26250	29300	32350
	maxi			23100	29200	32000	35200
m.v. 4dr. MV Auto	mini			22000	28150	30350	33600
	maxi			24150	30350	32520	36200
m.v. 4dr. Camper	mini			26250			
	maxi			28350			

See page 7 to adapt these figures.

2001 VOLKSWAGEN Eurovan

1998 VOLKSWAGEN Golf GL

Launched under this name in 1985, the Golf is available as a 3- or 5-door sedan or as a 2-door convertible. The GTI 16V came out in 1987, the VR6 engine in '94 and the latest body design in '95. In '99, two type of Golf were sold in the marketplace: the "Classic" Golf and the New Golf.

PROS

• **The huge cabin and trunk** give space in all directions and access is very easy from side and rear.

• **Handling** is clean and the sports models literally stick to the road, for they exhibit no sway or lean.

• **The last VR6** engine provides strong accelerations and pick-up.

• **Driving** is pleasant with such a nice cockpit, good visibility, crisp, sensitive steering and the straightforward, ergonomic instrument panel that has become quite attractive, by the way.

• **The economical,** remarkably sturdy Diesel engine that simply refuses to die.

• **Convenience** hasn't been overlooked, for the rear seat area has modular seats and storage compartments are well distributed throughout the cabin.

CONS

• **The Volkswagen reputation** for foolproof reliability is no longer what it once was, for bodywork is quite prone to rust and mechanical features aren't really dependable, and we might add, the quality of some components is pretty wishy washy.

• **Driving competence** varies with the years, models, the shape the original equipment or replacement parts are in, and tire quality.

• **High noise** really affects driving comfort.

• **The cabin interior** is smaller than average for this car category, because of the narrow body.

• **Gas engines** aren't economical, mostly the least VR6 which guzzles just like its american competitors.

VERDICT

The Golf lost its pristine reputation when it began to be built in Mexico, and in spite of technical improvements, it's less economical and less efficient than its rivals.

RECALLS

None during this period.

Golf   VOLKSWAGEN

RELIABILITY PROBLEMS

	1997	1998	1999	2000	2001	2002
Engine:	X	X	X			
Transmission:	-	-	-			
Suspension:	-	-	-			
Steering:	-	-	-			
Brakes:	X	-	-			
Electricity:	X	-	-			
Body:	-	-	-			
Accessories:	-	X	X			
Fit/finish:	-	-	-			

POWERTRAIN

Year	Type/ L/Camshaft/bhp	Drivetrain & gearbox
97-99	L4/1.8/SOHC/90-123	front-M5
		front-A3-A4
	L4/2.0/SOHC/115-133	front-M5
		front-A4
	L4D/1.9/SOHC/75-90	front-M5
	V6/2.8/DOHC/174-201	front-M5
		front-A4

PERFORMANCE

Acceler. 0/100 sec.	Top. speed km/h	Ave. Fuel consp. l./100 km
11.8	175	9.3
13.0	165	10.0
10.9	180	10.1
12.0	175	10.8
13.0	170	5.9
8.0	210	12.2
8.8	200	12.6

SPECIFICATIONS

Model 97-99	Wlb. mm	Lght. mm	Cb.wt kg	Brakes fr/rr	Steering type	Standard tires
con. 2dr.	2475	4020	1225	dc/dr	pwr.r&p.	195/60R14
sdn. 3dr. CL	2475	4075	1117	dc/dr	pwr.r&p.	195/60R14
sdn. 3dr. GTI	2475	4075	1043	dc/dc	pwr.r&p.	185/60R14
sdn. 3dr. GTI v6	2475	4075	1252	dc/ABS	pwr.r&p.	205/50R15
sdn. 5dr. CL	2475	4075	1173	dc/dr	pwr.r&p.	195/60R14

PRICES

Model / version		1997	1998	1999	2000	2001	2002
con. 2dr. Cabriolet	mini	9450	11850	13650			
	maxi	12100	14200	15950			
con. 2dr. Highline	mini	12500					
	maxi	15200					
con. 2dr. GLS	mini		14400	16800			
	maxi		16800	19100			
sdn. 3dr. CL	mini	5500					
	maxi	7350					
sdn. 3dr. GTI	mini	9000	11550				
	maxi	11150	13850				
sdn. 3dr. GTI VR6	mini	11000	13850	16800			
	maxi	13250	16500	18900			
sdn. 5dr.	mini		7900				
	maxi		10500				
sdn. 5dr. CL	mini	6100					
	maxi	7900					
sdn. 5dr. GL	mini	7050	8200	10000			
	maxi	9350	10500	12100			
sdn. 4dr. K2	mini	7050	8400				
	maxi	8900	10700				
sdn. 5dr. GL TDI	mini	7250					
	maxi	9450					
sdn. 5dr. Jazz	mini	7650					
	maxi	9750					
sdn. 5dr. Trek	mini	7900	11000	12600			
	maxi	10000	13350	14700			
sdn. 5dr. Wolfsburg	mini			9450			
	maxi			11550			
sdn. 5dr. 2.0L	mini						
	maxi						

See page 7 to adapt these figures.

VOLKSWAGEN   Jetta

1998 VOLKSWAGEN Jetta GL

The Jetta, that's inspired by the Golf, was first sold in 1975 and the GLX with VR6 engine was first available in '94. It comes in 2- and 4-door models, powered by gas or Diesel engines. In '99, two type of Jetta were sold in the marketplace: the "Classic" Jetta and the New Jetta.

PROS

• **Handling** on the models equipped with a 4-cylinder engine is clean, for there isn't much sway or swing.

• **The VR6 engine** is remarkable and yields very spirited accelerations and pick-up.

• **Driving** is enhanced by the nicely designed cockpit, good visibility, crisp and sensitive steering and a convenient, ergonomic and nice-looking instrument panel.

• **The Diesel engine** is economical and so robust that it just never dies.

• **The huge trunk** is characteristic of the Jetta and can hold heaps and heaps of luggage.

CONS

• **The Volkswagen reputation** for foolproof reliability is no longer what it once was, for bodywork is quite prone to rust and mechanical features aren't really dependable, and we might add, the quality of some components is pretty hit and miss.

• **Handling** on the GLX is very touchy with the VR6 engine that is just too muscular for this type of frame and undercarriage. So there's whopping torque and responses are rough around the edges, which could be problematic for an inexperienced driver.

• **High noise** really affects driving comfort on long trips.

• **The cabin interior** is smaller than average for this car category, because of the narrow body.

• **The 3-speed** automatic is poorly calibrated.

• **Gas engines** aren't economical.

VERDICT

The Jetta lost its credibility when it began to be built in Mexico, and in spite of improvements, it's less economical and less roomy than its rivals.

RECALLS

1999   A sound absorbing mat inside of the B-pillar side trim may have been improperly installed and could ignite in the event of a collision, resulting in vehicle fire.

Jetta   VOLKSWAGEN

RELIABILITY PROBLEMS

	1997	1998	1999	2000	2001	2002
Engine:	X	X	X			
Transmission:	X	X	X			
Suspension:	-	X	X			
Steering:	-	-	-			
Brakes:	X	X	-			
Electricity:	X	-	-			
Body:	-	-	-			
Accessories:	X	X	X			
Fit/finish:	-	X	X			

POWERTRAIN / PERFORMANCE

Year	Type/ L/Camshaft/bhp	Drivetrain & gearbox	Acceler. 0/100 sec.	Top. speed km/h	Ave. Fuel consp. l./100 km
97-99	L4/2.0/SOHC/115-133	front-M5	10.9	180	10.1
		front-A4	12.0	175	10.8
	L4D/1.9/SOHC/75-90	front-M5	13.0	170	5.9
	V6/2.8/DOHC/174	front-M5	8.0	210	12.2
		front-A4	8.8	220	12.6

SPECIFICATIONS

Model 97-99	Wlb. mm	Lght. mm	Cb.wt kg	Brakes fr/rr	Steering type	Standard tires
sdn. 4dr. GL	2513	4376	1279	dc/ABS	pwr.r&p.	195/65R15
sdn. 4dr. GLS	2513	4376	1283	dc/ABS	pwr.r&p.	195/65R15
sdn. 4dr. GLX	2513	4376	1369	dc/ABS	pwr.r&p.	195/65R15
sdn. 4dr. TDI	2475	4404	1254	dc/dr	pwr.r&p.	205/50R15

PRICES

Model / version		1997	1998	1999	2000	2001	2002
sdn. 4dr. GL	mini	7550	9450	11550			
	maxi	9650	11550	13650			
sdn. 4dr. GL TDI	mini	6950	10300	12600			
	maxi	9150	12400	14900			
sdn. 4dr. TDI DSL	mini	7900					
	maxi	11250					
sdn. 4dr. GLX VR6	mini	13250	14400				
	maxi	15450	16800				
sdn. 4dr. GT	mini	8100	10000				
	maxi	10200	11950				
sdn. 4dr. GLS	mini	8500	10500				
	maxi	10700	12600				
sdn. 4dr.Jazz/Treck	mini	8700					
	maxi	11000					
sdn. 4dr. K2	mini		10500				
	maxi		12600				
sdn. 4dr. Wolfburg	mini		11000	13450			
	maxi		13100	15350			

See page 7 to adapt these figures.

VOLKSWAGEN   New Beetle

2002 VOLKSWAGEN New Beetle

The Beetle is a Golf spin-off and its launch in 1998 was the automobile industry highlight of the year. Since that day, the New Beetle has won its right to be equipped with the sophisticated 150-bhp 1.8L turbo, borrowed from the Audi A4 mainly in order to create, once more, a bit of excitment for the brand's enthusiasts.

PROS

• **The style** is utterly irresistible, so this car sure gets noticed, thanks to the array of bright body shades.

• **Ultra-modern** technical features are real assets when it comes to safety and comfort, such as effective heating and air conditioning that do their stuff when it counts and the four airbags.

• **Safe travel** derives from clean follow-through, smooth and precise steering and brakes that really grip in most situations.

• **Front seats** are comfy and accessible, offer lots of toe, hip and headroom, seats are beautifully contoured and upholstered and the suspension is quite velvety.

• **The performance** of the 1.8L turbo engine is just so exemplary and truly dictates the selection of this engine above others.

• **The cabin design** is very plush and includes top-notch trim and neat finish touches, so the overall look is quite unique.

• **The rear hatch** is well integrated and meticulously crafted with the lock hidden under the brand crest, a real work of art!

• **The manual gearbox** is a driver's dream with such an accurate and well-honed shifter, a true VW beauty.

CONS

• **Convenience-wise**, there aren't enough storage spots, the rear seats are snug and hard to get to and the trunk holds enough luggage only when the seatbench is folded down.

• **Performance** is wimpy and breathless with both the 2.0L and 1.9L Diesel engines, linked to either the manual or automatic transmission.

• **Outward view** is hampered by the high body belt that cuts down on window size, massive roof supports and tiny mirrors.

• **Noise** is stereophonic due to the noisy, shaky engine, whistling mirrors and roaring tires.

• **It's hard getting comfy** behind the wheel and the driver feels really far removed from the windshield and from what's going on up front...

• **The dashboard** is absolutely huge for what it holds, so it makes the cabin look tinier than it actually is.

• **Disappointing:** rear windows that can't be opened, small sun-visors, insufficiently bright headlights, awkwardly located clock and the hardly practical cup-holders.

VERDICT

The Beetle is a winner due to its nostalgic style rather than for its overall practicality or fair performance.

RECALLS

1998   Wiring inspection and installation of modified battery casing.

RELIABILITY PROBLEMS

	1997	1998	1999	2000	2001	2002
Engine:		X	X	X	X	X
Transmission:		-	-	-	-	-
Suspension:		-	-	-	-	-
Steering:		-	-	-	-	-
Brakes:		-	-	-	-	-
Electricity:		X	X	X	X	X
Body:		X	X	X	X	-
Accessories:		X	X	X	X	X
Fit/finish:		X	X	X	-	-

POWERTRAIN   PERFORMANCE

Year	Type/ L/Camshaft/bhp	Drivetrain & gearbox	Acceler. 0/100 sec.	Top. speed km/h	Ave. Fuel consp. l./100 km
98-02	L4TD/1.9/SOHC/90	front-M5	13.0	170	5.6
		front-A4	14.2	165	6.9
	L4/2.0/SOHC/115	front-M5	10.6	180	9.9
		front-A4	11.8	175	10.5
99-02	L4T/1.8/DOHC/150-180	front-M5	8.0	210	10.2
		front-A4	NA	NA	NA

SPECIFICATIONS

Model 98-02	Wlb. mm	Lght. mm	Cb.wt kg	Brakes fr/rr	Steering type	Standard tires
sdn. 2dr. 2.0	2512	4092	1230	dc/dc	pwr.r&p.	205/55R16
sdn. 2dr. TDI	2512	4092	1260	dc/dc	pwr.r&p.	205/55R16
sdn. 2dr. 1.8T	2512	4092	1290	dc/dc	pwr.r&p.	205/55R16

PRICES

Model / version		1997	1998	1999	2000	2001	2002
sdn. 2dr. 2.0	mini		10200				
	maxi		12600				
sdn. 2dr. GL	mini			11550	13850	16000	17650
	maxi			13850	16000	19400	21200
sdn. 2dr. GLS	mini			12600	14900	17300	18700
	maxi			14900	17100	20500	22250
sdn. 2dr. TDI	mini		11850				
	maxi		14200				
sdn. 2dr. GLS TDI	mini			14200	16600	19400	20700
	maxi			16500	18700	22600	24000
sdn. 2dr. GLS 1.8T	mini			15750	17000	19850	21000
	maxi			18000	19200	23000	24350
sdn. 2dr. GLX 1.8T	mini			17850	20150	22800	24150
	maxi			20150	22350	25700	27500

See page 7 to adapt these figures.

2000 VOLKSWAGEN New Beetle

VOLKSWAGEN   New Golf

2001 VOLKSWAGEN New Golf

The last Golf derived from the former one. It is available as 3- or 5-door sedans with TDI or 2.0L 4-cylinder or 2.8L V6 gas engine.

PROS

• **Performance** of the GTi and GLX's VR6 is the most exciting. It provides the kind of acceleration and pick-up that makes you hate the sluggish 2.0L on the pretentious GTI GLS.

• **Handling** is stable and predictable thanks to efficient and sophisticated suspensions that result in precision driving. Although they tend to understeer, it's easy to control and are ideal for sporty drivers.

• **Steering** is precise and responsive. Assistance is just right and it makes driving on winding roads a very pleasant experience.

• **The fuel economy** of the Diesel engine's is more noteworthy than levels recorded for the less economical gasoline engines.

• **The presentation** is not as severe now that materials come in colors other than grey and black. Plastics and fabrics look significantly better than they did on previous models.

• **The standard anti-theft** system is far from a luxury. It's now part of standard equipment and will no doubt serve to decrease the number of thefts that once reached virtually epidemic levels.

• **The convertible** is the only one of its kind, with four seats, a roll bar and a lined top including a glass rear windshield featuring a defroster, a definite asset for problem-free in winter driving.

• **Bonus:** high praise for the diesel models' range and automatic windshield wipers that spring into action as soon as it begins to rain.

CONS

• **The price** of the Golf is yet high compared to some of their less problematic Japanese competitors.

• **The rear bench** is wider, but it isn't still long enough and only smaller passengers will feel comfortable.

• **Few exasperating problems** continue to plague Golf owners. Once you get past the product's good looks, you soon see that some manufacturing details could use improvement.

• **The performance** of the 2.0L engine is mediocre and acceleration and pick-up are both unenthusiastic.

• **Comfort** is no picnic; this car remains noisy, the engine and drivetrains vibrate, the suspension is very firm and seats are very hard.

• **Dashboard** wastes a lot of space and is a hazard for kneecaps.

• **To be fixed:** very weak headlights and slow windshield wipers, are dangerous, especially on the high-performance GLX versions

VERDICT

Improvements aside, the Golf are overvalued. Their reliability has not yet been proven undeniably and their performance levels and warranties fail to justify their price.

RECALLS

2000   One of the two brackets used to bolt the front control arm to the body structure may not have been welded properly and must be inspected and replaced if necessary.

00-01 One of two brackets use to bolt the front control arm to the body structure may have not been welded to specifications.

01-02 Dealers will replace the ABS command module on some vehicles.

New Golf   VOLKSWAGEN

RELIABILITY PROBLEMS

	1997	1998	1999	2000	2001	2002
Engine:			X	X	X	X
Transmission:			X	-	-	-
Suspension:			X	-	-	-
Steering:			X	-	-	-
Brakes:			X	-	-	-
Electricity:			X	X	X	-
Body:			X	X	X	-
Accessories:			X	X	X	X
Fit/finish:			X	X	X	X

POWERTRAIN / PERFORMANCE

Year	Type/ L/Camshaft/bhp	Drivetrain & gearbox	Acceler. 0/100 sec.	Top. speed km/h	Ave. Fuel consp. l./100 km
99-02	L4/2.0/SOHC/115	front-M5	10.9	180	10.1
		front-A4	12.0	175	10.8
	V6/2.8/DOHC/174-201	front-M5	8.0	210	12.2
		front-A4	8.8	200	12.6
	L4D/1.9/SOHC/90	front-M5	13.0	170	5.9
00-02	L4/1.8T/SOHC/150-180	front-M5	9.0	200	10.0

SPECIFICATIONS

Model 99-02	Wlb. mm	Lght. mm	Cb.wt kg	Brakes fr/rr	Steering type	Standard tires
con. 2dr. Cabrio	2474	4074	1398	dc/dr/ABS	pwr.r&p.	195/60R14
sdn. 2dr. GTI GLS	2511	4149	1253	dc/dr/ABS	pwr.r&p.	195/65R15
sdn. 2dr. GTI GLX	2511	4149	1311	dc/ABS	pwr.r&p.	205/55R16
sdn. 4dr. TDI GLS	2511	4149	1304	dc/dr/ABS	pwr.r&p.	195/65R15
sdn. 4dr. GL 2.0L	2511	4149	1235	dc/dr/ABS	pwr.r&p.	195/65R15
sdn. 4dr. GLS	2511	4149	1279	dc/dr/ABS	pwr.r&p.	195/65R15

PRICES

Model / version		1997	1998	1999	2000	2001	2002
Con .2dr. GL	mini			15200	17850	19200	20500
	Maxi			17550	19950	21500	23200
Con .2dr. GLS	mini			18400	21750	22350	23600
	Maxi			20700	24000	24900	26150
Con .2dr. GLX	mini					24450	25700
	Maxi					28900	29300
sdn. 2dr. GL 2.0L	mini			11550	12600	15100	16800
	maxi			13650	15200	17750	19650
sdn. 2dr. GL TDI	mini			12800	13850	16150	18000
	maxi			14700	16300	18800	20700
sdn. 2dr. GLS 1.8	mini				16800	19300	23300
	maxi				19400	21950	25950
sdn. 2dr. GTI VR6	mini						25400
	maxi						28000
sdn. 2dr. GTI GLS 2.0	mini			15450	15750		
	maxi			17300	18850		
sdn. 2dr. GTI GLS 2.8	mini			17850	19950	21950	
	maxi			19950	22450	24550	
sdn 4dr. 1.8T GLS	mini				15750	18250	
	maxi				18400	20900	
sdn. 4dr. GL 2.0L	mini						19100
	maxi						21750
sdn. 4dr. GL TDI	mini						20150
	maxi						22800
sdn. 4dr. GLS 2.0L	mini			13850	14700	17200	20700
	maxi			15750	17300	19850	23300
sdn. 4dr. GLS TDI	mini			14700	15200	17750	21200
	maxi			16800	17300	21400	23850

See page 7 to adapt these figures.

VOLKSWAGEN — New Jetta

2001 VOLKSWAGEN New Jetta

The new Jetta derived from the former one. It is available as 4-door sedan with 2.0L 4-cylinder or 2.8L V6 gas engine.

PROS

• **Performance** of the GLX's VR6 is the most exciting. It provides the kind of acceleration and pick-up that makes you hate the sluggish 2.0L on the GLS.

• **Handling** is stable and predictable thanks to efficient and sophisticated suspensions that result in precision driving. Although they tend to understeer, it's easy to control and are ideal for sporty drivers.

• **Steering** is precise and responsive. Assistance is just right and it makes driving on winding roads a very pleasant experience.

• **The presentation** is not as severe now that materials come in colors other than grey and black. Plastics and fabrics look significantly better than they did on previous models.

• **The standard anti-theft** system is far from a luxury. It's now part of standard equipment and will no doubt serve to decrease the number of thefts that once reached virtually epidemic levels.

• **The trunk** is smaller than on the previous model, but it has a respectable capacity and can be extended by lowering the backrest of the rear

• **Bonus**: high praise for the automatic windshield wipers that spring into action as soon as it begins to rain.

CONS

• **The price** of the Jetta is yet high compare to some of their less problematic Japanese competitors.

• **The fuel economy** of the gasoline engines is not obvious mostly if they are driven on the sports mode.

• **The rear bench** is wider, but it isn't still long enough and only smaller passengers will feel comfortable.

• **Few exasperating problems** continue to plague the Jetta owners. Once you get past the good looks of the product, you soon see that some manufacturing details could use improvement.

• **The performance** of the 2.0L engine is mediocre and acceleration and pick-up are both unenthusiastic.

• **Comfort** is no picnic; this car remains noisy, the engine and drivetrains vibrate, the suspension is very firm and seats are very hard.

• **Dashboard** wastes a lot of space and is a hazard for kneecaps.

• **To be fixed:** weak headlights and slow windshield wipers are dangerous, especially on the high-performance GLX versions

VERDICT

Improvements aside, the Jetta are overvalued. Their reliability has not yet been proven undeniably and their performance levels and warranties fail to justify their price.

RECALLS

01-02 Dealers will replace the ABS command module on some vehicles.

New Jetta — VOLKSWAGEN

RELIABILITY PROBLEMS

	1997	1998	1999	2000	2001	2002
Engine:			X	X	X	X
Transmission:			X	X	-	-
Suspension:			X	-	-	-
Steering:			-	-	-	-
Brakes:			X	X	-	-
Electricity:			X	X	X	X
Body:			X	X	-	-
Accessories:			X	X	X	X
Fit/finish:			X	X	-	-

POWERTRAIN / PERFORMANCE

Year	Type/ L/Camshaft/bhp	Drivetrain & gearbox	Acceler. 0/100 sec.	Top. speed km/h	Ave. Fuel consp. l./100 km
99-02	L4/2.0/SOHC/115	front-M5	10.9	180	10.1
		front-A4	12.0	175	10.8
	V6/2.8/DOHC/174-201	front-M5	8.0	210	12.2
		front-A4	8.8	200	12.6
	L4D/1.9/SOHC/90	front-M5	13.0	170	5.9
00-02	L4T/1.8/SOHC/150-180	front-M5	9.0	200	10.0

SPECIFICATIONS

Model 99-02	Wlb. mm	Lght. mm	Cb.wt kg	Brakes fr/rr	Steering type	Standard tires
sdn. 4dr. GLS TDI	2513	4376	1311	dc/dr	pwr.r&p.	195/65R15
sdn. 4dr. GL	2513	4376	1279	dc/dc	pwr.r&p.	195/65R15
sdn. 4dr. GLS	2513	4376	1283	dc/ABS	pwr.r&p.	195/65R15
sdn. 4dr. GLX 2.8L	2513	4376	1369	dc/dr	pwr.r&p.	195/65R15

PRICES

Model / version		1997	1998	1999	2000	2001	2002
sdn. 4dr. GL	mini			14100	15750	18400	19400
	maxi			15950	17850	20500	21500
sdn. 4dr. GL TDI	mini			15650	17850	20500	21500
	maxi			17450	19950	22600	23600
sdn. 4dr. GLS	mini			15100	17580	20500	21500
	maxi			17000	20250	22600	23600
sdn. 4dr. GLS TDI	mini			16000	18900	21500	25000
	maxi			18000	21000	23600	27300
sdn. 4dr. Wolfburg	mini					20500	
	maxi					22600	
sdn. 4dr. G:S 1.8	mini				17300	20700	22600
	maxi				19400	22800	24700
sdn. 4dr. GLS 2.8L	mini				17300	20500	23100	24700
	maxi				19400	22600	25200	26800
sdn. 4dr. Gli 2.8L	mini						25700
	maxi						27800
sdn. 4dr. GLX 2.8L	mini			20250	23850	23850	28350
	maxi			22000	25950	28900	30450

See page 7 to adapt these figures.

2001 VOLKSWAGEN New Passat

The Passat has been extensively redesigned while awaiting a full revamp. It remains available as a sedan or wagon with either a 1.8-liter L4 or a 2.8-liter V6. The 4Motion all-wheel drive system is optional.

PROS

• **The cabin and trunk** are roomy and make for a spacious and comfortable vehicle.

• **The V6** provides spicy performance and energetic full-stop and pick-up accelerations.

• **The Passat handles** with exemplary rigor, a Volkswagen trademark and one of the model's main advantages.

• **Ride comfort** is appreciable, although somewhat firm as is often the case with German automobiles.

• **The efficient brakes** are easy to gauge and work gradually to bring the car to a stop in a short and straight line.

• **The solid construction** and attentive finish are part of the quality image that Volkswagen is seeking to market.

• **The 4Motion** all-wheel drive system gives a whole new dimension to the mid-range family wagon, which is not as expensive as an Audi yet more prestigious than a Subaru.

CONS

• **The Passat doesn't come cheap** and is far from being an economy car.

• **The vague steering** feels disappointingly elastic in this otherwise rigorous package. This is mainly because of the poor-quality Continental tires that come as standard equipment.

• **The Continental Contact tires** do not provide adequate grip, even on dry roads. In the rain, they are prone to aquaplaning and are very noisy.

• **The Tiptronic transmission** is tiresome to use and is very less practical that equivalent systems developed by other auto makers.

• When coupled to the automatic transmission, the 1.8T produces timid performance given the high weight-to-power ratio.

• **The center console** is no model of ergonomics, with several out-of-reach controls.

• **The instruments** are lit in such a way that makes them difficult to read at night. The small digital screen lacks contrast and is impossible to decipher during the day.

VERDICT

The Passat remains the family wagon of choice for European car aficionados. It is built according to strict German construction standards but is far from economical.

RECALLS

None over this period.

RELIABILITY PROBLEMS

	1997	1998	1999	2000	2001	2002
Engine:					X	-
Transmission:					-	-
Suspension:					-	-
Steering:					-	-
Brakes:					-	-
Electricity:					X	X
Body:					X	-
Accessories:					X	-
Fit/finish:					-	-

POWERTRAIN

Year	Type/ L/Camshaft/bhp	Drivetrain & gearbox	Acceler. 0/100 sec.	Top. speed km/h	Ave. Fuel consp. l./100 km
01-02	L4T/1.8/DOHC/170	front-M5	9.2	200	10.5
	V6/2.8/SOHC/190 FWD	front-A5	9.7	220	13.1
	V6/2.8/SOHC/190 AWD	all-A5	10.5	200	13.7

PERFORMANCE

(merged into POWERTRAIN table above)

SPECIFICATIONS

Model 01-02	Wlb. mm	Lght. mm	Cb.wt kg	Brakes fr/rr	Steering type	Standard tires
sdn. 4dr. FWD	2703	4703	1452	dc/ABS	pwr.r.&p.	195/65R15
wgn. 4dr. FWD	2703	4703	1591	dc/ABS	pwr.r.&p.	195/65R15
sdn. 4dr. AWD	2703	4703	1634	dc/ABS	pwr.r.&p.	195/65R15
wag. 4dr. AWD	2703	4703	1704	dc/ABS	pwr.r.&p.	195/65R15

PRICES

Model / version		1997	1998	1999	2000	2001	2002
sdn. 4dr. GLS	mini					23650	25200
	maxi					26150	27800
sdn. 4dr. GLS V6	mini					26250	27600
	maxi					28900	29900
sdn. 4dr. GLS V6	mini					30450	28700
4M	maxi					32950	32000
sdn. 4dr. GLX V6	mini					27300	31500
	maxi					29800	34100
sdn. 4dr. GLX 4M	mini					35300	32550
	maxi					37150	35200
sdn. 4dr. W 8 4M	mini						45700
	maxi						48300
wgn. 4dr. GLS	mini					25700	26550
	maxi					28250	28900
wgn. 4dr. GLS V6	mini					29400	28350
	maxi					32000	31000
wgn. 4dr. GLS 4M	mini					35700	30450
	maxi					38200	33100
wgn. 4dr. GLX	mini					30450	31500
	maxi					33000	34100
wgn. 4dr. GLX 4M	mini					35600	34100
	maxi					37800	36750
wgn. 4dr. W 8 4M	mini						46700
	maxi						49350

See page 7 to adapt these figures.

VOLKSWAGEN   Passat

1998 VOLKSWAGEN Passat

First launched in Europe in 1980, these compact sedans and station wagons were equipped with 4-cylinder gas engines, for the Diesel and VR6 were only installed before these cars were revamped in '95. The Syncro all-wheel drive and the Tiptronic 5-speed automatic transmission made their debut in 1999. Would the new model objective be that the Passat will, from now on, "compete" against its more expensive sister, the Audi A4?

PROS
• **The cabin** is very roomy, considering the compact size of the car and the trunk is huge and can be extended.
• **The instrument panel** is practical, the cockpit is comfortable and there's good all-round outward view.
• **Power steering** is quick and accurate and with such a small steer angle, the Passat maneuvers in superb fashion.
• **Brakes** are muscular, but they're easier to control at high speed for the pedal is stiff at lower speed.
• **Handling** on curves is amazing for the car stays neutral before going gradually into understeer.
• **The 2.0L engine** is competent, but the VR6 is a better choice, even if it's not as spectacular as on the Golf/Jetta.
• **The all-wheel drive** on the Syncro models makes for safer winter driving.

CONS
• **Hit and miss reliability** has tarnished the reputation of this model and sales are confidential, even if it's been remarkably improved in many respects.
• **Poorly calibrated** gears force the driver to downshift all the time in order to get pick-up of any momentum.
• **The big headrests** obstruct rearward view.

VERDICT
The Passat doesn't deserve its sad lot, for the latest generation models are very state-of-the-art, but there's a price to pay for all the frustrations that besieged owners of former models.

RECALLS
1998 Air flow meter screen may be damaged.
98-99 A control valve in the vacuum hose connecting the brake booster to the intake manifold may cause loss of power brake assist at low temperatures.
2000 Fuel sending unit will be replaced by a redesigned one.

RELIABILITY PROBLEMS

	1997	1998	1999	2000	2001	2002
Engine:	X	X	X	X	X	
Transmission:	-	-	-	-	-	
Suspension:	-	X	X	X	-	
Steering:	-	-	-	-	-	
Brakes:	X		X	X		
Electricity:	X	X	X	X	X	
Body:	-	X	X	X	X	
Accessories:	-	X	X	X	X	
Fit/finish:	X	X	-	-	-	

POWERTRAIN

Year	Type/ L/Camshaft/bhp	Drivetrain & gearbox
97-98	L4/2.0/DOHC/110	front-M5
97-01	L4T/1.8/DOHC/150	front-M5
		front-A5
	V6/2.8/DOHC/172-190	front-M5
		front-A4/A5
	L4TD/1.9/SOHC/75-90	front-M5

PERFORMANCE

	Acceler. 0/100 sec.	Top. speed km/h	Ave. Fuel consp. l./100 km
	11.8	200	10.0
	9.0	220	11.3
	10.5	210	NA
	8.0	225	12.4
	9.3	220	13.2
	14.5	175	6.2

SPECIFICATIONS

Model 97-01	Wlb. mm	Lght. mm	Cb.wt kg	Brakes fr/rr	Steering type	Standard tires
sdn. 4dr. GLS	2705	4675	1200	dc/dc	pwr.r&p.	185/60R14
sdn. 4dr. GLX VR6	2705	4675	1250	dc/ABS	pwr.r&p.	215/50R15
sdn. 4dr. TDI	2705	4675	NA	dc/dc	pwr.r&p.	195/60R14
sdn. 4dr. 4Motion	2707	4669	1624	dc/ABS	pwr.r&p.	195/65R15
wgn. 4dr. GLX VR6	2623	4569	1480	dc/ABS	pwr.r&p.	215/50R15
wgn.4dr. TDI	2623	4569	1450	dc/dc	pwr.r&p.	195/60R14
wgn.4dr. 4Motion	2707	4669	1657	dc/ABS	pwr.r&p.	195/65R15

PRICES

Model / version		1997	1998	1999	2000	2001	2002
sdn. 4dr. TDI	mini	9750					
	maxi	12100					
sdn. 4dr. GLS VR6	mini		14500	17850	22600	24150	
	maxi		17000	20250	24550	26650	
sdn. 4dr. GLS	mini		13100	16600	20550	21500	
	maxi		15550	18700	22400	24000	
sdn. 4dr. GLS	mini				26800	28350	
4Motion	maxi				28750	31900	
sdn. 4dr. GLX	mini	12800	15950				
	maxi	15200	18400				
sdn. 4dr. GLX VR6	mini			20500	23600	25200	
	maxi			22900	25600	27700	
sdn. 4dr. GLX VR6	mini			23100			
Syncro	maxi			25400			
sdn. 4dr. GLX	mini				30650	32550	
4Motion	maxi				32950	35000	
wgn. 4dr. TDI	mini	10200					
	maxi	12600					
wgn. 4dr. GLX	mini	13750					
	maxi	16300					
wgn. 4dr. GLS	mini				27800	33600	
4Motion	maxi				29800	36100	
wgn. 4dr. GLS VR6	mini			18500	25400	27300	
	maxi			20800	27700	29800	
wgn. 4dr. GLX VR6	mini			23400			
Syncro	maxi			25700			
wgn. 4dr. GLS	mini			16800	22600	23600	
	maxi			19100	24600	26150	
wgn. 4dr. GLX	mini				31700	34650	
4Motion	maxi				34000	36000	
wgn. 4dr. GLX V6	mini				26450	28350	
	maxi				28750	30850	

See page 7 to adapt these figures.

VOLVO

40 Series

2001 VOLVO V40

Volvo finally found a successor to the former 240 to fill in its bottom end and attract a younger clientele. The 40 has been around in Europe for several years now, and it is the fruit of collaborative efforts between the Swedish auto maker and Mitsubishi.

PROS
• **The dimensions** are interesting, especially in the case of the wagon which is practical and highly appreciated by young families.
• **The impressive** list of passive security features are in keeping with Volvo's traditional philosophy.
• **The sure handling** can be attributed to an efficient rear-end geometry and good-quality shock absorbers.
• **Performance** is quite respectable given the vehicle's weight and the engine's displacement. Fuel consumption remains reasonable.
• **Presentation** has been polished to the slightest details. Also thanks to rigorous construction standards, the 40 is a small luxury car that stands in a class all its own.
• **The excellent** overall comfort results from the soft suspension, great seats and hushed cabin.
• **The 40's extensive equipment** list allows it to rival other established models.

CONS
• **The hefty overall weight** is the result of the body's structural rigidity capable of resisting high impacts.
• **Body roll** leads to important body motion, and the 40 models are sensitive to crosswinds.
• **The rear seats** are difficult to access and were designed more with children than with football players in mind.
• **The headlights** and windshield wipers are inefficient and make for uncomfortable driving in poor weather conditions.
• **The ergonomics** of the center console need to be improved. The window and radio controls are ill-located. Furthermore, there is no gear reminder for the automatic transmission.
• **Rearward** visibility is mediocre and hindered by the thick roof pillars and rear-seat headrests.
• **There is an inadequate number of storage spaces**, which takes away from this compact's practical side and reveals the age of its design.

VERDICT
The small Volvo will need to be slightly redesigned before it can truly conquer the North American market, where its name is not enough to ensure its success.

RECALLS
None over this period.

RELIABILITY PROBLEMS

	1997	1998	1999	2000	2001	2002
Engine:					X	X
Transmission:					X	-
Suspension:					-	-
Steering:					-	-
Brakes:					X	-
Electricity:					X	X
Body:					X	-
Accessories:					X	X
Fit/finish:					-	-

POWERTRAIN

Year	Type/ L/Camshaft/bhp	Drivetrain & gearbox
01-02	L4T/1.9/DOHC/165	front-A5

PERFORMANCE

Acceler. 0/100 sec.	Top. speed km/h	Ave. Fuel consp. l./100 km
8.8	200	10.5

SPECIFICATIONS

Model 01-02	Wlb. mm	Lght. mm	Cb.wt kg	Brakes fr/rr	Steering type	Standard tires
sdn. 4dr.	2562	4541	1255	dc/ABS	pwr.r.&p.	195/60R15
wgn. 4dr.	2562	4541	1280	dc/ABS	pwr.r.&p.	195/60R15

PRICES

Model / version		1997	1998	1999	2000	2001	2002
sdn. 4dr. 2.4L	mini					23100	26800
	maxi					26800	30100
sdn. 4dr. 1.8L	mini					24350	28350
	maxi					27500	31900

See page 7 to adapt these figures.

2001 VOLVO S40

2001 VOLVO S60

The S60 replaces the S70 sedans. Its components are borrowed from the former S70 and the current S80. The AWD version was introduced in 2002.

PROS

• **The lines** are very pleasing to the eye and are in keeping with Volvo's metamorphosis: from straight to rounded in the space of a few short years.

• **The array of mechanical options** to choose from offers an interesting range of choices that makes it easy to adapt the vehicle's character to that of its owner.

• **The T5** is capable of breathtaking performance and is a sports car in its own right, with muscular acceleration and pick-up.

• **Handling** is more sure than ever with the refined suspension components.

• **The excellent front and rear seats** are Volvo strong points, because they make for fatigue-free travelling over long distances.

• **Overall quality** has been improved once again. This in turn increases this model's resale value a little bit more.

• **The rear ventilation ducts** contribute to improving the comfort of rear-seat occupants.

CONS

• **Legroom and shoulder room** are at a premium in the rear sears, where access is not as easy as on previous models.

• **Maneuverability** suffers from the wide turning radius that forces the driver to sometimes attempt certain maneuvers several times before being successful.

• **There are too many options** to choose from, revealing a sales system that is typical to Ford.

• **The poorly designed steering wheel** is massive and uncomfortable to grasp.

• **Front and rear storage space** has been reduced to the strict minimum, which is unacceptable in a car of this price and status.

• **The wide center console** and the position of the hand brake take up previous front-seat space.

• **The spare tire** is located far under the trunk floor and is difficult to get at.

VERDICT

Although very refined and elegant, the latest Volvo is not as practical or roomy as its predecessor, a fact reflected by its declining sales figures.

RECALLS

None over this period.

RELIABILITY PROBLEMS

	1997	1998	1999	2000	2001	2002
Engine:					X	X
Transmission:					-	-
Suspension:					-	-
Steering:					-	-
Brakes:					X	-
Electricity:					X	X
Body:					X	-
Accessories:					X	-
Fit/finish:					-	-

POWERTRAIN

Year	Type/ L/Camshaft/bhp	Drivetrain & gearbox	Acceler. 0/100 sec.	Top. speed km/h	Ave. Fuel consp. l./100 km
01-02					
2.4	L5T/2.4/DOHC/168	front-M5	8.8	210	11.0
2.4T	L5T/2.4/DOHC/197	front-A5	8.5	210	11.4
2.4T	L5T/2.4/DOHC/197	all-A5	NA	NA	NA
T5	L5T/2.4/DOHC/247	front-A5	6.8	210	11.8

PERFORMANCE

SPECIFICATIONS

Model 01-02	Wlb. mm	Lght. mm	Cb.wt kg	Brakes fr/rr	Steering type	Standard tires
sdn. 4dr. 2.4	2715	4576	1427	dc/ABS	pwr.r.&p.	195/65R16
sdn. 4dr. 2.4T	2715	4576	1435	dc/ABS	pwr.r.&p.	205/55R16
sdn 4dr. T5	2715	4576	1450	dc/ABS	pwr.r.&p.	215/55R16

PRICES

Model / version		1997	1998	1999	2000	2001	2002
sdn. 4dr. 2.4L	mini					29900	33600
	maxi					33100	37300
sdn. 4dr. 2.4T	mini					32000	35700
	maxi					35200	39400
sdn. 4dr. TS	mini					34650	38850
	maxi					38000	42500

See page 7 to adapt these figures.

2001 VOLVO S60

VOLVO   70 Series

2001 VOLVO Cross Country

The 70 Series replaced the 850 line-up in 1998. It's a fresh remake of the previous models, but based on the same mechanical features. It's sold as a C coupe and convertible, S sedan and V station wagon which is available with 4-wheel drive since 1998.

PROS

• **The AWD version** opens up new vistas, since you can benefit from this feature without being at the wheel of a truck.
• **The fuller, rounder shape** is in keeping with traditional traits that give it an unmistakable Volvo look.
• **The superb Turbo engine** provides really thrilling sporty moves. The base model engine is less awesome, but fairly impressive even with the automatic gearbox.
• **Brakes** are among the best tested on a mass-produced car, yielding really trim stopping distances in spite of hefty vehicle weight and anti-lock system.
• **Handling** has been seriously improved with the really rigid structure and better suspension travel. The AWD is amazing on slippery surfaces and the vehicle holds the road just beautifully.
• **Cabin and trunk space** comfortably accommodate five passengers and their luggage.
• **Ride comfort** is super with the supple suspension of conventional engine models, the remarkable seat design, reasonable noise level at cruising speed and air conditioner that's easy to adjust as needed, no matter what the season.
• **The instrument panel** is more esthetic and ergonomic than on previous models.
• **Construction quality, finish job and trim materials** are comparable to those of some Japanese products and equipment is top of the line.

CONS

• **Upkeep** isn't cheap and resale value fluctuates quite a bit, so fans of these Swedish beauties have to cough up the cash to enjoy such a privilege.
• **The automatic shifter** is rougher around the edges with the base model engine than with the Turbo.
• You're in for a **far from smooth ride** on the sporty versions equipped with a stiffer suspension that faithfully transmits every single bump and crack.
• **Some components** seem to be poorly and loosely put together, since you can hear some strange squeaks and rattles.
• **Unusual controls** take some getting used to, such as for windows, mirrors, cruise control and low-slung sound system dials. The steering wheel is still too big and awfully wide.

VERDICT

The 70 Series models have a shapelier exterior and more ergonomic cabin design, yet boast of the zippy performance range of the 850 line-up.

RECALLS

1998 Incorrect "Vehicle Emission Control Information" label.(S&V)
98-99 Users of the third seat (V70) may come in contact with the tailpipe when entering or exiting the vehicle due to its location and the variability in its length.
1999 A fuel filter bracket must be installed on affected AWD vehicles.
2000 Defective tail gate locking mechanism will be replaced.

70 Series   VOLVO

RELIABILITY PROBLEMS

	1997	1998	1999	2000	2001	2002
Engine:			X	X		
Transmission:					-	-
Suspension:		X	X			
Steering:						
Brakes:		X	X	X		
Electricity:		X	X	X	X	X
Body:					-	-
Accessories:		X	X	X	X	X
Fit/finish:					-	-

POWERTRAIN / PERFORMANCE

Year	Type/ L/Camshaft/bhp	Drivetrain & gearbox	Acceler. 0/100 sec.	Top. speed km/h	Ave. Fuel consp. l./100 km
98-02	L5T/2.3/DOHC/240 (T5)	front-M5	7.8	235	12.3
	L5/2.4/DOHC/168	front-M5	8.9	205	11.9
	L5T/2.4/DOHC/190	front-A4	9.6	200	11.7
	L5/2.4/DOHC/190	front-A4	9.0	220	12.0
	L5T/2.4/DOHC/190 AWD	front/all-M5	9.6	210	12.3
	L5/2.3/DOHC/236 C70	front-A4	6.8	235	11.9
		front-M5	NA	NA	11.9

SPECIFICATIONS

Model 98-02	Wlb. mm	Lght. mm	Cb.wt kg	Brakes fr/rr	Steering type	Standard tires
con. 2dr.Cabrio.	2664	4720	1647	dc/ABS	pwr.r&p.	225/45R17
cpe. 2dr.	2664	4720	1458	dc/ABS	pwr.r&p.	205/55R16
sdn. 4dr. base	2664	4660	1413	dc/ABS	pwr.r&p.	195/60R15
sdn. 4dr. GLT	2664	4660	1450	dc/ABS	pwr.r&p.	195/60R15
wgn. 4dr. T-5R	2664	4711	1536	dc/ABS	pwr.r&p.	205/55R16
wgn. 4dr. AWD	2664	4711	1480	dc/ABS	pwr.r&p.	205/65R15

PRICES

Model / version		1997	1998	1999	2000	2001	2002
cpe. 2dr.	mini		23100	24800	29700	33600	39600
	maxi		27300	28750	33600	37300	42700
con. 2dr.	mini		27300	29000	33900	41350	46900
	maxi		32000	32750	37800	45150	50100
sdn. 4dr.	mini		12600	16700	22900		
	maxi		16500	20500	26900		
sdn. 4dr. SR	mini		13650				
	maxi		17650				
sdn. 4dr. SE	mini		15400				
	maxi		19100				
sdn. 4dr. GLT	mini		15550	20150	25900		
	maxi		19400	24150	29900		
sdn. 4dr. T5	mini		16600	21600	28000		
	maxi		20500	25400	32000		
sdn. 4dr. T5 SE	mini		17650				
	maxi		21500				
sdn. 4dr. T5 AWD	mini			23600	28550		
	maxi			27500	32450		
wgn. 4dr.	mini		14200	19600	24700		
	maxi		18000	23400	28650		
wgn. 4dr. SR	mini		15200				
	maxi		19100				
wgn. 4dr. SE	mini		16300				
	maxi		20150				
wgn. 4dr. GLT	mini		18400	22900	27300		
	maxi		22350	26800	31300		
wgn. 4dr. T5	mini		20250	24450		37800	42000
	maxi		24150	28350		41150	45150
wgn. 4dr. AWD	mini		20700				
	maxi		24700				
wgn. 4dr. XC AWD	mini		24450	26250	31500	40400	43600
	maxi		28350	30250	35600	43600	46700
wgn. 4dr. R AWD	mini		28000				
	maxi		32000				
wgn. 4dr. TBO R AWD	mini				30250	36550	
	maxi				34100	39400	
wgn. 4dr. 2.4L	mini					30650	34100
	maxi					34100	37300
wgn. 4dr. 2.4T	mini					33600	37800
	maxi					36950	40950

See page 7 to adapt these figures.

VOLVO 80 Series

2002 VOLVO S 80

The S80 has replaced the 900 Series as the top model of the Volvo line-up. It is available with a tranversal 6-cylinder in line engine, 2.9L atmospheric in the base or 2.8L turbo in the T6 version.

PROS

• **The styling** differs greatly from previous models that have been around for generations. With a more sculptured shape, the S80 is very similar to the 1992 ECC prototype.

• **The bucket seats** in the S80, as in all Volvos, demonstrate what comfort should be. The high back and well-shaped seat provide excellent support. And they're heated.

• **The trunk** is very deep and flat. Because of the 60/40 rear folding seat, storage space can nearly double.

• **Accelerating** and passing is highly inspiring in the bi-turbo version.

• **Handling** is very smooth. The suspension dampens any roll and minimizes bumps.

•**The rear bench** is very comfortable. There's enough room for heads, shoulders and legs. Headrests are adjustable, improving rear window visibility slightly, as long as no one is sitting there.

• **Bonus**: for detailed equipment, a logically laid out dashboard and powerful headlamps whose brightness and reach are both excellent.

CONS

• **The large turning radius** due to the transverse-mounted 6-cylinder in line engine, seriously hampers maneuverability.

• **Braking efficiency** is disappointing and emergency stopping distances are longer than average for this category.

• **Rear visibility** is seriously limited. The high trunk makes backing up an uneasy undertaking in this large car.

•**Steering** is overassisted and quickly becomes light and imprecise at center, to please the typical North American driver.

•**Performance** of the base S80 is uninspiring since both acceleration and passing are mediocre at best.

• The same tires equipped the base model and the T6 who delivered superior performance.

• **Minus**: wipers are too slow to keep up with heavy rain and a flat emergency tire that has no place in a car sold at this price.

VERDICT

This model has some fine qualities, but it has been created to please more the American than the Swedish...

RECALLS

99-00 Both front ball joint will be replaced with a reinforced version.

RELIABILITY PROBLEMS

	1997	1998	1999	2000	2001	2002
Engine:			X	X	X	-
Transmission:			X	-	-	-
Suspension:			X	X	X	-
Steering:			X	-	-	-
Brakes:			X	X	-	-
Electricity:			X	X	X	X
Body:			X	X	X	X
Accessories:			X	X	X	X
Fit/finish:			-	-	-	-

POWERTRAIN

Type/ L/Camshaft/bhp	Drivetrain & gearbox	Acceler. 0/100 sec.	Top. speed km/h	Ave. Fuel consp. l./100 km
99-02 L6/2.9/DOHC/197	front-A4	9.0	200	13.2
L6T/2.8/DOHC/268	front-A4	7.2	240	14.2

PERFORMANCE Year

SPECIFICATIONS

Model 99-02	Wlb. mm	Lght. mm	Cb.wt kg	Brakes fr/rr	Steering type	Standard tires
sdn. 4dr. 2.9L	2791	4822	1452	dc/ABS	pwr.r&p.	215/55R16
sdn. 4dr. T6	2791	4822	1492	dc/ABS	pwr.r&p.	225/55R16

PRICES

Model / version		1997	1998	1999	2000	2001	2002
sdn. 4dr. 2.9L	mini			25200	29400	36200	41700
	maxi			29200	33400	39700	44800
sdn. 4dr. T6	mini			28350	33600	40400	43600
	maxi			32350	37600	43350	46900
sdn. 4dr. T6 Exec.	mini					42000	
	maxi					44400	

See page 7 to adapt these figures.

2002 VOLVO S 80

VOLVO   850 Series

1997 VOLVO 850

The first front-wheel drive in Volvo history, the 850 came in 1993 as a sedan powered by a 2.4L 5-cylinder conventional engine. The station wagon and the Turbo engine were available in '94 and the T-5R model was sold in '95. In Sweden in '97, Volvo has revised its style in perspective of a total model rename that will take place the following year.

PROS
• **High-level safety** features with a very robust, reinforced body that has been imitated since, ABS brakes, standard dual airbags and front-wheel drive.

• **The typical Volvo** body design is still the same, but the angular lines have been softened and streamlined, especially with aerodynamics in mind.

• **The base model** is adequate, but not at all like the Turbo that really has get up and go.

• **Brakes** are strong and stable on sudden stops.

• **The cabin** accommodates five adults and the trunk holds all their baggage. The baggage compartment on the station wagon is more spacious and can be extended by lowering the rear bench.

• **Build is solid**, finish is impeccable and trim materials are spiffy.

CONS
• **The base engine** loses a lot of power with the automatic transmission and gears are sometimes cantankerous.

• **There's swing and sway** on the base model because of the soft suspension, so handling isn't great.

• **Some controls** aren't too ergonomic, like those for the windows, cruise control, rearview mirrors and sound system that are too low; and lastly, the steering wheel diameter is too wide.

• **Safety belts** are awkward on some models.

VERDICT
The 850 models are a good buy because they're really practical and they benefit from "à la carte" performance, depending on the engine model chosen.

RECALLS
None over this period.

RELIABILITY PROBLEMS

	1997	1998	1999	2000	2001	2002
Engine:	X					
Transmission:	-					
Suspension:	X					
Steering:	X					
Brakes:	-					
Electricity:	X					
Body:	-					
Accessories:	X					
Fit/finish:	-					

POWERTRAIN

Year	Type/ L/Camshaft/bhp	Drivetrain & gearbox	Acceler. 0/100 sec.	Top. speed km/h	Ave. Fuel consp. l./100 km
1997	L5T/2.3/DOHC/250 (R)	front-M5	7.8	235	12.3
	L5/2.4/DOHC/190	front-A4	9.6	200	11.6

PERFORMANCE

SPECIFICATIONS

Model 1997	Wlb. mm	Lght. mm	Cb.wt kg	Brakes fr/rr	Steering type	Standard tires
sdn. 4dr.	2664	4661	1446	dc/ABS	pwr.r&p.	195/60R15
sdn. 4dr. Turbo	2664	4661	1450	dc/ABS	pwr.r&p.	205/50R16
wgn. 4dr.	2664	4710	1480	dc/ABS	pwr.r&p.	195/60R15
wgn. 4dr. T-5R	2664	4710	1536	dc/ABS	pwr.r&p.	205/50R17

PRICES

Model / version			1997	1998	1999	2000	2001	2002
sdn. 4dr.	mini		8400					
	maxi		12600					
sdn. 4dr. GLT	mini		10400					
	maxi		14700					
sdn. 4dr. T5	mini		14200					
	maxi		18500					
sdn. 4dr. R	mini		18000					
	maxi		22450					
wgn. 4dr.	mini		9900					
	maxi		14200					
wgn. 4dr. GLT	mini		11350					
	maxi		15750					
wgn. 4dr. T5	mini		14900					
	maxi		19400					
wgn. 4dr. AWD	mini		18500					
	maxi		23100					
wgn. 4dr. R	mini		18600					
	maxi		23300					

See page 7 to adapt these figures.

1998 VOLVO S90

The 900 Series is inspired by the former 700 Series and was powered by a 4-cylinder engine when it was first sold in '91. The 6-cylinder in-line engine came out in '92. The 90 Series took over in 1998 with the same powertrain.

PROS

• **There's a wide variety** of choices in this model range that includes two body styles, three engine models, two suspension designs, two transmissions and six trim levels.

• **Preventive safety** features, body design and topnotch quality typical of Volvo products.

• **The efficiency** of the 2.3L multi-valve engine, the Turbos and the 6-cylinder in-line engine.

• **Driving is really** enjoyable because of the well-designed cockpit, excellent outward view, well-organized instrument panel, clean and smooth steering that also benefits from a small steer angle diameter, resulting in superb maneuverability.

• **Brakes are powerful**, predictable and stable, especially with ABS.

• **The cabin interior** has a nice layout, seat trim is attractive and the noise level is exceptionally low.

• **The luggage capacity** of the 900 models is generous, especially on the station wagon with its trunk that can be extended by lowering the rear bench.

CONS

• **The independent suspension** on the 960 really shows the deficiencies of the front end, that doesn't quite stick to the road.

• **The unimpressive** performance of the 4-cylinder conventional engine that shakes and roars as soon as it's solicited to do its job.

• **The interior cabin** design isn't very plush, considering the hefty price of the vehicle.

VERDICT

These are very classic cars, but they have a charm of their own and they're quite comfortable, especially with the 6-cylinder in-line engine that is silky smooth.

RECALLS

None over this period.